Myth and History in
the Contemporary Spanish Novel

Since the Civil War, Spanish novelists have produced a noteworthy body of fiction. In this book, Jo Labanyi provides detailed textual analysis of six of the most important novels to have been written during this period: Martín-Santos' *Tiempo de silencio*, Benet's *Volverás a Región*, Marsé's *Si te dicen que caí*, Cela's *San Camilo, 1936*, Juan Goytisolo's *Reivindicación del conde don Julián*, and Torrente Ballester's *La saga/fuga de J.B.*

The focus on myth as a response to history is intended as a corrective to archetypal myth criticism, and stresses the variety of ways in which contemporary Spanish novelists have resorted to myth, and the need to relate their use of it to the historical context of Francoist ideology. The book also raises important general issues about the ways in which fiction, as a form of mythification, relates to the real world.

Myth and History in the Contemporary Spanish Novel

JO LABANYI

Senior Lecturer, Birkbeck College
University of London

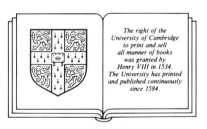

The right of the
University of Cambridge
to print and sell
all manner of books
was granted by
Henry VIII in 1534.
The University has printed
and published continuously
since 1584.

CAMBRIDGE UNIVERSITY PRESS

Cambridge

New York   New Rochelle   Melbourne   Sydney

Published by the Press Syndicate of the University of Cambridge
The Pitt Building, Trumpington Street, Cambridge CB2 1RP
32 East 57th Street, New York, NY 10022, USA
10 Stamford Road, Oakleigh, Melbourne 3166, Australia

First published 1989

Printed in Great Britain at the University Press, Cambridge

British Library cataloguing in publication data
Labanyi, Jo
Myth and history in the contemporary Spanish novel
1. Fiction in Spanish, 1900–. Critical studies
1. Title
863′.6

Library of Congress cataloguing in publication data
Labanyi, Jo.
Myth and history in the contemporary Spanish novel/Jo Labanyi.
p. cm.
Bibliography.
Includes index.
ISBN 0-521-24622-9
1. Spanish fiction–20th century–history and criticism. 2. Myth
in literature. I. Title.
PQ6144.L33 1989
863′.6′0915–dc19   88-23689   CIP

ISBN 0 521 24622 9

US

Contents

Introduction

The aim of this book is to provide a detailed study of six of the most important novels to have been written in Spain since the Civil War: *Tiempo de silencio* (1961) by Luis Martín-Santos, *Volverás a Región* (1967) by Juan Benet, *Si te dicen que caí* (1973) by Juan Marsé, *San Camilo, 1936* (1969) by Camilo José Cela, *Reivindicación del conde don Julián* (1970) by Juan Goytisolo, and *La saga/fuga de J.B.* (1972) by Gonzalo Torrente Ballester.[1] A large number of general surveys of the postwar Spanish novel have appeared over the last twenty years; their attempt to provide comprehensive coverage has left little room for textual analysis. To date, only two such surveys have appeared in English: one quite unreliable, the other useful but brief in its treatment of individual authors.[2] The only other book in English to discuss – alongside earlier texts – the postwar Spanish novel is Robert C. Spires' *Beyond the Metafictional Mode*, which gives detailed analyses of novels not included in this study. Four of the six novels studied here – those by Martín-Santos, Benet, Marsé and Goytisolo – have been translated into English.[3] It is hoped that this book will interest not only those with a specialist knowledge of Spanish literature but also a wider public curious to know how Spanish writers of the 1960s and 1970s succeeded in emerging from the cultural parochialism of the first two decades of the Franco regime. All quotations are given in English translation; in the case of longer quotations from the novels discussed, the Spanish is also given.[4]

I have devoted a chapter each to *Tiempo de silencio*, *Volverás a Región* and *Si te dicen que caí*; and have grouped together for briefer discussion in a final chapter *San Camilo, 1936*, *Reivindicación del conde don Julián* and *La saga/fuga de J.B.* My reasons for so doing are various. Firstly, the treatment of myth in the last three novels seems to me to be largely similar; by discussing them in conjunction I hope to point a contrast with the novels by Martín-Santos, Benet and Marsé studied in the earlier chapters. Secondly, of the three novels studied in the concluding chapter only *Reivindicación del conde don Julián* has been translated into English. Thirdly, Cela and Juan Goytisolo have already attracted considerable critical attention despite the fact that, in my opinion, they are less deserving of international recognition than Martín-Santos, Benet or Marsé. It must be said that Torrente Ballester – who I feel also merits international recognition – has been excluded from more detailed study with reluctance.

The subject of myth and history emerged as a way of relating the various novelists to one another and to the context of Franco's Spain: a historical period whose dominant ideology – like that of German and Italian fascism – was heavily charged with mythical resonances. My starting-point is the assumption that the literary use of myth inevitably – and particularly in the context of fascist ideology – has political connotations. One of the impulses behind this book has been a growing irritation with the school of myth criticism, largely practised in the United States under the aegis of Northrop Frye, which sets out to prove that the whole of world literature is the manifestation of a timeless, universal scheme of symbolic archetypes located in the collective unconscious, dissociated from the particularities of history. This study is not a work of myth criticism but a critique of its premises. My supposition is that all literature, being constructed out of the culturally-mediated instrument of language, entails an attitude – explicit or implicit – to history; and that this is particularly true of narrative, whose medium is time. The suggestion that individual writers can do no more than echo the archetypes of the collective unconscious is not only reductive but gives writers – and readers – little credit for critical intelligence. If all books are manifestations of the Universal Book, there seems little point in writing – or reading – anything new. What seems to me interesting about the literary appeal to myth is, first, what it reveals about the particular writer's attitude to history; and second, the different uses to which myth has been put by different writers. Myth critics, with their view of the writer as unconscious medium, have missed a fundamental point: that many contemporary writers have used myth ironically to expose its distortions or limitations.[5] It is for this reason that I have concentrated my analysis on Martín-Santos,

Benet and Marsé: writers whose ironic use of myth demonstrates the impossibility of denying history. All three writers regard fiction as, by definition, a form of mythification but they also point to the existence of a historical reality behind the masks, echoes or corruptions of the text. Cela, Juan Goytisolo and Torrente Ballester have been grouped together in the concluding chapter as examples of writers who, despite the presence of irony in their works, seek to create a mythical discourse that provides release from history. I make no secret of the fact that my sympathies lie with those writers for whom history, and not myth, is the measure of truth.

Anthropologists have long been divided over the issue of whether myth is a universal function of the human mind or the product of specific social circumstances. The briefest perusal of the bewildering proliferation of theories of myth makes it obvious that myth has meant different things to different people in different times and places. We should not be surprised to find that different writers have used it in different ways. It has been pointed out that, even in cultures where myth still thrives as part of a collective oral tradition, different versions of the same myth will vary wildly, depending on the individual story-teller and the circumstances of performance. In his wide-ranging study *Myth: Its Meaning and Functions in Ancient and Other Cultures*, Geoffrey Kirk concludes: 'I prefer to approach the general problem from empirical observation of the behaviour of story-tellers rather than from *a priori* convictions about the mode of operation of human minds.'[6] This pragmatic approach seems even more advisable when studying the self-conscious use of myth by writers. There is no point in trying to establish an objective, universally valid account of how myth functions: myth does whatever people expect it to do. Perhaps the only constant is that myth is always conceived as a way of dealing with historical problems. A particular society's conception of myth bears a direct relationship to its conception of its history. History – which the *OED* reminds us is 'the "formal" record of the past'; that is, a mental structuring of events – is as relative a concept as myth: in any given society the two depend for their definition on each other. The study of a society's myths helps us understand which aspects of its history it has chosen to define as problematic. Conversely, the study of a society's historical circumstances helps us understand the function of the myths it creates. My first two chapters are intended to set the use of

3

myth by Spanish novelists of the 1960s and 1970s in a historical context. Chapter 1 will sketch the evolution of the Western interest in myth, outlining the principal theories of myth on which contemporary writers can draw. Chapter 2 will discuss the role of myth in Spanish fascist thought and its largely unacknowledged traces in the postwar Spanish novel prior to the 1960s. It is impossible to understand the role of myth in the contemporary Spanish novel without some knowledge of its function in Nationalist ideology. Despite the fact that the novels studied here were written twenty or thirty years after the Civil War, it is the fact of Nationalist victory in 1939 that conditions the response of all their authors, whether they are trying to come to terms with Spain's particular version of the 'nightmare of history' or to escape it.

This book could not have been written without the generous financial assistance of the British Academy, and the equally generous verbal assistance of the following: Juan Benet, Juan Marsé, Carlos Castilla del Pino, José-Carlos Mainer of the University of Zaragoza, Donald Shaw of the University of Virginia, Colin Smith of Cambridge University, Leo Hickey of Salford University, Robin Fiddian and Peter Evans of Newcastle University, my colleagues at London University Edwin Williamson, William Rowe and David Henn, and above all my students at Birkbeck College, whose enthusiasm has sustained my own. I should also like to thank Margaret Jull Costa for her helpful editorial comments, and Katharina Brett of Cambridge University Press for her patience and efficiency in seeing this project through to completion.

I

The historical uses of myth

I am not concerned here with what myth has meant in pre-literate cultures, but in the meanings that have been invested in it by Western writers for whom its attraction has been the fact that it is a borrowing from an earlier or 'more primitive' culture. In this sense the use of myth by writers – whether creative writers or theorists of myth – is necessarily a form of cultural imperialism. It is no coincidence that it was the Renaissance that saw the beginnings of modern European imperial expansion and the first revival of classical mythology. As Jeffrey Perl remarks in *The Tradition of Return*: 'The idea of modernity has, since the Renaissance, been intimately tied to the notion of a classical rebirth.'[1] The rediscovery of the classical world provided Renaissance writers and artists with a set of *topoi* – historical and mythological – which gave their works the prestige of earlier imperial civilizations. The legitimizing function of classical history, acting as precedent, is obvious. Classical mythology was regarded as literally false but revealing a deeper symbolic truth, endowing it with the similarly legitimizing function of prophecy. Furthermore, allusion to classical mythology situated the contemporary writer in a supposedly universal tradition which sanctioned the worldwide imposition of European culture. The notion, inherited from the Renaissance, that myth confers universality has perhaps been its most insidious attraction: the claim to represent universal values has always been the mainstay of theories of Empire. If Spanish Falangists of the 1940s extolled Garcilaso as the model of the imperial poet, it was not only because he fought in Charles V's military campaigns in Europe and the Mediterranean, but also because of his use of mythological references. In addition the appeal to classical mythology allowed writers to voice imperialist doubt. This is not the place to explore the relationship between the use of classical mythology and the persistent theme of decadence found in so much seventeenth-century Spanish writing, but the shift to an increasingly burlesque mode suggests that it was precisely the gap perceived between the world represented by the mythological allusions and the present day that allowed myth to make a meaningful statement about contemporary history. The appeal to the mythology of a previous age ends up undermining the illusion of universality it had initially created.

It is this sense of a gap between historical present and mythical past that will intensify with the Romantic revival of interest in myth beginning in the late eighteenth century, and with all subsequent revivals. It is only in the Romantic period that the term 'myth' comes into use: it is this connotation of absence that distinguishes it from the earlier 'mythology'.[2] The Romantics reject the privileging of classical mythology in favour of 'primitive' myth: myth ceases to represent a past grandeur worthy of imitation and comes to stand for an original state of existence prior to civilization. If the Romantics conclude that man is condemned to live out a lie knowing the futility of the enterprise, it is partly because they are aware that the original state they have posited as an antidote to their contemporary sense of alienation is prior to civilization only in a metaphorical sense; in effect, it is the imaginary product of it. At the same time the Romantic belief that all knowledge is the product of the imagination leads to the suggestion that history is a dream, an exile from the source of truth, a fall from grace. It is a small step from here to the equation of history with decadence that will dominate the late nineteenth century. The central myth of Romanticism is that of Paradise Lost. Rousseau's notion that society is not the mirror of a natural order but the result of a contract entered into by the group so as to give order to natural chaos opens up a gulf between nature and society that will never again be bridged. 'Civilized' man is doomed to alienation as a result of his expulsion from an original oneness with nature. The rational urge to order nature being responsible for this alienation, it will be rejected in favour of irrationalism in an attempt to recapture the non-analytic perception attributed to 'natural man'. Myth comes to be valued not despite but because of its inability to stand up to rational proof. In order to escape the 'lie' of a history which is a distortion of natural origins, the Romantics opt for the lie of myth which at least has the merit of

6

being 'natural'. The fact that myth is associated with the beginnings of civilization leads to the assumption that it embodies an 'original' mode of perception essential to man's nature; and to the further notion that its function is to explain origins. The Romantic link between myth and origins will prove particularly long-lasting.

Foucault has argued that the notion of historical causality which underlies the nineteenth-century belief in progress, by requiring the return to original causes in order to understand the subsequent developmental process, leads to a converse obsession with origins.[3] There is however a fundamental difference between the historicist notion that the present is caused by the past and the mythical view that history is dissociated from origins. It can be more plausibly argued that the Romantic mythical view of history as the expulsion from the Garden of Eden gives rise to nineteenth-century historicism, in that it introduces the idea of irreversible change. There is no going back to the past; if there is to be a 'return to origins' it will have to take place in the future. Mircea Eliade has suggested that the linear concept of history is produced by the desire for a future Utopia in which man can re-establish the original Paradise from which he has been expelled.[4] Indeed, the Hegelian dialectic which informs much nineteenth-century historiography incorporates the mythical view of history as a rupture with origins into its causal vision, by positing a three-stage process of thesis–antithesis–synthesis, roughly corresponding to the mythical triad Paradise Lost–the Fall–Utopia. The nineteenth-century linear view of history as progress is subsumed into a cyclical vision whereby the goal of history is reintegration.[5] This cyclical vision is reinforced by the comparisons drawn by many nineteenth-century historians between the historical process and the lifespan of a biological organism, whether a human being passing through the stages of infancy–maturity–old age, or a plant passing through the stages of germination–growth–decay. Again history is divided into three stages, giving the impression that it comes full circle. The mythical resonances of this biological view of history are various. The insistence on a circular movement endows history with a completeness that echoes the wholeness of man's prelapsarian state. In the case of the comparison to the lifespan of a man, the equation of the first stage with infancy idealizes it as an age of lost innocence. The recourse to plant analogies tacitly 'roots' history within the natural state from which it is simultaneously

7

regarded as being an expulsion. As Hayden White has pointed out, such biological analogies lead to the fatalistic assumption that men do not choose their history but 'suffer' it.[6] At the same time the use of plant comparisons leaves open the possibility of decay leading to the germination of a new cycle, as in Burkhardt's vision of the Italian 'Renaissance'. In their anthology *The Rise of Modern Mythology 1680–1860*, Burton Feldman and Robert Richardson stress the redemptive quality of the Romantic concern with myth, in that it is seen as restoring man to the original health of the natural state.[7] The same redemptive urge underlies the triadic schemes of nineteenth-century historiography.

If the Romantic appeal to myth gives shape to nineteenth-century historical writing, it in turn is shaped by historical circumstances. Industrialization, a new social mobility and revolutionary political upheaval create a sense of divorce from nature and of individual and political insecurity that encourages the appeal to roots. It is noticeable that it is the age which produced liberal individualism and which saw a massive extension of literacy that turns to myth as the expression of a collective oral culture. More obvious still is the connection between the rise of nationalism and the Romantic emphasis on myth as the expression of the national soul, embodied by the uncultured and therefore 'natural', 'unspoilt' *Volk*. The contradiction between the view of myth as a universal mode of perception and as the expression of the national soul is only apparent: if myth is 'natural', it is the product of telluric forces and racial factors which in turn give shape to the national character. All nations produce myths, but in each case they will be different. The Romantics dedicate themselves to compiling anthologies of popular culture in order to boost the growing sense of nationhood. The notion that myth defines the nation gives the false impression that national boundaries predate history and have an essential, 'natural' status. Myth unifies the nation by grounding it in the wholeness of nature; in so doing it legitimizes international rivalries and divisions. The age of nationalism is also, from the Napoleonic period onwards, the great age of imperialist ventures. The fascination with myth as a primitive mode of perception stimulated interest in the discovery of previously unknown cultures; at the same time the definition of such cultures as 'primitive' justified their incorporation into 'civilization'. Curiously, the 'naturalness' of the *Volksgeist* gives it the right to colonize the 'naturalness' of the non-European world. The Romantic notion of the 'noble savage' idealizes 'primitive' culture by classifying it as childlike and therefore, like Rousseau's Emile, in need of tutorage. Mid-nineteenth-century popular anthologies of mythology, such as those produced by Bullfinch and Charles Kingsley, eliminate the violent aspects of 'primitive' myth to produce a sugary fairy-tale version that fosters the equation of the 'primitive' with the infantile.[8] It should be added that, even within Europe, the cult of the *Volk* has at no time – in the Romantic period or under twentieth-century fascism – been accompanied by the suggestion that the people should have political power.

The late nineteenth century will see a new burst of interest in myth, with the stress shifting on to its more disturbing, 'savage' aspects. Sir James Frazer described his monumental comparative study of myth *The Golden Bough* (first edition 1890, expanded third edition 1911–15) as a record of 'the long march, the toilsome ascent, of humanity from savagery to civilization'.[9] Frazer's view of myth as a survival from ancient fertility rituals – particularly that of the 'dying god' sacrificed to secure communal regeneration – in fact encouraged the contrary view that contemporary society, having lost touch with its 'primitive' past, had lost its capacity for regeneration. The Romantic view of myth as an antidote to alienation gives way to a new insistence on it as an antidote to decadence. Frazer's study seemed to confirm the controversial implications of Wagner's *Ring* cycle that a 'twilight of the gods' was necessary to restore the nation to its mythic integrity. Wagner's apocalyptic vision welcomes violence and destruction as an irruption of primeval energy into a degenerate, materialistic world. Feldman and Richardson stress Wagner's daring in highlighting the 'savage' aspects of Germanic mythology, concluding that 'after Wagner mythopoesis is not only a possible cure for modern problems, but an important cause of those problems'.[10] Wagner's equation of regeneration with a return to barbarism was given intellectual coherence by Nietzsche's suggestion that Christian morality had so repressed Western man's instinctual energies that it had made him into 'a sublime miscarriage'.[11] Nietzsche's originality is to make Christianity responsible for the fact that history is a fall from an original wholeness with nature. The remedy Nietzsche proposes for the 'disease' of civilization is a return to a healthy amorality that affirms the wholeness of body and mind,

9

an ideal represented for him by the pre-Christian world of Ancient Greece. Indeed Nietzsche takes his search for origins back one step further to the pre-Socratics, rejecting the whole of the post-Socratic rational tradition. For this reason he insists that history should consciously imitate myth, for positivistic historiography had succeeded only in presenting man with the balance sheet of a dead past. What Nietzsche meant by myth was a creative form of dreaming and 'willed forgetting' that would set man free from the illusion of progress and allow him to live the present to the full. It is this notion of the eternity of the present moment that he sought to stress with his doctrine of eternal recurrence. His insistence that the Apollonian concern with order, characteristic of Western rationalism, rejoin hands with the Dionysiac capacity for ecstasy from which it had become estranged led him to demand a 'rebirth' of tragedy not only because of the ritual, cathartic nature of Greek tragedy but also because violence and destruction are necessary if man is to affirm his wholeness. The antidote to the enervating repressions of civilization is the vital, energizing power of myth, which 'goes beyond good and evil' by showing both to be an intrinsic part of human nature. Nietzsche destroys the Romantic notion that natural man is good and that it is society which corrupts him, arguing that on the contrary civilization has meant man's 'fall' into a constricting goodness.[12] The fundamental lesson of Nietzsche's writings is that the 'primitive' – which nineteenth-century Europe had identified with the 'other' (whether the uncultured *Volk* or the non-European 'savage') – is to be found within. Nietzsche's exaltation of the early Greeks for their 'barbaric' wholeness destroys the illusion that European culture is founded on classical 'civilization'. The imperialist ventures which had seemed to prove Western man's superiority backfire by confronting him, in the image of the 'savage' he had scoured the globe to subdue, with the mirror-reflection of his hidden self.

Freud's discovery that man's sexual and aggressive urges can be traced back to the early stages of infancy – the desire to 'marry' the mother and kill the father that constitutes the Oedipus complex – dealt a definitive death-blow to the Romantic equation of origins with innocence: the child is innocent only in the sense that he has not yet learnt to feel guilt and repress his instinctual desires. At the same time Freud firmly located the 'primitive' within civilized man. It is his concern with the origins of neurosis in childhood that makes him take his terminology – 'Oedipus complex', 'Narcissism' – from Greek mythology, seen as embodying the mental life of 'original' Western man. Freud's concern to find biological explanations of mental life led him, like so many nineteenth-century historians, to draw an analogy between the individual human life-cycle and the historical development of nations. Myths were a throwback to the 'infancy' of civilization: 'the distorted vestiges of the wish-phantasies of whole nations – the age-long dreams of young humanity'.[13] Just as in the individual infancy represents an original state prior to repression, so Freud suggested that myth is a survival from an age when 'young humanity' had not yet learnt to repress its instinctual drives. The suggestion that civilization began when man learnt to repress his infantile urges had the advantage of appearing to give a scientific, causal explanation of the present in terms of the past, while at the same time appealing to the mythical view of history as a dissociation from origins. It has been suggested that Freud did not so much apply to myth his theory of the unconscious – that area of the psyche governed by the pleasure principle as opposed to the reality principle – as deduce his theory of the unconscious from the concept of a mythical imagination.[14] In *The Psychopathology of Everyday Life* (1901) he suggested that 'a large part of the mythological view of the world ... is nothing but psychology, projected into the external world'. In *Totem and Taboo* (1913) he would go on to argue that the task of the psychologist was 'to reverse the process and put back into the human mind what animism teaches us as to the nature of things'.[15] By this he did not mean that myth is the subjective projection of the historically-determined attitudes of individuals, but that it is the unconscious expression of a universal human nature prior to the socialization process.

If myth gives shape to the Freudian theory of the unconscious, conversely the latter – putting mythical thought forward as the key to understanding modern man – will be the major contributing factor to the modernist revival of interest in myth.[16] As Ruthven states in his useful handbook on myth: 'One need not read very far into modern literature to realize that a good deal of the mythology one encounters there owes its existence to the new perspectives opened up by Freudian psychology.'[17] The work that made Freud's theories available to a wide public was *The Interpretation of Dreams*

11

(1900). The suggestion that myth functions in the same way as dreams led to a positive valuation of its dislocated structures, now seen as a function of the displacement process whereby repressed emotions are transferred on to neutral objects. The ability of the unconscious to transform everything into something else suggested that poetic metaphor was the most 'natural' form of language. At the same time Freud's demonstration of the ambivalence of the symbolic language of the unconscious – able simultaneously to express conflicting emotions – suggested that myth, like dreams, provided a way of resolving the dichotomies of rational thought that Nietzsche had seen as the cause of Western man's alienation from Socrates onwards. Once again myth is seen as the key to wholeness, prized because it means nothing in particular but everything at once. Freud acknowledged that poets and artists had anticipated his theories, but his concern was to provide a scientific explanation of mental life. If writers and painters insisted on the illogical 'integrity' of the symbolic language of the unconscious, Freud was concerned with rationally analysing its underlying meanings. The surrealists in particular, with their insistence that their arbitrary metaphorical juxtapositions had no deep meaning, were guilty of a basic misreading of the Freudian theory of symbolism, according to which all language has an underlying unconscious meaning. More seriously, writers and artists chose to ignore Freud's view that reason was progressive and creative, and the unconscious regressive and destructive. Freud privileged childhood as the origin of subsequent mental life but, unlike writers and artists, he did not idealize it. His concept of the Oedipus complex – derived from myth – shows childhood to be a period of helplessness and terror. Just as Freud regarded his patients' tendency to revert to infancy as a sign of neurotic regression, so he saw myth – a 'distorted vestige' of the phantasies or dreams of 'young humanity' – as at best self-indulgent wish-fulfilment, at worst a sign of arrested mental development. The mythical notion of the 'eternal return' – the compulsion to regress to origins – is transformed by Freud into the law of the return of the repressed. In his more pessimistic and more political later writings, Freud became increasingly convinced that the urge to return to origins was biologically in-built. In *Civilization and its Discontents* (1930) he warned that Western civilization might one day have to pay for the centuries of repression on which it was based. The rise of Nazism in the 1930s was seen by him in *Moses and Monotheism* (written 1934–8) as an alarming sign of just such a regression to a primitive rule of terror. Jeffrey Perl stresses that Freud's major discovery was that of 'the psyche's reactionary instincts'.[18] Freud could see no way out of the problem created by the fact that civilization was founded on repression: his view of the destructive nature of man's instinctual urges ruled out the abolition of repression as a solution.

Freud's warning that a regression to the primitive would have dire consequences for contemporary history went largely unheeded by modernist writers and artists. Lawrence and Yeats turned to pre-Christian mythical archetypes in their works in order to give voice to the primal emotions and energies repressed by civilization: in many ways their use of myth is closer to Nietzsche than to Freud. The surrealists – in keeping with the mythical notion that death is the pre-requisite to rebirth – preached the destruction of bourgeois society and a return to unrestricted and indiscriminate sex and violence: Buñuel's aptly-titled *L'Age d'or* (1930) makes the link between aggression and the rejection of repression clear. The political ambiguities of the modernist appeal to the primitive are well known: Picasso's return to African art would culminate in his passionate attack, with his painting *Guernica*, on Nationalist destruction in the Civil War; while Dalí's attempt to express the contents of the unconscious would lead to a life-long admiration of Franco as the mythical hero who stands above the bourgeois rule of law. Conservative writers such as Thomas Mann saw myth as providing recognition of the fact that the present is a repetition of patterns consecrated in the past.[19] T. S. Eliot – a self-declared conservative – appealed to the mythic capacity to fuse oppositions as a way of healing the 'dissociation of sensibility' – the split between emotion and intellect – he had diagnosed in post-seventeenth-century literature; and seized on Frazer's notion of the 'dying god' to assert the hope that out of the 'wasteland' of contemporary life there might spring a spiritual rebirth. Frazer's emphasis on the seasonal pattern of decay leading to regeneration underlying fertility rituals, together with Freud's view of the unconscious as existing only in the eternal present of the pleasure principle, suggested to Eliot that the poetic use of mythical thought and structures might afford some kind of salvation from the condemnation to history by converting it into 'a pattern of timeless moments'.[20] Ignoring Freud and Frazer's stress on the violent

13

aspects of primitive thought, Eliot proclaimed in his 1923 essay on Joyce's *Ulysses* that 'the mythical method' was 'a way of controlling, of ordering, of giving a shape and significance to the immense panorama of futility and anarchy which is contemporary history'.[21] Eliot's declaration that the return to classicism which he attempted to achieve through myth 'is in a sense reactionary, but it must be in a profounder sense revolutionary' is disquietingly similar to the insistence by fascist thinkers of the 1930s on the revolutionary nature of the political 'return to roots'. In fascist terminology 'revolution' is used in its literal sense of a cyclical reversal. Perl traces the disquieting link between the modernist appeal to myth (what he calls the 'ideology of return') and fascism, pointing out that the return to roots – exemplified by Ulysses' return to Ithaca – necessarily requires the slaying of the rival suitors.[22] The best known case is that of Ezra Pound, who took to the extreme Eliot's attempt to revive the classical ideal of order by building his poetry on a complex web of mythical allusions, and who also went to the political extreme of championing Mussolini. The same longing for a return to classical order led Wyndham Lewis to flirt first with Mussolini and then with Hitler. Just as Mussolini appealed to Imperial Rome, so Hitler – in addition to his predilection for Wagner – staged the 1936 Berlin Olympics in an attempt to revive the Greek ideal. Charles Maurras, founder of the French fascist organization Action Française, likewise pleaded for a return to classical culture. It is one of the ironies of history that the advocates of fascist thuggery should have had a clearer understanding of the implications of the return to myth than did many intellectuals of the time.

The mythical appeal on the one hand to classical order and on the other to primal instinctual energies is not as contradictory as it might seem, for both are attempts to return to what is seen as an original wholeness. The contemporary sense of disintegration that had begun with the Romantic concept of alienation from nature and been compounded by the *fin-de-siècle* concern with decadence was made urgent by the senseless slaughter of the First World War. That the desire for a return to order tended to prevail, particularly among writers, is perhaps to be explained by the fact that the prospect of war had originally been hailed by poets as a return to the Dionysiac energies whose loss Nietzsche had lamented. The publication in 1918–22 of Spengler's *The Decline of the West* – which proposed that history was a series of biological cycles each ending in exhaustion, with the impetus for renewal passing to a new geographical centre of power – seemed to confirm that Europe was threatened with the definitive loss of its capacity for regeneration. The economic slump of the 1930s would suggest that even the Western world's economic superiority was in danger of collapse. It is perhaps not surprising that anthropologists between the two World Wars – with the exception of Malinowski, who pragmatically insisted that myth has the function of validating social institutions – should have either continued Frazer's emphasis on fertility rituals (as in the case of the Cambridge school of anthropologists represented by Jane Harrison and Gilbert Murray, both classical scholars), or opted for a return to the Romantic concept of myth as a numinous, redemptive force restoring man to a lost wholeness with nature. In *Language and Myth* (1925), Ernst Cassirer proposed that language had its roots in myth, since both were manifestations of man's capacity for symbolic thought. Mythopoesis affirmed the oneness of creation by refusing to admit the discrete categories of logical analysis. Myth was the expression of feeling and not of thought; as such it was the spontaneous manifestation of divine 'mana'. In *Primitive Mentality* (1922) and *The Soul of the Primitive* (1927), Lévy-Bruhl echoed this religious view of myth with his notion that it expressed a 'mystical participation', merging man with the natural world. This is another way of saying that myth is man's unconscious, but we are far removed from what Freud had in mind with his equation of the two concepts. Although writers of the inter-war period refer to Freud as the source of their interest in myth, the majority have more in common with the thought of his ex-disciple Jung, whose work represents a return to early nineteenth-century Romanticism.

Jung's insistence that the unconscious is ruled not by anarchic sexual and aggressive urges, but by a striving for spiritual self-realization, defuses the threatening aspects of Freudian theory. Jung also opposed Freud's pessimistic belief that the fact that civilization was founded on guilt made a regression to barbarism inevitable with the optimistic suggestion that the psyche is a self-regulating mechanism that naturally strives for balance. Jung regarded myths – like dreams – as 'messages from the unconscious', pointing man in the direction of wholeness. The Jungian concept of the unconscious fuses the antinomies of order and the irrational. Myth, by plunging man into the natural world of the unconscious, heals the 'divided self' of modern man. Jung rejected Freud's view of myth as an infantile vestige, insisting that its 'wholeness' was a sign of maturity. If Freud's scientific concern to explain the origins of mental life led him to Greek mythology, Jung's religious concern with man's spiritual goals led him to privilege the quest myth, in which the hero undergoes a series of trials whose successful resolution leads him to maturity or regeneration. Jung's influence here has been so pervasive that we often forget that the quest myth is only one kind of myth, and not the prototype of all myth. Particularly influential has been Jung's interpretation of the hero's descent into the underworld as a return to the maternal womb in search of rebirth. By this Jung was not advocating a regression to infantilism, but a conscious self-immersion in the 'womb' of the unconscious in order to emerge as a mature individual. The mythical descent into the underworld is a voluntary self-sacrifice or 'death of consciousness' in order to secure rebirth in the sense of putting oneself back in touch with the source of wholeness. Jung's view of the unconscious is not, however, entirely idyllic: the hero's encounter with a series of monsters represents the need to acknowledge the repressed dark side of oneself that Jung called the 'shadow'. For Jung, myth is valuable because it encompasses the whole of life – good and evil – and is therefore able to heal inner divisions through self-acceptance. Jung's concern with wholeness led him to postulate the concept of a 'collective unconscious' with an in-built predisposition to formulate archetypal patterns. Myth thus puts man in touch not just with his own nature but with the universal brotherhood of man. Jung's notion of the 'collective unconscious' suggests that men are 'naturally' at one with each other, and that it is the socialization process which introduces differences and discord. His theory of universal archetypes further implies that myth is an autonomous system whose contents may be affected by historical circumstances but whose archetypal forms are constant. Jung's theories were derived from his study of comparative religion, particularly of Eastern religious thought with its emphasis on the transcending of oppositions. Jung interpreted the Buddhist mandala as the visual equivalent of the quest myth, requiring the initiate to pass through its four cyclically-arranged sections in order to apprehend its totality. Far from releasing Dionysiac energies, myth has now been tamed to the extent of constituting a spiritual discipline, not unlike the spiritual exercises of St Ignatius of Loyola. It is not surprising that the Jungian theory of myth should have provided the basis of academic myth criticism in the 1950s. Its emphasis on man's spiritual strivings also offered an alternative model of religious thought at a time when established Christianity had lost its appeal: Frank Kermode has noted that writers began to turn to myth at precisely the point when theologians took to de-mythologizing Christianity.[23] One suspects that another reason why Jung's theories found such ready acceptance – particularly in the United States – was the liberal apoliticism of his view of myth as a 'science of universals'. In his last work – the introductory essay to *Man and his Symbols*, written in 1960–1 at the close of the Cold War – he proposes myth as an antidote to the 'terrible primitivity' of both Nazi Germany and the Soviet Union. His reference throughout to the Soviet Union as the 'shadow' of the Western world does not, one feels, imply that the West should accept communism as part of its 'whole' self.[24] As always, the universal appeal to myth conceals a political stance.

The other main influence on the postwar revival of interest in myth has been Mircea Eliade, like Jung a student of comparative religion. Eliade's anti-historicism is quite explicit, indeed militant. His fascination with myth as a universal mental disposition can be traced directly back to fascist thought of the 1930s: his work was produced in the late 1940s and 1950s in exile from his native Rumania, from which he was banned because of his fascist and anti-semitic activities prior to and during the Second World War.[25] Just as Jung privileged the quest myth, so Eliade privileges what he calls 'the myth of the eternal return'. In his book of the same name (1949) he studies the New Year rituals of different civilizations, concluding that man has always found it necessary to divide time into calendar years in order to impose a cyclical pattern on to the irreversibility of history. New Year rituals, celebrating the death of the old and the birth of the new, allow man to wipe clean the accumulated burden of history and start afresh. For Eliade, all myth has this function of 'undoing' history and re-enacting the original *illud tempus* prior to the erosion of time. He insists that all civilizations have, in one way or another, regarded history as the Fall because of the intolerable and arbitrary suffering it imposes. Eliade starts from the existentialist position (with which as a resident of postwar Paris he was familiar) that man is condemned to the absurdity and alienation of history; but he breaks with existentialism by insisting that man needs to believe that his condemnation to history has a meaning. Myth provides such a meaning by explaining suffering as the necessary expiation of collective guilt, a 'sacrificial death' that must be voluntarily undergone to secure regeneration. In a circular argument, the suffering that constitutes history becomes the means of undoing it. Eliade suggests that Judaeo-Christian thought radically altered Western man's perception of history by supposing that it is not an infinitely repeatable series of cycles but a straight line moving from the Fall at the beginning to the millennium or definitive abolition of history (the coming of the Messiah or the second coming of Christ) at the end. The Western linear concept of progress is thus a view of history as a single cycle: modern man, having lost faith in the possibility of securing regeneration in the here-and-now, has postponed it till the future. Eliade points out that both Marxism and fascism incorporate this millenarian belief in a future, final abolition of history. He sees the postwar vogue for existentialism, refusing the hope even of a future end to history, as symptomatic of a profound spiritual crisis. Eliade suggests that the return by many modern artists to a Nietzschean or Spenglerian cyclical vision of history, based on the notion that destruction is the prelude to rebirth, is a healthy attempt to reinvest history with a sense of purpose.[26] For all its illogicality, Eliade's argument that the way to give a meaning to history is to 'undo' it has been extraordinarily appealing. It is the same appeal of fascism's promise to undo the errors of modernity by returning to mythical roots. Just as Eliade proposes myth as an antidote to man's 'terror of history', so fascism inaugurated a reign of terror in order to exacerbate man's historical insecurity, enabling it to step in with the promise of salvation. Eliade's insistence on the 'myth of the eternal return', like fascism, requires the perpetuation of the equation of history with evil. Ironically Eliade's notion of the need for myth as an antidote to the evils of history, which can be seen as the direct offshoot of his previous involvement with the Rumanian fascist movement, was able to appeal to a postwar public for whom the evils of history had become equated with fascism.

Jung's liberal apoliticism and Eliade's militant anti-historicism join hands to form the basis of the school of myth criticism that rose to prominence in the United States in the 1950s. The leading myth critic John Vickery, in the introduction to his anthology *Myth and Literature*, asserts that 'myth criticism is non-ideological'.[27] Such claims can be seen as the academic counterpart of the pretension to represent 'universal values' of US foreign policy during the Cold War. Northrop Frye, in his classic theoretical work *Anatomy of Criticism* (1957), argued that all art – as the expression of the collective unconscious – obeys a set of universal structuring principles, of which the clearest manifestations are the archetypes of myth. The implication is that those elements of the work of art that deviate from the mythic norm are to be dismissed as 'inauthentic'; the task of myth criticism is to strip off such accretions to reveal the 'authentic' mythic kernel. It has been pointed out that Northrop Frye does not use myth to elucidate the work of art, but uses the work of art to illustrate the underlying mythical scheme.[28] Frye's repertoire of archetypal patterns – the dying and reviving god or 'scapegoat', the cyclical passage from decay to rebirth – is drawn from Frazer's *The Golden Bough*. In practice he further reduces it to fit the all-embracing structure of the Jungian quest myth, in which the hero descends into the underworld in search of regeneration. In *Fables of Identity* (1963) he will go so far as to say: 'It is part of the critic's business to show how all literary genres are derived from the quest myth.'[29] Frye's topology of genres sets out to fit the historical development of Western literature into a cyclical seasonal pattern, with contemporary literature standing at the point of transition from winter to a new spring. Frye's use of biological metaphor in his title *Anatomy of Criticism* is deliberate: he wants to show that the whole of world literature forms a single 'body' governed by immutable 'natural' laws. His appeal to biological analogies serves – as in nineteenth-century historiography – to fit his evolutionary theory of genres into a cyclical view of historical development. Frye's archetypal reductionism parallels the work of his fellow American myth critic Joseph Campbell, whose influential book *The Hero with a Thousand Faces* (1949) had popularized Jung's privileging of the quest myth as a universal structure of the human mind. Like Jung, Campbell interprets the hero's descent into the underworld as a return to the womb of the unconscious in search of wholeness. Campbell reduces all myth to what he blatantly calls 'the Monomyth', paraphrasing Tolstoy's opening of *Anna Karenina* to argue that 'Like happy families, the myths and the worlds redeemed are all alike.' Campbell insists on the therapeutic value of myth – and by derivation myth criticism – in that it puts the contemporary alienated individual back in touch with the 'total image of man' of which 'the individual is necessarily only a fraction and distortion'.[30]

The attempt by myth criticism to fit all literature into a universal scheme goes hand in hand with the assault on individualism that was to become the most controversial aspect of French structuralism in the late 1950s and 1960s. Structuralism can be seen as a direct heir of myth criticism, in that its claim to found criticism on a scientific basis echoes Jung's attempt to found a mythic 'science of universals'. The structuralist proclamation of the 'death of the author' is a new version of myth criticism's insistence on the literary text as an unconscious elaboration of archetypal structures. In a sense structuralism is an attempt to reduce literature to the status of myth, whose lack of an author gives it an impression of objectivity. Not for nothing did the structuralist attempt to 'rescue' literature from its subjectivity by reducing it to a universally applicable scheme derive its inspiration from Propp's *Morphology of the Folktale* (1928). There are striking similarities between Todorov's structural analysis of narrative and Campbell's reduction of myth to a set of variants on an archetypal pattern, with the hero crossing a threshold with the aid of a magic helper, undergoing an ordeal, receiving his reward and returning to his point of departure with a boon or elixir.[31] The structuralist concern to establish a universally valid typology of genres can also be seen as the direct legacy of Northrop Frye.[32] It is not coincidence that the most influential structuralist thinker should have been an analyst of myth: the anthropologist Lévi-Strauss. At the same time Lévi-Strauss marks a radical break with the Romantic theory of myth which had dominated Western thought for a century and a half. Structuralism, like myth criticism, appealed to universalists who preferred to regard literature as an autonomous system independent of historical circumstances; but its roots in Russian formalism of the 1920s also attracted Marxist thinkers who believed that the literary work was the product not of an individual mind but of a conflicting set of cultural codes. Lévi-Strauss' theory of myth represents a curious blend of the universalist and Marxist strands of structuralism.

Lévi-Strauss shares with Romanticism the view that myth represents a universal structure of the human mind, but he turns Romantic theory upside down by proposing that myth is the product not of an irrational perception that can offer an antidote to the alienating excesses of the intellect, but of reason. Myth is a form of taxonomy, an attempt at logical classification. As Lévi-Strauss insists in his most famous work *The Savage Mind* (1962): 'The thought we call primitive is founded on this demand for order.'[33] As a result the whole Romantic concept of myth as an original state of mind prior to civilization collapses. Lévi-Strauss suggests that myth, as an analogical mode of thought, is parallel – and not prior – to the causal analysis of science. He rejects Lévy-Bruhl's idea that 'primitive' man enjoyed a naive 'mystical participation' in nature, arguing that on the contrary myth represents his attempt to mediate the contradiction between culture and nature, of which he was all too aware. For Lévi-Strauss the universal tendency of the human mind illustrated by myth is not an ability to apprehend wholeness, but the propensity to create binary oppositions which then require mediation. The mythical recourse to analogy is based on the prior perception of difference. Lévi-Strauss' Marxist antecedents are evident in his dialectical refusal to see myth as a fusion of opposites, insisting that 'mediation' is the imaginary resolution of a real contradiction: 'the purpose of myth is to provide a logical model capable of overcoming a contradiction (an impossible achievement if, as it happens, the contradiction is real)'.[34] Lévi-Strauss' definition of myth is thus a version of the Marxist definition of ideology as 'a solution in the mind to contradictions which cannot be solved in practice; ... the necessary projection in consciousness of man's practical inabilities'.[35] He insists that no society, however 'primitive', lives 'prior to' or 'outside' history, but that certain societies resort to myth in order to suppress contradiction and thus minimize the consequences of historical change: 'All peoples live in history but some try to annul the effects of history on their equilibrium; while others make the historical process the mainspring of their development.' 'Primitive' societies are not those at an earlier stage of evolution but those which 'try, with a dexterity we underestimate, to make the states of their development which they consider "prior" as permanent as possible'.[36] Lévi-Strauss rejects the idea not only that myth reflects an 'original' pre-historical state of mind but also that its function is to explain origins; indeed he suggests that it does not set out to illustrate any pre-existing idea, but that its internal structures are a way of ordering elements from reality in such a way that a new perception of them emerges. Myth has no 'original' meaning; its function is to create meaning where before there was none. Lévi-Strauss thus resorts to a comparative analysis of myth on the assumption that the existence of similar structures in different myths, no matter how disparate their cultural provenance, supposes that they have a common function. Despite Lévi-Strauss' Marxist insistence that myth is an imaginary solution to real problems, his comparative method leads him increasingly to study myth as an autonomous universal system, disregarding the specific historical context of individual myths. He will end up concluding that the function of myth is not to tell us about the outside world but to illustrate the functioning of the human mind. In *The Raw and the Cooked* (1964) – the first volume of his massive comparative *Science of Mythology* – he will claim that myth is an autonomous self-referential system which 'thinks itself' through the medium of man's unconscious. The comparison he draws is with music, the least referential of the arts.[37] Kirk criticizes Lévi-Strauss for contradicting his useful notion of myth as the imaginary resolution of a real contradiction by arguing that it is an unconscious universal system, pointing out that this is a relic of the Romantic view of myth as a spontaneous configuration of the human spirit, and of the Jungian theory of archetypes.[38] Jorge Larrain has also pointed out that Lévi-Strauss contradicts his Marxist premises – whereby myth is a response to a real contradiction – by going on to state that contradiction does not exist in nature but only in the mind, and that myths therefore 'try to explain facts which are themselves not of a natural but of a logical order'.[39] Lévi-Strauss' rejection of the idea that myths refer to a pre-existing 'original' reality leads him to draw his famous analogy with *bricolage*, whose ingredients are oddments left over from past manufacturing processes: likewise myth does not draw on nature directly but on the 'debris' of past cultural systems. In this sense myth can degenerate from being 'a way of thinking' into being 'a way of remembering'. But myth will always be a failed form of memory because – being built on the relics of past cultural systems which themselves are at a remove from nature – it can never be more than an echo of irretrievably lost origins. The Romantic view of myth as a return to origins – which Eliade develops to the full with his notion of the re-enactment of an original *illud tempus* – is shown by Lévi-Strauss to be a logical impossibility.[40]

Lévi-Strauss' view of myth as a second-degree cultural system, which does not deal with reality as such but manipulates pre-existing cultural stereotypes, echoes that of Roland Barthes in his seminal collection of essays *Mythologies* (1957). Barthes's structuralist analysis is firmly rooted in Marxism, regarding myth as synonymous with ideology. His interest is not 'primitive' myth but the falsification of consciousness by bourgeois capitalist society, particularly in its contemporary mass-media version. Like Lévi-Strauss, Barthes sees myth as an attempt to deny the contradiction between culture and nature, but he suggests that this is done not by mediating the two concepts but by presenting as 'natural' that which is cultural. In this way the ruling élite can give the impression that social structures are not man-made and therefore changeable, but 'essential' and therefore immutable. Western capitalism, having 'colonized' nature through technology and imperialist expansion, attempts to reconvert its products back into nature in order to legitimize the process. For Barthes myth is always authoritarian in that it denies ambiguity and the possibility of alternatives, and creates a solid world of fixed, 'eternal' values. Barthes agrees with the Romantic theory of myth inasmuch as he regards it as an attempt to return to nature in order to deny historicity. But if for Romantic thinkers this made myth an antidote to alienation, for Barthes – in keeping with the Marxist theory of ideology – it is myth which produces alienation. In Barthes's analysis, myth is not an attempt to overcome the irreversibility of time but precisely the pretence that history could not be otherwise. Barthes rejects the notion of mythical archetypes: 'Ancient or not, mythology can only have an historical foundation, for myth is a type of speech chosen by history: it cannot possibly evolve from the "nature" of things.' Myth is a 'corruption' or 'prostitution' of language, a 'depoliticization of the word'; in short, an 'alibi'. The Romantic notion that myth explains origins is fraudulent because myth posits the contradiction-in-terms of 'eternal origins', making the question 'how did things come into existence?' unaskable. Myth gives the impression of objectivity and universality because it conceals the voice that speaks and passes itself off as a 'natural' statement.[41] Barthes's analysis of myth provides a devastating political critique of the Romantic view that myth puts man back

23

in touch with his origins in nature and reveals a set of eternal, universal truths. Barthes is perhaps the only structuralist critic to avoid the mythical temptation to construct a 'science of universals'.

Structuralism can now be seen to have been very much a product of the 1960s. Its uneasy mixture of Marxism and universalism characterizes the explosion of radical thought that culminated in the events in Paris of May 1968. The proliferation of Trotskyist student movements and the revival of anarchism in the 1960s is curiously inseparable from the contemporaneous proliferation of religious cults based on a revival of interest in pre-Christian and Eastern religion, witchcraft and the occult. Fringe politics and fringe religion meet in the utopian rejection of an alienated capitalism in favour of a return to 'natural' forms of collective existence. Underlying both is the equation of civilization with sickness, and of the natural with the healthy, that has explicitly or implicitly characterized mythical thought since the Romantics. Not for nothing was contemporary Soviet communism rejected for a revival of interest in the utopian socialists of the Romantic period, William Morris' arts-and-crafts movement, medieval millenarianism – popularized by Norman Cohn's *The Pursuit of the Millennium* (1957) – and third-world revolutionary movements which seemed to have harmonized Marxism with the 'natural' existence of peasant communities. The political and religious thought of the 1960s is literally 'radical' in that it demands a return to roots. Nowhere is this mythical desire to recover a lost wholeness more marked than in the 'revolution' in sexual attitudes. The rejection of sexual repression binds together the political and the religious because it puts sexuality – being biological and therefore organic – at the root of all human activity. The key feature of the 1960s was the insistence that neither political nor religious fulfilment are possible without sexual fulfilment. If the religious revival attempted to fuse Freud's view that man's basic impulses are sexual with Jung's belief in the primary nature of the religious, so political thinkers attempted to reconcile the Freudian theory of sexual repression with the Marxist analysis of capitalist exploitation and alienation. In *Eros and Civilization* (1955) – which was to become a key textbook of the 1960s – and his later *Essay on Liberation* (1969) – written in the wake of the events of May 1968 – the Californian political philosopher Herbert Marcuse argued that Marxism had gone wrong because it had failed to take into account the revolutionary implications of Freud's equation of civilization with repression. Marcuse knowingly makes the same misreading of Freud that had been made by the surrealists, twisting Freudian theory to argue for the abolition of repression and the reversion to a Narcissistic infantile 'polymorphous perversity' that will at the same time mark the breakdown of capitalism and the inauguration of the Marxist millennium. The sexual liberation movement of the 1960s also derived its inspiration from Wilhelm Reich, an exile from Nazi Germany whose classic works *The Function of the Orgasm* (1942) and *The Mass Psychology of Fascism* (1946) had argued that fascism was the product of sexual repression. Far from releasing man from the 'nightmare of history' by returning to a primal wholeness, it sublimated impotence and guilt by channelling repressed libidinous energies into aggression and authoritarianism, transforming sexual repression into political repression. Somewhat naively, Reich con-cluded that the achievement of orgasm by all would automatically lead to the end of repressive political structures. The mythical dimension of this equation of political liberation with sexual libera-tion is made explicit by the North American classicist Norman O. Brown, whose brilliant and influential *Life against Death: The Psycho-analytical Meaning of History* (1959) – together with its sequel *Love's Body* (1966) – stressed that the abolition of repression would mean not only an end to capitalism but an end to history altogether. For Brown, the Western linear view of time is necessarily repressive because it is the postponement of pleasure that creates the concept of the future as a time when fulfilment can be achieved. Sexual repression – particularly anal retentiveness – is the basis of the capi-talist notion of the accumulation of surplus profit, whereby resources must be hoarded and expenditure indefinitely postponed. The concept of progress is founded on the notion of jam tomorrow instead of jam today. Brown goes on to argue that it is not just linear time that is the product of repression, but also the cyclical view of time which Eliade had proposed as an antidote to the 'terror of history'. He points out that Eliade's analysis of New Year rituals shows that 'primitive' man also equated history with guilt: it is not that 'primitive' man was less repressed but that he had faith in his ability to annually wipe out the burden of history – a faith which modern man has lost. Brown is opposed to any such notion of the need to 'undo' history in order to expiate guilt, for this perpetuates belief in the inevitability of guilt; here his analysis is in line with Reich's suggestion that the fascist desire to 'undo' history compounds repression. But Brown's demand for an end to time – whether linear or cyclical – is in effect another version of the mythical desire to 'undo' history, in that it seeks to return to the 'original wholeness' and 'eternal present' of bodily pleasure as experienced in infancy. The release of bodily fluids is the release from history into a timeless world of ecstasy. Brown's chapters are titled 'The disease called Man', 'Neurosis and history', 'The way out', 'The resurrection of the body'. Despite the appeal to Freudian theory, Nietzsche is the more important influence. Brown revises Freud's conclusions, arguing that psychoanalysis strives for an end to repression and the repetition-compulsion which founds historical time, in order to enter the 'realm of Absolute Body' – in which 'joy wants itself, wants eternity, wants recurrence, wants everything eternally the same' – that Nietzsche had proclaimed with his doctrine of the Eternal Return. It is likewise Nietzsche and not Freud who is speaking when Brown insists that the function of memory, in enabling the neurotic to relive and understand his past, is to liberate him from 'the burden of his history, the burden which compels him to go on having (and being) a case history'.[42] Brown takes up Freud's definition of the life instinct (Eros) as a tendency towards inertia which joins hands with the death instinct (Thanatos), to argue that fulfilment means accepting the indivisibility of life and death, inasmuch as both are forms of release from the burden of history. Brown's insistence that the death of consciousness – inasmuch as the latter represents ego-control – is necessary to achieve the ecstatic 'free play' of the body is another version of the mythical notion that death is the prerequisite to rebirth and the recovery of wholeness. It is significant that the catchphrase of the 1960s was not 'freedom' (implying the ability to participate fully in history) but 'liberation' (implying release). Brown's marriage of Marx and Freud emphasizes the mythical substratum of their thought – the former's belief in a future definitive end to history; the latter's suggestion that the psyche is prior and in opposition to the socialization process – in order to argue against the view of both thinkers that man is inserted in a historical process. It is easy with hindsight to see why the political revolt of the 1960s degenerated into the cult of the social drop-out. The critic Frederic Jameson – also concerned to marry Marx with Freud – has criticized the appeal in much contemporary thought to what he calls the 'autonomization of sexuality', whereby sex is separated out from the public sphere and designated an 'autonomous' area of private experience, enabling it to be invested with symbolic meaning as the mythical 'ground' of human existence. Jameson points out that 'such allegories of desire (generally the products of the Freudian Left) have a great deal more in common with Jungianism and myth criticism proper than they do with the older orthodox Freudian analyses'. The 'Freudian Left', Jameson notes, perpetuates the mythical notion that 'desire is always outside of time, outside of narrative: it has no content, it is always the same, in its cyclical moments of emergence'; and that history is defined as being that which stands as an obstacle to desire. In this way, Jameson argues, the 'Freudian Left' disallows the possibility that desire might be historically conditioned, and that history might offer the means whereby it is able to find fulfilment.[43]

The neo-modernist return to myth by writers of the Latin American 'boom' coincided with the utopianism of the 1960s, and can be understood only in its context. The fringe cults of California, Paris or Berlin appealed to a continent which saw itself as being on the fringe of Western civilization, while at the same time wanting to be part of it: the assimilation of 1960s 'hippy' culture allowed Latin American writers to be Western and anti-Western at the same time. Particularly appealing to a continent struggling to emerge from colonial structures was the marriage of political radicalism with the demand for a return to roots, whether in the form of nature or human nature. The belief that sexual liberation was the key to political liberation offered an apparent answer to intractable economic problems by locating the solution in the individual and not in governments. The equation of governments with political corruption, plus the rejection of former colonial and subsequent imperialist domination as an 'inauthentic' imposition on to a 'natural' indigenous culture (a contradiction in terms, since culture can never be 'natural'), made Latin America particularly receptive to the mythical notion that history is a deviation from roots. The Cuban-born critic González Echevarría has insisted on the importance of the fact that the sense of national identity of Latin American countries was formed in the Romantic period, at the time of independence from Spain and Portugal: as a result national identity was from the start seen in terms of the mythical appeal to telluric essences.[44] In his book *The Making of New Cultures*, Colin Partridge shows that new-world cultures have generally gone through an initial stage of idealizing mythical roots, in order to affirm an independent identity.[45] The peculiarity of Latin American culture is perhaps the persistence of what elsewhere has been an initial stage. The so-called 'geographical novel' of the 1920s was rejected by later writers because its mythification of telluric essences was complicated by its depiction of Latin American nature as 'barbaric' (Gallegos' *Doña Bárbara*, Rivera's *La vorágine*), or by its view of nature as the founding step in the ascent towards culture (Güiraldes' *Don Segundo Sombra*). It could be argued that the ambiguous presentation of the nature/culture dichotomy by writers of the 1920s shows a greater understanding of the complexity of the issues involved than the often simplistic equation of roots with good and history with evil found in much Latin American writing of the 1960s. The most extreme case has been the Cuban Fernández Retamar's defiant assertion, in his essay *Calibán* (1971), that Latin America should not attempt to be a civilized 'Ariel' – as the Uruguayan Rodó had argued in his 1900 essay of that name – but should assume the role of Caliban: the primitive, monstrous 'other' of the Western world. The greatest influence in propagating the mythical view that Latin America's history is an inauthentic deviation from essences has, beyond doubt, been the Mexican Octavio Paz, whose seductive essay *El laberinto de la soledad* (1950) argued that Mexico's current identity was, as a result of a succession of foreign impositions, a 'mask' concealing a suppressed indigenous self. Much like Eliade, Paz insists that the Mexican strives – through the *fiesta* – for a release from the burden of an inauthentic history: a release which is found through the cult of death, seen as the other face of rebirth. Most seductive of all has been Paz's equation of the conquest of Mexico by Spain with the Fall: somewhat twisting the Genesis myth, he casts La Malinche – Cortés' Indian interpreter and concubine – in the role of Eve, and Cortés in the role not of Adam but – as violator of a pre-conquest Eden – of serpent. Paz blends Freud with existentialism to argue that Mexicans suffer from ontological insecurity because they can identify neither with their violator–father (representing culture) nor with their violated mother (representing nature) who lost her virginity to become a whore. Like Eliade, he misuses the existentialist notion of the inauthenticity and alienation

28

of history, insisting on the Mexican's need for roots. It is no coincidence that Paz should be a Mexican. Post-revolutionary Mexican governments had camouflaged their failure to better the lot of the Indian population with a rhetoric based on the mythification of indigenous culture as the 'essential' expression of the national soul. Another Mexican, Carlos Fuentes, has built his voluminous literary output on Paz's analysis of national schizophrenia (the split between the 'mask' of history and a suppressed 'essential' self). His most ambitious attempt to overcome historical alienation *Terra Nostra* (1975) will re-write or 'undo' both European and Mexican history in order to find the lost 'universal' roots of both. If Paz's poetry appeals to Aztec mythology (affirming the cyclical wholeness of death and rebirth) and Eastern religion (stressing sexual ecstasy as a release from the oppositions of rational thought), Fuentes attempts a fusion of Aztec mythology with the European millenarian tradition (which merge via a common cult of sex and death). The concept of millenarian revolt has fascinated contemporary Latin American writers and film-makers, with its irrationalist equation of political liberation with spiritual release: apart from *Terra Nostra*, see Vargas Llosa's *La guerra del fin del mundo* (1981) and Glauber Rocha's films *Deus e o diabo na terra do sol* (1964) and *Antonio das Mortes* (1969). The marked irrationalism of contemporary Latin American literature finds justification in the notion that it was the imposition of Western rationalism on to Latin America that produced the historical dissociation from 'natural' origins; in fact, such irrationalism derives directly from the European surrealist movement, whose valuation of the 'primitive' gave Latin American writers in Paris – Asturias, Carpentier, Cortázar – a new sense of cultural pride. It is also worth noting that the political radicalism of the writers of the Latin American 'boom' goes hand in hand with the influence of reactionary European thinkers such as Spengler (whose *Decline of the West* suggested that the time had come for the American 'New World') and Eliade. Thus García Márquez's *Cien años de soledad* (1967) will combine a radical desire to correct the official mythifications of Colombian history with a cyclical vision which curiously imposes the Spenglerian notion of decadence on to its depiction of the underdeveloped continent of Latin America. The concept of myth put forward by Latin American writers is almost exclusively based on Eliade's insistence on myth as a return to origins, fused with the

Jungian notion – relayed via Joseph Campbell – of the quest myth as a return to the 'womb' of the unconscious in search of rebirth. The few exceptions who turn to indigenous myth rather than to European notions of 'the mythical mind' – the Guatemalan Asturias or the Peruvian Arguedas, both anthropologists and the latter brought up by Quechua Indians – are a healthy reminder that myth does not need to be concerned with 'undoing' history.[46] The Jungian theory of myth has appealed particularly in Argentina, a country where psychoanalysis has a high status and where massive immigration from different European countries, combined with the virtual extinction of the indigenous population, created an acute sense of lack of roots. Jung's view of mythical archetypes as the expression of a universal 'collective unconscious' has also enabled Latin American writers to reconcile their urge to recover indigenous mythical roots with the fact that they are mostly of European extraction and keen to be regarded as part of the Western intellectual mainstream. This is particularly clear in the case of Carlos Fuentes, whose critical essays *La nueva novela hispanoamericana* (1969) put forward the contradictory view that myth allows a return to Latin American origins and at the same time gives contemporary Latin American writers a new universality.[47] Ruthven shrewdly observes that myth, by promising access to a superior source of wisdom, has a snob appeal for writers anxious to make their mark on the world.[48] In the same way the use of classical mythological references – and the frequency of these in Latin American literature is notable – singles the author out as the product of a superior European-based education, while at the same time flattering the reader by supposing he has the cultural equipment necessary to spot the allusions. Latin American writers who have turned to myth – Fuentes is a prime example – are impressively difficult because of the vast array of cultural allusions with which their works are littered.

If the reader has come to expect contemporary Latin American literature to reduce history to a cyclical pattern whereby Paradise Lost is projected on to the future in the form of Utopia, it is largely because critics – under the influence of North American myth criticism, with its insistence that all literature of worth conforms to the structures of the quest myth – have bent over backwards to find such archetypal patterns so as to prove Latin American writers deserving of international attention. The works of Paz, Fuentes, Neruda,

Carpentier, Cortázar, Rulfo, García Márquez do contain mythical structures but – with the exception of the first writer – they also contain a degree of ironic awareness of the limitations of the mythical return to origins. In *Terra Nostra* the desire to 'undo' history leads in practice to an eternal repetition of suffering; the mythical equation of sex and death as a release from time leads to an ambiguous 'final solution', with the millennium ushered in to the twin accompaniment of Narcissistic erotic play and the gas-chambers. In his quest in *Alturas de Macchu Picchu* (1950) for an original Latin American identity, Neruda will discover that the continent's history is founded not on unhewn rock but on the blood and sweat of the Indian labourers who built the ancient city: there is no 'original nature' prior to culture, no 'wholeness' prior to aliena-tion. The attempt of the narrator–protagonist of Carpentier's *Los pasos perdidos* (1953) to give voice to a 'virgin' nature unsullied by civilization is ironically undercut by his inability to free himself from cultural preconceptions; while the parallel attempt of Oliveira, in Cortázar's *Rayuela* (1963), to 'undo the course of civilization' does not rescue him from an alienating intellectualism but turns him into a monster of egoism on the verge of breakdown. Critics have tended to ignore the ambiguous endings of the novels of Carpentier and Cortázar, which by no means present the attempt to convert Paradise Lost into Utopia as entirely positive: see, for example, Esteban and Sofía's senseless death as they attempt to revive lost heroic ideals at the end of Carpentier's *El siglo de las luces* (1962). In the same way *Cien años de soledad* (1967) can be seen as a critique of its characters' mythical obsession with converting history into a sterile cyclical process of 'making in order to unmake'. Incest (return to the 'womb' of the unconscious) is not put forward as a solution to the alienation of history, but is the founding crime on which Macondo is built and which causes its final destruction: the implication is that the 'original sin' of Latin America is not the loss of origins but precisely its obsession with origins.[49] Rulfo's *Pedro Páramo* (1955) can also be interpreted as an implied critique of the return to roots, which in this case leads to a father figure who turns history into an eternal present of death. It is only recently that critics have begun to suggest that Latin American writers do not always turn to myth to recreate the Jungian archetypes dear to myth criticism. In her latest book *Utopía, paraíso e historia*, Aronne Amestoy suggests that Rulfo is criticizing his characters' antihistorical obsession with Paradise Lost.[50] Similarly González Echevarría's recent collection of essays *The Voice of the Masters* demolishes many of the critical assumptions about the use of myth in Latin American literature.[51]

This revision of critical attitudes towards myth is the direct result of the deconstructive demolitions in the 1970s of Derrida, who has mercilessly exposed the illusory nature of Western civilization's obsession with origins and wholeness.[52] The term postmodernist' is an apt one to describe deconstruction, for it represents a major break with the modernist appeal to myth as an antidote to the alienation of modern life. Derrida insists that the only primary reality is difference; there is no escape from the instability and contradiction that comprise history. Another more basic, but probably more serious, blow to the Romantic concept of myth has been dealt by Walter Ong, whose work in the 1960s and 1970s on the transition from oral culture to literacy led him to the sensible conclusion that the constitutive features of myth can be explained – with no need to posit the existence of a privileged 'mythical mentality' – as an inevitable consequence of oral performance. Ong's insistence that oral culture lacks the notion of underlying symbolic meaning which is the hallmark of literacy shows the Romantic theory of myth to be a modern 'reading' of it: ironically, the Romantics' appeal to an oral culture threatened by the new extension of literacy only confirmed the extent to which literacy had shaped their sensibility.[53] Just as the 1970s have seen a reaction against the Romantic concept of myth, so postmodernist critics have set about debunking the concept of history, showing it to be 'mythical' in the sense that it is a verbal construct. In *The Order of Things* (1966), Foucault deconstructed the arbitrary nature of the classification systems which in different periods have constituted Western man's view of history. (Borges had, of course, made the same point earlier: the exclusive interest of Latin American myth critics in Jungian archetypes led them to omit Borges from their discussions.) In his two books *Metahistory* (1973) and *Tropics of Discourse* (1978), the American historian Hayden White – taking up Lévi-Strauss' comments at the end of *The Savage Mind* – has deconstructed the 'tropes' or rhetorical devices used by historians to give their accounts of the past the illusion of authenticity. Particularly interesting (if schematic) is his reduction of nineteenth-century historiography to Northrop Frye's four 'universal' genres of Romance, Comedy, Tragedy and Satire, in turn derived from the seasonal pattern which informs the mythical cyclical vision.[54] The historian of Arab culture, Bernard Lewis, has also made the point that history is often used to 'recover' a past that had been forgotten or 'lost' during an intervening period which comes to be regarded as a 'usurpation', just as myth – in its Romantic version – seeks to 'undo' an 'inauthentic' history in order to recover 'authentic origins'. Lewis' analysis suggests a reason for the perennial appeal of the *Odyssey*, with its threefold pattern of loss of roots/usurpation by the suitors/return to roots and slaying of the usurpers. Lewis points out that revolutions and invasions have a special need to disguise their illegitimacy as 'usurpers' by spawning a historiography that postulates their descent from – and return to – some lost founding tradition, which they claim had been 'usurped' by their predecessors: the mythohistoriography of the Franco regime is a perfect example. Lewis' warning about the temptation felt by newly independent nations to 'decolonize' the past by creating a mythical Golden Age prior to conquest is equally pertinent to Latin America. History, in Lewis' view, is all too often invested with the mythical function of providing a 'foundation' for those in authority – or for those seeking to assert an alternative authority.[55] It seems that use of the terms 'myth' and 'history' – which started life meaning 'utterance' and 'tale' respectively, without distinguishing between 'true' and 'false' – has come full circle. It would however be a mistake to conclude that the 'mythical' nature of historical writing makes the terms 'myth' and 'history' interchangeable. History may be 'myth' in the sense that it is a verbal construct, but myth affirms cyclical recurrence and supposes that history is dissociated from origins, while historical writing – when not used in the mythical manner described by Lewis – affirms linear progress and continuity. Myth is concerned with the eternal and the universal, and attempts to neutralize change; history is concerned with the temporal and the particular, and stresses the importance of change. Both are ways of organizing reality into a meaningful structure that may have little to do with reality as it is experienced, but they remain in opposition to

33

one another. The warning uttered by Philip Rahv in his 1953 essay 'The myth and the powerhouse' still holds true:

> Myth, the appeal of which lies precisely in its archaism, promises above all to heal the wounds of time. For the one essential function of myth stressed by all writers is that in merging past and present it releases us from the flux of temporality ... Hence the mythic is the polar opposite of what we mean by the historical, which stands for process, inexorable change, incessant permutation and innovation. Myth is reassuring in its stability; whereas history is that powerhouse of change which destroys custom and tradition in producing the future ... In our time the movement of history has been so rapid that the mind longs for nothing so much as something permanent to steady it. Hence what the craze for myth represents most of all is the fear of history.[56]

Eliade's insistence that myth provides an antidote to the 'terror of history' is correct; whether he was right to advocate such an antidote is another matter.

Myth and Nationalist Spain

An understanding of the role played by myth in provoking the Civil War and consolidating Nationalist victory is essential to an understanding of its use by writers in the postwar period. As in the case of fascism in Italy and Germany, the ideology of the Spanish fascist movement Falange Española was based on the mythical notion that the nation's history was an inauthentic deviation from origins. Fascism would 'save' the nation by returning it to its 'essential nature'. This mythical view of history was not a borrowing from Italian and German fascism, as Spanish fascist thinkers rightly stressed, but can be traced back to the analysis of Spain's 'decadence' undertaken by the so-called 1898 Generation and by Ortega y Gasset. In *En torno al casticismo* (1895), Unamuno had divided the 'sea of history' into the 'superficial waves of change' and the 'eternal tradition' – represented by the folk – lying in its depths. Unamuno's insistence on the need to plunge into the depths of the ocean (the *pueblo*) reads like a version of the Jungian quest myth in which the hero plunges into the depths of the collective unconscious.[1] In his *Idearium español* (1897), Ganivet likewise divided Spanish history, not into an 'above' and a 'below', but into a 'before' and an 'after', creating the same mythical dissociation between an inauthentic history and authentic origins. Ganivet suggested that the nation's course since 1492 (the beginning of imperial expansion) had been a 'mistake' or 'deviation' from its essential 'territorial spirit', to which it must return. His view that the 'territorial spirit' had determined, not what happened in Spanish history, but what should have happened but didn't, makes it clear that his pretence of positivistic geographical determinism is a mask for mythical thinking. In *Meditaciones del Quijote* (1914), Ortega would similarly advocate the need to 'burn' the 'dross' of Spain's historical past in order to recover 'the primary substance of the race', 'the iridescent gem of the Spain that might have been'.[2]

Such ideas enabled the founder of the Falange, José Antonio Primo de Rivera, to insist 'we love Spain because we don't like her', differentiating a rejected historical reality from an 'authentic' 'original' Spain. The Falangist intellectual Pedro Laín Entralgo, twisting existentialist argument like Eliade, would claim that fascism saved man from the inauthenticity of history by restoring him to lost eternal values: 'we are thrust into time – into history – but our substance is eternity'. The avant-garde writer Giménez Caballero, the major literary exponent of fascist thought in Spain, made explicit the equation of history with the Fall by calling José Antonio the 'Agnus Dei qui tollis peccata Hispaniae'. In his book *España y Franco* (1938) he would compare Franco's smile to the Virgin's mantle holding out the promise of redemption; while in an article of 1937 he railed against a besieged Republican Madrid as a biblical Sodom and 'whore of Babylon' paying the price for her sins.[3] His best-known work *Genio de España* (1932) set out to denounce 'three centuries of bastardization', calling for the 'cleansing' of the nation from the 'drugs' that had 'poisoned' its soul, and a return to 'the genital root of the nation's essence'.[4] Franco's sister Pilar would give characteristically blunt expression to the notion that Nationalist victory had 'cured' Spain from the 'sickness' of history when she declared: 'Ortega y Gasset diagnosed Spain as invertebrate; my brother tried to fit her with an orthopaedic corset.' Just as Mussolini had said that 'Today, in Italy, we are not living the time of history but of myth', so the Falangist Rafael García Serrano would say in 1935: 'We shall create a new mythology, which this time will be fullbloodedly romantic.' Fascism is indeed the ultimate expression of the Romantic appeal to myth in that it takes literally and puts into practice the urge to 'undo' history and return to origins. The Romantic longing to recover lost purity finds its political equivalent in the Comisiones de Depuración ['Purification Committees'] set up in all walks of life after Nationalist victory.[5]

The notion that Spanish history since the Catholic Kings had been a long process of decadence led to the conclusion that the nation must undergo a 'sacrificial death' to hasten 'rebirth'. The fascist exaltation of violence has a mystical note: the proclaimed 'return to barbarism' is at the same time called a 'Crusade'. The

Nationalist 'myth of the Crusade' has been savagely demolished by Herbert Southworth.[6] Franco himself would betray the reality behind the myth of a return to spiritual values when he declared 'Our Crusade is the only struggle in which the rich who went to war came out of it richer.'[7] The cult of sacrificial death and its corollary of rebirth is a salient feature of Falangist ideology. The Moroccan divisions under Franco's command proclaimed themselves the 'Bridegrooms of Death'; their rallying cry 'Viva la muerte' expresses the notion that death is the pre-requisite to salvation. In *Genio de España*, Giménez Caballero asserted that the 'true, eternal life' of a nation is embodied in its dead, going on to demand a 'resurrection' of the national soul. The book ends with its author in Nietzschean fashion heralding the fiery sunset over the Monte de El Pardo in Madrid – his 'Mount Tabor' – as an annunciation of the apocalyptic battle to come.[8] The terms 'youth', 'dawn', 'spring' recur throughout *Genio de España*, as throughout Falangist ideology in general. The words of the Falangist anthem 'Cara al sol' proclaim that the blood of the fallen heroes will 'blossom' in a new 'spring'. José Antonio would encourage the ideal of heroic death by insisting that the future Spain would be built on 'the blood of our dead', and that 'death is an act of service'. His mystical conception of violence as the prelude to rebirth is epitomized by his famous description of Falangist militants as 'half-soliders half-monks'. Franco would dedicate his 1941 film-script *Raza* (whose thesis is the need to return to 'essential' racial virtues) 'To the youth of Spain, whose blood paved the way for our rebirth.'[9] By 'rebirth' José Antonio had in mind a return to 'barbarian' virility; what Franco meant was a return to purity in the sense of puritanism. Despite the Nietzschean streak that remained in Nationalist ideology even after the war – when propaganda was put in the hands of the Falange – it was the Francoist and official Catholic interpretation of spiritual rebirth that prevailed in practice. The tension between the Nietzschean and the classical strands of the modernist appeal to myth come to the surface in the growth and final emasculation of Spanish fascism.

The political ambiguity of the fascist appeal to myth was in fact its main attraction, allowing it to claim that it transcended the divisions between Right and Left, restoring the nation to a lost 'organic wholeness'. The emphasis on 'unity' – which in practice meant the suppression of regional separatist movements – is entirely in keeping with the appeal to myth as a source of wholeness. The original Falange – before its domestication by Franco on his assumption of overall command of Nationalist forces in 1937 – was, like its original Italian and German counterparts, opposed both to communism and to capitalism. It mobilized Right-wing opposition to the modification of traditional class structures at the same time as appealing to the popular notion of millenarian revolt. Not for nothing did the Spanish peasantry divide its allegiance between fascism and anarchism: both movements with a strong millenarian appeal. The Falange promised to transcend class conflict by uniting employers and workers in state-controlled 'vertical syndicates' (the only part of the original Falangist platform that was put into effect under Franco). Its dream was the return to a paternalistic feudalism in which the people – seen as the repository of the nation's spiritual values – would be 'saved' from the divisive evils of progress and returned to their 'oneness' with nature. The one concrete demand in José Antonio's political programme was for an agrarian reform that would produce 'a genuine return to Nature, not in the sense of the eclogue, as found in Rousseau, but in that of the georgic, with its deep, austere, ritual understanding of the earth'.[10] This emphasis on a return to 'natural wholeness' is seen in the Francoist proclamation of a 'totalitarian' state based on 'organic' laws. José Antonio's meaningless but evocative definition of the nation as an organic 'unit of universal destiny' became the chief catchphrase of Nationalist propaganda. The notion of unity is linked to that of imperialism: the return to 'natural', 'organic' values gives the nation a universality that legitimizes the imposition of its culture on other nations. In his indispensable *Literatura fascista española*, Rodríguez-Puértolas demonstrates that the emphasis on organic unity was inseparable from the desire to make Spain once again an imperial power.[11]

The Falangist appeal to 'wholeness' attracted certain avant-garde writers – notably the surrealist Giménez Caballero, editor of the leading avant-garde magazine *La Gaceta Literaria* which published writers of all political persuasions including Alberti and Lorca, and founder of Spain's first cinema club and modern art gallery – for whom the irrationalism of myth offered a way of resolving the dichotomies of rational thought. It is this that is meant by José Antonio's definition of the Falange in his founding speech as 'a poetic movement'. Laín Entralgo would describe fascism as a 'style' appropriate to 'poets writing a vast communal poem'. José Antonio, himself a minor poet, surrounded himself with a literary 'court' to whom he turned for political advice. His speeches abound in vacuous poetic statements such as: 'in History and in politics the shortest route between two points is via the stars'. The lack of content in his political programme was a deliberate rejection of a divisive rationalism for the 'organic integrity' of poetic speech: 'People say we have no programme ... When did you ever see matters of importance, eternal matters like love, life and death, organized according to a programme?' The other side of this cult of irrationalism was a rabid anti-intellectualism. Giménez Caballero – a friend of Goebbels, the Nazi Minister of Propaganda who declared 'When I hear the word culture I reach for my gun' – would proclaim 'the mystical doctrine of anti-culture', insisting that rational thought should be replaced by a state of 'exaltation', defined as 'a return to the vital world of fanaticism'.[12] His *Genio de España* – one of the most remarkable political tracts ever written, and a textbook example of the modernist revival of myth – bears the subtitle *Exaltations to a National and Universal Resurrection*. This anti-intellectualism would finally alienate the vast majority of Spanish writers and thinkers. It was the cry 'Death to intelligence' that led Unamuno – himself a champion of the irrational – to retract his initial support for Franco in his Salamanca speech of October 1936.

In keeping with this rejection of rationalist argument, the political rallies of the Falange – not for nothing founded in 1933 in a Madrid theatre – were cultivatedly spectacular. José Antonio's love of ritual would see its apotheosis at the end of the Civil War with the torchlight procession transporting his body from Alicante to be buried in the Escorial. This cult of pomp and ceremony would be continued by Franco, notably with his erection of the Valle de los Caídos, to which José Antonio's body was transferred and where Franco made provision for his own burial. Appropriately this monument to the 'national resurrection' secured by the blood of the Nationalist 'martyrs' was built by Republican prisoners of war 'expiating their sins'. The same monumental style and appeal to ritual shaped artistic tastes in the Nationalist zone during the war. In his manifesto *Arte y estado* (1935), Giménez Caballero – who unsuccessfully asked for the post of Minister of Propaganda – had put art at the service of the fascist State 'in accordance with the almost mythical, propagandistic impulse in the phalanxes of art today ... Art is propaganda ..., but with a transcendental basis ... Its true origins are religious. *Propaganda fide.*' Giménez Caballero pleaded for the integration of the avant-garde in painting, architecture, music and drama into a grandiose Wagnerian art that would be at once religious and popular. Falangist writers turned particularly to the theatre as a collective spectacle, reviving the allegorical *auto sacramental* of Spain's Golden Age to create what the young Falangist dramatist and theorist Gonzalo Torrente Ballester – later to emerge as one of Spain's most talented novelists – termed the 'Liturgy of Empire'. Torrente Ballester called for a return to the 'epic' theatre of classical Greece with its heroic protagonists, and its chorus which 'redeemed' the masses by giving them a corporate identity. In his important theoretical article 'Razón y ser de la dramática futura' (1937), he summed up his vision of the new fascist theatre as 'Myth, Magic, Mystery. An epic of national endeavour.' To achieve this the poet Dionisio Ridruejo – head of the Nationalist Press and Propaganda Services from 1938 till 1941, after which he broke with the Franco regime – set up the Compañía del Teatro Nacional de Falange Española Tradicionalista y de las JONS (the full title of the Nationalist political movement formed from the forced merger in 1937 of Falange Española y las JONS – itself formed from the merger in 1934 of Falange Española with the rural-based Juntas de Ofensiva Nacional Sindicalista – with the Carlist Comunión Tradicionalista). Interestingly, in its desire to create a popular collective art this Nationalist Theatre Company borrowed many of the ideas of the prewar Republic's state-funded touring company La Barraca, which under Lorca's direction had set out to take culture to the masses. The fusion of the Greek ideal with Catholic ritual led to a playing down of the Nietzschean 'Dionysiac' aspects of Greek tragedy in favour of a classical appeal to 'unity' and 'order'. Greek tragedy provided the inspiration for Nationalist writers such as José María Pemán, who wrote the plays *Antígona* (1945), *Electra* (1949) and *Edipo* (1953) as well as poetic drama mythifying glorious episodes from national history. Torrente Ballester's play *El retorno de Ulises* (written during the Civil War, published in 1946) turns the Homeric theme into an allegory of contemporary Spanish history, with the absent hero Ulysses representing José Antonio – 'the Absent One' as he was called in Falangist rhetoric

40

after his execution in a Republican prison in 1938 – who will one day return to succour Penelope, representing the abandoned Motherland.[13] This predilection for myth was to last throughout Torrente Ballester's literary career, though from 1942 onwards the seeds of political disenchantment would introduce an ironic note. Another Falangist writer who started publishing during the war, Alvaro Cunqueiro, would subsequently devote himself to the writing of mythical novels – the best known being *Las mocedades de Ulises* (1960) and *Un hombre que se parecía a Orestes* (1969) – again turning to classical Greece. Cunqueiro's irony derives from the supposition that history is the enactment, frequently self-conscious, of pre-ordained mythical roles. Despite his exploitation of the comic possibilities of anachronism, his novels affirm a mythical view of history as eternal recurrence, in which different historical periods become interchangeable.[14] Both Torrente and Cunqueiro would combine their taste for myth with a love of folklore, particularly that of their native Galicia. The cult of folklore by the Franco regime – especially by the Women's Section of the Movimiento Nacional (as the Falange was re-named in 1958), headed by José Antonio's sister Pilar – constitutes a particularly interesting attempt at defusing the separatist implications of regional culture by incorporating it into a popular vision celebrating 'national essences'. The Nationalist protection of folklore parallels its political 'protection' of the *pueblo* from the dangers of modernity. As the original revolutionary aspirations of the Falange gave way to the consolidation of bourgeois capitalism, the ideal of a mythical, epic theatre was replaced by folkloric spectacle and a return to bourgeois comedy. The poetic cult of Garcilaso as imperial soldier–poet – known as 'garcilasismo' – evolved into an inward-looking lyricism concerned to express the more anodyne 'universal values' of human sentiment. In the field of the novel, the official insistence on the need to create a non-elitist, popular culture would lead to a rejection of modernism in favour of a return to bourgeois realism: see, for example, the novels of Zunzunegui and Gironella. Perhaps nowhere is the Francoist betrayal of the original Falange's anti-bourgeois revolutionary ideals seen more clearly than in the field of literature.

If officialdom began by preaching the need for a mythical, epic literature but in practice ended up turning to bourgeois realism, conversely the new generation of opposition novelists that emerged in the 1950s would preach the need for social realism (censorship did not permit the Marxist term 'socialist realism') but in practice produced works with strong mythical undertones. The term 'social realism' is inadequate to describe any of the novels written in the 1950s that can still be read with pleasure.[15] It is not surprising to find an officially approved writer such as Delibes – coming from the rural area of Old Castile which had formed the stronghold of the JONS – producing novels such as *El camino* (1950) and *Las ratas* (1962) in which realistic description combines with nostalgic evocation of a country childhood and 'natural' way of life threatened by the advent of adulthood and progress respectively. As late as 1979 Delibes will be commissioned to produce the anthology of excerpts from his fictional work *Castilla, lo castellano y los castellanos*, proving the continuing demand for such evocations of an essential national character. Despite Delibes' insistence that he is not opposed to progress, his choice of excerpts perpetuates all the Nationalist clichés about the capacity for endurance of the Castilian peasant. Neither is it surprising that Camilo José Cela – who like Delibes fought when young for the Nationalists, refusing exemption from conscription on grounds of tuberculosis and in 1938 offering to denounce acquaintances to the Nationalist Government in Burgos, later in the 1940s working as magazine censor and enjoying the literary patronage of the Falangist head of press censorship Juan Aparicio – should produce a novel such as *La familia de Pascual Duarte* (1942) where the depiction of rural deprivation is subsumed into a mythical vision of history as evil, strongly reminiscent of Greek tragedy; or *La colmena* (1951) whose hyper-realistic description of the monotony of Madrid life takes place in an ahistorical vacuum, structured in a series of overlapping circles. Cela's ahistorical attitude is made explicit in his foreword to the second edition of *La colmena*, where he expresses his cynical amusement at the eternal recurrence that constitutes human behaviour.[16] But what is surprising is that Delibes' evocation of a Paradise Lost and Cela's cyclical vision recur in the work of younger writers such as Jesús Fernández Santos, Rafael Sánchez Ferlosio, and the brothers Juan and Luis Goytisolo, all of whom were regarded – and regarded themselves – as members of the opposition. Up to a point it can be argued that the presence of mythical characteristics in the work of such opposition writers functions as a covert criticism of prevailing Nationalist ideology. But the lack of any counterbalancing historical vision – Luis Goytisolo is an exception here – makes one suspect that it is perhaps a case of contagion by a generation which had received its schooling in the 1940s when education was synonymous with indoctrination (only in 1956 would the Department of Propaganda be separated from education and put under the control of the new Ministry of Information and Tourism). In his important article 'Dictatorship and literature: the model of Francoist Spain', Paul Ilie has argued for a study of 'the mythohistoriography arising after history is absorbed into ideology', pointing out that the obsession with childhood and the treatment of father and mother figures in the postwar novel can be related to Nationalist ideology. A disproportionate number of postwar novels – and films – do indeed opt for a child's perspective.[17] Writers such as Ana María Matute – belonging to the new generation of novelists that emerged in the 1950s – will, by concentrating on the treatment of childhood, express a disconformity that does not go beyond the inner realm of personal sensibility, thus echoing the 'intimismo' that characterized official poetry of the postwar period. In a film such as Víctor Erice's *El espíritu de la colmena* (1973), the child's uncomprehending perspective of postwar repression increases the poignancy but one also feels it is a way of avoiding a political focus, lifting events out of the realm of history into that of myth. The repeated adoption of an infantile perspective is a way of getting past the censor precisely because it conforms to the official requirement that culture be depoliticized. Ilie notes that writers under censorship resort to a 'new mythography' in order to counter official myths, but that at the same time myth is a 'vehicle of last resort' to which writers turn to provide imaginary solutions when real solutions seem impossible.[18] Indeed the use of mythical patterns in the novel of the 1950s seems to reflect a fatalistic belief that not even imaginary solutions are possible. Dionisio Ridruejo, Franco's first head of censorship, has argued that the censors approved the publication of the majority of so-called 'social realist' novels of the 1950s because they felt their fatalistic presentation would encourage resignation rather than rebellion.[19] It is worth noting that Cela's *La colmena* – published first in Argentina and banned in Spain till 1955 – experienced more problems with the censor than did novels such as Fernández Santos' *Los bravos* (1954), Juan Goytisolo's *Duelo en el Paraíso* (1955), Sánchez Ferlosio's *El Jarama* (1956) or Luis

Goytisolo's *Las afueras* (1958).[20] Rather than attempt here to give an overview of the Spanish novel of the 1950s, I shall restrict myself to an examination of these four novels, which provide instructive examples of the contradictory juxtaposition of a supposedly social realist aim with an underlying mythical vision.

In all four novels, the desire to expose the evils of the Franco regime leads to the equation of contemporary history with the Fall, echoing the mythical view of history that characterized Falangist ideology. The difference is, of course, that the Falange identified the Fall with progress and looked back to the Paradise Lost of traditional values, whereas the novels of the 1950s identify the Fall with Nationalist victory and look back to the Paradise Lost of the Republic. The frequency of the Paradise Lost theme in the postwar novel has been noted by Gonzalo Sobejano.[21] What has not been pointed out is that this mythical view of contemporary history constitutes a revised version of Nationalist ideology. Rather than reject the mythical view of history instilled into them at school, the generation brought up after the war – which after all was not taught to analyse history as an interplay of political and economic forces – simply inverts the terms of the Nationalist version of Genesis, idealizing as Paradise Lost what the latter regarded as the Fall. It is perhaps not coincidence that the majority of young writers in the 1950s were born into Nationalist families: their lack of access to alternative explanations of history makes inversion of their elders' values the easiest form of rebellion. Ignacio Soldevila has pointed out that the communist sympathies proclaimed by many of the 'angry young men' of the 1950s were often based on the assumption – shared with officialdom – that any dissident line was Marxist.[22] It is noticeable that the Paradise Lost theme is absent from a genuinely social realist novel such as *La mina* (1959) by Armando López Salinas, from a working-class background and a member of the Central Committee of the banned Spanish Communist Party. (It must also be said that López Salinas' orthodox Marxist vision makes for much less interesting reading.) In a perceptive piece of self-criticism, Juan Goytisolo would later point out the dangers of this rejection of the present in favour of an idealized past, suggesting that Spanish dissidents were so fixated with clinging to the ideals of their Paradise Lost that they failed to notice that postwar Spain was changing and got left behind in the 'rear carriage' of the train of history.[23] Indeed it could be said that the use of the Paradise Lost theme by novelists of the 1950s leads to an even greater ahistoricism than that found in Falangist ideology. The Nationalists believed that it was possible to 'undo' the evils of history in order to return to lost origins, and fought their 'Crusade' to achieve this. But in the novels of the 1950s Paradise tends to be a futile dream located in an irretrievable 'before' or an inaccessible 'somewhere else'. Their cyclical vision does not suppose that history can be undone but that it is revolving on the spot. This sense of a paralysis of time equates the present with the decadence of the Fall and at the same time with the eternity of Paradise. Such a contradictory view of Franco's Spain as an 'eternal decadence' is the inevitable result of the inversion of Nationalist ideology: if the 'myth of the Crusade' claimed to have restored Spain to the Paradise Lost of her 'eternal values', the younger generation of opposition writers would regard Nationalist victory as a 'fall' into 'eternal values'. When events do take place in this paralysed world, they take the form of death or crime. The impression often given is that Spanish history is under a curse, sentenced to an eternal recurrence of disaster without even the possibility of redemption held out by Nationalist ideology. It is interesting that the same entirely negative cyclical vision should be put forward by Cela, despite his links with a regime for whom the cyclical view of history meant the return to a new 'dawn' or 'spring'. The only dawns or springs that occur in the novels of the 1950s are undercut by irony. Just as the chapters of *La colmena* end with a series of dawns that hold out false hopes or – in the closing pages – illumine a cemetery at the onset of winter, so *Los bravos* ends with a dawn that marks the first day of autumn and a return to the initial status quo; *Duelo en el Paraíso* opens with a dawn – again in autumn – sullied by the death of a child; and the central story of *Las afueras* – set in spring – tells of old age and death, while the final dawn scene ushers in a prosperous but empty future, once more set against an autumn background. *El Jarama* is also set in autumn, with no dawn but only a nightfall. The decadence of the present is eternal not only because it represents the imposition of Nationalist 'eternal values' but also because it is inescapable. It is perhaps not so surprising after all that the censors should have found such historical pessimism acceptable in opposition writers, but been alarmed by it in a writer such as Cela whom they regarded as one of their own.

If the temporal sequence of *La colmena* follows the circular spatial meanderings of its characters, in *Los bravos* the chronological presentation of the action is undercut by the circular trajectory of the characters, as the doctor assumes the role of the landowner Don Prudencio, and Amparo that of the spinster Pilar. The novel does not so much tell a story as describe a routine existence where the only option is to 'seguir el curso de la rueda: girar, girar' ['go round and round like a wheel'].[24] Just as the narrator looks back to better times before the Civil War, so the characters dream of escape to the city, representing progress. But all the city brings them is the swindler, who takes what little wealth they had. Don Prudencio's trip to the city will confirm his imminent death and lead to his abandonment by Socorro. As Pepe prepares to emigrate, he is met by the returning migrant worker who warns of failure ahead. There is a world of progress outside the eternal decadence of the village, but it brings only crime, death, loss and failure to compound the existing paralysis (represented by Amador's bed-ridden child). Despite the detailed description of material conditions, the accumulation of disasters makes the reader feel the village is under a curse: an impression confirmed by mention of a mythical lake beneath whose waters lies a village submerged by Christ in punishment for its meanness, and by the novel's epigraph 'El destino de un pueblo es como el destino de un hombre: su carácter es su destino' ['The destiny of a nation, like that of a man, lies in its character']. In keeping with the Nationalist view of rural Spain as the repository of an 'essential' national character (albeit in this case negative), the message seems to be that it is not material conditions that have created the villagers' closed attitudes, but vice versa. The absence of possible redemption is suggested by the dereliction of the church and lack of a village priest. The superimposition on to the description of material conditions of this mythical view of present history as a curse is made inevitable by the fact that, while Fernández Santos is appalled by the devastation brought by historical disaster (specifically the Civil War), at the same time he rejects progress because it means the end of rural Spain. Rejection of the Franco regime's evolution towards capitalism would, in other writers of Fernández

Santos' generation, prove an obstacle to the acceptance of a forward-moving historical vision. If both decadence and progress are rejected, there is no way out but a fatalistic view of history as evil. It was the inability of the Left to come to terms with the fact that Franco's Spain was progressing materially that was to produce the splits and expulsions that weakened the Spanish Communist Party in the 1960s.

In *El Jarama*, the chronological narrative sequence is likewise subsumed into a closed cyclical pattern: that of one day's events from morning to night, framed by the arrival and departure of a group of youngsters from the capital. This circular frame is in turn contained within the description of the course of the River Jarama, implying that human activity is a parenthesis in an unchanging natural cycle, and – as the river finally flows out into the sea – that if there is an end to the cycle it is death: the reader is inevitably reminded of the fifteenth-century poet Jorge Manrique's famous lines 'Our lives are rivers/that flow into the sea/of death.' Indeed the only event in the novel is the death of Luci, just as in *La colmena* the only event was the murder of Doña Margot. If ignorance of the motives for Doña Margot's murder increased the impression that events are arbitrary, so the accidental nature of Luci's death makes the incident appear 'natural' rather than the product of historical circumstance: the culprit is the river. The main function of the river is as a Heraclitan symbol of the dual nature of time as irreversible flow and eternal recurrence. A similar opposition is created at the end by the division of the characters into 'los que se van' ['those who depart'] and 'los que se quedan' ['those who stay'], reminding the reader of Unamuno's division of time in *En torno al casticismo* into 'lo que pasa' ['what happens/passes'] – i.e. history – and 'lo que queda' ['what remains'] – i.e. intrahistory or mythical repetition. The novel's juxtaposition of a linear historical vision with a cyclical mythical vision serves to inscribe the former within the latter. For if the irreversible nature of time is represented by Luci's death, the concept of eternal recurrence is illustrated by the fact that her death is a repetition of the deaths of Spanish soldiers in the Battle of the Jarama in the Civil War. Historical and mythical time, both being represented by death, become indistinguishable. Repeated mention of the Civil War does not so much turn the novel into a historical allegory, as has been suggested, as incorporate history into the eternal recurrence of

47

myth.[25] This cyclical impression is reinforced by the circular comings and goings of the characters, the repeated passing of trains in both directions, and the idle meanderings of the conversation. As in *La colmena* and *Los bravos*, circularity does not mean that decay leads back to renewal but that the characters are living in a limbo or 'tiempo muerto' revolving on the spot: a sensation reinforced by the juxtaposition of conversations taking place simultaneously. If the youngsters escape the empty routine of their city lives by turning their Sunday outing into a 'return to nature' that attempts to deny the existence of time (defined by one of them as 'cosas feas' ['nasty things']), so the older countryfolk indulge in idle chatter to obliterate the pain that history – in the form of the Civil War – has brought them.[26] On the one hand, Sánchez Ferlosio's novel provides a devastating critique of the emptiness of life in the depoliticized, ahistorical world of postwar Spain; on the other, the repeated use of omens gives the impression that – as in *Los bravos* – events are caused by fate, confirming the depoliticized, ahistorical vision that is criticized. The River Jarama is presented as an anthropomorphic mythical monster waiting to devour its latest victim. Its symbolic presence in the novel, reminding the reader of the Civil War, suggests that Spanish history – doomed to repeated destruction – is under a curse. As the innocent victim of an impersonal, natural principle of evil, Luci is a mythical sacrificial scapegoat: her death is undeserved but required by an implacable deity. The mythical dimension introduced by the river gives *El Jarama* its power, but it works against the novel's effectiveness as social criticism.[27]

In *Las afueras*, the characters are not victims of a curse but of class divisions. The fact that Luis Goytisolo was not just a fellow traveller but an active member of the Catalan Communist Party, imprisoned in 1960, no doubt helps account for the attention given to the economic underpinnings of class structure, and for the depiction of Catalan society in the 1950s as a dynamic interplay of contradictory forces. The division of the text into seven interrelated stories – whose overlappings are such that the whole has to be regarded as a novel – allows the author to show the plurality of contemporary Catalonia, offsetting the decadence of the bourgeoisie and the oppression of rural and urban poor with the upward social mobility of a new generation of entrepreneurs (Tonio) and professionals (Alvarito). Nevertheless the novel has the most complex cyclical structure of any written in the 1950s, with the repetitions of names for characters in different stories belonging to the same class and generation, implying a view of history as an eternal recurrence of class and generational conflict; and with an end (Alvarito setting off from the village to make it in the city) which foreshadows the opening story (Víctor returning to the village having made it in the city), implying that the future will be a repeat of the past. This impression of inevitability is reinforced by the text's inscription within a seasonal cycle going from autumn to autumn. As in *Los bravos*, the end marks a confirmation of the initial state of decadence, as new prosperity is shown to perpetuate old class structures. There is however a fundamental difference in that Luis Goytisolo distinguishes between the material progress of capitalism (represented by the shallow Alvarito) and that brought about by the peasant Tonio's setting up of a rural cooperative (presented as positive). Despite the fact that the novel ends with Alvarito in autumn, it does not sentence the whole of Catalan society to eternal decadence but offers a positive historical alternative. The narrative moves to and fro between city and country, but each individual story traces a one-way movement: the cyclical spatial pattern does not so much represent a society going nowhere as a dialectical process composed of individual linear movements going in different directions. Where the novel comes closest to the static cyclical vision of *Los bravos* and *El Jarama* is in its treatment of time, as the narrative sequence in each story (with the exception of the third, which nonetheless ends with a return to the opening situation) doubles back on itself in a series of loops to recount earlier events. Sometimes these are prior to the beginning of the story, but at other times we have a re-take of events described at an earlier stage, increasing the sense of time revolving on the spot. On certain occasions the characters are responsible for the flash-backs, implying criticism of them for living in terms of the past; but on others they are recounted by the narrator, implying that he shares their regressive tendencies. This recourse to multiple flash-backs creates the impression that the characters are living in a limbo exiled from a Paradise Lost, often represented by the social harmony of a childhood which had not yet learnt the meaning of class divisions. (Interestingly, all the child characters – unlike the adults – have related names regardless of class.) The fact that the child characters have lost their parents (Bernardo) or have a father in

49

prison (Dina, Bernardino) reinforces the sense of 'orfandad' or loss. The notion that the present is the result of a 'fall' is related to the Civil War in the central story where the servant Domingo's thoughts constantly return to the diving or 'falling' ('caer en pico') of the planes which killed his son in an air raid. The child Bernardo's obsessive poring over his atlas further gives the impression that the emptiness of the present can be made tolerable only by escape to a more exciting world elsewhere: a world to which several of the adult males mentioned in the text have emigrated. Here again Luis Goytisolo differs from other writers of the 1950s who use the Paradise Lost myth, in that he shows that it is possible to reach the outside world of history. Regardless of whether this juxtaposition of a regressive and a progressive vision is deliberate or a sign of Luis Goytisolo's mental contradictions, the novel provides an acute depiction of the contradictions of postwar Spain, torn between a regressive ideology and a reality of incipient development. *Las afueras* is perhaps the only novel of the 1950s to succeed in integrating a mythical vision into a historical vision, rather than vice versa.

Duelo en el Paraíso, by Luis Goytisolo's better known brother Juan, could not be more different. Despite the fact that it purports to be a historical novel – set in the last weeks of the Civil War – the mythification of history is total. The title makes it clear that the 'fall' of Catalonia to Nationalist troops, described in the novel, is symbolic as well as literal. As in *La colmena* and *El Jarama*, the only event is a death – the murder of the mythically named child Abel – reinforcing the equation of history with evil. Critics have supposed that Goytisolo presents Nationalist victory as the loss of Paradise. It is however made clear that Nationalist victory is to be seen as a 'fall' into Paradise: the false Paradise represented by the static, puritanical world of the bourgeois Doña Estanislaa, whose estate is named El Paraíso. Abel is an orphan not in the sense that he is exiled from a Paradise Lost but in that he is imprisoned in the false Paradise of the bourgeoisie, cut off from the fallen world of history. The novel's description of the house and garden of El Paraíso as a mixture of timelessness and decay makes explicit the contradictory view of Franco's Spain as an 'eternal decadence' found implicitly in other works of the period. The mythifications of Doña Estanislaa are ridiculed both because of her obsession with the past and because of her puritanical morality. At the end of the novel she retreats into her mythical world accompanied by a Nationalist soldier, making explicit the link between her mythifications and Nationalist ideology. The entry of Nationalist troops coincides with the stopping of the Republican soldier Elósegui's watch, while in each chapter the narrative sequence consists of a series of flashbacks provoked by the Nationalists' interrogations of the various characters: the Nationalists' victory is – as they themselves proclaimed – an 'undoing' of history. This parody of the Nationalist 'myth of the Crusade', purporting to return Spain to a Paradise Lost, is supplemented not by a contrary historical vision but by an inverse mythification of the Republic. The parody of Nationalist ideology requires the equation of the Republic with the Fall; but Goytisolo seems to agree with the equation, siding with the Republic precisely because it represents the fallen world made taboo by Nationalist puritanism. It is true that, as critics have unanimously stressed, the novel shows how the horrors of war pervert the Republican children.[28] But there is also a sneaking admiration for their animal-like behaviour, which the Nationalist child Abel finds liberating in comparison with the restricting purity of his class. If the Nationalist child is called Abel and the Republican children are equated with Cain, it is in order to vindicate the latter. The equation of the Republic with sexual freedom – the Republican schoolteacher Dora is pregnant with an illegitimate child – is fair enough; but Goytisolo goes further, identifying it also with crime. Dora is awakened to political commitment at the start of the Civil War by the murder of the male members of her landowning family by the hired farmhands. Conversely the Republican child Pablo, after witnessing the shooting of a striker and the clamouring of the workers for vengeance, will found his Sadeian 'Society of Crime'. If Pablo is the tempting devil who seduces and corrupts Abel, it is because moral corruption is more seductive than purity. Abel is a mythical scapegoat in the sense that he chooses to take the burden of evil on his shoulders in order to be accepted by the degenerate Republican children. There is nothing in the novel to substantiate the view, held by critics, that the Nationalists are to blame for the degeneracy of the Republican children: on the contrary, their murder of Abel is a direct response to the Republic's war propaganda, urging its supporters to 'Kill a Nationalist'. The arrival of Nationalist troops – as in the 'myth of the Crusade' – brings 'redemption', putting an end to their degeneracy and restoring lost moral values. The seduction, corruption and final killing of Abel may be horrific, but it is more an echo of the surrealists' scandalous notion that the perversion of a child is the ultimate weapon of attack on bourgeois society than a denunciation of Nationalist violence in the war. Indeed the war is viewed almost entirely through the eyes of Abel, who mythifies it as a superior world of action, contrasting with the emptiness of life in El Paraíso. The fallen world of history is preferred to Paradise precisely because – as in Nationalist ideology – history is equated with evil. The use in *Duelo en el Paraíso* of mythical references constitutes a savage attack on the puritanism of Nationalist Spain, but the antidote it proposes to the return to Catholic 'eternal values' is not historical progress but an alternative 'return' to the animal side of human nature. In the latest volume of his autobiography Juan Goytisolo recognizes that his early fiction had little to do with the Marxist analysis given in his political articles of the 1950s.[29]

The change of course taken by the Spanish novel in the 1960s and 1970s is perhaps best described not as the abandonment of realism but as the abandonment of the pretence of realism, as the mythical undertones of the 1950s are replaced by overt recourse to myth. This move coincides with the 'boom' of the Latin American novel, largely promoted by the Barcelona publishing house Seix Barral. The critical notion that the use of myth by contemporary Latin American writers had given their work a universal quality was bound to be taken up by Spanish writers at a time when economic boom and tourism were starting to open the doors to the outside world, forcing them to recognize the provincialism of contemporary Spanish culture and creating an urgent desire to join the international mainstream. As in Latin America, critics have played a dominant role in stressing the need for the 'demythification' of the novels of the 1950s to be accompanied by a contrary process of 'mythification'.[30] What critics have not perceived – again as in Latin America – is that the recourse to myth by Spanish novelists of the 1960s and 1970s is often ironic. The aim continues to be that of 'demythification', with the important difference that novelists now show an awareness of the fact that language inevitably mythifies reality and that the writer approximates to reality not by 'describing it as it is', but by exposing the falsifications perpetrated by language – that of others and the writer's own. It has been pointed out that the postwar German novel has been more concerned with demythification than mythification as a result of the abuse of myth by Nazism.[31] I suggest that the same abuse of myth by Nationalist ideology accounts for the frequently ironic use of myth by contemporary Spanish novelists. It seems not to be coincidence that, of the three writers grouped together in my final chapter on the grounds that in their novels mythification prevails over demythification, two – Cela and Torrente Ballester – began their careers as members of the Falangist literary establishment. The third – Juan Goytisolo – has devoted his life to attacking the official values of Francoism. In his case, the rejection of history for myth is explained partly by disillusionment with Left-wing politics but also by his concern – as a resident of Paris from 1957 – for international recognition and by his friendship with Carlos Fuentes, who included a chapter on him in the book *La nueva novela hispanoamericana* in which he elaborated his theory of the universalizing function of myth. Both Goytisolo and Torrente Ballester (who has also lived abroad, in the United States) accompany their mythifications with a display of international cultural references. Recourse to myth did indeed rescue the Spanish novel of the 1960s and 1970s from the provincialism of the immediate postwar period. Moreover it can be argued that the mythical undertones of the novels of the 1950s – whatever ideological contradictions they may introduce – give them more of a universal appeal than has perhaps been recognized. There are, however, two ways in which the use of myth can give a novel a relevance that goes beyond the bounds of the society depicted in it: by denying history, or by critically exposing the universal human tendency to mythification. The mythical substratum of the novels of the 1950s seems to me to have the former function. I wish now to examine three novels which fall into the latter category.

3

Fiction as mask: *Tiempo de silencio*

Critics of postwar Spanish literature are unanimous in singling out Luis Martín-Santos' novel *Tiempo de silencio* (1961) as the first to break with the anachronistic realism advocated – if not always practised – by novelists of the 1950s. They are also unanimous in stating that it does so by resorting to myth. Myth is indeed central to the novel but what must be stressed is that its use is ironic. Far from being a mythical novel, *Tiempo de silencio* accuses postwar Spain of abandoning history for myth. It is by exposing the falsity of the characters' mythifications of reality that Martín-Santos is able to break with realism. His novel is an indictment both of the mythical view of history as a return to origins put forward in Nationalist ideology, and of the realist notion that truth in literature is measured in terms of its fidelity to an original. At the end of the novel, the symbolically named Pedro ['foundation stone'] will return to the traditional cradle of Spanish history in the *meseta* of Old Castile: the return to origins is shown to be a rejection of the insecurities of history for the immutability of barren rock. Pedro's search for security is undermined by the text, which refuses to give the reader the security of feeling that what he is reading is the reflection of a pre-ordained, fixed original. If the characters' lives are shown to be founded on alienation, the text points to the divorce between language and reality. *Tiempo de silencio* is a political novel in its depiction of human behaviour and in its use of language. Not for nothing did Martín-Santos play a leading role in the banned Socialist Party (PSOE), which he joined in 1957 and on whose Executive Committee he served from 1961 till his death in a car crash in 1964.[1] The novelists of the 1950s, in their eagerness to expose the 'true reality' concealed by official propaganda, were attracted to realism because of its unproblematic, authoritative mode of narration. The more lucid among them – the Goytisolo brothers, Sánchez Ferlosio, García Hortelano – realized that recourse to an authoritative narrator only served to reproduce the authoritarianism they wished to denounce, and in the second half of the 1950s – under the influence of Italian neo-realist cinema – opted for what became known as 'objectivism': the reduction of the narrator's role to that of impassive camera lens (Spanish 'objetivo').[2] In practice this aggravated the problem, for there is no authority more insidious than that of an invisible narrator whose utterances appear to be 'natural' and 'given'. It is just such a lack of a visible narrator that gives mythical narrative its appearance of 'natural-ness'. The narrator of *Tiempo de silencio* makes his presence felt through the use of rhetoric in order to make the reader aware that what he is reading is not 'natural' but man-made. Indeed the ironic nature of much of the text forces the reader to challenge its authority, replacing its literal sense with an alternative version. The characters use language as a tool of mythification to give their lives a false appearance of solidity; the reader learns to recognize that truth lies in the ambiguous zone of silence and darkness between and beneath words. It is by ironically exposing the ways in which language allows man to mythify the world that Martín-Santos destroys the realist notion that words reflect reality.[3]

Tiempo de silencio systematically sets out to denounce the myths of Nationalist ideology. Several critics have noted echoes in the novel of the writers of the 1898 Generation and Ortega y Gasset, but it has not been pointed out that their presence is due to the fact that their ideas were taken up by the founders of the Falange in the 1930s and came to constitute the backbone of Nationalist ideology.[4] The fact that the Falange was given control of propaganda after the war led to a split between theory and practice, since it was the radical sectors of the Falange that provided the main source of internal opposition in the 1940s. The radical Falangists turned back to the roots of Falangist ideology in the 1898 writers and Ortega in order to vindicate the anti-capitalist platform of their founder José Antonio, which they felt Franco had betrayed. Such writers were regarded as radicals – and in some cases had their works banned – despite the fact that their ideas formed the basis of official ideology. It was the ideas of the 1898 writers and Ortega that formed the basis of what became known as the debate on the 'Spanish problem', which monopolized political discussion in the first two decades of the Franco regime.[5] Martín-Santos had firsthand experience of this debate while at Madrid University in the late 1940s, as the supervisors of his doctoral thesis in psychiatry – Pedro Laín Entralgo and Juan José López Ibor – were its leading antagonists. Laín Entralgo – Professor of History of Medicine, from 1951–6 Rector of Madrid University, and a liberal Catholic Falangist – took a critical stance, insisting in his books *La generación del 98* (1945) and *España como problema* (1949) that the problems the 1898 writers had diagnosed still needed solving. López Ibor – Professor of Psychiatry and a member of the National Council of the Falange – justified the status quo, arguing in his book *El español y su complejo de inferioridad* (1951) that what the 1898 writers had seen as problems were in fact signs of Spain's superiority. Martín-Santos was also friendly with Rafael Calvo Serer, a member of the Catholic pressure group Opus Dei, whose book *España, sin problema* (1949) insisted – in reply to Laín Entralgo – that any problems Spain might have had had been solved by the Civil War. Despite his friendship with Calvo Serer, Martín-Santos defended Laín Entralgo's position.[6] *Tiempo de silencio* makes it clear that postwar Spain is afflicted by serious problems, the chief one being its insistence 'que no está tan mal todo lo que verdaderamente está muy mal' ['that things are not so bad when really they are very bad'] (20). The Spanish problem is, precisely, its refusal to recognize the existence of problems.

In a speech given in San Sebastián in 1961, shortly before the publication of *Tiempo de silencio*, Martín-Santos praised the 1898 writers for their concern at Spain's backwardness but criticized them severely for their political confusions and fatalism.[7] Despite a youthful admiration for Ortega, his reaction when he heard him speak in person – at the lecture parodied in the novel, which Martín-Santos attended in 1949 with Juan Benet – was one of ridicule.[8] If the 1898 writers and Ortega were able to be a source of inspiration both to the internal opposition and to official ideology, it was because of the political confusions which Martín-Santos rightly noted. Nowhere are these more evident than in what was to be their main legacy to Spanish fascism: their explanation of the country's problems in terms of the myth of an essential national character or 'destiny'.[9] This myth is the principal object of satire in Martín-Santos' novel.

The 1898 writers claim to be guided by scientific deterministic principles, but their suggestion that national character is determined not by history but by the fixed 'original essences' of geography and race is a throwback to the Romantic view of the *Volksgeist* as a mythical emanation of telluric forces. Their reduction of history to geography and biology is a perfect example of the reduction of culture to nature, presenting the man-made as given and immutable, that Barthes has proposed as the main characteristic of myth. Indeed the 1898 writers reduce the varied features of the Spanish landscape to one in particular: the immutable rock of the Castilian *meseta*. In keeping with this emphasis on fixed 'original essences', stoicism – *amor fati* or the capacity to remain faithful to an essential destiny – is put forward as the basis of the national character. Unamuno would recommend 'freedom through submission', while Ortega would define man as 'the being condemned to translate necessity into freedom', meaning that, of the historical alternatives open to the individual, only one will coincide with his 'authentic' inherent destiny or 'vocation'. Ortega's main contribution to Spanish fascism was his definition of national destiny as 'a suggestive project for communal living' in which the nation pledged fidelity to its essential destiny.[10] The Nationalist apologue Manuel García Morente, a pupil of Ortega, would justify Franco as the instrument of Ortega's concept of the 'national project'.[11] This advocacy of stoic *amor fati* legitimizes not only those who impose their will on the pretext that they embody the national destiny, but also those who are forced to submit. It is this justification of resignation in the name of stoicism that formed the basis of Martín-Santos' hostility to the 1898 writers, whom he criticized in his San Sebastián speech for idealizing – via their obsession with the Castilian landscape – a backwardness they felt unable to remedy. His novel will end on the same note, as Pedro – leaving Madrid for a mediocre future as a village doctor, in the footsteps of the stoic hero of Baroja's novel *El árbol de la ciencia* (1911) – resorts to stoic withdrawal as an unheroic defence against failure. The other model for this final section is the epilogue to Laín Entralgo's *La generación del 98*, in which Laín – like Pedro – leaves Madrid by train for Old Castile, reflecting on the landscape of the *meseta* whose austerity he sees as a consoling mirror of his own sense of failure.[12] The concluding image of the Escorial also refers indirectly to Laín as editor of the Falangist literary magazine *Escorial*. A favourite image of the 1898 writers in their exaltation of

57

stoic austerity, and the inspiration for Ortega y Gasset's reflections on the national temperament in *Meditaciones del Quijote*, the Escorial became the aesthetic ideal of the classical strand within the Falange.[13] The classical symmetry of its architecture – modelled on the grid-iron on which its patron St Lawrence was martyred – is mockingly transformed by the closing words of the novel into the symmetry of passively 'turning the other cheek'. The Castilian *meseta* is shown not to be the 'paisaje masculino nunca castrado nunca' ['masculine landscape never castrated never'] (294) that Pedro does his best to see, but represents precisely the castration of the country's – and Pedro's – potential. In an unfortunate phrase López Ibor had described stoicism as the adoption of an 'erect position'; Pedro, by opting for stoicism, becomes a 'eunuch' (293).[14]

Throughout the novel Pedro resorts to the stoic concept of the free acceptance of an adverse destiny to justify the disasters that befall him. That his argument is insincere is shown by the fact that he also claims to be a victim of fate. Thus in prison he will start by lamenting 'El destino fatal' ['The hand of fate'] and will end up persuading himself he wants things to be the way they are (215–17). The same sour-grapes appeal to stoicism characterizes the rest of Madrid society, which insists on its freedom of choice when it can choose only between a multiplicity of futile options (17–18). Ortega's notion of freedom as the choice of an inherent vocation is parodied by the suggestion that a reluctant prostitute 'lacks vocation' (109), while his definition of an 'essential' national destiny is ridiculed by the mock-heroic 'collective project' (29) uniting – or failing to unite – Pedro and Amador on their journey to the shanty-town. The boarders at the *pensión* are sarcastically described as 'martyrs' whose deprivation has made them 'the essence of a country that is not Europe' (72). Dorita's grandmother in particular is a genius at the art of making a virtue of necessity. It is important that her husband should have fought in the 1898 disaster in the Philippines as this links her stoicism with the inheritance of the 1898 Generation: her personal inheritance from the events of 1898 is sterility as a consequence of venereal disease contracted by her husband from a Filipino prostitute. The narrator insists that there is no hope for the future until the 'passive consenting classes' stop rationalizing deprivation and face their problems: 'Es preciso ... suspender el juicio ... hasta que los que ahora ríen tristemente aprendan a mirar cara a cara a un destino mediocre' ['Judgment ... must be suspended ... till those who now just laugh sadly learn to look a mediocre destiny in the eye'] (16–17).

The lower classes are also attributed with a stoic acceptance of adversity, but in this case the criticism is aimed not at them but at the 1898 writers and their heirs. When the narrator attributes the use of improvised building materials in the shanty town to 'the spiritual values other nations envy us' (52), he is sarcastically echoing the view that the Spanish people have an innate spiritual vocation for poverty enunciated by writers from Unamuno to García Morente and even the exiled Republican historian Américo Castro. It was, of course, convenient for Nationalist ideology to propagate such a myth. The mock-bucolic description of Muecas' 'contented days' in the shanty town (70) parodies Menéndez Pidal's definition of stoicism as 'contented poverty' in *Los españoles en la historia* (1947), written on return from exile to secure reinstatement as President of the Real Academia Española. Menéndez Pidal saw the Spaniards' innate stoicism as part of their Roman inheritance, incarnated by the Spanish-born stoic philosopher Seneca whom Ganivet had singled out as the supreme representative of the national character.[15] Further evidence of the Roman inheritance – a topic dear to Spanish fascism, from the start closely allied to Mussolini – was seen by Menéndez Pidal in the alleged democratic tradition of the Spanish people, by 'democracy' meaning not the right of the people to make the law but their right to implement it: i.e. popular support for authority. In the novel, the episode of the musical revue shows how authority propagates the myth of Spain's democratic tradition with the spectacle of the 'feudal history' of 'plebeian infantas who hold their own fans' and 'duchesses who pose naked for commoners' (273). The favourite example of the popular nature of Spanish history was the revolt of 2 May 1808 against the occupying Napoleonic troops which had ousted the tyrant Ferdinand VII: the narrator reminds the reader that the same *pueblo* welcomed Ferdinand VII back with the cry 'Vivan las caenas' ['Long live our chains'] (273). Cartucho's revenge on the social superior he suspects of offending his honour is reminiscent of the plays *Fuenteovejuna* and *Peribáñez* by Lope de Vega and *El alcalde de Zalamea* by Calderón, upheld by the 1898 writers and Nationalist ideology as illustrations of the democratic temperament of the Castilian peasant. Cartucho's revenge, clinched with a quote from Tirso de Molina's rather less heroic Golden Age play *El burlador de Sevilla*, does not restore justice but confirms the rule of brute force.

The 1898 writers contradict their belief in the inherent stoicism and democratic spirit of the national character by also attributing to it an anarchic individualism that needs controlling by a 'man of steel'. Baroja's novel *César o nada* (1910) – much quoted in the Nationalist anthology of Baroja's work *Comunistas, judíos y demás ralea* (1938) – proposed that Spaniards, being individualistic, needed 'the iron military discipline' of a tyrant they could then 'have the pleasure of devouring'.[16] The exiled historians Américo Castro and Claudio Sánchez Albornoz – despite their opposition to the Franco regime – perpetuate this myth by arguing that Spaniards, being individualists, have an innate tendency towards authoritarian forms of government.[17] The same contradiction characterizes the thought of Ortega who defended liberal individualism while at the same time expressing his fear of the individualistic insubordination of the masses. In *España invertebrada* (1921), Ortega ascribed Spain's problems to a predominance throughout history of the masses and a corresponding lack of 'great men' to form a ruling elite.[18] The myth that Spaniards' individualism makes them innately suited to authoritarian government, particularly as formulated by Ortega, comes in for savage attack in Martín-Santos' novel. Ortega's view of his own superior mission is satirized by the comparison of his appearance on the lecture platform – as the unnamed but clearly recognizable 'maestro' – to God creating light (162). The 'select minority' advocated by him appears in the form of the pretentious clients of the literary café, whose ideas are described as forming a future elite (79). Ortega's influence on Laín Entralgo is parodied with the nickname 'el hombre' ['the great man'] given to the head of the research institute – the Patronato Ramón y Cajal of the Consejo Superior de Investigaciones Científicas where Martín-Santos had worked as a research student under Laín's direction – who proclaims the need for an intellectual 'priesthood'. Martín-Santos shows the true face of Ortega's elitism by relating his 'divinity' to the 'divine' authority of the police: the 'theogony' of the Barceló Cinema – where Ortega transferred his lectures after being banned from Madrid University – has its counterpart in the vertical hierarchy of the prison (159–61, 208–10). This vertical hierarchy is repeated within each social class:

Martín-Santos accuses Ortega of justifying the concept of the vertical state that was the most genuinely fascist aspect of Franco's Spain. The novel suggests that the Spanish problem is the result not of a 'rebellion of the masses' – as Ortega had claimed in his bestseller of the same title – but of a vertical hierarchy that condemns the individual to passive submission. When the narrator describes the 'helpless masses' in the Goya painting – whose description merges with that of Ortega's lecture – as 'revolucionadas', he is using the term sarcastically to mean not 'in a state of revolution' but 'writhing in a heap' at the feet of the far-from-divine authority of Ortega in the guise of cloven-hoofed devil (157).

By explaining Spanish history in terms of a mythical national character, the 1898 writers and their heirs necessarily end up advocating authoritarian solutions, for their appeal to racial determinism supposes that the people are incapable of improving themselves. Racial argument is invoked in a contradictory fashion: on the one hand it is claimed that the essential virtues of the race have been corrupted by an inauthentic history, on the other it is suggested that the national character is congenitally flawed. In both cases a redeemer is needed to save the nation: the positivist concept of racial determinism leads to the mythical concept of *mesianismo*. *Tiempo de silencio* reminds the reader that the Spanish obsession with racial purity goes back to the expulsion of the Moors and the persecution of Jews by the Inquisition, which the narrator – via the German painter – relates to Nazism (89). The emphasis of the 1898 writers and their heirs on Spain's Castilian heritage was a continuation of this anti-semitic tradition, voiced most eloquently – in agreement with Nationalist ideology – by the exiled historian Sánchez Albornoz who argued that the Arabs and Jews had corrupted Spain's authentic inheritance, constituted by the 'original' racial substratum of Celtiberian, Roman and Visigoth.[19] Such racialist myths are parodied in the novel by the description of Muecas' 'age-old gestures inherited by the peasants of Toledo' (58), which in this case are a sign not of superior Visigothic blood (Toledo having been the Visigothic capital) but of St Vitus' Dance caused by malnutrition. As an Asturian ('Celtiberian'), Amador regards himself as superior to 'the mass of aborigines from the steppes' (191), while the inhabitants of the shanty town regard themselves as racially superior to the newly-arrived migrants from the 'semitic' south (70). The novel reminds us that the expulsion of the Arabs changed Spain from a fertile into a barren country (121, 294).

Martín-Santos' main concern is the use of racial theory to explain Spain's apparent intellectual inferiority in the scientific field. Some thinkers – such as Ramón y Cajal and Laín Entralgo – had insisted that this was a cultural problem, but the majority claimed that Spaniards had a congenital incapacity for – or at best disinclination towards – science. Such was the thesis maintained by López Ibor – known as a psychiatrist for his belief in biological determinism – in *El español y su complejo de inferioridad*. Even the Republican exile Américo Castro would declare that 'Spain always upheld its right to live on the fringe of an industrialized, scientific Europe'.[20] In *Tiempo de silencio*, Pedro echoes this view when he claims he wants to be a failed scientist. Like the protagonist of Baroja's *El árbol de la ciencia*, Pedro reflects his author's negative experience of medical education at Madrid University. Baroja attributed Spain's poor record in science to her semitic racial inheritance (forgetting that the Arabs in Spain were responsible for introducing Greek science to Europe). Ortega – like Baroja a Germanophile – agreed that the predominance of Latin blood in the Spanish race made it congenitally irrational. In *Meditaciones del Quijote*, Ortega classified Europeans into two racial types: the intellectual Aryan and the sensual Latin, arguing that Spain's problem was that she had forgotten the Germanic (Visigothic) element in her racial make-up. In the later *España invertebrada*, Ortega took a more negative view of Spain's Germanic inheritance but still saw it as the key to the nation's problems, claiming that Spain's decadence was due to the inferior nature of the Visigoths who invaded Spain, whose Germanic 'virility' had been 'alcoholized' by contact with the decadent Latin culture of Rome.[21] In *Tiempo de silencio*, the description of Goya's painting of the witches' sabbath – in which the satanic he-goat blurs with Ortega – accuses the latter of having given fascism a theoretical justification by insisting on the racial inferiority of the Spanish people. The narrator assumes Ortega's voice in order to parody his argument that Spaniards are congenitally 'stupid' because of 'their poor-quality Gothic and Mediterranean blood' (158). Ortega's racial explanations are satirized by the comparison of the guests at the reception in his honour to different bird species perching on different levels of the Tree of Knowledge (165–7). Ortega's superiority over his Visogothic and Latin compatriots is 'explained' by attributing to him a 'Celtiberian mind' (161).

Martín-Santos criticizes Ortega for resorting to mythical racial explanations to distract attention from economic problems resulting precisely from the vertical class system Ortega advocated. In the description of the Goya painting, Ortega bewitches his female worshippers so they forget the corpses of their infants. The scene sarcastically ends: 'te perdonarán los niños muertos que no dijeras de qué estaban muriendo' ['the dead children will forgive you for not saying what they were dying of'] (159). The narrator does specify the cause of their death: a malnutrition that leads to over-inflated 'elephantiasic geniuses' (157). The chain of association leading from elephantiasis to the Temple of Elephanta concludes with an extended comparison of the vertical structure of Spanish society to the Hindu caste system. The racial term 'casta' – and its derivate 'casticismo' – had been much abused by Spanish thinkers from Unamuno to Américo Castro. The novel suggests that the 'castes' of Spanish society are the product not of racial difference but of a rigid class system: the 'segmentation' of the *pueblo* is likened to that of a worm, designed for crawling along the ground (157). The 'pueblo castizo' portrayed by writers and painters is not a racial type but a social class determined by poverty: 'casta pordiosera, casta andariega, casta destripaterrónica, casta de los siete niños siete, casta de los barrios chinos de todas las marsellas y casta de las trotuarantes mujeres de ojos negros de París' ['caste of beggars, caste of migrants, caste of earthscratchers, caste of bandits of Ecija, caste of red-light districts in every Marseilles, caste of black-eyed Parisian trottoir-walkers'] (158). The list ends with two non-Spanish examples, for it is a matter not of race but of class. In his description of the shanty town the narrator sarcastically laments the fact that Spaniards are not as fortunate as other nations in being able to attribute class divisions to colour or other ethnic differences, suggesting that anyway the proverbially 'narrow foreheads' of the Spaniards can perhaps be expanded (71). The narrator goes on from this refutation of racial theory to compare the inhabitants of the shanty town to an African tribe (71–2), partly to parody the myth of racial inferiority he has just refuted but also to emphasize the country's backwardness. *Tiempo de silencio* suggests that conditions in the shanty town are worse than those in the Third World (52–3). At the end of the novel we are reminded that the nations of Africa have an advantage over Spain in the 'hungry years' after the war when the novel is set: that of membership of the United Nations, from which Franco's Spain was excluded until 1955. Not only has Spain failed to develop but she has regressed to an animal level of existence. The construction of the shanty town is compared to the nest-building activities of ants, bees and beavers (a comparison borrowed from the turn-of-the-century reformer Macías Picavea).[22] Muecas' wife is described in entomological and vegetable terms, with her fly-coloured skirts wrapped round her like onion skins (61). Muecas' wife – 'este ser de tierra' (247) – is an extension of the earth; her daughter is called Flora. This return to nature – anything but idyllic – is symbolized by the incest linking Muecas' family with the mice (64). The biological and botanical analogies with which the 1898 writers and Ortega adorned their racial theories are turned upside down in the novel to show that Spain's backwardness is not naturally determined, but is the result of man-made conditions that have led to the abandonment of civilization for nature.

The reduction of history to biology effected by the myth of a racially-determined national character was supplemented by appeal to the medical terminology dear to nineteenth-century positivist thinkers. Even those turn-of-the-century reformers who saw Spain's problem as one of economic backwardness liked to refer to it as the 'Spanish disease': as in the title of Lucas Mallada's *Los males de la patria* (1890), or in Joaquín Costa's advocacy of a 'surgical policy' to be implemented by an 'iron surgeon'.[23] The family in the *pensión* and Muecas look vainly to the surgical skills of Pedro for their salvation. The theme of cancer in the novel is obviously reminiscent of earlier writers' insistence on describing Spain's problems as a disease. (One thinks also of Camus's *The Plague*, where disease functions as a metaphor for fascism.) The 1898 writers' use of racial argument had led them to diagnose the disease as congenital and therefore incurable. The type of cancer Pedro is studying is hereditary, but he hopes to prove that it is caused by a virus because 'then you could discover a vaccine' (242). In other words, if it can be proved that the 'Spanish disease' is not congenital but environmentally caused, it can be cured.[24] Pedro does not of course succeed in proving that cancer is a virus. But this does not mean that the 'Spanish disease' is after all congenital. The cancer is transmitted genetically by the mice only as the result of human intervention, through a strictly-controlled process of incestuous inbreeding. It is Spain's inward-looking iso-lationism and backward-looking regression to nature – man-made and therefore controllable factors – that are the cause of the disease.

However the narrator declares that not only are racial factors (skin colour, shape of the skull) insufficient to explain why Spaniards are like they are; so too are economic factors (poverty, malnutrition) (224). The implication is that psychological factors must also be taken into account. In an article Martín-Santos suggested that one can psychoanalyse nations as well as individuals, concluding 'Every nation has its complexes.'[25] The phrase he uses is not 'national character' but 'national complexes'. A complex is not congenital but the consequence of the individual's response to a problematic environment. Martín-Santos' psychiatric writings are devoted to refuting deterministic explanations of human behaviour. The psychological analysis he undertakes of the 'Spanish disease' in *Tiempo de silencio* is diametrically opposed to that offered by the 1898 writers in its rejection of the myth of an essential national character. Martín-Santos shows Spain's problem to be not a congenital infer-iority, but an inferiority complex. Another name for which is the Oedipus complex: the complex of the child unable to assert its independence from parental figures.

The references in *Tiempo de silencio* to the Oedipus myth can be understood only in terms of Martín-Santos' professional training as a psychiatrist. His psychiatric career is marked by a growing, but critical, interest in Freud, whose work was banned in Spain when Martín-Santos was a student at Madrid University. It is important that Martín-Santos should have come to Freud relatively late after a grounding in existential psychiatry, which rejects the Freudian notion that human behaviour is determined by biological factors and in infancy, and insists that neurosis is the result of a free choice made by the individual in response to present – and future – circum-stances. Martín-Santos criticized Freud for his use of mythological analogies to give a fixed, universal, biological explanation of human behaviour. If he rejected Freud's tracing of neurosis back to infancy, he shares his refusal to idealize childhood and the irrational. This is decisive in shaping his attitude to myth. In his major work *Libertad, temporalidad y transferencia en el psicoanálisis existencial*, published post-humously, Martín-Santos insists that the goal of psychoanalysis is 'the destruction of the magical universe of the primitive or of the child', in order to free man from the 'mythical eternal return' to infantile obsessions and enable him to accept responsibility for making rational decisions.[26] In this work Martín-Santos talks a great deal about the Oedipus complex, understood in terms of existential psychiatry according to which the child's fixation with parental figures is not a sexual response but a response to authority.[27] The incestuous desire for the mother represents a desire for the protection of the maternal womb; the desire to kill the father represents a desire to assert independence. The incestuous impulse leads not to parricide, as in Freud, but to its opposite: submission to authority out of fear of castration by the father. Incest and fear of castration both represent the regression to infantile dependence. Thus paternal authority – contrary to Freud's analysis – encourages incest. The existential interpretation of the Oedipus complex supposes that man's basic instinct, encouraged rather than repressed by society, is a fear of freedom. *The Fear of Freedom* is the title of Erich Fromm's classic analysis of Nazism in terms of the Oedipus complex. Fromm's book, published in the United States in 1942, was widely read in Franco's Spain in the banned Argentinian edition. Martín-Santos is known to have been familiar with Fromm's work; in the view of his friend and fellow psychiatrist Carlos Castilla del Pino, it is inconceivable that he had not read *The Fear of Freedom*.[28]

Fromm develops the more political interpretation of the son's parricidal urge given by Freud in *Totem and Taboo* and *Moses and Monotheism*. Here Freud suggested that civilization began when the sons rebelled against the 'father of the primal horde', whose monopoly of the mother represented his monopoly of the land, in order to institute a society based on shared fraternal rights. Parricide is thus necessary to civilization. Like Freud, Fromm suggests that fascism reawakens the primitive, infantile desire for submission to patriarchal authority. In his later book *The Sane Society* (1955), Fromm described this urge to submit to authority as a form of religious idolatry, encouraged through recourse to ritual and mythology. As in existential psychiatry, Fromm supposes that the maternal figure threatens castration as much as the father, in that the incestuous return to the womb reduces man to dependence. Father and mother are simultaneously desired and feared, for they offer protection at the expense of castration. For Fromm the incest taboo is a historical

necessity; incest is opposed to progress. Fromm re-interprets the
Genesis myth, suggesting that the expulsion from Paradise symbolizes the expulsion from the womb. The avenging angel at the gates
to the Garden of Eden who forbids the return to nature and obliges
man to face the insecurities of progress is the enforcer of the incest
taboo. Fromm points out that, according to the Genesis myth, man
was expelled from Paradise for disobeying God's paternal authority:
historical progress is inaugurated by an act of rebellion. Fromm
speculates bitterly that it may be obedience that puts an end to
history. The return to Paradise offered by fascism is, Fromm
suggests, a regression to the hell of dependence. Fromm notes that
submission to authority is counterproductive because, by increasing
dependence, it increases the original fear of insecurity. This produces
a sado-masochistic relationship in which the powerful and the
impotent need each other but resent their mutual dependence. Both
the leader and the led claim to be determined by an outside force
beyond their control. For Fromm, this belief in an external fate is the
most corrosive feature of fascism.[29] Fromm's analysis of fascism in
terms of the Oedipus complex provides a valuable insight into its
mythical urge to 'undo' history by returning to the 'womb' of
origins. The result is shown to be not rebirth but castration.

The Oedipal implications of the demand for a return to origins
emerge clearly in Nationalist ideology, which – like Nazism – was
based on the appeal to matriarchal and patriarchal images. The
Nationalist 'Crusade' was an attempt to return to the 'cradle' of
Spanish history, incarnated in the maternal myth of Isabel la
Católica, who in turn stands for the 'motherland' in the form of the
Castilian *meseta*. Both Isabel la Católica and the Castilian *meseta* are
images of sterility, for the mother who offers protection to her
children also represents the castrating hand of punishment. The
castrating maternal myth of the Castilian *meseta* was to have been a
central theme of Martín-Santos' unfinished second novel *Tiempo de
destrucción*. The maternal myth was inseparable from the paternal
myth of the *caudillo*, who saves the mother of the race at the price of
subjecting her. In *Genio de España*, Giménez Caballero announced
the return of the national hero Don Juan, who would express the
strength of his passion for the motherland by 'conquering her,
forcing her – sublime enemy! – into submission and, in the supreme
ecstasy of genital triumph, branding her mouth with an indelible,

burning kiss'.[30] As in Fromm's analysis, the mother race worships the conquering hero as saviour. The use of religious terminology was stronger in Nationalist ideology than in Nazism not only because of the enforced marriage of the Falange with the Catholic Carlists and Monarchists, but also because of the insistence of the 1898 writers and their heirs on the need for a 'redeemer' or 'messiah'. The *caudillo* is seen as the instrument of an external fate in the form of divine providence, whose bounty is tempered with severity and who is to be feared as much as revered. Thomas Mermall has noted the obsession in Nationalist rhetoric with patriarchal figures. Mermall's analysis of the work of the Catholic humanist Rof Carballo – one of the few Falangist psychiatrists to take an interest in Freud – provides a useful foil to Martín-Santos' use of Oedipal imagery in *Tiempo de silencio*. For Rof, the myth of Oedipus illustrates the importance of the parental home. Oedipus' tragedy is his ignorance of his origins, which sends him in search of the truth that destroys him. Rof re-christens the Oedipus complex the 'Segismundo' complex: the complex of the foundling child. He suggests that modern society suffers from the 'double castration of matriarchal and patriarchal symbols', and insists that a healthy society must be founded on the 'rock' of patriarchal tradition.[31] The home ('hogar'), under paternal authority, did in effect constitute the basic legal unit of Francoist society.

The text of *Tiempo de silencio* abounds in Oedipal references to incest and castration. As in Fromm's *The Fear of Freedom*, incest is presented as a form of castration. The symbolic relationship between the two concepts is illustrated by what appears to be a Freudian slip on Martín-Santos' part. Matías refers to Electra as Oedipus' daughter and to Clytemnestra as Oedipus' mother (109–11, 199), when they are, of course, sister and mother to Orestes. The existential psychiatrist Rollo May has suggested that the myth of Orestes complements that of Oedipus because it shows the need to rebel against the mother as much as the father, for the mother also castrates. Indeed the myth of Orestes better illustrates the need for rebellion, since Orestes killed his parent knowingly.[32] In *Tiempo de silencio*, the castrating effect of the incestuous fixation is illustrated by the description of Pedro's figurative returns to the womb as a series of journeys to the grave or to hell. The 'welcoming penumbra' of the *pensión* is a 'dark cave' into which Pedro plunges each night 'con

68

alegrías tumbales' ['with sepulchral rejoicings'], emerging each morning 'con dolores lucinios' ['with delivery pains'] (31). By offering him its 'visceral-cum-psychological protection', it deprives him of his freedom. It is worth noting that Pedro is pleased to descend into the world of the dead and finds his daily rebirth painful. On his traumatic Saturday night he will discover that the darkness does not give him the anaesthesia he seeks but confronts him with an 'inferno'. The brothel is both 'protecting womb' and 'Stygian lake' (105). Doña Luisa – a Queen of Hades in her brothel basement – will offer her maternal protection to Pedro at the price of 'damning' him to an 'underground' existence as a backstreet abortionist. The subterranean cell in the police station (the Dirección General de Seguridad which Martín-Santos knew from personal experience) is not the protecting womb Pedro tries to turn it into, but a devouring stomach entered via the jaws of hell (209). The sexual refuge offered by Dorita is another devouring mouth: '*Vagina dentata*, emotional castration, possessive emasculation' (198). The recurring image of the siren, as serpent–woman, likewise offers pleasure at her 'python's breast' at the price of destruction (198).

The fact that the protection of the womb is a form of castration explains the symbolic relationship in the novel between incest (return to the womb in search of protection) and abortion (destruction as a result of expulsion from the womb). Incest leads to abortion because it destroys man's potential. Also – as in Fromm's analysis – incest increases the insecurity it is intended to relieve, thus expelling man back into the anxieties of the outside world. This in turn creates renewed desire for the protection of the womb: hence the plot of the novel – at a symbolic level – leads from incest to abortion and back to further incest in an ever-repeating vicious circle. The same infernal night will take Pedro from figurative incest with Dorita to Florita's abortion. In scraping Florita's womb he performs a macabre inversion of his penetration of Dorita, leading this time not to pleasure (Eros) but to death (Thanatos). In the brothel Matías undertakes a metaphorical return to a 'cradle' rocked by a maternal figure who is 'caressing, soothing' but also 'stifling'. Matías' failed attempt to find solace in the brothel is described as an 'aniquilación inversa en que el huevo ... se escinde en sus dos entidades previas y Matías ha desempezado a no existir' ['inverse annihilation in which the ovum ... splits into its two prior units and Matías has unbegun to not exist'] (105). This last phrase is reminiscent of the exiled Republican historian Américo Castro's suggestion – disquietingly similar to fascist thought – that Spaniards are characterized by a tragic but heroic urge to 'vivir desviviéndose' ['unlive life'] in order to annul the errors of their history.[33] The brothel does not provide the desired solace but expels Pedro back into the outside world. On his second visit to the brothel seeking refuge from the police, Pedro will be offered the protection of the womb by the castrating 'phallic mother' Doña Luisa at the price of asphyxiation: 'le parecía que había dejado de respirar y que quedaba inmóvil en aquel espacio sumergido en que todo (el alimento, el aire, el amor, la respiración) se lo introducían por un tubo de goma mientras que él permanecía inerte' ['he felt he had stopped breathing and moving in that submerged space in which everything (food, air, love, life) was fed into him by a rubber tube while he remained inert'] (187). His refuge in the brothel will – logically – lead to his imprisonment. Even in prison Pedro attempts to turn his forced passivity into a 'Return to the cradle. To a womb' (219). When he claims he is more free in prison than in the outside world, he is confusing freedom with the liberation from responsibility that is the other side of dependence. Not even prison will offer him a permanent refuge from insecurity: his release is experienced by him as an abortion, hence his first urge is to throw himself into Dorita's arms. The symbolic link between incest and abortion will lead to Pedro's final expulsion from the city, as the corollary to his repeated attempts to return to the womb. Florita's literal incest leads to her literal abortion. Pedro's figurative incest leads to his figurative abortion. On his 'abortion' by the city at the end of the novel, Pedro is explicitly described as a castrated 'eunuch'. Even after his definitive emasculation Pedro will once more attempt figurative incest, this time with mother nature in the form of the Castilian *meseta*, as he plunges with the 'gigantic organ' of the train into 'the sierra's womb' (291).

In *Libertad, temporalidad y transferencia*, Martín-Santos defines neurosis as 'a prolonged infancy'.[34] Pedro's figurative incest symbolizes that of a society which has regressed to infantile dependence. Pedro's scientific training is preparing him to be an 'architect of the future' (254), but in the course of the novel he becomes an abortionist. Florita's incest and abortion show how – 'in a paradoxical backwards march' (69) – Spain has regressed into underdevelopment.

The 'exogamy necessary to the forwards march of the species' (79) is represented in the novel by the intellectual promiscuity of the Café Gijón, while 'a sagacious process of endogamic breeding' (67) produces an Orteguian 'select race' of cancerous mice. Pedro's final incest with the Castilian *meseta* shows that not only is he regressing to his personal origins but Spain too, instead of following the path of progress, has regressed to a sterile natural state. *Tiempo de silencio* shows how psychological dependence compounds economic dependence.

The society depicted in the novel contains a number of maternal figures – literal or symbolic – but, in keeping with Rof Carballo's analysis, it is a 'society without a father'. The only father to appear is Muecas: an inverted Oedipus who seduces not his mother but his daughter.[35] Muecas' incest represents the violation by paternal authority of the future. Muecas is the father of the primal horde, feared as castrating father by Cartucho and a 'biblical patriarch' monopolizing all the women (66). It is appropriate that the inhabitants of the shanty town should be described as a primitive tribe, and that Muecas' wife and his daughter Florita – the women he monopolizes – should represent nature. Muecas' family stands as a degraded image of the patriarchal authoritarianism of Franco's Spain. The fact that, with the exception of Muecas, Madrid society should be devoid of fathers does not indicate a freedom from paternal authority but, on the contrary, a chronic insecurity alleviated by submission to a symbolic father. The entire life of the *pensión* is geared to the search for 'el hombre' who will right the lack of fathers in previous generations. The postwar generation was indeed a generation of orphans; the novel implies that Francoism took advantage of this to offer itself as a substitute paternal authority. In *Tiempo de silencio* the lower classes (the shanty town), the middle classes (the *pensión*) and the upper classes (the reception for Ortega) coincide in their adulation of a patriarch, whether present (Muecas, Ortega) or absent (as in the *pensión* which tries to make Pedro fit the role of founding father). In all three cases the 'saviour' is surrounded by a primal horde not of rebellious sons but of prostrate women.

The reflection on Goya's painting constitutes a savage denunciation of patriarchal authoritarianism. The he-goat – an image of malevolent male potency – is surrounded not only by prostrate women but also by stillborn infants: like incest, submission to the father leads to abortion. This scene highlights the sadomasochistic relationship between the powerful and the powerless: the latter create the image of an omnipotent, oppressive figure in order to compensate for – and justify – their own impotence. The messiah also needs his worshippers as his power is derived from their 'centripetal adoration' (155). The mutual dependence of leader and led is illustrated by the fact that not only does Pedro turn others into paternal as well as maternal figures, but others also turn him into a saviour. For the three women in the *pensión* he is an 'angel of the annunciation', an 'epiphany' and a 'transfiguration' respectively (44). Pedro in turn will convert them into goddesses. Likewise Pedro sees Muecas as the saviour able to bring his dead mice back to life, just as the latter sees Pedro as the saviour able to resuscitate his daughter. Amador is a 'blessed' saviour for his wife, Muecas and Pedro, who from the start – inverting their relationship as superior and subordinate – shows a total dependence on him. The use of religious terminology in the novel is not an attempt to create the ritualistic atmosphere of myth, as has been suggested, but an ironic exposure of Spain's tendency to 'mesianismo'.[36] In the course of the novel Pedro encounters a series of 'divinities' whose prestige is bestowed on them by his attitude of reverence. He always supposes that others have an omnipotence that obliges him to bow to their will. Pedro's evening 'ritual' with the three 'goddesses' in the *pensión* constitutes a consecration of social convention (41–9), just as the 'priestesses' and their 'worshippers' in the brothel (99–104) represent the institutionalization of personal relations. Postwar Spain is accused of consecrating authority in order to compensate for its insecurity.

This consecration of authority is an attempt to 'undo' history. The women in the *pensión* see Pedro as the 'magic helper' who will 'reverse the whole course of the family destiny' (43–4). Matías appeals to his prestigious contacts 'to make the waters return to their source, reversing the course of history' (231). The purpose of submission to paternal authority is incest: it is apt that the only father in the novel should be the incestuous Muecas. The redemption promised by the saviour is the other face of castration. The promised land to which Amador points turns out to be a hell. All the 'divinities' in the novel are infernal figures. Muecas does not offer Pedro salvation but is a nocturnal emissary who leads him to perdition; the three 'goddesses' in the *pensión* are also the three Fates. Likewise Pedro does not save Dorita but leads her to her death. The patriarchal 'divinities' of the Dirección General de Seguridad are 'punishing Joves' who encourage Pedro's incestuous tendencies by treating him like a child and constructing the concrete bed in his cell so he is obliged to curl up in a foetal position (211). The paternalistic head of the research institute will similarly suggest that Pedro 'undo' his life by returning to his origins in the provinces. Martín-Santos' use of Oedipal references shows how the 'mythical eternal return' leads to destruction.

The idolatry of patriarchal authority represents not only the transference of power on to a fetish object, but also a transference of guilt. The messiah figure is closely related to that of the scapegoat which, according to Sir James Frazer's *The Golden Bough*, is the prototype of the mythical sacrificial hero. Frazer's analysis of scapegoat rituals in volume 9 of his massive study has been central to the use of myth in twentieth-century literature; it also formed the inspiration for Freud's analysis of authoritarianism in *Totem and Taboo* and *Moses and Monotheism*. Freud noted the similarity between Frazer's emphasis on the scapegoat's function as substitute and his own theory of sublimation. According to Frazer, the scapegoat was originally a king sacrificed in memory of the mythical god who had died to regenerate the world, but later kings started the practice of buying a further substitute to die in their place.[37] Freud observed that, according to Frazer's analysis, the sacrificed scapegoat represented authority but the purpose of the sacrifice was to secure the continued existence of authority. The scapegoat ritual thus seemed to offer an explanation of man's contradictory desire to rid himself of authority and at the same time submit to it. According to Freud, the sons' murder of the father of the primal horde gave rise to guilt feelings which required expiation. The scapegoat ritual allowed the sons to worship the dead father and at the same time sublimate their anti-authoritarian sentiments by providing a symbolic representation of the original parricide.[38] The analysis of the bullfight in *Tiempo de silencio* is based on Freud's interpretation of the scapegoat ritual. The novel depicts a society united in guilt for the crime not of rebellion against the father but of submission to patriarchal authority. The sons' inability to kill the father leads them to kill a

73

substitute. In *Genio de España* – again under the influence of *The Golden Bough* – Giménez Caballero had seen the bullfight as the sacrifice of the 'dying god' or messiah who gives his life to redeem the nation.[39] Martín-Santos insinuates a contrary explanation of the bloodshed provoked by the Nationalist 'Crusade': it is because of its incapacity for parricide that the Spanish nation has opted for the substitute of fratricide.[40]

Earlier in the novel Pedro, after succumbing to Dorita's lure, had had a nightmare vision of himself as a bullfighter stabbing at a bull which finally kills him (120–1). Pedro here explicitly refers to the Mithraic rite of the *taurobolium* which Freud had analysed as a symbolic representation of parricide; in an inversion of Freud's interpretation, it is Pedro and not the bull (representing authority) who is killed.[41] In the narrator's later analysis, it is the bullfighter who – as 'scapegoat for the people's hatred' (225) – represents authority, but the ritual is still a celebration of the failure to commit parricide. In desiring the bullfighter's death, the *pueblo* is sublimating its anti-authoritarian urges; but it does so at the cost of final submission, since the bullfight will end with the bullfighter's triumph. Hence the collaboration – noted by the narrator – of police, press, armed forces, Church and Civil Governor. It is pointed out that the bullfight became institutionalized in the eighteenth century, coinciding with the beginnings of imperial decline. The bullfight constitutes a sublimation of historical failure: a 'symbolic channel' which 'exorcizes' mass frustration (224). This sublimation process is described as a consecration of authority:

Que el acontecimiento más importante de los años que siguieron a la gran catástrofe fue una polarización de odio contra un solo hombre y que en ese odio y divinización ambivalentes se conjuraron cuantos revanchismos irredentos anidaban en el corazón de unos y de otros no parece dudoso.

(224–5)

That the major event of the years following the great catastrophe was the polarization of hatred for a single man and that this ambivalent hatred and deification exorcized the unallayed thirst for revenge harboured by all and sundry seems beyond question.

The words 'a single man' must refer to Franco: it is surprising that they were not cut in the heavily censored early editions of the novel.[42] The projection of the nation's hatred on to Franco consecrated him in authority since, by putting all the blame for the country's ills on to him, the people – in a process of 'ambivalent hatred and deification' – attributed to him a divine omnipotence. The implication is that even those Spaniards who did not accept Franco as their messiah contributed to his authority by holding him responsible for their destiny.

The function of the bullfight is thus to neutralize the *pueblo*'s desire for vengeance. The novel ends with an act of vengeance, with Cartucho's killing of Dorita. Cartucho's success in exacting revenge contrasts with Pedro's 'impotent resentment' (171). But Cartucho's vengeance is not a genuine act of rebellion either, because he again sacrifices an innocent scapegoat instead of punishing the superior power responsible. The person on whom Cartucho ought to exact revenge is of course Muecas, the father of the primal horde. Cartucho also fails to rebel against authority, becuase he does not know who to direct his hatred against. As his nickname ('Cartridge') suggests, Cartucho represents brute force which is useless because it is blind.

The scapegoat figure, sublimating the guilt of impotence rather than that of rebellion, occurs also with the satanic goat in Goya's painting.[43] The narrator notes that he is not a genuine scapegoat, for he clearly runs no risk of being sacrificed. He is a scapegoat only in the sense that the 'helpless masses' regard him as the omnipotent source of their ills. It is the 'helpless masses' with their dead children who are sacrificed as the innocent victims of authority. It is in this sense that Pedro – punished by the head of the research institute despite being found innocent by the law – becomes the scapegoat of society.[44] Pedro agrees to take on the role of sacrificial victim by voluntarily leaving Madrid for a barren future. At the same time he turns authority into a scapegoat by putting the blame for his fate on to its shoulders. The subject of the political manipulation of guilt had been dealt with by Sartre – Martín-Santos' favourite author – in his play *The Flies*, written under Nazi occupation. Sartre's play is a reworking of the Orestes myth: Aegisthus secures absolute power by uniting the people of Argos in expiation for Agamemnon's murder, for which he and Clytemnestra are responsible. By opting for expiation the people become the tyrant's scapegoat, as well as turning him into a scapegoat who explains all their ills. Orestes saves the city by killing Aegisthus and Clytemnestra and taking the curse of the furies on his own shoulders, refusing to expiate a crime which was his responsibility.[45] At the end of the novel Pedro presents himself as an Orestes pursued by the furies (285). But his position is rather that of Sartre's Electra, who opts for the consoling role of expiation rather than face guilt. Like Electra, Pedro in prison declares that punishment is a 'consolation' and 'remedy' (244) to guilt. The tendency to opt for expiation to free himself from guilt characterizes him throughout the novel. After seducing Dorita he washes as if bathing in the River Jordan or in a blood sacrifice (121). In the novel water and blood do not act as purifying agents. The 'ocean' of Madrid is a 'Dead Sea' (121). The baptism by blood that Pedro seeks will be Florita's haemorrhage. By seeking purification from guilt, Spanish society has fallen into the fatalistic belief that only an external power can redeem it: 'como si una maldición los persiguiera y sólo la negra y fresca noche pudiera limpiarles del mismo modo que limpia el océano' ['as if pursued by a curse with only the cool, black night able to cleanse them as the ocean cleanses'] (111).

A third kind of scapegoat is referred to in the novel, whereby guilt is projected not on to an external body but on to a part of oneself that is disowned. This concept of an internal scapegoat had been analysed by the existential psychiatrist Igor Caruso, whose work Martín-Santos mentions in *Libertad, temporalidad y transferencia*. Caruso calls this process 'angelism' – the denial of one's own capacity for evil – and notes that it is a characteristic of totalitarian thought.[46] Like Caruso, Martín-Santos insists that the neurotic must recognize that he is not an 'angel', pointing out that this is the same as Jung's insistence on the need to accept one's shadow.[47] Throughout the novel Pedro attributes responsibility for his acts to a 'tú' which he dissociates from his 'yo'. By fleeing the 'hell' of the shanty town, he is trying to ignore not only the evil that exists within society but also his own inner demons. His 'witches' sabbath' will plunge him into the inferno of his own irrationality, forcing him to wander round an instinctual labyrinth leading from Eros (Dorita) to Thanatos (Florita), which threatens to destroy his 'angelic' self-image as a rational intellectual. Pedro's vain attempt to flee his inner demons is symbolically represented by his pursuit by Cartucho, the 'man dressed in black' who lives in a 'semi-cave' (143). Cartucho literally shadows Pedro round Madrid; he can also be seen as Pedro's 'shadow' in the Jungian sense. Cartucho's final revenge shows that man cannot ignore his inner demons with impunity. Pedro does not see Cartucho once in the novel, not even when he exacts his revenge. Pedro is not the 'angel of the annunciation' the women in the *pensión* try to see in him, but a 'lamentable image of the human and far-from-divine condition we have inherited from our forefathers' (142). The womb is associated with hell not only because incest is a form of castration but also because the womb symbolizes the unconscious: a subterranean zone of guilt. The incestuous attempt to return to the womb does not protect man from the dangers of existence but exposes him to the dark impulses that seek to destroy him from within. Pedro is criticized not so much for his journeys into the unconscious as for failing to recognize that it is an infernal zone. His repeated descents into hell show that man's attempts to avoid the source of his guilt only lead him back to it once more.

This interpretation of Pedro's Oedipal urge to return to the womb as a journey into the unconscious coincides with the analysis of Nazism in terms of the Oedipus complex given by the Jungian analyst Ernst Neumann in his book *Depth Psychology and a New Ethic* (1949), translated into Spanish in 1959. Neumann's best known work *The Origin and History of Consciousness* (also 1949) likewise consists of an analysis of the Oedipus complex. Neumann suggests that the Oedipus complex passes through various stages on the passage from infancy to maturity. He develops Jung's notion – derived from his reading of mythology – that the incestuous return to the womb is a journey into the underworld of the unconscious but, unlike Jung, stresses the negative aspects of the unconscious which must be overcome. For Neumann, maturity is achieved by consciously undertaking the journey into the unconscious in order to conquer its regressive pull. Neumann distinguishes this 'active incest' from two earlier negative stages. The first he calls 'uroboric' incest: the child's passive refuge in the womb in search of protection. The second he calls 'matriarchal incest', in which the child experiences the return to the womb as a castration. Pedro's incestuous regressions are a combination of these two infantile stages. The novel contains an ironic reference to the uroboros – the serpent swallowing its tail, representing in Jung's reading of mythology the undifferentiated continuum of the unconscious – with the whiting biting its tail which Pedro eats for supper before embarking on his various journeys to the underworld. According to Neumann, Oedipus was

77

not a genuine hero because his incest was not undertaken consciously. Neumann rejects the traditional interpretation of the end of the Oedipus myth according to which his self-inflicted blindness – a symbolic castration – represents a new inner enlightenment, and suggests that his blindness is better seen as his attempt to ignore guilt.[48] This interpretation fits the end of *Tiempo de silencio* where Pedro also castrates himself in order to declare himself impotent and thus free of responsibility. Neumann suggests that fascism was the price Western man had to pay for not having undertaken the conscious journey back to the unconscious to overcome its dangers. Fascism is the revenge of man's inner demons. Neumann advocates a new humanism based on the recognition of evil, since man can learn tolerance of others only if he learns to accept the existence of evil within himself.[49] In *Tiempo de silencio*, Pedro's example shows that man can accept himself, and thus others, only when he frees himself from the delusion that he is a superior rational being. Pedro evades both his personal and his social responsibility by ignoring Cartucho, the symbol of his inner demons and of the repressed unconscious of society.

Juan Villegas has attempted an analysis of *Tiempo de silencio* in terms of the Jungian interpretation of the quest myth, as popularized by Joseph Campbell, according to which the descent into the underworld represents the plunge into the unconscious in search of spiritual regeneration. Villegas admits that Pedro does not find regeneration, but argues that his contact with his unconscious gives him a new self-awareness.[50] It seems to me that, at the end of the novel, Pedro is more concerned than ever to blind himself to unpleasant truths. If Martín-Santos stresses the hellish aspects of Pedro's descents into the underworld, it is to emphasize the destructive nature of the unconscious. Julian Palley has also seen the novel as a latter-day quest myth leading to self-knowledge, pointing out the existence of a network of references to Homer's *Odyssey*. This leads Palley to suggest that Martín-Santos modelled his novel on Joyce's *Ulysses*, mentioned admiringly in the text (81). Palley recognizes that Homeric parallels can be found only for certain sections of *Tiempo de silencio*, but notes that Martín-Santos' Madrid – like Joyce's Dublin – is constantly compared to an ocean around which the characters voyage like Ulysses round the Mediterranean; that Dorita – like Molly Bloom – can be seen as both Calypso and

Penelope; that the brothelkeeper Doña Luisa echoes Joyce's 'Circe' Bella Cohen; that Florita's funeral and Pedro's imprisonment jointly correspond to the Hades episode in *Ulysses*; that Florita – like Joyce's Gerty McDowell – is a parodic Nausicaa; that Cartucho – like Joyce's Irish Nationalist – represents the brute force of the Cyclops; and that Ortega y Gasset – like Joyce's Professor MacHugh – is Aeolus, the god of wind.[51] Curiously Palley does not pick up the comparison of Matías seeking help from his prestigious contacts to Telemachus consulting Nestor (231), nor the various references to sirens and to fate. That Joyce's *Ulysses* was the inspiration for the Homeric references in *Tiempo de silencio* seems irrefutable; whether their function is the same in the two novels is another matter. The question is complicated by the fact that critics of *Ulysses* differ in their view of the function of the Homeric references in Joyce's novel. If T. S. Eliot saw Joyce's use of myth as a way of imposing an ordered classical framework on to the chaos of modern life, Jung – despite his predilection for spotting mythical archetypes – could not find any symbolic intention in *Ulysses*, which he dismissed as soulless and formless.[52] Stuart Gilbert, with Joyce's apparent authorization, launched the popular but not unchallenged view that the subject of *Ulysses* was Stephen–Telemachus' quest for a father in the form of Bloom–Ulysses. There is no consensus as to whether Joyce's use of mythical references represents a belief in the nobility of the everyday or an ironic comment on contemporary mediocrity, most critics concluding that Joyce was attracted to myth because it could do different things at once, allowing him to achieve his goal of multivalence.[53] Recent critics, influenced by the Post-Modernist debunking of the mythical quest for origins and wholeness, have insisted that the Homeric references in *Ulysses* are a jocular exercise in cultural displacement.[54] All views have in common the supposition that, if Joyce is using myth ironically, it is to make a critical comment on modern life or on culture; no critic has suggested that his irony is directed against myth. The latter seems to me to be Martín-Santos' principal aim.

There is no sense in which *Tiempo de silencio* can be said to resort to the *Odyssey* in order to show the nobility of the everyday. It does however point an ironic contrast between the degradation of post-war Spain and the heroic world of epic. Pedro is an anti-Ulysses 'putting on his nylon socks' as he embarks on his 'periplus' to meet his 'Nausicaa' who, far from being a virginal princess washing the royal linen, is soiling her family's only sheet as she bleeds to death after her bungled abortion (124–5). Unlike Homer's 'wily Ulysses', and in a modest way Joyce's Bloom, whose resourcefulness allows them to outwit a malevolent destiny, Pedro is a blunderer who blames his ills on fate in order to delegate responsibility to a superior power. But what is most striking is that the references to Homer – like those to the Oedipus and Orestes myths – emphasize the negative aspects of the mythical prototype. Palley notes that Pedro descends into the underworld not once but twice; in fact all the mythical locations he visits on his 'periplus' are infernos of one kind or another. Doña Luisa is more explicitly a Queen of Hades than a Circe. The sirens, who lure man to his destruction, likewise occur not once but repeatedly. Whatever Joyce's intentions, *Ulysses* contains a number of references to the importance of paternity (Bloom–Ulysses) and the need for the protection of the maternal womb (Molly–Penelope); in *Tiempo de silencio* both are destructive images of authority. If Martín-Santos omits the son's search for the father (his Telemachus being Pedro's friend Matías), it is because his theme is the need to reject paternal authority. The allusions in his novel to the abuse of mythical thought by Nationalist ideology give his use of mythical references a political dimension lacking in that of Joyce. Certain of the Homeric references bring Ortega to mind as much as Joyce or Homer. The sirens that tempt Pedro recall Ortega's suggestion that the way to resist the sirens' song – which for him represented the seduction of history – was to sing it backwards; in *Tiempo de silencio* the sirens represent precisely the regressive urge to 'undo' history which must be resisted.[55] Similarly the 'ocean' around which Pedro voyages refers to Homer and Joyce via Ortega's aphorism that 'life is not just a perilous sea but also a welcoming shore'. In *Tiempo de silencio* there is no refuge from the perils of the ocean: the 'shore' of the literary café is an 'octopus', as is the 'womb' of the *pensión* (78, 120). Pedro's 'Ithaca' is not the *pensión* – as Palley suggests – but the barren Castilian *meseta* to which he returns on his final expulsion from the city. It is worth noting that, in his use of Homeric references, Martín-Santos omits not only the son Telemachus but also the usurping suitors (included, though not slain, by Joyce in the form of Blazes Boylan) whose presence in the Ulysses myth has allowed it to be interpreted politically as an illustration of the need to 'undo' the 'usurpations' of the immediate historical past in order to restore a lost founding tradition (Giménez Cabellero's demand in *Genio de España* for the return of the founding father who will end three centuries of 'bastardization' being a prime example). Regardless of whether or not Joyce is appealing to myth as a founding tradition, it seems clear that his novel is an attempt to transcend the linearity of history: the 'nightmare' from which Stephen is 'trying to awake', and from which H. C. Earwicker would be 're-born' in *Finnegans Wake*. Unlike *Ulysses*, *Tiempo de silencio* has a logically-developed plot, for its theme is the inescapability of history. History is a nightmare but one that has to be faced. Pedro's encounter with the shanty town confronts him with 'el aspecto bestial e hinchado de los fantasmas que aparecen en nuestros sueños y de los que ingenuamente suponemos que no existen' ['the bestial, distorted visage of the ghosts which inhabit our dreams and which we naively suppose not to exist'] (53–4). The point, as Pedro discovers, is that they do exist and there is no escaping them.

In his comparison of *Tiempo de silencio* to *Ulysses*, Alfonso Rey wisely concentrates not on the mythical references but on the use by both writers of a variety of styles and narrative points of view, which problematize the relationship between language and reality.[56] It is this notion of language as a multivalent construct that constitutes Martín-Santos' chief debt to Joyce. Again, however, there are important differences. Joyce is fascinated by the possibilities of double meaning offered by the pun. The notion of duplicity is also central to Martín-Santos' use of language, but with a stronger emphasis on the moral sense of the word. As a psychiatrist with a growing interest in Freud, he is concerned with the ways in which language betrays hidden unconscious meanings which the speaker is seeking to repress. In Joyce's work, the different layers of meaning are not mutually exclusive. Martín-Santos' language is two-dimensional in the sense that the surface meaning is a falsification which stands in opposition to the hidden underlying meaning. Martín-Santos is concerned with double meaning not in order to show how language can take off from reality to generate meanings of its own making, but in order to reveal the reality that lies hidden beneath the surface mythifications of words. *Tiempo de silencio* is an anti-mythical novel above all in its exposure of the mythifications of language.

As an existential psychiatrist Martín-Santos saw neurosis not as biologically-determined but as a refusal to face reality on the part of the individual. Neurosis is thus defined as a willed falsification of meaning: what Sartre – in the section of *Being and Nothingness* that most influenced existential psychiatry – called 'Bad Faith'.[57] Existential psychiatry has in common with psychoanalysis the fact that it is a 'talking cure': if language, by falsifying meaning, has caused the problem language is also the means by which it can be solved. Existential psychiatry is based on that branch of phenomenology which insists that all perception is subjective and as such liable to falsification: this notion formed the basis of Martín-Santos' doctoral thesis *Dilthey, Jaspers y la comprensión del enfermo mental*. In his later work, Martín-Santos emphasized the additional importance of Freud's notion of the symbolic nature of language, which allows it to operate simultaneously on two levels, one conscious, the other unconscious.[58] The function of the psychoanalyst is to expose the hidden meaning repressed by the patient. In the same way *Tiempo de silencio* is designed to reveal those areas of meaning obscured by the surface mythifications of the text.

Tiempo de silencio bears witness to Martín-Santos' insistence in his psychiatric writings on the subjective nature of perception. Situations are always described from the point of view of a character, whether via interior monologue or free indirect style. These subjective points of view are unreliable, for the characters use language in Bad Faith to justify themselves. It is commonly held – as Derrida has pointed out – that the reproduction of thought in interior monologue gives the reader access to the character's 'true' inner self.[59] The truth revealed about the characters by the interior monologues in *Tiempo de silencio* is that they are not to be trusted. The dissociation between self and language is emphasized by the suppression of the names of the characters responsible for the interior monologues. A similar dissociation is created by the use of impersonal expressions, as in Pedro's monologue in prison (215), his meditation on guilt (285–6), and the grandmother's triumphal cry on Dorita's seduction (118–19). On Pedro's return from the brothel, his words are detached from him by a string of impersonal gerunds (112). Muecas' wife's flashback over her life also consists of a series of impersonal expressions (248), in this case because she is divorced from language in the sense of being totally inarticulate. This dissociation between language and speaker is reinforced by the attribution to characters of inappropriate language. The speech of even the least educated characters contains erudite language that can be explained only as an intrusion on the narrator's part. The shifting narrative perspective means that we are often not sure whether the narrator or a character is talking.[60] Just as the characters' Bad Faith intrudes into the narrator's reflections on Spain's problems, so the latter's criticisms of Spanish society intrude into Pedro's monologues. The particular difficulty of distinguishing between Pedro's language and that of the narrator has led one critic to suggest that Pedro is the narrator of the whole novel.[61] I would argue that the novel confuses the language of the different narrative voices in order to make the point that words are not an accurate reflection of the speaking self. It is the incongruities of the inconsistent narrative perspective that allow the reader to read between the lines of the text's surface falsifications.

It is because Pedro – as an intellectual – is articulate that he is able to manipulate language to rationalize his behaviour: the more he resorts to words, the less he understands himself and his situation. Being illiterate Cartucho is able to translate his intentions directly into action, while Pedro gets tied up in knots by his flair for words. But even Cartucho's monologues – like those of Dorita's grandmother – serve the purpose of self-deception rather than of self-expression. Muecas' wife, alienated from language rather than by it, has a sincerity lacking in the other characters: her inability to manipulate language does not allow her to deceive herself or others. She alone gives an honest account of her life because she does so in the form of visual images which the narrator verbalizes on her behalf (247). The duplicity of language is illustrated in the interior monologues by the use of free association, leading the characters back to the reality they are trying to conceal with words. Language serves the dual purpose of mythification and demythification. Pedro's idealization of rural life will thus lead him from frogs to vivisection and back to Florita's death, which he is trying to forget (287–8). Man uses language to control his life but discovers that language is controlling him. The policeman interrogating Pedro takes advantage of this, knowing that if he encourages him to talk freely he will betray himself involuntarily. The confession dictated to Pedro by the police shows that they have a masterly understanding of the Freudian theory of the symbolic nature of language, whereby its literal meaning is undermined by an underlying level of involuntary implications.

Freud likened the unconscious to a censored text. Claude Talahite aptly refers to the hidden meaning of the text of *Tiempo de silencio* as its 'repressed discourse'.[62] By repressing unpleasant truths, language functions on a conscious level as an expression of the pleasure principle; but on an unconscious level, by referring in between the lines to that which is repressed, it functions as an expression of the reality principle. The Freudian theory of the symbolic nature of language is a theory of irony, in that it supposes that surface and underlying meaning are in contradiction, and that as a result language frustrates the expectations it sets up. The use of symbolism in *Tiempo de silencio* is ironic in both these senses. The novel repeatedly resorts to the notion of the mythical archetype to show how language, being in the service of desire, idealizes reality. The mythical archetype affords a Jungian insight into man's essential nature only in the sense that it reveals his essence to be his urge to mythification. The recurring image of the siren illustrates Pedro's urge to project an archetypal image of desire on to an undesirable reality, whether it be his prison cell or the fact that Dorita is not the kind of woman he wants (220, 114–16). The image of the siren also occurs in connection with the brothel where it forms part of a list of archetypal images of desire – the phallic symbolism being so overdone as to become ludicrous – whose function is to eclipse the images of revulsion which also insist on coming to mind (105). The red light in the brothel will give free rein to 'the inner archetype after which the spirit tirelessly yearns' (203), because the clients cannot see properly in the half-light. The audience at the musical revue will likewise project an archetypal image of desire on to the dancers, with the leading lady dressed in 'fish scales' like a siren, and the chorus-girls corresponding to the image of 'a more essential being' contained not in their undernourished bodies but in the collective unconscious of the spectators (270–1). This episode shows how society encourages the individual to fall for the glossy images of desire it holds out to him to distract his attention from the reality of frustration. The women in the *pensión* dangle the desirable image of Dorita in front of Pedro to secure his capitulation. Matías will compare the luxury goods in the shop windows in the centre of

Madrid to Platonic archetypes (233) because they correspond to an essential image of desire which in practice is inaccessible. The image of the siren is apt because, as an image of desire, it lures man to his destruction. What is important is that the symbolic images of pleasure in the novel are ironically undercut by a contrary set of symbolic images of destruction: the womb is also a devouring stomach; Dorita and society are tempting sirens but also octopuses (78, 120).

The Cuban writer Severo Sarduy has related the Freudian notion that language simultaneously conceals and reveals to the Baroque use of artifice. Several critics have noted the 'Baroque style' of *Tiempo de silencio*. Fernando Morán has suggested that Martín-Santos' use of latinisms and syntactical inversions parodies the inflated rhetoric of Francoist officialdom.[63] But the use of Gongorisms also points to the existence, beneath the exaggeratedly artificial surface of the text, of a repressed level of meaning. The Baroque is an ironic style which deceives the spectator through its use of *trompe-l'œil* perspective, offering him an illusion of solidity which turns out to be a façade. Sarduy notes the frequency in Baroque art of the ellipse which lacks a fixed centre, its centre being the gap between two displaced centres. Michael Ugarte has observed that the construction of *Tiempo de silencio* depends on the displacement of symmetrical structures.[64] The Gongoresque juxtaposition in the novel of images of petrification and shipwreck symbolizes a world whose apparent solidity masks an underlying precariousness. Góngora's image of the shipwrecked mariner – found throughout *Tiempo de silencio* – has been seen as a symbolic representation of man's hybrid nature: part-conscious (land), part-unconscious (sea). For Sarduy, this duality finds visual expression in the two displaced centres of the Baroque ellipse. Sarduy suggests that the Baroque technique of chiaroscuro – focussing light on one centre in such a way as to plunge the other into darkness – is a stylistic representation of the Freudian notion of consciousness as an area of apparent clarity which monopolizes attention by repressing the contents of the unconscious.[65] The images of light ('sun') and darkness ('night') in *Tiempo de silencio* have the same function. The sun – a 'great liar' (181) falsely embellishing the sordid reality of the Calle Atocha (30), the shanty town (139) and the cemetery (178) – creates a deceptive luminosity, thus repressing the darker side of reality. In *Libertad, temporalidad y transferencia,*

Martín-Santos warns that clear explanations are usually false.[66] Pedro's monologues distance him from reality by trying to impose a false clarity on to what is confused. The narrator however resorts to a labyrinthine syntax – at the same time constructed according to a rigorous logic – that enables the reader to make sense of the text without imposing a false sense of clarity.

The novel insists on the need to recognize the dark areas of reality, but it never suggests that darkness is a source of truth. The unconscious is likened to night because it falsifies reality as much as the false clarity of reason. The daylight gives a false air of innocence to the prostitutes, but the night turns them into equally false 'lascivious houris' (181). The 'third eye' of desire which guides Pedro to Dorita's bed does not help him see in the dark but makes him a prisoner of his darker urges. Sun and night deceive in different ways: the sun by concentrating attention on the surface of things, ignoring their underlying meaning; the night by subordinating the reality principle to the pleasure principle:

El gran ojo acusador [el sol] consigue llevar hasta el límite su actividad engañosa porfiando tercamente ... para hacer constar ... que es real solamente la superficie opaca de las cosas, su forma, su medida, la disposición de sus miembros en el espacio y que, por el contrario, carece de toda verdad su esencia, el significado hondo y simbólico que tales entes alcanzan durante la noche.   (180)

The great accusing eye [the sun] successfully perpetrates its deceptions by insisting ... that only the opaque surface of things, their shape, measurements and spatial organization are real, and that on the other hand their essence, the deep symbolic meaning they take on at night, is entirely devoid of truth.

According to this, the 'essence' of reality is the 'deep symbolic meaning' it has for man. This 'essence' is a falsification because it is located in the 'night' of the unconscious which projects a false image of pleasure on to reality. The 'night' referred to here is the false night which the brothelkeeper creates by drawing the curtains to shut out the light of day. The underlying meaning of existence must be sought in the unconscious, in the knowledge that the latter is a zone of darkness.

The antithesis 'sun'/'night' is supplemented by the antithesis 'speech'/'silence'. The meaning of the text lies beneath the visible surface, in what is not spoken. The novel's title refers to the silence of conformism. By this Martín-Santos is referring not only to official censorship but also to the way the individual censors his vision of the world. This self-censorship can be the conscious product of Bad Faith, but it is also partly inevitable in that the unconscious is by definition a 'censored text'. The silences at the soirée in the *pensión* show that its hidden meaning lies in the unvoiced desires of its participants (45). The conversation is compared to a 'work of art' because there is a 'deep truth' – embodied by the characters' 'ardent desires' – underlying the 'deceptive, shifting reality' of the words spoken (48). According to this, the function of the literary text is to offer the reader a fictitious construct which reveals an underlying, unspoken truth. Dorita is the 'true (dumb) axis' of the soirée because, by remaining silent, she is best able to express the unconfessed desires of all present. Since the meaning of words lies not in what they say but in what they represent symbolically, Muecas' wife does not need to understand her husband's conversation with Pedro to appreciate its import (63). It is because she is inarticulate that she is able to give a howl of protest, instead of resorting to words to silence the truth.[67] The silence of conformism does not consist of an absence of words but of the proliferation of words in order to erect a defensive barrier between man and reality. By saying one thing and meaning another, words not only serve conformism by rationalizing that which is unjustifiable, they also serve authoritarianism by manipulating others without appearing to do so. Dorita's grandmother traps Pedro by giving him to understand that she knows he has seduced her granddaughter, without actually saying so (119). The police secure his capitulation by means of a series of innuendoes (207). The meaning of Dorita's conversation with the police also consists in what is not said (222–3). Silence is not a lack of meaning but the relegation of meaning to a subterranean zone. In the subterranean cells of the police station, Pedro will discover that the apparent silence conceals a multiplicity of voices which reveal the reality of oppression (214).

Silence functions in the novel in two ways. The characters use language to silence truth. The narrator, by making the reader aware that meaning must be sought in what the words do not say, turns silence into a critical instrument. Some critics have seen the fact that Pedro opts for silence at the end of the novel as a sign of hope.[68] There is nothing positive about Pedro's final silence because it represents the silencing of truth. The characters do not want to be understood, the narrator does. It is the difference between lying and irony.

Martín-Santos' Freudian understanding of the way language simultaneously conceals and reveals makes irony fundamental to *Tiempo de silencio*. Even when the irony takes the straightforward form of social satire – in which the exaggerated surface idealizations point to the clear existence of a less attractive underlying reality – the reader is obliged to work out for himself what the unspoken reality might be. The reader is thus forced to reject the authority of the text and take responsibility for the production of meaning. The indirect description of reality via a falsely embellished account also has the advantage of making the reader suspect the existence of something more terrible than could be conveyed by literal statement. Pedro, confronted by the women in the *pensión*'s idealized version of their lives, will imagine the worst (48). The realist novels of the 1950s failed in their political mission because the social problems they depicted were insignificant in comparison with those that existed in real-life Spain. By falsely idealizing reality, Martín-Santos is able to approximate to it. Satire is a particularly appropriate method for conveying the problems of underdevelopment: just as the meaning of the text consists of what is not said, so the underlying reality of postwar Spain is shown to consist of a lack. In the case of the satire of the upper classes we are made aware that reality consists of a lack in the different sense that, behind the social masks of Matías and his mother, there is nothing of substance. The fact that the middle classes (Dorita's grandmother) and the lower classes (Muecas, Cartucho) are satirized via their monologues – direct or reported – makes the reader view their verbal falsifications from their vantage-point, forcing him to recognize that truth, being dependent on point of view, is not fixed and stable. In the case of the intellectual Pedro, his self-justifications are so articulate that he is able to convince not only himself but also the inattentive reader. The majority of critics have failed to perceive the Bad Faith of his sophisticated appeal to existentialist argument to claim that he is more free in prison than in the outside world, and that it is a good thing for him to abandon his ambitions for a mediocre life as a village doctor.[69] The lack of a clear-cut boundary between truth and falsity makes the reader aware that truth is not only relative but also ambiguous.

Irony, by refusing all certainties, is alien to myth in which everything is unquestioned and given. Myth deals in one-dimensional absolutes; irony is two-dimensional and relative in that it juxtaposes two opposing levels of meaning both of which are valid from different points of view. If the function of myth – in Lévi-Strauss' definition – is to mediate contradiction, contradiction is the stuff of which irony is made: whether it be the contradiction between what is said and what is meant that constitutes verbal irony, or the contradiction between expectations and outcome that constitutes situational irony. Myth deals with larger-than-life heroic characters; irony thrives on the human weaknesses that create misunderstandings and miscalculations. If myth claims to offer access to eternal truths, irony thrives on deafness and blindness. *Tiempo de silencio* is an ironic novel – and an anti-mythical novel – in that it describes a world where there are no certainties but only ambiguities, for truth resides in silence and in night. The absolutes of truth and falsity blur as the hidden meaning of reality is shown to lie in the unconscious, which is deaf and blind to reality. The existence of the unconscious inevitably creates a situation of irony, since man is ignorant of his essential being. The conflict between consciousness and the unconscious creates a particularly complex irony, since the two are in conflict yet at the same time in complicity in their attempt to mythify reality in accordance with the pleasure principle. William Empson singles out the Freudian concept of emotional ambivalence as the most extreme type of ambiguity, since man ironically desires what he fears.[70] Pedro's desire for the castration he fears is a perfect example. The existence of the unconscious also creates an ironic situation by making human behaviour counterproductive. Pedro's search for protection leads to his castration. Man is a victim of irony in that he discovers his acts obey different impulses from those which he thought motivated him. Pedro thinks he is motivated by a rational project, but discovers he is motivated by irrational urges. Man is also a victim of irony because his regressive instincts undo his efforts to progress. Pedro's desire to win the Nobel Prize leads to the destruction of his career. The Freudian analysis of human behaviour is based on the double ironic contradiction between lucidity and blindness, and between progress and regression. In his book *The Compass of Irony*, Muecke points out that Oedipus is the quintessential ironic hero because he is blind to his crimes and commits them while trying to avoid them.[71] Pedro is an Oedipus in both these senses. In perhaps the greatest irony of all, the Oedipus myth undermines the certainties and belief in the need to return to origins that are myth's hallmarks. *Tiempo de silencio* puts forward an ironic view of existence by contradicting the expectations and hopes of all its characters: Pedro, Cartucho, the women in the *pensión*, Muecas' family are all confronted with an unforeseen tragedy. Dorita's entirely unexpected death takes place as she and Pedro embark on their 'nocturnal periplus through the mother's absence' (284): the novel portrays an insecure world in which nothing has a firm foundation.

Pedro's behaviour is doubly ironic in that his blindness to his errors is the result of an ironic attitude to life. Pedro makes the mistake of equating irony with superiority. Throughout the novel he reflects on his own life and that of his fellow-citizens from a superior position that detaches him from the objects of his criticisms: when seducing Dorita, he looks down from the ceiling on his body's actions as if it did not belong to him (117). The morality of the ironist has been the subject of much debate. Michael Ugarte accuses Martín-Santos of nihilism because of his use of irony.[72] In his famous treatise on irony Kierkegaard distinguished between two categories: one immoral, the other moral. The former – which he accuses of arrogance – is Romantic irony, according to which man is free to dissociate himself from reality and opt for the world of imagination since all knowledge is illusory. The latter – which Kierkegaard praises for its humility – is Socratic irony, in which the ironist adopts a position of part-detachment part-commitment by feigning ignorance in order to provoke others to reflection. For Kierkegaard, Romantic irony is a denial of history because it declares that everything is an illusion. Whereas Socratic irony, by encouraging man to adopt a critical stance while at the same time refusing to impose dogmatic solutions, affirms history by asserting freedom and the need for change.[73] In dissociating himself from his situation, Pedro is guilty of Romantic irony. While the narrator, by adopting a position that is part-detached part-involved, adopts a position of Socratic irony. In *Libertad, temporalidad y transferencia*, Martín-Santos insists that the analyst must take an omniscient, detached stance but that he must also accept that he is 'inside the process of which he claims to be narrator'.[74] The analogy drawn between the role of analyst and that of narrator is interesting: the narrator of *Tiempo de silencio* adopts the same ambiguous position. At times omniscient, at others he will recognize his limitations; at times invisible, at others he will make his presence felt; at times critical of his characters' Bad Faith, at others he will assume it parodically. Martín-Santos ends *Libertad, temporalidad y transferencia* with an analogy between the ironic stance of critical detachment combined with acceptance of responsibility which the analyst encourages in his patients and the aesthetic response of catharsis, which he defines as 'the coming to terms with one's own tragic destiny as a result of seeing it enacted by symbolic figures'.[75] *Tiempo de silencio* produces just such a response in the reader. The oscillation between third person and first person narration places him in a position that is simultaneously detached and involved. He is asked to reflect critically on how Spanish society survived 'in what they themselves called the hungry years', while the next sentence – beginning 'In this way we can understand' – includes him in the characters' situation (18). The first person plural, involving the reader, occurs precisely at the points of maximum critical detachment: in the meditations on Madrid, on Goya's painting and on the bullfight; the descriptions of the cemetery and the musical revue; and Pedro's final reflection on a 'time of silence'.

Octavio Paz has claimed that irony, being based on contradiction, affirms movement and change as opposed to analogy, which strives to eliminate differences and seeks a static point of reconciliation. Irony is the substance of history; analogy is the substance of myth.[76] If Paz favours analogy and myth, Martín-Santos favours irony and history. Martín-Santos is not interested in reconciliation (the 'symmetry' mocked at the end of the novel) but in contradiction and change. Muecke points out that irony is opposed to stability and is thus subversive. In its supposition that nothing is fixed and everything is liable to turn out otherwise, irony affirms the inevitability of change. Irony is based on a tragic view of life, but it supposes that man is worth saving from his illusions.[77]

The characters' mythical urge to escape the insecurities of history by returning to the womb and submitting to authority is countered by the temporal flow of the narrative. The past is mentioned only in the characters' interior monologues, with the result that it is viewed in the light of their present situation and hopes for the future. The one exception is the narrator's meditation on the city of Madrid (15–19): Talahite has noted how the temporal perspective here moves to and fro between past, present and future.[78] Narration in the past tense tends to slip into the present, while the repeated rhetorical questions – 'How shall we ever ...?' (8), 'What shall we do to ...?' (290) – incorporate the future into the text. The use in the interior monologues of free association also produces a temporal fluidity which not only recreates the sensation of Bergsonian 'lived time' but also shows how meaning is created through the interrelation of different points of time. Pedro's final monologue provides a brilliant demonstration of the tension created by his attempt to stop time by turning the future into an end and the temporal flow of his thoughts which prevents him from doing so. The rhythm of the moving train, which Pedro forms into different patterns, becomes a symbol of temporality: man is free to create a 'different rhythm' but he must 'form a rhythm' (292). All attitudes are attitudes to time. Pedro is free to opt for a 'time of silence' but he cannot opt out of time. It is important that at the end of the novel Pedro should not have been able to resolve his contradictions: his inability to escape contradiction represents his inability to escape history.

In an article Martín-Santos defined man as 'a being who is duration, who is time, who is movement and change'.[79] The notion of time is central to his work: the words 'time' and 'temporality' appear in the titles of his two novels and in that of his major psychiatric work. In his doctoral thesis on the thought of Dilthey and Jaspers, he insists that the present always contains elements of the past and the future: time is neither a straight line travelling from past to future nor a cyclical return to origins, but a dialectical flow moving simultaneously in all directions.[80] Thus *Tiempo de silencio* will be based on the dialectical juxtaposition of the characters' regressive tendencies with the narrator's chronological treatment of the plot. In *Libertad, temporalidad y transferencia*, Martín-Santos shows neurosis to be a denial of the possibility of change: the neurotic imprisons himself in a fixed form of behaviour and projects his own inflexibility on to the outside world, in order to have the security of knowing what is what. The analyst makes the neurotic accept change by undermining the false sense of security he derives from his neurosis, and forcing him to face what Martín-Santos calls the 'insecure ocean' of existence.[81] In one of his few recorded statements of his literary views, Martín-Santos spoke of his wish to create a 'dialectical realism' which showed the contradictory nature of both individual and society.[82] *Tiempo de silencio* creates such a 'dialectical realism' by showing that existence is based not on the fixed categories of myth but on the contradictions which make change inevitable. Critics who have seen *Tiempo de silencio* as a mythical novel have been misled by Martín-Santos' statement that he regarded the social function of the novelist as being the combined one of destroying myths and of creating a new 'progressive Mythology' that would act as a stimulus to social change.[83] The phrase 'progressive Mythology' shows that what Martín-Santos had in mind is very different from the mythical regression to origins that has appealed to so many twentieth-century writers. If *Tiempo de silencio* compares Pedro's voyage round Madrid to that of Ulysses round the Mediterranean, it is not in order to create a mythical novel in the Romantic or Jungian sense of the term, but in order to demonstrate that man's life – despite his search for security (the petrification of the Castilian *meseta* and the Escorial) – is an 'insecure ocean'. If Unamuno rejected the surface agitation of the sea of history for its immutable mythical depths, *Tiempo de silencio* insists that man, like it or not, is a shipwrecked mariner floundering in the waves of time. It is important that Martín-Santos should use the same image of the ocean to symbolize temporality and the unconscious: the latter may – as in Unamuno's concept of 'intrahistory' – be an attempt to deny the temporal nature of existence, but it is precisely man's unconscious urges that undermine his rational intentions and turn his life into an 'insecure ocean' inhabited by sirens and octopuses.

The characters use language to mythify reality not only in the sense of falsifying it but also in the sense that they petrify it by reducing its ambiguities to words that have the appearance of being fixed and solid. In *Libertad, temporalidad y transferencia*, Martín-Santos described Bad Faith as the adoption of a mask (the Jungian 'persona'), whose rigidity is an attempt to deny the ambiguities of social existence.[84] All the characters in the novel wear masks in the sense that they play roles, either to manipulate others or to conform to others' expectations. The novel strips off the character's masks, revealing their underlying lack of essential definition: at the reception for Ortega Pedro sees an entirely different Matías from the one he had accompanied to the brothel (170). The interior monologues will further show that man is defined by his contradictions. In the same way the language of the novel functions as a mask concealing not an essential truth but an underlying silence and darkness. The disquieting 'truth' revealed beneath the mask of the text's surface mythifications is that reality can be defined only in terms of what it is not: as being other than what the characters think or say about it. Hence the frequent recourse to description by negation, the nicest example being the definition of Spain as 'a country that is not Europe'. Octavio Paz has described language as a mask obscuring an essential reality inaccessible to words: the function of the poetic image is thus to create a set of correspondences evoking that which cannot be expressed explicitly.[85] Martín-Santos also believes that language speaks more through insinuation than through literal statement, but he is concerned not with the associations created through the use of analogy but with the underlying implications created through the use of irony. For Paz, the writer's goal is to eliminate the opposition between surface and depth by making the opaqueness of language 'transparent'. For Martín-Santos, language produces meaning through the contradiction that exists between surface falsification and underlying implication. Fiction is a mask that mythifies reality, but through irony it can expose the uncertainties behind the wall of words that man erects to give his life a comforting appearance of solidity.

4

Fiction as echo: *Volverás a Región*

Juan Benet has stated that his first novel, *Volverás a Región* (1967), was influenced by a reading of *The Golden Bough* and that the figure of Numa who presides over the text was intended as an updated version of the guardian of the sacred grove at Nemi with which Frazer opens his study.[1] It has become a critical cliché to describe the work as a mythical novel. In using this term critics refer to its enigmatic features, implying that they have in mind the Romantic view of myth as the intuitive expression of that which escapes rational understanding. The only critic to have attempted a sustained analysis of the novel's use of myth – Robert Spires – interprets it as the dramatization of a Jungian descent into the underworld in search of regeneration, noting however – as Villegas was forced to do with *Tiempo de silencio* – that regeneration is absent from the text.[2] I shall argue that Benet's view of myth is anti-Romantic and anti-Jungian in that, like Lévi-Strauss, he sees it as the product of reason. I shall also argue that the novel is not so much an attempt to recreate mythical thought as a critical examination of its insufficiencies: in other words, that its use of myth is ironic. Mythical thought is shown to be a failed attempt to impose ordered structures on to an unstable history. The novel is as much about history as it is about myth, in that it takes the Civil War as an allegory of the devastation caused by the passage of time. If *Tiempo de silencio* offers a political analysis of a specific period of Spanish history, *Volverás a Región* uses a specific period of Spanish history as the pretext for a philosophical inquiry into the problems posed by temporality. Like his close friend Martín-Santos, Benet suggests that man's condemnation to time produces an insecurity that leads him to turn to the fixed categories of myth. But while *Tiempo de silencio* is characterized by an optimistic belief in the value of historical change, *Volverás a Región* suggests that change is synonymous with destruction and that the concept of history as progress is another form of myth. *Tiempo de silencio* is an anti-mythical novel; *Volverás a Región* is a sceptical examination both of myth and of the forward-moving linear view of history that has dominated Western culture. Martín-Santos' use of irony is constructive; that of Benet is not so much destructive as – in Derrida's sense of the term – deconstructive: doubtful of reason's ability to reconstruct the world, but confident that it can at least expose the illusory nature of the dichotomies by which it seeks to order experience. *Volverás a Región* is a study of the mythical boundaries between opposing categories which reason erects to contain the chaos of reality. The key mythical element in the novel is the boundary, guarded by the keeper Numa, that separates the mythical world of Mantua from the historical world of Región. The opposition between myth and history is itself shown to be mythical, for both are rationalizations of the only universal truth: the fact of loss.

The obviously mythical figure of Numa is just one of a series of mythical references in the novel, some explicit and others implicit. In fact Numa is the name not of the priest of Nemi but of the legendary second King of Rome who was by tradition supposed to have consorted with a water-nymph in the grove at Nemi. Frazer explores the parallels between the two legends.[3] The choice of the name Numa was no doubt forced on Benet by the fact that the priests of Nemi were anonymous. It also has the advantage of linking the keeper of the sacred grove with the attributes for which King Numa was renowned: notably his championship of law and order, which provided wartorn Rome with one of its rare periods of peace, and his responsibility for founding the religious institutions of Rome, including the worship of Terminus, the god of boundaries.[4] Benet's Numa, as an amalgam of priest and king, is an image of the theocratic state. The aspects which Benet has taken from the priest of Nemi are his defensive role and his association with the oak-tree, of which various species abound in Numa's forbidden forest.[5] There is also frequent mention of mistletoe, which Frazer links with the oaks at Nemi and which he also equates with the golden bough that, according to Virgil's *Aeneid*, provided a passport to the underworld.[6] A version of the golden bough appears in the novel with the gold coin which the boatwoman – an obvious incarnation of Charon, the ferryman to the underworld – gives to the Gambler as a talisman.

That the natural image of a gold branch should be replaced by the financial image of a gold coin is no doubt a comment on the degraded character of modern man's fetish objects. The infernal associations of the gold coin are made explicit by the description of its owner, the boatwoman, as an image of the 'perverse laughter' that rules the 'land of the damned' (198). The Gambler, gold coin in hand, takes the boatwoman's ferry every night to return to the subterranean world of the mine, situated on the other side of the River Torce at the point of its confluence with the Tarrentino, whose source lies in the Collado de los Muertos ['Mount of the Dead'] (209). It is not for nothing that Numa's forbidden territory, beyond the River Torce, should be called Mantua: the birthplace of Virgil, author of the *Aeneid* in which the golden bough is mentioned, and Dante's guide to the underworld in the *Inferno* where he is referred to as a 'son of Mantua'.[7] As befits an image of the underworld, Mantua is peopled by the souls of the dead. No one who crosses its boundary is seen alive again. The traveller who crosses the River Torce in the boatwoman's ferry senses that he has entered another world (198). Colonel Gamallo's daughter Marré likewise speculates that her journey to Mantua – passing an inn with a ghostly clientele situated at a 'crossroads to purgatory' – is a journey to the land of the dead (128).

If the boatwoman – linking Mantua and civilization – is associated with the gold coin and the mine, Numa – defending Mantua against civilization – is associated with nature. His accomplices in luring the traveller to his death are the wasteland plateau, the treacherous marshlands and the insect with the lethal sting. His revenge is preceded by the blossoming of the hyacinth and an accursed red flower said to contain the blood of various legendary heroes and of the victims of Spanish history (142, 189–90). These omens occur in April, while Numa's shots are heard in September: spring flowers do not signal rebirth but foreshadow autumn destruction. The mythical world of Numa is associated with a natural cycle from which regeneration is absent. As Numa himself will say in the later story named after him, he is not a messiah offering salvation.[8] On the contrary his function is to 'naturalize' disaster by confirming destruction as a natural law. He intervenes in history to give refuge to the defeated – the Visigoths, the Carlists, the Republicans in the Civil War – not to regenerate them but to put the final seal on their defeat. It is implied that the refuge he gives is death: as the remains of the Republican army disappear into the hills, unidentified shots are heard as when any other traveller crosses his boundary. Ricardo Gullón has suggested that, in keeping with the Romantic definition of myth, Mantua represents the promise of paradise: it would be more accurate to say that it represents the certainty of damnation.[9] The myth of Mantua offers redemption only in the sense that it saves man from the torment of hope. As in Dante's *Inferno*, entry to Numa's Virgilian realm is marked by the instruction 'Lasciate ogni speranza'.[10]

It is precisely because of its certainty that Numa's law of destruction appeals to the people of Región. The fact that his shots can be expected in September contains disaster by reducing it to an orderly seasonal pattern. It is however implied that Numa's shots are regular only because they are the projection of a desire for certainty: proof of their existence is provided by 'their repetition in memory and hope' (14). The falsity of the supposition that nature reduces change to a predictable pattern is made clear by the geographical descriptions in the novel: the wayward River Torce, the malignant north wind which comes just at the wrong moment, the mirages that falsely raise the traveller's hopes. The geological descriptions show the natural world of Mantua to be just as capricious and turbulent as Región's history: 'La sierra de Región se presenta como un testigo enigmático, poco conocido e inquietante, de tanto desorden y tanto paroxismo' ['The Región Mountains stand as a little known, disturbing, enigmatic witness to all that chaos and convulsion'] (39). It is important that Benet should describe the geological formation of the area because this shows that nature is not a static seasonal cycle but the result of a long evolutionary process. It is interesting to contrast his descriptions with those of the 1898 Generation, designed to justify the 'eternal Castile' of the unchanging *meseta*. Nothing could be more different than Benet's images of incessant geological upheaval. The implication is that the attempt to counter change by appeal to a fixed natural order is illusory because there is no such thing as natural order: only natural history. Order exists only as a mythical projection of the human mind. The opposition between nature and history is a false one.

Benet's notion of myth as a demand for order is close to that of Lévi-Strauss, but Benet is more sceptical about its value. For Lévi-

Strauss the function of myth is the mediation of the opposition between nature and civilization, achieved by projecting on to civilization the order discernible in nature.[11] Benet, however, implies that myth establishes an artificial opposition between nature and civilization in order to create the semblance of an order lacking in both civilization and nature. For Benet myth has a compensatory function that makes it suspect. There is much in Benet's analysis that anticipates Derrida's equation of the binary oppositions of Western rational thought with the psychological process of repression. Benet goes further than Lévi-Strauss' suggestion that mythical thought is rational; like Derrida, he suggests that all rational thought is mythical inasmuch as it depends on the invention of imaginary dichotomies. Derrida shows how the binary oppositions of Western thought constitute an attempt to contain the threat of that which is disturbing by defining it as the negation of that which is reassuring, and thus relegating it to an exclusion zone. In this way evil is kept at bay by being defined as the negation of good; the irrational is repressed by being defined as a negation of the rational. In fact – Derrida suggests – the supposedly primary term is derived from the excluded one: good is an abstraction invented to counter the presence of evil; the rational is posited as a check on the irrational.[12] The exclusion zone of Mantua is a perfect example of Derrida's thesis. Mantua represents the taboo: that which is threatening and must therefore be kept out of bounds. It is a mythical underworld not in the Jungian sense of a store of unconscious collective wisdom, but in the sense that it contains all those disquieting elements society needs to repress. Hence, in accordance with the law of the return of the repressed, its habitation by ghosts that return to haunt the present (89). Having relegated its repressed urges to the underworld of Mantua, the people of Región need to invent Numa to police the boundary between the two areas. As a combination of the guardian of the sacred grove at Nemi and the Roman king who instituted the worship of Terminus, Numa is the perfect candidate for the job. The No Trespassing sign that forbids entry to his realm stands as an image of the boundaries which reason erects to exclude the dangers it cannot eliminate. Without the securely guarded exclusion zone of Mantua, society would have to admit that danger lies within as well as without. The function of myth is shown to be not the mediation of contradiction, but the suppression of internal contradiction by means of the creation of an external contradiction. It is the timeworn political ploy of inventing an external enemy to distract attention from trouble at home. There are frequent references in the novel to reason's habit of inventing decoys that distract attention from the real source of danger. Mantua is a myth in the sense that it is an alibi.

Stephen Summerhill has suggested that Mantua represents nature in the sense of natural instinct: the wild, primitive forces society needs to prohibit. He argues that the people of Región fear Numa and relegate him to exile in Mantua because they see him as an embodiment of instinct.[13] While Summerhill's central thesis is correct, this last point needs modification. It is not the people of Región who banish Numa, but Numa who prevents them from entering Mantua. A distinction needs to be drawn between Mantua and its keeper. Mantua does indeed represent the repressed natural urges of society but Numa is society's policeman who, by guarding Mantua, enforces the taboo. The people of Región fear him not as an embodiment of that which is repressed but as the agent of repression who, by containing the irrational forces of nature, suppresses a fundamental part of themselves. It is appropriate that he should be a shepherd: the tamer of nature whose job is to keep the wolf at bay.

In his brilliant collection of essays *El ángel abandona a Tobías*, Benet analyses the systematic way in which Western thought, since the Greeks, has falsified what he calls the 'continuum' of reality by dividing it into opposing categories.[14] That society is not a zone of rationality clearly separated off from an external zone of irrationality is shown in the novel by the chaos of Región's history (seen in terms of the opposition between Republican Región and Nationalist Macerta). Despite its invention of the myth of Numa/Mantua, society fails to suppress its internal contradictions. Nor does it succeed in keeping the boundary between society and nature intact. Numa's task (as an incarnation of order who polices the boundary) is undermined by the existence of a second mythical figure: the boatwoman (an incarnation of the absurd who ferries people across it). The principal reason why the rational and the irrational cannot be kept apart is that they create each other. Dr Sebastián points out that reason is the product of the irrational – a 'bolt-hole' manufactured by man to escape his 'inner demons' – and conversely that the suppression of the irrational leads to its resurgence in the form of a 'nostalgia for fear' (138). The fact that the principal violators of Numa's realm are scientists illustrates how reason, having suppressed the dangers within, turns to exploring the *terra incognita* without. At the same time the more the irrational is relegated to an exclusion zone, the more it threatens to reassert itself at home. Dr Sebastián suggests that the advance of science has freed society from an elementary fear of the unknown only to create a more serious 'fear of oneself and of one's fellow men' (218).

It is essential to recognize that Numa is not an incarnation of the irrationality of the Mantuan underworld, but of the rational desire for order which requires him to keep the boundary between the rational and the irrational intact.[15] I use the contradiction in terms 'rational desire' deliberately: Numa is the mythical projection of reason, but reason is itself the rationalization of an instinctive fear. To be more precise: reason and instinct are two different manifestations of fear. In *El ángel abandona a Tobías*, Benet draws a distinction between 'miedo' (fear in the sense of an instinctive reaction to immediate danger) and 'temor' (fear in the sense of a rationalization of previous experiences of 'miedo', leading to a defensive attitude to reality in general).[16] The two terms are used in the same way in *Volverás a Región*. Numa is a projection of the collective 'temor' of the people of Región, which in turn is a rationalization of the 'miedo' history has instilled in them. In the same book of essays, Benet insists – in keeping with Frazer – that religion is a response to fear, but – unlike Frazer – he regards it as rational in that it is an abstraction from experience and not an instinctive response.[17] The myth of Numa is an illustration of man's need for religious belief; the point is that it is not a spontaneous act of faith but the defensive rationalization of a long history of disillusionments. As Dr Sebastián says: Numa is not a product of nature or even of the Civil War, but the outcome of 'a long, organized religious process' (221).

That Numa is the mythical projection of the collective 'temor' of the people of Región is implied by the fact that no one has ever seen him, and that his shots are produced 'to relieve their unease' (21). Dr Sebastián speculates that he perhaps exists only as a 'crystallization' of 'temor' (221). The recurrent mention of boundaries in relation to the characters' private lives also suggests that Numa's No Trespassing sign is the external projection of a psychological condition. Marré's expedition to the aptly named Hotel Terminus teaches her that she cannot cross the 'impregnable boundary' that separates her rational self (the 'usurper') from the passionate self (the 'recluse') that has been repressed since the Civil War, because of the existence of an internal policeman or 'referee' (149–50). In order to defend himself from passion, Dr Sebastián marries the daughter of the railway worker whose job is to keep the level-crossing barrier permanently closed. It is implied that such boundaries, however arbitrary, are inescapable. The sequence of guardians who inhibit Marré's movements is unending (276–7). Even when she surrenders to sexual instinct, there will be a sentry 'ever leaning in the omnipresent doorway' (155). Later, with Luis Timoner, she will discover there are certain boundaries that can never be crossed:

Y la joven malcriada que, sin saber cómo, ha logrado romper las barreras impuestas por su casta ... contempla por primera vez la línea real del horizonte más allá de la cual jamás verá nada por mucho que sea su atrevimiento: una piel ... perfilada en las tinieblas como la línea de la cordillera donde habita esa gente y esa raza maldita.   (167)

And the spoilt young girl who has somehow managed to break down the barriers erected by her class ... has her first glimpse of the real horizon beyond which she will never see, try as she may: the profile of a body ... outlined in the dark like the silhouette of the mountains inhabited by his folk and their accursed race.

It is appropriate that Luis – symbol of a psychological *terra incognita* – should come from and return to Mantua, and that his middle initial should be I. for incognito. Physical images of restriction are frequent in the novel, symbolizing mental restriction. Dr Sebastián's shuttered house, where the action of the last three chapters takes place, stands as the image of a shuttered mind. At the end of the novel the orphan breaks free from the bonds that tie his wrists, but he is unable to break out of the house. Marré does succeed in leaving the house but only – it seems – to be shot by Numa as she attempts to cross his boundary. The most frequent image of the boundary in the novel is that of the doorway, whether literal or metaphorical. The doorway is a useful symbol because it combines the dual elements of the threshold (which promises liberation) and the frame (which contains). Characters in *Volverás a Región* are never described in the process of crossing thresholds; the most characteristic posture is that of the static figure poised in the doorway as if frozen.

The Janus-like nature of the doorway image emphasizes the fact that the territories on either side of the boundary stand in a complementary relationship to one another. Given the existence of a barrier, there are two options: to maintain it or to break it. As Numa points out in the story dedicated to him, the custodian of the boundary needs the transgressor in order to fulfil his function, just as the transgressor needs the custodian.[18] The central episode of Gamallo's card game with the Gambler illustrates the fact that, in any drama, there have to be two antagonists. The solitary orphan will divide himself in two in order to be able to continue his game of marbles (17). The need for binary oppositions is internal as well as external. The boundary image in *Volverás a Región* provides a psychological model for the national schism that produced the Civil War: the Nationalists correspond to the custodians of the boundary, the Republicans (at least the younger ones) to the transgressors. It is implied that the conflict between the two is the historical projection of an internal dichotomy that persists even in time of peace. Chemical metaphors of precipitation are applied both to individual psychology and to the Civil War in order to suggest that, when a catalysing agent breaks down the emulsion of antagonistic elements, the effect is not to eliminate either element but to produce an equilibrium in which they neutralize each other (183–4, 272). Franco's peace does not represent the elimination of conflict, but its stabilization. The figure of Numa, who enforces immobility by preserving divisions, is an appropriate emblem.

The principal reason for the necessary existence of both the custodian of the boundary and the transgressor is that the exclusion zone represents not only that which is feared but also that which is desired. In this sense Ricardo Gullón is right to talk of Numa's realm as Paradise, provided one remembers that the people of Región, because of their fear of desire, need to regard it as hell (Mantua) in order to declare it out of bounds. In *El ángel abandona a Tobías*, Benet endorses Frazer's view that the taboo and the sacred are the same thing since that which is worshipped on account of its special powers needs, for that reason, to be kept under control. At the same time, if the sacred were not kept separate from everyday reality by being declared out of bounds, it would cease to be special.[19] In *Volverás a Región* the Nationalists are primarily motivated by fear, the young Republicans by desire: both, for different reasons, have an interest in the continuing existence of the boundary. The historical positions of the two sides in the Civil War are shown to be dependent on a mythical belief in Numa.

The novel suggests that the usual association of the Republic with history (belief in progress) and of the Nationalists with myth (belief in the need to return to a Paradise Lost) is based on a false dichotomy. In *El ángel abandona a Tobías* Benet argues that the concepts of progress and the Fall do not represent an opposition between history and myth, but that both are myths which have historical repercussions. Indeed, it is the mythical concept of cyclical time that gives birth to the historical concept of linear time, for the desire to recover a lost past requires the concept of the future as a time when this can be achieved.[20] In *Volverás a Región*, the Nationalists are shown to be motivated by a mythical desire to save the nation from decadence, but their objective in rejecting the present for the past is not to abolish linear time but to restore a capitalism threatened by economic decline. Their position is complemented by that of the older generation of Republican reformers who also reject the present, in their case for the sake of a future utopia. In both cases, belief in myth coincides with belief in the historical concept of progress. The Republic is, however, mainly represented in the novel by the young idealists striving for liberation from moral repression. The young Republicans reject both the traditional morality of the Nationalists and the reforming zeal of the older Republicans, because they see both as representing the sacrifice of the present. In rejecting the concepts of both past and future in order to enjoy the pleasures of the present, they reject the historical process for the eternal present of myth. The positions of the Nationalists, the older Republicans and the young Republicans are all mythical in different senses: the Nationalists in their desire to undo decadence, the older Republicans in their desire for a future utopia, the young Republicans in their desire for an eternal present. It is however only the young Republicans who reject the historical concept of linear time. By suggesting that it is the young Republicans and not the Nationalists who reject history, Benet reverses the usual assumptions. The Nationalists and the older Republicans, with their belief in linear time, represent reason (the postponement of pleasure); the young Republicans, with their cult of the present moment, represent passion (the immediate satisfaction of pleasure). The various positions are shown to be inadequate because, in different ways, they represent an attempt to free man from the inevitable destruction caused by the passage of time. But it is the young Republicans, who want to abolish time altogether, who suffer the greatest defeat. The novel shows the historical concept of linear time to be inescapable, but this is not a cause for optimism.

The Nationalists are associated with the capitalist notion of material progress through the description of traditional morality in terms of economic metaphors. The Nationalists' defence of honour is shown to be based on the capitalist doctrine of thrift ('ahorro'), which requires emotional and financial resources alike to be accumulated and not expended. Honour conserves the moral capital of the past by sacrificing present enjoyment for the sake of future gain. Colonel Gamallo's aunts write him a letter 'like a bank statement', reminding him that 'today's sacrifices and savings' are 'tomorrow's wealth and honour' (73). In the same way Dr Sebastián's mother invests in the future by having her son trained as a doctor, in return for which she expects him to sacrifice his youth 'in repayment of the debt' (130–1). The equation of the moral concept of duty with the economic concept of debt (the Spanish for both is 'deber') is common to both the Gamallo and Sebastián households. The two families represent the two sides of a capitalism forced on the defensive by economic decline: Gamallo's aunts represent a *rentier* class struggling to conserve its dwindling fortunes; Dr Sebastián's mother an emergent middle class struggling to achieve status.

The debt morality of capitalism is shown to be necessarily opposed to pleasure, inasmuch as this involves the dissipation of resources.[21] The conflict between the Nationalists and the young Republicans is that between conservatism and liberalism in the sense of the urge to retention and the urge to prodigality. It is in this sense that the Nationalists are the custodians of Numa's boundary and the young Republicans its transgressors. It is appropriate that the enemy of the future Nationalist commander Gamallo should be the Gambler. Gamallo's loss of María Timoner to the Gambler is just punishment for his procrastination of their marriage: he has rebelled against his aunts' morality of thrift by becoming a gambler, but he has not learnt to free himself from their doctrine of the postponement of pleasure. Unlike his opponent, he gambles not for pleasure but to defend his past winnings and to gain the gold coin. The sacrifice of present enjoyment in order to conserve past earnings and ensure

future gain is shown to be counterproductive in every case. Gamallo's defensive card-playing makes him lose to the Gambler who is not
afraid to stake all. Gamallo's aunts condemn themselves to a future
of barren spinsterhood for fear of losing their money on marriage: it
is implied that they appeal to Numa to shoot the pleasure-seeking
suitor of the younger sister (70–2). The miserliness of Dr Sebastián's
mother leads her to make a disastrous investment in an abortion
clinic: thrift leads not to future prosperity but to the destruction of
life (121).

The defensive capitalism of the Gamallo and Sebastián households is contrasted with the ethos of risk of the miners who formed
the basis of Región's earlier period of economic boom. For the
miners (whose favourite pastime is playing cards) capitalism is not
an investment in the future but a gamble to be enjoyed for its own
sake. It is appropriate that the Gambler should come from the mine,
and that the mine should be situated in Mantua, for it represents the
enjoyment of the present moment which the Nationalists repress and
hence relegate to a subterranean zone. The wealthy families who
continue to send their sons to work in the mine are all Republican;
Eugenio Mazón and Captain Asián, whose moral formation was
acquired in the mine, are the leading lights of the young Republicans seeking moral emancipation. The fact that the mine was the
source of Región's period of economic boom suggests that capitalism
was not originally founded on a calculating morality of thrift but
only subsequently, when threatened, did it appeal to reason to
suppress pleasure. It is implied that economic boom – like the
Gambler's winnings – is bound to be shortlived because the attempt
to carry the past into the future necessarily destroys the present.

Just as the subterranean world of the mine shows that capitalism is
founded on a suppressed irrationality (the love of risk), so it is made
clear that the Nationalists, fighting to vindicate capitalism, are in
practice driven by irrational factors. Gamallo's fellow officers claim
to be fighting for rational principles, but their unnecessary prolonga-
tion of the war shows them to be motivated by petty jealousies (65).
Gamallo himself has no illusions about the irrational nature of his
motivation: his plan for the capture of Región is a self-confessed
'folly' (74). It is his clarity about the nature of his objectives that
enables him to win, whereas the previous Navarrese colonel's
judgment is clouded by his unquestioning belief in the rationality of

his strategy. The earlier dishonour brought on Gamallo by the Gambler has made him cynical about the value of honour; nevertheless he sides with the Nationalists because the experience has left him with a wounded pride that requires him to defend himself against passion. His plan to drive the Republicans behind Numa's boundary can be seen as a symbolic attempt to banish the last remnants of passion from himself. Despite his cynicism, he is still fighting for the triumph of reason. His plan is a 'folly' but it is meticulously calculated. The surprise guerrilla raid that kills him in the flush of victory shows that no amount of rational calculation can save man from the fact that life is a gamble.

The Nationalists may be fighting a military offensive but their motives are defensive. Their triumph represents the vindication of Numa's boundary. Luis Timoner intimates that it will be a hollow victory because it represents the repression of passion (176–7). At the same time, it is implied that the Nationalists are bound to win inasmuch as their defensiveness is a basic human urge. The same economic terminology that is used to show the mean-mindedness of traditional morality occurs in passages of psychological analysis, without any apparent pejorative intention. Despite her rejection of her repressive upbringing, Marré finds it necessary to appeal to the notions of debit and credit to explain her behaviour (115, 164, 169). The abandoned orphan is incapable of self-analysis, but even at an unconscious level he keeps a reckoning of his emotional savings and expenditure (18–19). Both characters represent a will to survival that makes self-defence necessary. The fact that, in the orphan's case, the process is unconscious shows that the urge to build defences is in the first instance an instinctive reaction of 'miedo' which only later is rationalized to produce a code of morality based on 'temor'. The struggle between the Nationalists and the Republicans is not just a conflict between reason and passion; at a deeper level it is a struggle for control between the two conflicting instincts of fear and desire. That the defensive will to survival always asserts itself is not a cause for celebration because, being based on fear of the unknown, it requires the destruction of the future. Hence the orphan, with his retarded development, can survive only at the expense of clinging to the past. Likewise, the siege morality of the tenant farmers of Región – under attack from history and geography – enables them to secure a 'peaceful coexistence' at the cost of rejecting change and perpetuating their existing poverty (49). The implication is that the 'peaceful coexistence' secured by Nationalist victory is based on a similar defensive appeal to a fixed order, which far from vindicating progress confirms decadence.

The defensiveness of the Nationalists is echoed by that of the older Republicans, who insist on defending Región to the last as opposed to the younger Republicans who are in favour of surrender. The older and younger Republicans are united by their belief in the need for a society based on love but, while the younger generation are fighting for sexual liberation, the older generation are fighting for the abstract concept of the 'family of man'. Dr Sebastián suggests that this kind of utopianism is just as repressive as his own family background, because it requires the subordination of the individual to the group and the suppression of immediate pleasure for the sake of the future (139). The rational nature of this concept of a society based on mutual love is exemplified by the elderly Republican intellectual Señor Rumbal, whose lack of individuality is illustrated by the hesitations over his name and by his subordination to his authoritarian wife Adela. Rumbal's dark glasses suggest that his visions of the future depend on his blindness to the immediate moment. The repressiveness of this socialistic strand of Republicanism is shown by the dogmatic Republican commander Julián Fernández, the rigidity of whose rational principles drives his followers to a futile death, still defending their positions. Only the younger Republicans, who put pleasure before principles, will succeed in abandoning their defensive positions and crossing Numa's boundary.

The younger Republicans represent the libertarian strand within the Republic. Benet shows evident sympathy for the libertarian position, inasmuch as it puts the individual before the group and immediate happiness before future good. Contrary to the defensiveness of both the Nationalists and the older Republicans, the young Republicans represent the desire to break down barriers. Eugenio Mazón's motor car, in which they achieve their liberation, is another of the various motor cars in the novel that try to violate Numa's boundary: in this case figuratively rather than literally. Benet implies, however, that the young Republicans are doomed to failure, because they ignore the defensive side of human nature. They naively believe that their desire for liberation is compatible with the older Republicans' doctrine of a society based on mutual love, thinking that their pursuit of passion, by breaking down moral barriers, will overcome individual isolation (78). Marré will discover with Luis Timoner that love does not overcome individual isolation; indeed, that it creates a new defensiveness as the lover becomes obsessed with fear of losing the loved one. The young Republicans' pursuit of passion necessarily makes them subversive of all forms of political commitment, whether progressive or reactionary. Their main contribution to political life in Región is a transgressive sense of fun, created by the revolting bird they set loose at their political opponents' rallies. The target of their mockery is the notion, common to progressive politics and to traditional morality, that today must be sacrificed for tomorrow (160). Their belief that passion will free them from the constraints of historical existence by giving them access to a mythical eternal present outside time is, however, shown to be a delusion. The owner of the inn of ill fame where Marré has her idyll with Luis Timoner – appropriately situated in the mythical zone of Mantua – is called Muerte ['Death']. Marré will find that Mantua is not inviolate to history: the inn is set in the thick of the devastation of the Civil War. In fact, all the successive wars that have punctuated Región's history have violated Numa's boundary (41). The implication is that the breakdown of law and order that occurs in war releases the subterranean energies normally confined to Mantua and shows the boundary that separates society from its mythical exclusion zone to be a false one. Or to put it the other way round: passion, as the release of society's 'infernal' energies, necessarily signifies an irruption of violence. Thus Marré is able to fulfil her desires only during the Civil War. Indeed it is precisely because the war makes it uncertain whether there will be a tomorrow that she is able to abandon herself to the present moment (160). The closer the end of the war comes, the more she becomes obsessed by fear of losing Luis and falls prey to the calculating debt morality against which she has rebelled.

The other important point about Marré's idyll is that it is achieved not out of free choice but as a hostage of the Republicans. It is only because her defences have been destroyed that she is able to abandon herself. The suggestion is that no one overcomes his defensive urges voluntarily. Marré experiences happiness because she has nothing left to lose. With the end of the war she finds herself on the winning side, and spends the rest of her life tormented by the defensive barriers that prevent her from experiencing happiness again. Her final decision to return to Región to cross Numa's boundary is no longer an attempt to recover happiness; it is because she has lost all hope of it that she again finds herself in the position of having nothing left to lose (311). The fact that her specific aim is to return to Muerte's inn, situated in the underworld of Mantua, suggests that she is seeking the release of death. The novel implies an equation between passion and death, not only because passion depends on the heightened sense of temporality that occurs in war, but also because it depends on the surrender of one's defences: that is, the destruction of self. Marré describes herself after the war as being torn by two irreconcilable urges: 'the desire to possess and the desire to surrender' (172). This, basically, is the conflict between the Nationalists and the young Republicans. The Nationalists' defensiveness represents a will to survival; the young Republicans' desire to lose their defences logically requires them to fight for self-destruction. As Luis Timoner says (echoed by Dr Sebastián):

la mejor razón para prolongar un combate era siempre derrotista y ... en nuestro caso era absolutamente preciso continuar la guerra hasta ser merecedor de la completa derrota. (161)

the best argument for going on fighting was always defeatist and ... in our case it was absolutely essential to continue the war till we had earned total defeat.

The Nationalists are fighting an offensive for defensive reasons; the young Republicans are defending Región in order to surrender. Constantino – who, as a miner, personifies the love of risk – insists that surrender is not a pacifist stance but something that has to be fought for (86). Surrender means staking all. The gambling motif is central to the novel. Selflessness can be experienced briefly – and only imperfectly – through passion; the only lasting experience of it is in death.[22] María Timoner – the symbol of desire who is the helm ['timón'] directing the course of all the characters in the novel – will surrender to the Gambler in Mantua at the price of contracting a fatal disease. In an inversion of the Jungian quest myth, those who descend into the underworld of passion find annihilation. Numa's boundary is necessary to survival.

It is also worth noting that Marré's idyll with Luis takes place in a brothel. The implication is that emancipation is a form of corruption. The fact that it would not be possible without a boundary to transgress confirms the boundary as much as it violates it. It is appropriate that all the attempts to cross Numa's boundary should be made in autumn: the season of decay. Marré asks for payment from Muerte like a common prostitute, to have proof that she has committed an act of transgression. Surrender to passion confirms corruption also in the sense that it requires the surrender of mind to body, and the body – as Marré points out (156) – is by definition subject to decay. Mind and body constitute two different forms of self-destruction: the mind, an urge to self-preservation which leads to a fear of change and therefore to stagnation; the body, an urge to dissolution in the moral and physical senses of the word. The Nationalists confirm economic decadence through their defensiveness; the Republicans confirm moral decadence through their surrender of mind to body. The temporality of history intrudes into Numa's mythical zone not only with the destruction wrought by the war but also in the form of the inescapable law of decay, as is shown by its habitation by decrepit, bearded ghosts.

The novel suggests that the decadence of Spain is only partly the fault of the triumph of the defensive morality of the Nationalists. In the long run, the young Republicans' attempt to create a Paradise based on enjoyment of the present moment produces much the same result: enjoyment of the present not only eliminates the future but, as the present inevitably slips into the past, also leads to the cult of a past now lost. Luis Timoner is wrong when he tells Marré that the only people to gain from the war will be those who, like herself, will emerge from it freed from illusions (176–7): her loss of faith in the future does not set her free to enjoy the present because she becomes a prisoner of the past. Having failed to perpetuate her mythical eternal present, she becomes obsessed with the mythical attempt to return to the past. The result is that she, like the orphan, grows old without experiencing the present. In both cases, living in terms of the past does not bring rejuvenation but premature senility (92, 297). Towards the end of the novel Marré laments the fact that her liaison with Luis Timoner did not produce a child: that is, that it led only to sterility (307–8). Her wish to return to the past is, in a sense, more regressive than that of the Nationalists because she is not trying to recover progress but to abolish time. She spends her adult life struggling to preserve desire, while they struggle to preserve themselves from it; but in order to survive she, like them, is forced to appeal to reason to rationalize her emotions. Her final return to Región to cross Numa's boundary is no longer motivated by the transgressive desire to recover passion that had dominated her adult life, but by a rational decision to free herself from the past by eliminating desire once and for all (311). Marré, too, comes to rely on Numa to save her from passion.

If Marré represents the point of view of the young Republican idealists, seen with the hindsight of thirty years' disillusionment, Dr Sebastián represents the point of view of an older generation of Republicans who, unlike Rumbal and Julián Fernández, had rejected reason for passion but had already become disillusioned by the time of the war. Marré's life is ruined by the fact that she has lost happiness; Dr Sebastián's by the fact that he has never achieved it. Loss of María Timoner puts him in the same sceptical position with regard to the young Republicans as it does Gamallo with regard to the Nationalists: Gamallo continues to defend himself against passion while having lost faith in the rational concept of honour; Dr Sebastían continues to reject reason while having lost faith in passion. The difference between the two is that Gamallo still believes in the value of revenge, while Dr Sebastián has come to the conclusion that nothing is worth fighting for. Dr Sebastián's position is that of the majority of the people of Región – Republican by default rather than by conviction – who do not want their hopes raised in vain:

un pueblo que durante treinta años no había deseado otra cosa que carecer de deseos ... que como mejor solución a las incertidumbres del futuro y a la sentencia de un destino inequívoco, había elegido el menosprecio del presente y el olvido del pasado. (34)

a people who for thirty years had desired only to be freed from desire ... and who, as the best way of relieving the uncertainties of the future and the verdict of an unequivocal destiny, had decided to scorn the present and forget the past.

The older, disillusioned Republicans are – like the young Republicans – fighting to lose: in their case not in order to surrender their defences, but in order to destroy the last remnants of hope. Unlike that of the young Republicans, their defeatism is a pacifist stance.

Their self-destruction is not, like that of the Nationalists and the young Republican idealists, the counterproductive result of a will to survival or to happiness: it is deliberate. It is the older, disillusioned Republicans who most desperately need to believe in Numa's boundary. They turn to reason without any enthusiasm for it, in full knowledge of its repressive function. Dr Sebastián is speaking for himself when he says of Región that a cowardly people 'prefers repression to uncertainty' (222). At the end of the novel he will join the rest of Región in praying to Numa to defend his boundary, knowing that Numa exists only as a projection of collective fear. His youthful experiences working with the terminally ill and as an abortionist have turned him into the contradiction in terms of a doctor who does not believe – or want to believe – in the possibility of a cure (101).

The fact that Dr Sebastián is a doctor is important. The novel describes the ills afflicting the Republic as a cancer, reminding the reader – as in *Tiempo de silencio* – of the 1898 writers' habit of applying medical terminology to the nation's problems. Dr Sebastián's belief that there is no cure by implication refers to the Spanish disease of decadence. Like Pedro in *Tiempo de silencio*, he ends up confirming decadence by becoming an abortionist. His fatalism is shown to be the result of the disillusionments of a generation – that succeeding the 1898 Generation – who grew up in the early part of the century at a time of affluence and optimism, but whose hopes were subsequently shattered. The novel associates this disillusionment with the onset of economic decline around 1925, the date of Gamallo's loss of his fortune to the Gambler. It is implied that this loss of prosperity created an uncertainty about the future which manifested itself in different ways: the Nationalists' defence of traditional morality; the young Republicans' cult of the present moment; the older Republicans' loss of faith. For all three, the Civil War fulfilled the function of destroying the future, putting an end to uncertainty. Franco's peace is dominated by the figure of Numa, to prevent the possibility of hope re-emerging.

The novel implies, however, that the future cannot be destroyed. For good or ill, the irrationalism of history asserts itself over the rationalizations of myth. Both Dr Sebastián and Marré sense the dawning of a new age, which they view with alarm (140, 160). The comforting fatalism offered by Numa's unerring law of destruction is undermined by a conflicting concept of fate represented by the boatwoman, whose grotesque antics make her a symbol of the absurd. Numa never appears physically in the novel, while the boatwoman does. As a projection of wish-fulfilment, Numa can exist only as an absence; as the thwarting of desire, the boatwoman makes her presence felt all too well. The boatwoman's protection of the Gambler indicates that she represents chance: a perverse variety that ensures that the winner loses and the loser wins – only to lose once he has become a winner. The gold coin she gives the Gambler wins only when he stakes all, and the winnings it earns him – including María Timoner – are instantly lost. In the same way the young Republicans discover they can gain happiness only by staking all and fighting for defeat. Marré loses happiness once she is on the winning side. The sceptical Gamallo wins where the confident Navarrese colonel failed, but is prevented from reaping the rewards of victory. Just when Dr Sebastián thinks he has succeeded in eliminating desire, Marré arrives to rekindle old emotions. His apparent murder by the orphan – who, at the expense of losing his reason, has refused to give up hope – is just punishment for his confidence in his fatalism. Dr Sebastián's cohabitation with the orphan, whom he has to subject forcibly, symbolizes his unresolved struggle to eliminate hope. The arrival of an external threat in the form of Marré distracts him from the enemy within and leaves him vulnerable. The same ironic twist of fate will befall Numa in the story of that name, where he is distracted from his watch for the intruder destined to kill him by an external threat in the form of the building of a reservoir. It is interesting to note that the adjective 'zumbón' ['teasing'] is used to describe the buzzing noise of the construction work which distracts Numa: the words 'zumbón' and the similar sounding 'zumbido' ['buzzing'] occur in Volverás a Región whenever the quirks of fate frustrate the expectations of a character (125, 198, 219).[23] The buzzing of the telegraph wheel of Dr Sebastián's father – an updated version of the medieval wheel of fortune – indicates its love of macabre pranks (125). That the wheel of fortune should be represented by a machine suggests that material progress is having a joke on those who have been foolish enough to put their trust in it. The first joke played by the telegraph wheel is a double bluff: it offers Dr Sebastián's father an alibi for leaving his wife by predicting he will end his days in Jaén, and then prevents him from enjoying his

freedom by making the prophecy come true. The second joke is on
Dr Sebastián, who is led to believe by the wheel that he will die a
violent death in Región in the 1960s, in a woman's lap (126): his
confidence in the prophecy leaves him open to attack by the orphan.
The notion of Fate the Trickster recurs with the figure of death
which confuses María Timoner with a patient by the related name of
Gubernäel (Spanish 'timón' meaning 'helm' and 'gobernar' – from
the Latin 'gubernare' – 'to steer') (237–8). When death does strike
María down it will be as a result not of the disease foreshadowed by
the deathly apparition, but of a stupid accident. It is appropriate
that this accident should be the result of her son's desire to possess the
gold coin originally given the Gambler by the boatwoman. At
certain points in the novel laughter is heard from behind the bushes,
implying that Fate the Trickster is watching from the wings (224,
259). Marré describes fate as a joker concerned not to determine but
to conceal man's destiny (165). Dr Sebastián defines it as 'not what
man is destined to be but the gap between what he is and what he
would like to be' (257). Contrary to the certainty of Numa's law of
destruction the wheel of fate can go up or down, but what goes up
must then come down: the only certainty is that all expectations will
be frustrated. Like Martín-Santos, Benet suggests that history inevitably triumphs over the rationalizations of myth because it is
characterized by irony. But for Benet this fact is tragic.

Perhaps the biggest joke of fate is that Numa is guarding a
territory which is empty. Mantua exists only as an absence, not only
because it is a fictitious alibi designed to distract attention from
problems at home, but also because – as the refuge of the ghosts of
history – it is the repository of a lost past. It is an external projection
of the unconscious in the double sense of man's irrational urges and
the painful experiences – national and personal – he has repressed.
With the passing of time, the aspiration to eternal pleasure necessarily turns to pain because it is either never realized or lost: the
Mantua that initially offers the promise of Paradise inevitably turns
to a hell that has to be declared out of bounds. The María Timoner
who offers the promise of pleasure to the young Gamallo and Dr
Sebastián stands for the rest of their lives as a reminder of pain. As
befits her association with Mantua, she is always out of bounds: first,
as an image of unattained desire watching the contest for her hand
from the shadows of another room; later, as an image of mourning

concealed by a veil. She is the key to the whole novel and yet she never appears except via other characters' memories of her. It is important that the last three chapters should consist almost entirely of the memories of Dr Sebastián and Marré: the present moment of the novel is governed by the ghost of an absent past, of which María Timoner is the cipher. The geological strata of the mountains of Región provide an image of the sedimentation process that is memory: the point is that the upper layers bury those below. Mantua, whose rock formations do not solve the enigma of its geological origins, represents a past which is not recovered but suppressed by memory. It is interesting that Lévi-Strauss' interest in myth – conventionally seen as the attempt to recover a lost past – was initially stimulated by his knowledge of geology, the science of origins.[24] As a civil engineer, Benet has a professional formation in geology. In *El ángel abandona a Tobías* he insists that all theories of origins are defective because origins are by definition a mythical absence prior to 'the implacable erosion of history'.[25] By positing Mantua as the mythical projection of an absent past, *Volverás a Región* equates myth with memory but, contrary to the usual definitions, suggests that its principal function is the repression of the past. Numa's boundary divides experience into a 'before' and 'after' in order to keep the past at bay.

In *El ángel abandona a Tobías*, Benet laments the fact that man has segmented experience into the separate categories of past, present and future, and notes that the distinction 'before'/'after' represents the application to time of the spatial locations 'behind'/'in front'. Numa's boundary is an image of this spatialization of time. In the same essay Benet suggests that memory is a rational process in that its division of time into a 'before' and 'after' is an abstraction from experience deduced after the event. In this sense memory (what Benet calls 'intellectualized time') is radically opposed to the continuous experience of time as it is lived (what, echoing Bergson, he calls 'instinctive time'). For Benet, memory is not so much an attempt to recapture the eternal present of lived time as an attempt to rationalize the fact of loss.[26] Félix de Azúa has jokingly called Benet a 'Proust with a lousy memory'.[27] But if for Benet memory fails to recover lost time it is because it is not primarily designed to do so. Benet's equation of myth with memory coincides with the Romantic view of myth as the memory of a Paradise Lost, but he turns the

Romantic definition upside down by depicting memory as reason's method of relegating to oblivion a Paradise Lost that has become hell. Numa is the avenging angel at the gates to the Garden of Eden, whose function is to prevent man from returning to the past. The return motif referred to in the novel's title is fundamental to Benet's conception of myth but it is in many ways ironic: man finds himself condemned to return to the past despite the fact that he has invented Numa to prevent him from doing so.

For if memory relegates the past to the exclusion zone of Mantua, this only serves to inscribe it on the unconscious; it is thus always liable to be reactivated. The past is kept alive also by the fact that man wants, at the instinctive level of desire, to sustain the hope that what has been lost in the past can be recovered in the future. But, in a vicious circle, hope increases fear that the previous loss may be repeated, thus reinforcing the defensive urge to relegate the past to an exclusion zone. The conflict between the urge to transgress Numa's boundary and the urge to defend it is repeated within memory. The suppressed memories of the inhabitants of Región are triggered off by the intrusion of a series of motor cars (symbolizing the desire for transgression) bound for Mantua; in order to protect themselves from the pain caused by this involuntary reawakening of desire, they appeal to Numa to cut short the journey to the past.

That memory is designed to keep the past at bay is illustrated chiefly through Gamallo and Dr Sebastián. Both are motivated by the need to suppress the pain caused by the loss of María Timoner. The Gambler's contest for María's hand becomes an allegory of time: the continuous present of the ever-repeated game in the casino is suddenly brought to an end by the irreversible fact of loss, henceforth dividing time into a 'before' and 'after'. Once lost, María has to be confined to Mantua to make the loss bearable. Gamallo's rationally conceived plan to raze Región to the ground and drive its surviving inhabitants behind Numa's boundary represents his attempt to banish the past. The same willed inducement of oblivion is found in Dr Sebastián, whose anaesthetization of the orphan, with his retarded development, can be seen as his attempt to anaesthetize a past which has persisted in surviving into the present. There is, however, another way in which the past can be banished to an exclusion zone and that is through the mythical cult of the past, replacing the actual past with an idealized substitute. This is the method generally favoured by the people of Región, enabling them to provide a rational explanation for their present desolation:

probablemente nunca ... sonaron los cascos de los caballos ni las cornetas y disparos de Mantua, pero lo que ayer no fue hoy tiene que haber sido; como no hubo grandeza hoy son necesarias las ruinas. (247)

there was probably never any such sound of horses' hooves and horns and shots from Mantua, but what did not exist in the past needs to have existed today; the lack of past magnificence makes ruins necessary now.

Accordingly Marré wonders whether her past idyll with Luis Timoner might not be a mythification invented by a 'depraved memory' so as to make the emptiness of her later life bearable (301, 115).

Despite Gamallo and Dr Sebastián's attempts to banish the past to an exclusion zone, it persists within them at an unconscious level. Dr Sebastián describes memory as 'a stone covering an anthill' (181). The arrival of Marré reactivates a past which he has suppressed but not effaced (143). Marré points out that it is precisely the fact that the doctor has devoted his life to anaesthetizing the past that indicates how much it still hurts him (105). In the same way it is the numbness of the scar left in Gamallo by the past that indicates the depth of the wound: the persistence of painful memories in his unconscious is signalled by the involuntary twitching of his numb right hand, left semi-paralysed by the knife-wound inflicted by the Gambler. The same image is used in connection with the orphan's memories of abandonment by his mother, which remain in his unconscious as 'the scar of the past whose numbness corresponds to the gravity of the wound' (98). The rational urge to banish the present to an exclusion zone, seen in Gamallo and Dr Sebastián, is matched in the orphan by a biological defence mechanism which coats the surfaces of the brain with a 'protective film' whose function is to filter out unwelcome impressions (92–3). Thus the orphan's memory does not register the day the war ended because it was not accompanied by his mother's return (23–4). At the same time his abandonment by his mother is conserved in the unconscious by 'otra memoria – no complaciente y en cierto modo involuntaria, que se alimenta del miedo y extrae sus recursos de un instinto opuesto al de la supervivencia' ['another memory – uncompliant and in a sense involuntary, feeding on fear and drawing its energies from an instinct opposed to the instinct for survival'] (93). It is not however simply a matter of the conflict between a defensive urge to suppress the past and a self-destructive insistence on retaining it. The orphan also needs to retain the past in order to preserve his identity. He will thus sacrifice 'a reason free of memories' so as to 'maintain the integrity' of a self defined by abandonment (19). The mythical urge to suppress the past and the mythical urge to relive it are both, in different ways, defence mechanisms designed to secure survival. Marré will also talk of 'the urge to hoard secreted by the soul in its anxiety to cling to what little it has left' (116). Dr Sebastián, despite his suppression of the past, notes the existence in man of a biological 'defence valve' which conserves the past so as to allow reason to go on believing it can be repeated (127).

Just as the attempt to suppress the past is frustrated by its preservation in the unconscious, so the attempt to relive the past is frustrated by the fact that happiness, as the physical sensation of an eternal present, is not retained by memory which is the mental record of time passing. The only thing that memory can register is the failure to achieve happiness or its loss. In the case of Gamallo and Dr Sebastián memory is necessarily a record of pain because neither has experienced happiness. The orphan and Marré both want to relive the happiness they experienced before abandonment, but in both cases they find that the image of the loved one is absent from memory. The orphan cannot remember his mother's physical presence but only symbols of her absence such as the car, the brooch or the game of marbles. Hence his inability to tell whether any of the various women who subsequently return is his mother. In the same way Marré can remember trivial incidents from the past but is unable to reproduce the ecstasy she experienced with Luis Timoner because, as a physical experience which 'abolished time', it was not registered by memory (266, 304). In *El ángel abandona a Tobías* Benet speculates that heaven, as the projection on to the future of a continuous present that has been lost, ought logically to consist of the resurrection of the body without the soul because only the body is capable of experiencing time as an indivisible whole. Conversely, hell must be full of souls without bodies because hell is memory: the indelible record of loss.[28] It is presumably for this reason that Marré describes Región – living in empty memories – as purgatory. Mantua, with its ghosts of the past, is an embodiment of the hell that is memory.

The fact that memory is the record of loss has important conse-quences not only for Benet's view of myth but also for his view of history. History, as the record of the past, is the product of memory because it is an a posteriori linear reconstruction based on the sequence 'before' and 'after', as opposed to the continuous exper-ience of events in the present. The fact that history is a product of memory means that it too is a failed form of myth, for all that can be reconstructed of the past is the fact of loss. Historical events are non-events because only 'lo que no pudo ser' ['what failed to happen'] is preserved by memory (115). As a linear sequence, history is created by memory also in the sense that the concept of the future is brought into being by the desire to repeat a lost past; but all that memory can recover from the past is loss. Hence history – like memory – is 'the revenge of that which failed to happen' (115). The historical events in the novel consist of the destruction wrought by the Civil War, which in turn is a repetition of the destruction wrought by previous wars. More specifically, Spanish history is shown to be a repeated cycle of lost wars: 'el tiempo es todo lo que no somos, todo lo que se ha malogrado y fracasado' ['time is all that we are not, everything that has gone wrong or failed'] (301–2). In postwar Spain the position of the hands of the clock is irrelevant because all that matters is 'their never-ending circular movement', illustrating 'the void that envelops us' (246). The cyclical nature of time in postwar Spain does not mean that the nation has abandoned history for myth but that it is living the worst of both worlds, sentenced to linear time by the fact of loss, and sentenced to cyclical time by the fact that the future is a repetition of the past. For the linear concept of time on which history is based, as the projection on to the future of memories of a lost past, is identical with the mythical concept of time as repetition. Hence the Civil War brings loss but changes nothing: for all its upheavals, it is unable to put an end to the orphan's game of marbles (178). The paradoxical mixture of destruction and perma-nence which characterizes Spanish history is represented symboli-cally by the stationary peasant whom Marré, returning at the end of the war, sees silhouetted against the burning ruins of Región 'as if meditating on the passage of time' (178). The ruins left by the war are emblematic of the permanent record of devastation that is history. The fact that history is the product of memory – a failed form of myth which recovers only loss – means that it consists of a cumulative process of decadence, without hope of regeneration. One is reminded of the concept of an 'eternal decadence' found in the novels of the 1950s. But if the earlier writers had seen this as a 'Fall' from a better prewar world, for Benet the Civil War is merely the latest stage in a repeated cycle of destruction stretching back into prehistory. *Volverás a Región* echoes the mythical equation of history with evil, but it insists that the process of loss that is temporality has no beginning and has no end.

The fact that history is the mythical record of 'what failed to happen' means that it becomes indistinguishable from fiction. Here Benet echoes Lévi-Strauss' suggestion that historians mythify the past by imposing a false linear sequence on to events which at the time are experienced as a continuum. Lévi-Strauss insists that the original moment which both myth-makers and historians seek to recover remains forever absent: all they can do – much like the writer of fiction – is produce a reasonably convincing imitation.[29] In his novel Benet mixes analogies drawn from the Old Testament and from classical historians, implying that there is no difference between mythical and historical accounts of the past, and that both are comparable with his fictional text. The obvious reason why myth, history and fiction are all attempts to produce an absent original is that they are all textual versions: attempts to reproduce experience in language. In *El ángel abandona a Tobías* Benet suggests that all language is a form of memory because it attempts to reconstruct a prior intuition which, however, remains elusive to verbal expression. Language does not create thought but is an attempt to make it intelligible in rational terms. As a rational instrument – that is, an abstraction – language inevitably establishes a distance between itself and the original it is trying to reproduce; it then has to try to efface this distance by creating an illusion of immediacy. Despite the fact that language creates the problem it sets out to solve, Benet insists that it is the only means we have of understanding experience.[30] *Volverás a Región* can be called a mythical novel in the sense that it is the reconstruction of an absent original but, unlike myth proper, it declares that it is a failed reconstruction.[31]

The openings of the successive chapters indicate that the further the text progresses, the less it is able to establish a definitive original version of events. Chapter 1 starts with the words 'Es cierto' ['The fact is']; chapter 2 with 'Ciertamente era un coche parecido' ['Indeed it was a similar car'], the point being that it is not the original car; chapter 3 with 'No sé si sería cierto' ['I don't know whether it was true']; and chapter 4 – marking the final stage in the progression from certainty to uncertainty – with 'No lo sé – podía haber replicado ella' ['"I don't know," she might have replied']. A disconcertingly inconsistent blend of omniscience and fallibility characterizes the whole narrative, mixing insights into the characters' repressed or unconscious thoughts with hypothetical alternative versions of events introduced by the qualifications 'perhaps' or 'no doubt'. The text creates the illusion that it will gradually fill in all the missing details by constantly announcing in advance episodes that will be narrated at a later stage – as with the gambling scene in the casino, finally narrated in chapter 3 – but the more information we accumulate, the less certain we become of what 'really happened'. Similarly when re-takes occur later in the novel of episodes narrated earlier on, the different versions usually conflict. The first time we are told of Dr Sebastián's marriage to the level-crossing keeper's daughter, it appears he married her the same day he was abandoned by María Timoner (111); later we read that he married her three days after being abandoned (255–7); while the final re-take situates the marriage after the birth of Luis Timoner (275–6). It is important that these inconsistencies should involve dates: by giving us precise information about dates the text creates an illusion of historicity, but when we try to work out the linear sequence we find the figures do not tally. The most glaring inconsistency occurs in connection with Luis Timoner: if María Timoner eloped with the Gambler in mid to late 1925 (224, 262), Luis cannot have been born before 1926; this does not match the subsequent information that he had his ninth or tenth birthday before the advent of the Republic in 1931 and that he was aged between 19 and 21 when he was a captain in the Republican Army during the Civil War.[32] Certain loose ends are never tied up: we never find out how Gamallo came to marry Marré's mother or how she died, nor who was the mysterious older man mentioned at the end of chapter 1 as being at Luis Timoner's side throughout the war.

In similar fashion, confusion with characters' names is created by duplication – as with the variants on the name of Señor Rumbal, the two Adelas or the confusion of Colonel Gamallo with the previous Navarrese colonel (53–4) – or by omission.[33] The possibility of omitting the subject pronoun in Spanish is exploited to the full so that often we do not know who the subject is, or do not notice that it has changed in the course of the paragraph. Even when the subject pronoun is given, it is often not clear who it refers to. The same occurs with the use of the object pronoun. When Marré switches from the third person singular polite form she uses with Dr Sebastián to the familiar second person singular, we have to guess that she is talking to a Luis Timoner who, despite the impression of immediacy, is not there. The possessive adjective 'su' is likewise used so that it is unclear whether it means 'his' or 'hers'. The difficulty of knowing who the words refer to is matched by that of knowing who is speaking.[34] There is no ostensible difference between the language of Dr Sebastián and Marré, who function as narrators for most of chapters 2–4. Nor is their language ostensibly different from that of the external narrator, except in the case of the battle scenes and geological descriptions where the external narrator's language is characterized by the precision one might expect to find in a historical account or a scientific textbook – mixed however with extravagant figures of speech quite out of character with historical or scientific writing. The fact that the first chapter is narrated entirely by the external narrator and the rest of the novel mostly by two character–narrators is upsetting precisely because it makes little difference. The first person narrative of Dr Sebastián and Marré, far from creating the impression of immediacy we expect of direct speech, is totally unnaturalistic in tone, vocabulary and syntax. The fact that the character–narrators talk for many pages at a time, sometimes without a break of paragraph, makes the reader lose track of which of them is speaking or wonder whether the external narrator has taken over at some stage, as is sometimes the case: the section that runs from p. 206 to p. 216 starts with the doctor speaking but ends up narrated by the external narrator, without any evidence of a change of narrative voice. The fact that the character–narrators' dialogue consists of two alternating monologues, with little or no evidence that the interlocutor is listening (at one stage Marré falls asleep), indicates that language is not serving its supposed function of communicating information. At the same time the fact that we forget who is speaking undermines the notion that speech is the immediate expression of a character's presence. The more the characters talk, the more their words appear to emanate from a void. When their long discursions are punctuated by a brief exchange of 'natural' conversation (as when the doctor asks Marré if she wants another drink), this has the effect not so much of rooting the language in a recognizable human situation as of making us even more aware, through the triviality of the exchange, of the void in which the conversation takes place. This impression is reinforced by the fact that a large proportion of the brief exchanges of speech consist of unanswered questions or comments on the silence. It is significant that the dialogue is several times broken by Marré's repeated – and again unanswered – question as to the source of the cries heard in the distance. The orphan's inarticulate cries from the locked attic illustrate the fact that speech, far from conveying the presence of a speaker, serves mainly to remind us of his inaccessibility.

In a provocative essay on Joyce, Benet has argued that the attempt to create naturalistic interior monologue is pointless because 'natural' speech is mostly banal; written language, he suggests, is infinitely richer in its expressive possibilities.[35] In *El ángel abandona a Tobías* he reinforces this assertion on the grounds that, paradoxically, speech is less concerned than writing with recapturing the immediacy of experience, as is evidenced by the fact that speech rarely uses the present tense. Whereas the main characteristic of much twentieth-century writing has been its exploitation of the present tense. In other words, speech uses language to fulfil its natural function of rationalizing experience, whereas the writer is able to use language self-consciously to disguise the fact that language is a rationalization. Benet points out that the verb is central to all linguistic theories because the main problem of language is that of recapturing the continuous experience of time as it is lived. He suggests that tenses can be used in two ways: to differentiate between past, present and future (as is normal in speech), or (by using language 'unnaturally' as is possible in writing) to blur the distinction between temporal categories. Such 'unnatural' use of tenses cannot recreate the continuous present of lived time because language is by definition an abstraction from experience, but it can produce a passable imitation of it. The temporal

fluidity of much modern writing is thus a substitute for an immediacy which remains irrecuperable.[36]

The title *Volverás a Región* – replacing the earlier 'less dynamic' *La
vuelta a Región* – indicates from the start Benet's concern to create an
illusion of fluidity through the use of verb forms.[37] That the sections
of the novel narrated by Dr Sebastián and Marré should give an
impression of temporal fluidity is not surprising as they are recon-
structing events through memory: they therefore intersperse the
narration of past events with anticipations of what was to happen
later and with a large amount of commentary in the present tense.
The use of the present tense for commentary tends to spill over on to
the surrounding narrative, so that at times we are not sure whether
what we are reading is narration of what happened in the past or
current analysis. The fact that most of the events narrated by the
characters consist of things that failed to happen means that there is
frequent usage of the conditional perfect and imperfect subjunctive,
enhancing the sense of indeterminacy. What is interesting is that the
same temporal fluidity is found in the sections narrated by the
external narrator. The implication is that all language is a form of
memory because it is a reconstruction. The first chapter alternates
between passages of narrative (e.g. the battle scenes) predominantly
in the preterite, creating a fast-moving linear sequence of events, and
passages of description (geological, climatological, etc.) predominantly in the present tense, giving an impression of changelessness.
But the distinction is by no means absolute. Description can slip from
the present into the imperfect or pluperfect; conversely the narration
of events can move from the preterite to the present and future. It is
appropriate that the section narrating the abandonment of the
orphan – who refuses to establish a clear distinction between past
and present – should consistently mix past and present tenses.

This last-mentioned section is also a good example of a structural
device used to create a sense of fluidity: that of temporal duplication.
The passage starts with the narration of what we later discover is the
arrival of Marré's car, which takes us back to the mention in the
previous section of the various cars that pass through Región on their
way to Mantua. The second paragraph goes on to narrate the
previous arrival, also in autumn, of another car: that in which the
orphan's mother left. The rest of the section follows on from

this point in a linear sequence – albeit interrupted by frequent digressions – until the last paragraph, which gives a rapid re-take of the orphan's parting from his mother and his life for the rest of the war, continuing in chronological sequence up to Adela's departure which initially appears to be a re-take of his mother's departure, then – when she returns – appears not to be, but finally – when she dies – is confirmed as a repetition of the earlier abandonment. In similar fashion the battle sequences in chapter 1 begin with Gamallo's 1938 campaign, doubling back to the narration of the earlier 1937 campaign and then resuming narration of the 1938 campaign from the point where the narrative had previously left off. Gamallo's final capture of Región will be given a rapid re-take in chapter 4. This technique recurs throughout the novel with the constant anticipations and re-takes of episodes narrated elsewhere, giving the impression that time is both advancing and going round in circles. Lévi-Strauss points out that mythical narrative employs a historical linear sequence only to negate it through the use of repetition.[38] The use of repetition in *Volverás a Región* does not so much negate history in favour of myth as reinforce the point that history and myth are identical because the linear concept of progress represents the attempt to repeat a lost past. The chief episode to which the narrative constantly returns is, of course, the loss of María Timoner, illustrating the fact that language is a linear sequence which at the same time attempts to recover a lost original. The distinction between the cyclical and the linear is further eroded by the imperceptible transition from the description of repeated occurrences to the narration of specific events, as when we pass within the same sequence from the description of the orphan's endlessly unchanging days with Adela to the narration of the intrusion of the man we later learn is Juan de Tomé: a transition signalled only by the unobtrusive shift in mid-paragraph from imperfect to preterite tense (23–4). The enormously long and complex sentences, together with the need to cross-reference bits of information given at different points, force the reader to go back over the text, turning the act of reading into a circular process as much as a linear one. The use of multiple parentheses gives the sentence structure the form of a set of concentric circles as much as that of a straight line. Luis Costa has pointed out that the meanderings of the reader trying to follow the convolutions of Benet's prose echo the meanderings of the Traveller trying to reach Numa's boundary.[39] The comparison is apt: just as the Traveller is striving to reach a past made taboo by fear, so the language of the novel forces the reader to struggle to reconstruct past events which remain out of bounds.

Accordingly the text will tease the reader with a profusion of apparent clues which encourage him to search for hidden explanations only to discover the impossibility of doing so. David Herzberger has argued that Benet's avoidance of causal explanation is an example of 'magic realism', which presents events as 'given' or 'natural', requiring no explanation.[40] It seems to me that the novel stimulates the reader's desire for causal explanation as much as it frustrates it, showing that language – like myth – is an attempt to rationalize experience which, however, fails. The narrator compares Dr Sebastián's interest in deducing Marré's hidden motives to that of the viewer of a mythological painting, the clue to whose understanding lies in a dim figure in the background (142). Like the mythological painting referred to, the novel asks to be read as a cipher but with the difference that it sets out to lead the reader astray, providing clues that do not lead to answers. The narrator tells us that, in order to arouse Marré's interest, Dr Sebastián has littered his account of the past with clues in the form of red herrings and veiled allusions which frustrate the same curiosity they awaken (136). Key 'facts' in the novel are tucked away in marginal comments. These may take the form of footnotes (as in the case of that which runs from p. 275 to p. 277 and which provides vital information about Luis Timoner and his mother's death) or of parentheses (as with the information about the attempt to barter Marré as a prisoner of war, mentioned in parenthesis on p. 66 when we do not as yet have sufficient information to understand what is being referred to). The names of the characters, when given at all, are mentioned in passing at points in the novel when we are not looking out for them. Both Dr Sebastián and Marré enjoy only one incidental mention in chapter 1, belying the fact that they will be the principal characters. María Timoner's name is not given till p. 111, despite the fact that repeated mention of her loss has been made since the start of the novel. Conversely Luis Timoner's name is mentioned as early as p. 36, at a stage when we have no idea he is essential to the plot and fail to register it. The best illustration of the way the text conceals vital 'facts' is provided by the way we deduce that Marré's lover in the war was Luis Timoner by piecing together the information, scattered throughout the novel, that a Luis I. Timoner (I. for incognito) was in the Republican Army; that a godson of Dr Sebastián was among the Republican deserters last sighted near Muerte's inn; that María Timoner had a son by the unknown Gambler and that Dr Sebastián became his godfather; that Marré had intimate conversations in the war with the doctor's godson; that both Marré and the doctor have photographs of a certain person; and finally that a photograph of Luis Timoner existed on the warrant for his arrest issued at the end of the war. By concealing the vital pieces of information, the text reduces 'facts' to the status of 'clues': the 'facts' are never fully recovered. We can never be completely certain that Luis was Marré's lover. Even the photograph of Luis which Marré presents to Dr Sebastián is described variously as a 'photograph' and a 'card': the key document on which the unravelling of the plot depends is itself open to question. Appropriately, the clues betraying the Gambler's whereabouts consist of a trail of gaming counters leading to the boatwoman in disguise, embodying Fate the Trickster. The gaming counters do not lead Gamallo to the gambler, but only to the scene of his disappearance.

The notion of language as cipher – reproducing clues rather than facts – is reinforced by the use of symbolism: that is, a language of suggestion rather than of statement. The most noticeable feature of the symbols that occur throughout the novel is their visual character. If language cannot directly represent facts, the best it can do is provide a substitute which attempts to deny its linguistic nature by simulating pictorial representation. Of course paintings cannot reproduce the original model any more directly than writing, but painting has the advantage over writing of being non-linear. In *El ángel abandona a Tobías* Benet points out that all language, and narrative in particular, creates a discontinuous series which is incapable of representing the continuous experience of lived time, whereas painting is able to capture the eternity of the passing moment. The writer thus strives to emulate the condition of painting in order to overcome the seriality of his medium.[41] The narrative of *Volverás a Región* has a strong cinematic quality in the sense that the movement will suddenly freeze as if a camera lens were homing in on a particular detail to give it symbolic prominence. What we get is not, in fact, so much a cinematic sequence as a set of stills.[42] Characters are caught in a series of static postures, such as the 'awful negative' of Gamallo's aunts fanning themselves in the shadowy hallway which engraves itself on his mind (70); or the repeated image of Dr Sebastián sitting with his holdall at the crossroads waiting for María Timoner. This last example illustrates the technique of giving concrete pictorial form to what are abstract mental processes: instead of saying that Dr Sebastián found himself at an emotional crossroads in his life, the text shows him sitting at an actual crossroads. In the same way Marré's indecision is given concrete pictorial representation in the scene where she hovers on the threshold of the Hotel Terminus. This tendency towards pictorial representation not only makes the abstract analysis more intelligible but it also mitigates the linearity of the narrative by lifting certain scenes outside of time. The narrative sequence is frequently interrupted by parenthetic descriptive passages, producing a tableau effect. Often such parentheses lack a main verb, increasing the sense of timelessness, for example:

Todos los años de internado – corredores de azulejo chillón, delantales de mahón y un olor a rancho ... y los pasos susurrantes de los hermanos violentos y las tardes de los domingos lluviosos, contemplando cómo en el patio se formaban los charcos y los regueros – transcurrieron en la espera de un envío de dinero. (72)

All his years at boarding school – garish blue-tiled corridors, twill uniforms and the smell of cooking ..., the rustling footsteps of the ill-tempered monks and rainy Sunday afternoons watching puddles and rivulets form in the playground – were spent waiting for money.

A similar effect is created by the sudden switch to the pluperfect tense, giving the impression that time has halted. The habit of giving pictorial form to psychological states produces confusion between the literal and the figurative as it becomes hard to distinguish those images which are symbolic representations of an emotional condition from those which depict events. We are given so much detail about the wife visited by her wounded husband's ghost (21) and the girl looking in the mirror who hears the click of the door latch (249) that we begin to think they may be characters in the novel, rather than symbolic images of abandonment. Conversely, when at the beginning of the novel we find 'the dust trail left by the riders' listed as one of a series of visual images contained in the memory of the people of Región, we do not yet have sufficient information to categorize it as referring to a 'real' event (Gamallo's pursuit of the Gambler) and thus dismiss it as 'merely symbolic' (14). The point is that the distinction is a false one, for all language – like memory – is a symbolic substitute for something that cannot be reproduced directly.

The image of the dust trail is emblematic of the pictorial representations found in the novel, illustrating the fact that, as symbolic images, they are traces of an original that has disappeared from view. The photograph of Luis Timoner emphasizes the fact of his loss, just as the portrait of the unknown figure over the bed in Dr Sebastián's clinic reinforces the desolation (119–20). Perhaps the most poignant example of the visual memento which evokes only absence is the proliferation of cushion-covers embroidered by Dr Sebastián's wife as a token of her abandonment. Indeed, in Dr Sebastián's house the chief mementoes of the past are not objects but the empty spaces left on the walls by the mirrors, pictures and diplomas that are no longer there (94). As evocations of absence, the most eloquent symbols are those which state the least but suggest the most. María and Luis Timoner take on a symbolic value because they barely speak: both decide the fate of others through silent gestures. Throughout the novel physical gestures acquire a ritualistic quality, implying that the non-verbal speaks more than words. The orphan, incapable of reason, develops with Adela a sign language which is superior to language in that it enables them to anticipate sounds before they are heard (21–3). Through his use of visual symbols which suggest without explaining, Benet is able to minimize the fact that language is a rational explanation of experience, while at the same time pointing out that all it can reproduce is absence.

Apart from the dust trail, the most frequent images in the novel are those of the door or window and the echo. The last three chapters are narrated from inside Dr Sebastián's house, through whose doors and windows the outside world is indirectly perceived in the form of echoes in the night. The original events which give rise to the echoes remain out of view: all we get is their reverberation against the inner wall of the mind. Doors and windows are constantly shown swinging open to reveal a void: as empty frames, their function is to give form to the absence beyond. Benet is fond of referring to Faulkner's image of the candle whose light serves to increase the horror of the darkness.[43] In the same way the repeated use of echoes in the novel makes us more aware of the surrounding silence. The image of the echo occurs most frequently in connection with the sound of the various motor cars journeying to Mantua and with Numa's shots. Both are heard via echoes because they represent the twin aspects of memory: the cars stand for the attempt to recover a past which cannot be reproduced directly, while Numa's shots symbolize the suppression of the past. Even at the time, the Civil War is experienced only as the echo of distant gunfire because history consists of loss. The most vivid illustration of the use of empty window frames and echoes to evoke the surrounding devastation occurs at the end of chapter 2, where the loss caused by the Civil War is conveyed symbolically by the gaping façades of the buildings of Región, the echo of invisible snipers' bullets and the reverberation of the screams of a boy racing round the streets. By 'shattering the silence', the boy's screams make us all the more intensely aware of it (177).

Many of the images used in the novel involve the graphic representation of language, whether printed, engraved or inscribed. In every case we are given snatches of words or initial letters dislocated from their context, suggesting that language functions as an echo of that which is absent. One of the most suggestive recurring images is that of the fragment of newspaper blowing in the wind, evoking absence not so much by the announcement of death it sometimes contains as by the fact that it is torn out of context (21, 140). The desolation of Región is symbolically represented by the initial letters of the scientific formulae left on the school blackboard which, in turn, are converted into the unexplained political acronyms whose remnants on the torn street posters stand as an emblem of the devastation of the war (30, 33). The sense of loss evoked by Luis Timoner's photograph is reinforced by the partly deleted and faded jottings on its reverse (312). Dr Sebastián's abandonment of his wife is highlighted by the cursory messages on the postcards he sends her (106–8). Gamallo's suppressed past is evoked by the fragmentary inscriptions entered on his ordnance survey map (67), while the irrecuperability of Mantua's mythical past is illustrated by the rocks and tombstones engraved with 'some indecipherable Sufic inscription or meaningless date' (210). The cryptic messages punched out by the telegraph wheel – 'a demented echo in a demented land' (124) – provide a concrete illustration of the way words function as remnants of a prior reality which resists intelligibility. Another machine whose function is supposedly communication – the telephone – fails to reunite Marré with her absent father because all that comes out of the receiver are disembodied words (158–9, 271).

The same impression of words in a void is created by the use of quotations from other texts. On three occasions the authors of the quotations (Stefan Andres, Faulkner, Nietzsche) are listed in a footnote, but in most cases they are not identified: the words stand as relics of a lost source. The majority of these quotations refer to the echo of solitary dogs barking in the night, emphasizing the fact that language is an isolated echo which only intensifies the surrounding silence. The fact that in this case the lost original is another text means that what we have is an echo of what itself is the echo of an absence. This notion that language is the echo of an echo is reinforced by the deliberate literariness of the text, mediating its attempt to express experience through reminiscences of other texts. In addition to the cultivated use of melodrama and stock literary situations (particularly in the gambling scene), the text has a slightly archaic quality which echoes the work of earlier writers. The convoluted syntax is reminiscent of Proust and perhaps even more so of nineteenth-century prose style.[44] Two specific nineteenth-century writers leave their traces throughout the text. The influence of Sir James Frazer is found not just in the figure of Numa but also, more fundamentally, in the digressive sentence structure and graphic use of landscape description.[45] Benet himself has acknowledged his debt to the nineteenth-century Brazilian Euclides da Cunha's *Os sertões* [*Revolt in the Backlands*]. The structural parallels between the two texts have been studied by Malcolm Compitello; however it is again at the level of style that the reminiscences are strongest, both in the description with its mixture of scientific precision and extravagant analogies, and in the battle scenes with their comparisons to ancient history.[46] Perhaps the clearest vestige of Frazer and Cunha's texts in *Volverás a Región* is the constant reference to the unnamed Traveller journeying to Mantua, echoing the two nineteenth-century writers' appeal to the reader as a traveller undertaking a voyage of discovery.

The image of the Traveller is crucial to the novel. The text is 'about' its subject-matter not in the sense that it contains it but in the sense that it wanders round it as an absent centre (represented symbolically by María Timoner). It provides us not with a gradual recovery of past events but with a series of digressions 'around' them. All that we are given are clues and remnants of an irretrievably lost original: 'words, snatches of memory, hints of false abortive recollections and misleading echoes' (114). Lévi-Strauss has defined myth as a piecing together of remnants from a previous cultural order.[47] *Volverás a Región* is a mythical novel in the sense that it is built of the trail of debris left behind by a past that has vanished. At the same time it is a historical novel in that it shows history also to consist of the trail of devastation left behind by a series of military losses. As a work of fiction it is about 'what did not happen' not in the sense that it does not refer to a historical reality but in the sense that all it can do is provide a substitute which evokes symbolically that which it cannot reproduce directly. In *El ángel abandona a Tobías* Benet argues that the goal of language is silence, for its aim is to convey that which words cannot reproduce.[48] *Volverás a Región* shows language to be a mythical instrument whose suggestive power lies, paradoxically, in its ability to make us aware of its failure to recover an absent original. The novel ends with a sequence of desolate echoes intensifying the surrounding silence:

Durante el resto de la noche en la casa cerrada y solitaria, casi vencida por la ruina, sonaron los pasos apresurados, los gritos de dolor ... Hasta que, con las luces del día, entre dos ladridos de un perro solitario, el eco de un disparo lejano vino a restablecer el silencio habitual del lugar. (291)

In the locked, abandoned, derelict house, the sound of hurtling footsteps, howls of pain ... continued throughout the night. Till, at dawn, framed by two solitary barks, the echo of a distant shot returned the spot to its habitual silence.

The text functions as the echo of a past suppressed by Numa's shots. All it can salvage from history is the debris left by the Civil War, whose spluttering again serves to make us aware of the surrounding silence:

un montón de piedras calcinadas y humeantes, salpicadas de harapos y cadáveres, que al caer la noche se sumirá en el silencio – alterado solamente por el chisporroteo de las vigas, los lamentos de los heridos, el intempestivo y alocado tableteo de los peines quemados – del que no emergerá en el resto de los días. (61)

a pile of charred, smouldering rubble, strewn with corpses and scraps of clothing, that at nightfall would be swallowed up by the silence – broken only by the crackling of burning timbers, the moans of the wounded, the abrupt, demented rattle of exploding cartridge clips – from which it would nevermore emerge.

Fiction is the mythical echo of a history that consists of loss.

5

Fiction as corruption: *Si te dicen que caí*

Both Martín-Santos and Benet are intellectual writers whose novels require the reader to be familiar with classical mythology. In Juan Marsé's novel *Si te dicen que caí* (1973) the mythical models the reader is required to recognize are of a very different order. Martín-Santos and Benet had the advantage of relatively privileged backgrounds and a university education; Marsé was brought up in a working-class district of Barcelona and left school to work at the age of thirteen. The mythology on which his novel draws is in part that of Francoist ideology but more fundamentally that of the movies, comics and pulp fiction that coloured the imagination of a working-class boy growing up in Barcelona in the 1940s. This appeal to the popular imagination produces an important shift of focus. If Martín-Santos and Benet describe a society that has largely rejected historical change for the static world of myth, the adolescents in *Si te dicen que caí* create a mythical counter-culture that enables them to achieve a degree of mobility in a society threatened by paralysis: whether that of official Francoist values (represented by the cripple Conrado) or that of an ageing political opposition (represented by the resistance fighters living in terms of the past). Like Benet, Marsé breaks down the barrier between myth and history by showing how the opposing social groups that comprise the historical reality of Franco's Spain are governed by myth in one form or another. But Marsé's treatment of myth is more positive than that of either of the two writers previously studied. *Si te dicen que caí* is a denunciation of those backward-looking forms of myth that lead to stagnation, but it suggests that myth can also be forward-looking and creative. Which is not to say that the novel gives an unambiguously favourable view of progress. On the contrary those who regress and those who progress are shown to be equally corrupt; but those who progress are

135

at least able to turn corruption to their advantage. As in *Tiempo de silencio*, the treatment of myth has political implications. But if Martín-Santos shows myth to be the means whereby authority reduces the individual to impotence, Marsé suggests that it can provide an alternative source of power for the dispossessed. His novel describes a world where the key to power lies not in truth but in its absence. Such power, being based on the falsehoods of myth, is necessarily corrupt; but for those born into deprivation it can provide a release from impotence by creating an alternative reality that looks forward to the future. Myth is a lie but, when it does not degenerate into nostalgia, it is an attempt to master the world. In the hands of authority, myth is a source of power in the sense of exploitation. But in the hands of the dispossessed it becomes the expression of a collective will to be. *Si te dicen que caí* is a mythical novel in the sense that it puts forward a collective, popular vision. It is precisely because the mythifications of its working-class adolescent characters do not have the backing of authority that they are creative. The novel is a celebration of that kind of myth which has no pretensions to speak with the voice of authority; that which parades itself as a lie or fiction. By eliminating the concept of narrative authority, the novel undermines the concept of political authority.

The novel spans the period from the Civil War to the beginnings of economic boom in the 1960s, concentrating on the immediate postwar years when official propaganda and censorship reduced historical fact to the status of myth in the sense of ideology. The novel continually pokes fun at Nationalist propaganda. The patriotic postcards sold by Sarnita turn the 'saviours of the nation' into comic cardboard figures (258–9). The instructions on the postcard of José Antonio Primo de Rivera inviting the beholder to stare fixedly at the image so that, on looking up at the ceiling, it will still be before his eyes – a mockery of the Falangist chant 'José Antonio ¡presente!' – reduce official ideology to the level of childish superstition (218, 258). The boys are forever being reprimanded for urinating on the Falangist symbol of the yoke and arrows (popularly known as 'la araña' because of the resemblance of the crossed arrows to spider's legs) daubed on the wall. The Baroness' husband falls asleep reading the Falangist magazine *Vértice*, while her musical cigarette-case plays a kitsch version of the patriotic anthem 'Isabel y Fernando' (151–2). There is an implicit reference to Franco in the suggestion that

Conrado has Parkinson's disease (331): the depiction of Conrado, representing Falangist officialdom, was the reason given by the censor's office for originally banning the novel in Spain.[1] The most elaborate mockery occurs with the sarcastic weaving into the text of quotations from the Falangist anthem 'Cara al sol'.[2] When quoted out of context in the title of the novel, the words 'Si te dicen que caí' ['If they tell you I have fallen'] – originally referring to the heroic fall of the Nationalist 'crusaders' in battle – take on the inverse meaning of the Fall into corruption. When Java talks of taking up 'the place reserved for us on high' (299), he is referring not to the heavenly legions but to his future career as a homosexual prostitute. The repeated variations on the phrase 'Volverá a reir la primavera' ['Spring will smile again'] are clearly sarcastic when applied to the destitution of the 1940s: as, for example, in the description of 'that spring whose smiling face was plastered with sunshine like the face of a cheap whore' (64; also 16, 279, 299). Geneviève Champeau has suggested that the novel's persistent use of infernal motifs – subterranean locations (the bomb shelter, the morgue), fire symbolism, references to the Fall and to serpents, Java's role as Lucifer, the Church of Las Ánimas, descriptions of the characters as ghosts or shadows – represents an ironic inversion of the Nationalist claim to have restored Spain to a Paradise Lost. The 'myth of the Crusade' is replaced by the contrary myth of the descent into hell.[3]

The Francoist press, in particular, is singled out for giving a distorted view of history. Palau dismisses it as an unreadable mixture of propaganda and old wives' tales (358). Newspapers are put to a variety of uses in the novel, none of which have anything to do with providing information. The children in the poor districts of Barcelona turn them into kites (136). The tramp Mianet uses them to keep warm (237). Marcos whiles away his time in his hideout by making them into paper birds (262). It is important that the newspapers referred to in this last example should be piled up on the floor of the rag-and-bone merchant's hovel: news in Franco's Spain is mythical in the sense that it is gleaned from fragmentary remnants of the past, which have passed through many hands before reaching their final destination as rubbish. And yet such news, like myth, has some basis in historical fact: the problem is the impossibility of knowing where fact stops and fiction starts. Apart from the autobiographical basis of Marsé's depiction of life in the Barrio de Gracia in the 1940s – the orphanage in the Calle Verdi, the Church of Las Ánimas with its underground bomb shelter – the main events of the novel are based on historical fact. All the urban guerrilla attacks were carefully documented by Marsé from press reports of the time. The murder of Menchu is based on that in 1949 of the high society prostitute Carmen Broto. As in the novel the murder took place in the Solar Can Compte off the Calle Legalidad (next to the flat where Marsé lived as a boy), the victim was the mistress of the manager of the Tívoli Theatre, and the murderer Jaime Viñas committed suicide leaving a note with the words 'Life is a dream'.[4] Reference to this documentation is incorporated into the novel in such a way that the frontier between fact and fiction disappears. Luisito's mother is kept awake at night by the press reports she has read about the urban guerrillas, who are her husband's associates (182–3). Sarnita unfolds the paper birds made by Marcos to read out 'news' about characters and events in the novel (75); indeed many of the stories ('aventis') told by the boys are related while sitting on the piles of newspapers in the rag-and-bone merchant's hovel. Perhaps the most sarcastic comment on the Francoist news media is provided by the insertion of one of the most far-fetched stories told by the boys into the interval that occurs when a power cut interrupts the No-Do: the notoriously propagandistic newsreel (Noticiarios y Documentales Cinematográficos) shown obligatorily in all Spanish cinemas from 1943 onwards, replacing the German newsreels shown prior to that date.[5] The implication is that there is little difference between the boys' tall stories and those told by the officially controlled media.

The frequent reference to historical figures who have acquired legendary status in the popular imagination further blurs the boundary between myth and history. The real-life Robin Hood figure Quico Sabaté is mentioned several times as one of the urban guerrillas operating in Barcelona; he takes part in two of the armed raids described in the novel (162, 186, 307, 308, 322–3).[6] Aurora's boyfriend Pedro and her uncle Artemi Nin are said to have belonged to the libertarian youth movement Amigos de Durruti; it was to the legendary anarchist leader Durruti that Aurora was supposed to deliver the microfilm sewn under her skin (286). Artemi Nin's surname inevitably brings to mind the equally legendary leader of the Catalan Trotskyist Party (POUM), Andrés Nin, who died during the Civil War after undergoing torture at the hands of

Stalinist agents. (Artemi's wartime comrade Marcos originally went into hiding to escape Stalinist persecution.) The description given in the novel of the notorious shoot-out between the POUM and the Communists in Barcelona in May 1937 contains another historical/legendary reference with the mention of 'the Englishman on the roof of the Poliorama Cinema' (249), clearly identifiable as George Orwell whose *Homage to Catalonia* made this unfortunate episode known to the world.[7] The reason why figures such as Sabaté, Durruti, Nin and Orwell acquired legendary status was, of course, because the Francoist censorship forbade mention of their names; but the references to Nin and Orwell remind the reader that the Republic too was guilty of replacing fact with fiction. Orwell wrote *Homage to Catalonia* to expose the lies concocted by the Communists during the Civil War. While the official Communist version of Nin's death – according to which he had been 'rescued' from detention in Alcalá de Henares by a supposedly pro-Nazi German Commando of the International Brigades, who then allegedly shot him and buried him in an inner garden of the Pardo Palace – outdoes any of the 'aventis' told by the boys in the novel.[8] As the narrator observes, 'their fantastic adventures fed off a world more fantastic than their imaginings' (39–40). Myth plays a central role in history.

It is important to remember that the novel shows both political Right and Left to be guilty of mythification. Indeed it could be said that the resistance fighters, as survivors of a defunct Republic, are living in a world more unreal than that of Francoist ideology. The Republican press is shown to be as useless as that of the Franco period: both are piled up in the rag-and-bone merchant's hovel and both serve Marcos as material for making paper birds. The main reason why the Republican press gives a mythical view of the past is because the lack of information available about the Republic after the war has reduced it to leftover fragments which, seen in the context of postwar austerity and repression, look pathetically unreal. The 1930s press cuttings pinned on the wall of Marcos' hideout – with their photos of actresses and sports idols (262–3) – might as well be stills from a Hollywood movie. The images of Republican Madrid – proletarian beauty queens, demonstrations, socialist summer schools – glimpsed by the Baroness as she leafs through her prewar collection of the magazine *Crónica* (later sold to Java as rubbish) reduce history to a series of disconnected clichés (158). Even without the problem of censorship, the press of the past converts history into myth in that it reduces it to a collection of isolated remnants uprooted from their context and consequently indistinguishable from fantasy images.

This reduction of history to the isolated visual image is vividly illustrated with the sole surviving photograph of Marcos during the war, pinned up in the rag-and-bone merchant's hovel. The photograph – normally regarded as a form of documentary evidence – acquires mythical significance for the boys because it is a relic from a bygone age shrouded in mystery. Its function is not to provide factual information but to stimulate the imagination: Sarnita literally adds touches of colour – 'honey-coloured curtains', 'red kerchief', 'gilt frames' – to his description of what must have been a black-and-white photograph (264). The boys disagree as to whether the location is a real historical setting that exists outside the novel (the Moncloa Palace), a real historical setting that also exists inside the novel (the Bishop's Palace in Barcelona) or a fictional setting (Conrado's flat). Its documentary nature is further undermined by the inconsistencies in its description: initially (263) it appears to be on the wall inside Marcos' hideout which the narrator Sarnita has never entered; subsequently (264) it appears to be in the main living quarters of the rag-and-bone merchant's hovel next to the anachronistic calendar set at June 1937 (the date Marcos went into hiding), stressing the fact that both photo and calendar are pieces of debris dislocated from their context. In addition the photograph is 'explained' by Java's grandmother who we are immediately reminded is dumb (264, 266). The photograph does not explain anything but stands as an archetypal image of war. It is in this sense, above all, that it reduces history to myth.

A similar reduction of history to the archetype occurs with the repeated references to the design in the carpet in Conrado's bedroom, based on the famous painting *The Execution of General Torrijos and his Comrades* by Antonio Gisbert (1835–1905), depicting the liberal revolutionary facing the firing squad on the beach at Málaga after his ill-fated landing of 1831. On the one hand the reference to Torrijos' death serves to set the political persecution of the postwar period in a broader historical perspective; on the other hand it can be seen as a statement about the ways in which history is passed down to posterity. Again we have an archetypal view of repression where the factual elements – the firing squad, the sea, the dawn – take on a symbolic significance transposed on to the characters of the novel. History is perceived as a symbolic abstraction which tells us about the present rather than the past. If the photograph presents us with a 'documentary' record of a fictional happening, the design in the carpet gives us an artistic elaboration of a historical event. As such it is not just a symbolic abstraction but a secondary version of events. Or rather, as a design based on an original painting, it is a secondary version of an original that is itself a secondary version: historical fact recedes. But if neither the photo nor the design in the carpet give a factual account of history, that does not mean that they are 'untrue': their truth – like that of myth – is of an archetypal, symbolic order.

The design in the carpet is important also because it introduces the theme of betrayal: it was as a result of an act of betrayal that Torrijos was captured and shot. The theme of betrayal is central to the novel: in the double sense of moral betrayal and of the betrayal of truth. The two concepts are linked. The replacement of fact by fiction is the result not just of censorship and propaganda but, more specifically, of the political witch-hunts of the immediate postwar years which – as Sarnita and Java note – encouraged citizens to inform on their relatives and neighbours (75, 238). At the same time the fact that Marcos has had to go into hiding twice – after the events of May 1937 as well as at the end of the war – reminds the reader that this climate of suspicion ('espionitis') was the product not only of Nationalist repression but also of the factional in-fighting that occurred on the Republican side during the Civil War. The blurring of the distinction between political Right and Left increases the impression of a world lacking in fixed values, where anything can be believed of anyone.

The fact that the fictions of the text are the product of a political situation in which denunciations and interrogations are everyday currency is stressed by the repeated use of the confession formula, occurring most explicitly with Paulina's confession to the priest and the confessions of Tetas, Sarnita and Java to the Falangist delegate El Tuerto. It is important that Paulina and Sarnita's confessions should be imaginary versions of a future (possibly hypothetical) event, that Java's confession should be narrated via Sarnita's reconstruction of it as he lip-reads Java's words from a distance, and that there is no way of knowing who relates Tetas' confession to the reader: in all cases the reliability of the confession is undermined. What we have is not a Rousseauesque baring of the soul, but the picaresque use of the confessional form as a vehicle for self-justification.[9] Even Paulina, whose confession is the only one not extracted under threat of physical violence, covers up her own secret crime and limits her confession to informing on others. The confessions of Paulina, Tetas, Sarnita and Java are, of course, about the torture sessions during which the boys have themselves extracted confessions from the girls at the orphanage, which in turn are re-enactments of the wartime *chekas* (secret political prisons) which the boys know about through hearsay. The chain of confessions is interminable: there is no 'truth' at its source, only another confession (which, being known solely through hearsay, cannot even be accorded the status of an event). The point of the confession becomes the fabrication of an artistic elaboration which manipulates the listener's response through its use of stock narrative conventions. Thus Sarnita clinches his confession to El Tuerto with a clichéd spy-story account of how Aurora got her scars: like Scheherazade in the *Arabian Nights* he spins out his tales in order to survive, by distracting attention from the immediate situation. Perhaps the best example of the ironic twist whereby the confession comes to stand for the fabrication of a mythical version of events is provided by the narration of Luisito's interrogation by El Tuerto (chapter 21). The interrogation is recounted at several removes via Sarnita's reconstruction of the dead Luisito's supposed after-the-event account, with the result that it is impossible to tell what is embroidery on the part of Sarnita or of Luisito, and what – if anything – took place. The mythical nature of the episode is further highlighted by its description in terms of a horror movie, complete with Gothic castle, dungeons and vampires.

Indeed all the multiple variants on the story of Aurora and Marcos which comprise the novel take the twin form of the betrayal of truth and the betrayal of others. On the one hand they are fabricated by the boys as a string of red herrings designed to help Java spin out the tales he is reporting back to Conrado's mother; on the other hand the information he gives Conrado's mother serves to denounce Aurora and Marcos. The terms 'narrator' and 'informer' become synonymous: not for nothing has the principal teller of 'aventis', Sarnita, learnt his craft from his father who is a police informer. The title of the novel likewise links the concept of the corruption of truth (the dubious reported form 'If they tell you that ...') with that of moral corruption ('... I have fallen'). The characters acquire what measure of power they have not only by behaving in a degraded manner (informing on others, prostitution, sexual perversion, black-marketeering) but also by denying access to the truth (whether through official propaganda or, in the boys' case, through the fabrication of red herrings). This is not to say that authority in the sense of power has ceased to be linked with authority in the sense of truth; but it is by keeping the source of truth permanently at a remove that the characters are able to make others dependent on them. A parallel exists between the invisible chain of command which creates power in the novel – emanating from the largely unseen Conrado to El Tuerto to La Mastresa to Java – and the way in which Java succeeds in stringing along Conrado's mother by indefinitely postponing the final revelation of truth. Authority consists of 'the shadowy command from behind the curtain' (127) both in the literal sense that Conrado (representing Falangist officialdom) is for most of the novel hidden behind a curtain, and in the figurative sense that it depends on the permanent veiling of truth. The fascist emblem of the 'araña' functions as a symbol of this invisible 'web' of power. The confessions of Paulina, Tetas, Sarnita and Java – which indefinitely defer the truth – are made to authority figures (the priest, El Tuerto) who remain outside the narrative: it is through their absence that their power is felt.

The link between the deferral of truth and the invisibility of authority figures is reinforced by the fact that the majority of characters are orphans (Java and Marcos, the girls from the orphanage including Aurora, Menchu and La Fueguiña) or have lost their fathers (Conrado, Sarnita). The lack of paternal authority figures enhances their prestige but it also makes authority and absence synonymous. It is the boys' desire to create substitute authority figures that leads to their cult of the hero in their stories. The principal story-tellers are Sarnita and Java who have lost their fathers. Even the two boys whose fathers are present in the novel – Mingo and Luisito – feel betrayed by them. Luisito, who had idolized his father while absent in prison, feels rejected by him when on his release he greets him with a callous display of heroics. Palau – otherwise depicted as an endearing character – betrays his son

Mingo by involving him in his armed robberies, with the result that the boy loses his job and is sent to a reformatory.[10] This sense of betrayal by the father is aggravated by the fact that the victors in the war have usurped the paternal role by obliging the Republican war orphans to repudiate their fathers. A speaker at the inauguration of a charitable body states that its function is to teach Republican orphans to be grateful to the Nationalists for having shot their fathers (225). Accordingly the orphan Juanita, when asked about her father, will reply that he deserved to be shot by Franco's troops (51). The Nationalists undermine the prestige of the children's fathers in order to offer themselves as a substitute authority based on the falsehoods of myth. This produces an ambiguous attitude to father figures and authority in general. The boys will create a set of counter-myths to reinstate the Republican resistance fighters – at least two of whom are their fathers – in the paternal role of hero figure; at the same time they undermine the resistance fighters' heroic status by stressing their impotence. Conversely, the boys' 'aventis' undermine the authority of the Nationalist victors by presenting the war hero Conrado as literally impotent; while the story of El Tuerto's torture makes him into a heroic figure (albeit a villain) whose authority (represented by his gun) is clearly admired by Sarnita, for all his mockery (270).

The ambivalence displayed in the novel towards the hero figure can perhaps be explained by the centrality of the myth of the hero both to popular culture and to Nationalist ideology. The heroes and heroines of the 'aventis' fall into two categories – the persecuted and the collaborators – which are systematically juxtaposed: the chapters telling the story of Aurora (persecuted) also tell the story of Java (collaborator), while those telling the story of the urban guerrillas (persecuted) also tell the story of Menchu (collaborator). The hero figure both represents and betrays popular values. The form taken by the hero myth in Nationalist ideology was, of course, that of the Nietzschean superman whose innate superiority made him a natural leader of the masses. This myth was propagated not only by the imposition from above of official propaganda but also, more insidiously, by the cultivation and manipulation of popular culture, whose exaltation of the outcast who mocks the law could easily be made to coincide with the fascist exaltation of the *caudillo* who stands above the law. It was this populist aspect of Nationalist ideology –

based on the myth of the individual hero – that facilitated Spain's transition in the late 1950s from the values of feudalism to those of capitalism. Java and Menchu's rise from rags to riches takes place in the late 1940s (Menchu is murdered in 1949; Java's upwardly mobile career will continue on into the 1960s). Marsé suggests that the germs of the later evolution of Franco's Spain towards capitalism that would take place so spectacularly with the economic boom of the late 1950s and 1960s were present from the start of the postwar period.

The novel explicitly links the hero myth to popular culture: both in the sense of culture provided for the masses and in that of the popular imagination. As in real life, the two blur. Marsé has stated that he conceived the novel as a vindication of 'the popular memory' of Spain's postwar history, in opposition to 'the official Francoist version of events'. In Marsé's collection of satirical articles *Confidencias de un chorizo*, Sarnita will write a spoof letter to the press justifying his 'aventis' as his revenge on 'a system that warped my childhood and adolescence' and insisting that 'the day will come when officialdom has to bow to the collective memory'. The novel failed to progress till Marsé hit on the idea of narrating events via the 'aventis' told by a group of working-class adolescents: events are viewed from a perspective that is marginal, popular and collective.[11] The adolescent propensity to fantasy and hero worship merges with the stereotyped vision transmitted by the movies, comics and pulp fiction of the 1940s. The Spanish film industry of the 1940s devoted itself to patriotic epics about the heroes and heroines of national history. In addition, from 1943 onwards – when Allied victories led Franco to look increasingly to the United States – Spain saw a flood of imported (and censored) Hollywood movies, set in a far-removed, glamorized world that distracted attention from problems at home.[12] The paucity of Spanish fiction in the 1940s was compensated by imports of second-rate escapist literature: thrillers, westerns, romances. (The works of major foreign writers were mostly banned.)[13] In his book *Los comics del franquismo*, Salvador Vázquez Parga has described how, in the 1940s in particular, State and Church edited children's comics and magazines to instil the values of Nationalist ideology into the young populace, the best known of these official publications being *Flechas y Pelayos* (formed from the merger in 1938 of the Falangist *Flechas* with the Carlist *Pelayos*). A

Spanish version *Juan Centella* was produced of the Italian fascist comic *Dick Fulmine*. The most popular comics were privately produced though subject to strict censorship, such as *El Guerrero del Antifaz* (1944–66), set at the time of the Reconquest of Spain from the Moors. Vázquez Parga notes that the Spanish Middle Ages were by far the most popular setting, giving way in the 1950s and 1960s to North American locations. Predictably the central theme of children's comics in the Franco period was 'the myth of the hero', initially a crusading version of the Nietzschean superman, subsequently fading into Superman American-style. Pertinent to *Si te dicen que caí* is the fact that such comics coincided with official ideology in dividing the world into 'goodies' and 'baddies' (Marsé will systematically blur such distinctions) and that, despite strict censorship in sexual matters, they consistently depicted scenes of extreme violence: it was only with new regulations introduced in the early 1960s that violence started to be censored. This violence is mirrored in the boys' 'aventis' (though of course they do not share the sexual prudery enforced by the censor).[14]

Sarnita, the chief teller of 'aventis', runs a stall selling comics – *Merlin, Flash Gordon, Tarzan* – and paperbacks in the Plaza del Norte, which the other boys take it in turns to man. The comics and books sold by Sarnita are secondhand and avidly circulated among the adolescent characters. The vision of reality they derive from their reading of comics is a collective one, and one which is at a remove from reality not only because it is stereotyped but also because it has passed from hand to hand. Old comics and movie magazines are piled up in the rag-and-bone merchant's hovel alongside the newspapers (15, 39): as far as the boys are concerned, they have the same status. Juanita will agree to be tortured in exchange for two issues of *Merlin* and receives *Monito y Fifí* as a bonus (50); Java takes comics to the orphanage (one of those in demand is *El Guerrero del Antifaz*) in exchange for junk (193). Mingo describes Conrado's signed photo of Mussolini on a motorbike as being of Juan Centella (81, 200), while Tetas says that Java dressed as Lucifer looks more like Captain Marvel (115). The boys are familiar with thrillers and westerns: Mingo echoes Sherlock Holmes with his 'elementary, my dear Tetas' (333), while Sarnita describes Java talking to El Tuerto as 'Flecha Negra and Crazy Horse' smoking the pipe of peace (283): a nice jumble of Falangist and Red Indian names illustrating the mixture

146

of Nationalist and American ideology that dominated postwar Spain. The clichéd language and vision of pulp fiction is frequently evident in Sarnita's tales, particularly when dealing with the love story of Aurora and Marcos. Marsé has said that he first became addicted to novels as a result of reading popular fiction in his teens: before the creation of Alianza Editorial's paperback series in the early 1960s, there was in fact little good literature available in cheap editions.[15] In particular Marsé has singled out his love of detective stories: the tale of Marcos and Aurora – 'the man in hiding and the whore on the run' (267) – has all the ingredients of a popular thriller.[16]

Inseparable from the influence of popular fiction is that of the music hall and cinema. At one point in her career Menchu will work as a chorus girl: the lyrics she sings are incorporated into the narrative, their sentimentality adding a sarcastic gloss to the harsh reality of prostitution underlying her glamorous image (315). The same ironic juxtaposition of romance with economic realism occurs when Menchu returns the open cheque sent her by an admirer with a verse from the song 'La bien pagá' ['The Rewards of Love'] (223). The description of the sentimental sketches which Conrado has La Fueguiña perform under the name Magnolia is interwoven with quotations from songs of the period. The epithet 'sailor' given to Marcos – contrary to fact – situates him in a stock cabaret tradition: cf. Brecht's 'Bilbao Song' or 'Surabaya Johnny'. His description is, in fact, taken from the 1940s song 'Tatuaje' ['Tattoo'].[17] The girls in the orphanage hide novels and songbooks under their mattresses, together with pin-ups of singers and movie stars, and know by heart the words of 'Perfidia' and 'Bésame mucho' (194).

Of all the forms of popular culture referred to in the novel, it is the cinema that makes its presence felt most strongly. Marsé has himself written commercial film scripts.[18] Sarnita trades not only in comics but also in postcards of movie stars (173), and gets free passes for the Rovira Cinema where his mother works as a cleaner (258). A large number of episodes take place in or outside cinemas: the glamour of the silver screen is undermined by constant mention of the 'pajilleras' (among them Aurora) eking out a living by masturbating clients in the back rows. Scenes of torture in the alleged *chekas* of wartime Republican Barcelona – the basis of many of the boys' fantasies – were a stock ingredient of early Nationalist propaganda films.[19] The boys' tortures of the orphan girls are also based on the American films *Marked Woman* (144), *The Prisoner of Zenda* (173), *Suez* (229), *The Drums of Fu Manchu* (259), *Guadalcanal Diary* (282), plus *La corona di ferro* (229) made in Mussolini's Italy. The influence of English-language films is shown by the 'Yes, hay mar de fondo' and 'Yes, coño' (255) with which Sarnita imagines himself braving El Tuerto (with his black patch over one eye, a classic movie villain). The girls from the orphanage – like the girls on whom the tramp Mianet spies – stare at the stills displayed outside the cinema in anticipation of next week's programme (193, 235): likewise each of the 'aventis' constitutes a kind of trailer for stories to come. The boys are conscious of modelling their 'aventis' on films. Sarnita interrupts the story he is telling in the rag-and-bone merchant's hovel with the words 'Clear the auditorium' (17). (The attraction for him of the cops-and-robbers movie is still evident in the 1960s when, as the adult Ñito, his memories of his boyhood 'aventis' blur with the images of *Ironside* he is watching on TV [102].) The boys declare that they find their 'aventis' as gripping as the films they have seen; indeed the criterion of excellence is that they should be 'just like a movie' (103, 130).

An essential ingredient of the 'aventis' is the Hollywood pin-up. The Republican priest Ramón is tortured psychologically – in addition to his physical tortures – by the photo of Ginger Rogers whose presence in the torture chamber represents a world of luxury tantalizingly out of reach (319). This torture scene forms part of the story of Luisito's interrogation, narrated in the form of a horror film: the juxtaposition of the two contrasting cinematographic codes suggests that in some disturbing way they implicate each other. It is the Americanized glamour image of the pin-up that is incarnated by Menchu, whose rags-to-riches story takes the form of a series of movie stills. With her mink coat and jewels, her 'silken knees' always slightly apart and her room at the Ritz, she is the archetypal Hollywood temptress. It is important that her glamorous image should be systematically juxtaposed with the equally archetypal image of the luckless 'tart with a heart', incarnated by Aurora. Aurora's sob story – which Sarnita inserts into a description of the sob stories told by down-at-heel whores in general – reads like a cross between a sentimental war movie (with her fiancé being killed on the Aragonese front) and a gangster movie (with her involvement in the death of Conrado's father, which takes place 'by the roadside, at night, in the glare of the car headlamps' [211]). The cinematic nature of Aurora's story is made explicit by its parallel with the film *Arsène Lupin* which Aurora sees with Java (176).[20] Sarnita's account of how she got her scars (268–9) reads like a spy film: indeed a piece of film, sewn under her skin, is the central motif of the story. Menchu and Aurora are equally clichéd figures which, as inverted mirror images, complement and undermine each other.

The episodes about the urban guerrillas are equally cinematic in inspiration. Sentimental touches are still present – as with Taylor's girlfriend Margarita – but the dominant note is that of the slick gangster movie. Indeed the urban guerrillas are described as consciously acting out the role of gangsters in a film. Or rather, they act out the part of actors playing the role of gangsters in a film, with Meneses explicitly playing Robert Taylor and the cynical Palau implicitly imitating the deadpan style of Edward G. Robinson or Humphrey Bogart, complete with mackintosh and wisecracks. Palau reveals his priorities when he excuses himself for failing to carry out a political mission on the grounds that he had to take his son to the cinema. Several guerrilla raids take place in or near cinemas, notably the shoot-out outside the Teatro Cómico, presided over by the giant cardboard cut-out of the actress Carmen de Lirio's legs (185). The descriptions of the violence – with their emphasis on the various cars driven by the guerrillas – read like sequences from a Hollywood gangster movie. This cinematic quality serves to underline the artificiality of the guerrillas' heroics, motivated more by their desire to cut a fine figure than by the requirements of the political situation.[21]

If the urban guerrillas are implicitly criticized for modelling themselves on movie heroes, there is no suggestion that the boys are at fault in re-casting the reality around them in cinematic form. The difference is that the urban guerrillas (with the exception of Palau, largely exempted from criticism) take themselves seriously, whereas the boys' 'aventis' poke fun at the official Francoist version of history by likening it to a B-movie. Officialdom's promotion of forms of popular entertainment that encouraged stereotyped thinking is turned against it. Despite its hackneyed vision, the Hollywood movie – with its cult of fantasy images – stimulates in the boys a freedom of the imagination that saves them from the effects of propaganda and censorship. The boys prefer the 'aventis' that are most extravagant because 'nothing at that time made sense' (39–40). Their defiance of empiricism is a refusal to compromise with the sordid world around them (327). The boys are aware that, in a society where empirical verification of the truth is made impossible, fantasy provides the only access to truth. When Martín is congratulated on producing an 'aventi' as good as a film plot, he will reply 'Some films are true' (103).

The appeal to popular culture undermines the myth of the hero as much as it propagates it not only because the urban guerrillas are criticized for their heroics, but also because the characters' stereotyped nature detracts from their individuality. Like the celluloid images of the cinema, they are one-dimensional clichés who cannot act independently of their prescribed role. It is for this reason, and not only because of the political situation, that they are described as trapped. The sensation of being the prisoner of a set of self-reflecting mirror-images is experienced explicitly by Conrado – the voyeur is another stock cinematic personage; one thinks of the disabled voyeur in Hitchcock's *Rear Window* (1954) – and Menchu (199, 222). The scorpion bracelet that binds Menchu to the urban guerrillas – Java explains that the scorpion stings itself with its own tail when trapped (129) – symbolizes the fact that, as stock screen characters, they are trapped in the vicious circle of their image. Even Java, the hero figure who comes nearest to achieving a degree of individuality, performs roles dictated by others (Conrado, Señora Galán) and in the end is unable to escape the fate of Lucifer whose role he rehearses in front of a mirror (90), or of Torrijos – another doomed rebel – whose portrait reflects his mirror-image back at him from the carpet (285).

The stereotyped hero figures of the novel are those not only of the mass media but also of traditional oral culture. The fact that the boys read cheap paperbacks shows that they are literate but their deprived upbringing makes them an example of what Walter Ong, in his book *Orality and Literacy*, describes as 'residually oral subcultures in dominantly high-literacy societies'.[22] Of all the mass media, it is those that are visual – the cinema, the comic – that most appeal to them. Ong suggests that the absence of logical analysis and coherence characteristic of myth is best explained not as the result of a primitive, pre-rational mentality but as the inevitable consequence of oral transmission. Myth is necessarily oral: as soon as it is written down it becomes adulterated. *Si te dicen que caí* is a mythical novel in the sense that it attempts to capture the process of oral story-telling; however, as a printed book, written by a literate for other literates, it can be no more than a simulation. Ong insists that the absence of causal sequence in much twentieth-century fiction is essentially different from that in oral narrative since it depends for its effects on the reader's literate expectations, which are frustrated. *Si te dicen que caí* incorporates oral story-telling techniques, but for the purpose of achieving effects diametrically opposed to those of oral narrative.

Ong's study points out that the distinctive features of oral narrative can be explained by the story-teller's reliance on memory and by his need to make his tale clear to listeners who have no text to consult in case of confusion. The characters of oral narrative have to be larger than life in order to be, quite literally, memorable. Subtle psychology is out of the question – indeed Ong suggests that the whole concept of depth psychology could not have developed without print – for characters must always act true to type in order to be recognizable. There is no hidden meaning to the text, to be prised out through subsequent analysis, for once each sentence has been uttered it ceases to exist. The process is performance-oriented and not information-oriented: each telling of the tale will consist of variant versions. Indeed there is no correct version, for there is no original text. Instead the story-teller has at his disposal a set of formulae which he rotates according to the requirements of the moment. These consist both of stock situations and of set phrases or epithets which allow the audience instantly to recognize what or who is being described. These formulae are linked in associative clusters rather than by causal sequence: the organization of the *Iliad* is thus that of 'boxes within boxes as created by thematic recurrences'. There can be no chronological, logically developed plot not only because the characters must remain static, but also because on each narration the story-teller will introduce different episodes in a different order, depending on how and when they spring to mind and on the mood of the audience. Oral narrative is thus 'aggregative' rather than logically coherent. The notion of originality consists not in the capacity for departing from the standard pattern, but in the ability to adjust spontaneously to audience demand. This performance-orientation also leads to a tendency to dramatic pres-

entation, both with the story-teller narrating the hero's acts in the
first person, and with a preference for dialogue over description.
Oral narrative is a collective enterprise both in the sense that the
story-teller draws on a repertoire elaborated by others before him,
and in the sense that audience reaction plays a large part in the
shaping of the tale.[23]

The relevance of Ong's analysis of oral narrative to *Si te dicen que
caí* is immediately obvious. All of the above features characterize the
'aventis' but, in almost every case, the effect is not so much to
produce instant recognition and immediacy as confusion and distance. The two traditions – that of oral narrative and that of the
printed book – are played off against one another, for the 'aventis'
have a double audience: the boys who listen to them live and the
reader who turns the pages of the book. The novel frustrates the
expectations built up by its use of oral techniques by appealing to the
conventions of the printed book, and conversely frustrates the
expectations of the reader by appealing to the conventions of oral
narrative. This double game makes the novel doubly mythical: its
use of oral techniques reproduces the narrative structures of myth;
but its frustration of both oral and literate conventions undermines
the realist suspension of disbelief, making the reader critically aware
of the fictional nature of what he is reading.

The fact that the 'aventis' have a double audience brings them to
life for the reader as he puts himself in the place of the boys to whom
they are told, but it also sets them at a remove in that the reader is
not in fact listening to them but reading about the characters
listening to them. This chain of oral transmission – simultaneously
creating immediacy and distance – is reproduced within the 'aventis'
themselves inasmuch as they are stitched together from snatches of
hearsay: 'hablar de oídas, eso era contar aventis' ['bits of gossip,
that's what our stories were'] (38). The 'Si te dicen que caí' formula
of the novel's title recurs throughout, as in 'lo dijo uno que dicen que
es rojo' ['so somebody said who they say is a red'] (51), or ' – Este
loco, dicen que gritaba llorando – dice Ñito' ['"A madman they say
she kept screaming and crying," says Ñito'] (35) where Ñito reports
the ambulance men's report of the girl in the sports car's report of
Java's accident. The conditional formulation of the title is apt: often
it is not made explicit that a certain episode is based on hearsay
although we suspect that this is the case. The description of

Conrado's flat in chapter 1 is presented without explanation; only as we read on do we discover that Tetas and Amén (who assist at mass in the family chapel) and La Fueguiña (who looks after Conrado) have reported back on the flat to the other boys (81, 200). The fact that everything said in the 'aventis' appears in the final instance to be based on hearsay creates an impossible tangle of fact and fiction, for hearsay is at the same time both and neither. The 'aventis' are unreliable but neither are they complete fabrications: 'not a lie but a story, it's not the same', Sarnita will insist (257). If a story is corroborated by verbal evidence given by someone else we give it more credence; at the same time its doubly verbal nature makes it doubly unreliable. The double-edged nature of verbal evidence is summed up by Java's ironic allegation to El Tuerto that he is telling the truth when patently he is not: 'que fue la última noticia que se tuvo de él, palabra' ['that was the last we heard of him, on my word'] (291).

It is not just that the reader cannot tell how much of the hearsay is based on fact; neither can the boys. Apart from the political suppression of truth, as adolescents the boys are partly included in and partly excluded from participation in the adult world. The lurid sexual details in their 'aventis' are largely based on adolescent myths created either by ignorance or by adult mystification: halfway through the novel we are told that Sarnita has never been to a brothel and Java is still a virgin (242). Sarnita states that prostitutes have to be careful not to wear out their sexual nerve-ends and that sex gives you TB (248, 21); while the other boys insist that La Fueguiña is not a virgin as she wears a bandage round her ankle 'because of the time of the month' (334). This dubious chain of oral transmission extends outside the novel. According to Marsé, two of the most extravagant 'aventis' in the novel – those of Java's seduction by the bishop and of his sexual performance with Aurora for Conrado – were based on real-life rumours that the Bishop of Barcelona in the 1940s was a homosexual, and on the detailed verbal account given him by a male prostitute from the *barrio chino* of how he had been hired in his youth to perform for the painter Dalí.[24]

As in oral narrative, this hearsay is mostly presented in dramatic form. The 'aventis' reproduce a dialogue between two or more characters, within which previous episodes will be recalled which are interpolated also in dialogue form as if taking place at the same time.

This increases the immediacy of the text for everything is presented live; but at the same time the practice of presenting reported sequences in dramatic form makes us start to suspect that everything presented live may be hearsay. This encapsulation within a frame story of various interpolated stories presented in dramatic form is reminiscent of the Peruvian novelist Vargas Llosa's use of what he calls 'Chinese boxes'.[25] In Vargas Llosa's novels – as in oral narrative – the effect of such Chinese boxes is to create a sense of dramatic immediacy such that we forget we are reading a series of reported versions. But in *Si te dicen que caí* we are never allowed to forget that everything is mediated via a chain of narrators. In chapter 4 in particular, a sensation of infinite regress is created by the profusion of boxes within boxes: within Marcos' account of Palau's account of what, on examination, turn out to be not one but a series of different encounters with the other guerrillas stretching from 1939 (mention of the Nationalist victory parade) to 1942 (mention of the Allies), we then have Meneses' account of his previous life as a village school-master (63–5). This process of infinite regress, relegating everything to the dubious status of hearsay, is summed up by Java: '¿Qué se puede decir de una aventi de Sarnita que empieza diciendo qué se puede decir de una puta roja que empieza diciendo qué decir del hombre que amo ...?' ['What can I say about a story of Sarnita's that starts by saying what can I say about a red whore who starts by saying what can I say about the man I love ...?'] (292).

The fact that the characters become narrators in turn makes it difficult – if not impossible – to tell the difference between frame story and stories contained in it, leaving the reader unsure as to how many levels of fiction separate him from events. This problem is compounded by the fact that the boys include themselves as characters in their 'aventis': they thus stand simultaneously inside them and outside them. In addition, the tellers of the 'aventis' – as in oral narrative – frequently slip into the first person when narrating their characters' acts. Thus, in the 'aventis', reference to one of the boys in the third person does not preclude the possibility that he may also be telling the story; conversely reference to one of the boys in the first person by no means implies that he is the narrator. Sarnita's 'aventi' about Java's sexual performance with Aurora for Conrado will alternate between first and third person narration even within the same sentence (19–31), creating an impossible blend of immediacy and distance. Similar doubt as to the reliability of what we are reading is created by the shifting use of tenses. The 'aventis' usually start in the future tense (indicating that they consist of speculation on the part of a boy telling the story), then slip into the present tense (giving a sense of immediacy such that we forget there is an intermediary narrator), finally slipping into the past (which we associate with the voice of an omniscient narrator, forgetting that the story started as speculation on the part of one of the boys). The frequent omission of speech punctuation – again as in Vargas Llosa – further erodes the distinction between narrative and speech, making us aware that the dramatic immediacy of the text is an illusion.

The difficulty of distinguishing between frame story and interpolated stories is complicated yet more by our gradual discovery that the external narrator of the chapters relating the boys' 'aventis' – the morgue attendant Ñito – is the same person, now an adult in the 1960s, as Sarnita, the chief adolescent teller of 'aventis' in the 1940s. The outer frame of Ñito's conversations with Sor Paulina in the hospital morgue in the 1960s might have been expected to give coherence to the text by locating the confusing proliferation of narrative levels within a single perspective. But it turns out to be as unstable as any other narrative frame in the novel. The transition from Ñito in the 1960s to the boys in the 1940s is frequently imperceptible, as when mention of Java's autopsy fades into a description of the boys playing 'doctor' with Juanita (42–3). It is extremely difficult to establish how much of the text Ñito is responsible for. In oral narrative, the story can be loosely constructed because the voice of the story-teller provides continuity. Printed fiction has to simulate continuity by inventing a personalized narrator – either a character or an external narrator with a clearly defined set of opinions – who is made responsible for relaying the story to the reader. This personalized narrator can be unreliable in the sense of being biased, for the reader becomes familiar enough with his quirks to be able to correct the bias. He can even be an outright liar, because the reader then knows that all he says can be dismissed as 'fiction'. But his presence must be felt throughout so that the reader knows how to interpret everything he reads. The fact that in *Si te dicen que caí* we are often unsure who is speaking means that we have no way of assessing whether what we are reading is 'true' or 'false'.

The presence of a frame narrator is clearly established by the opening words of the novel: 'Cuenta que ...' ['He relates how ...']. But we are unable to personalize the narrator because it is not till the second chapter that we discover the subject of 'Cuenta' is Ñito. Only on p. 159, when 'la Preñada' – mentioned on the first page as Ñito's mother – is introduced as Sarnita's mother do we deduce that Ñito and Sarnita are the same person. Final proof comes only on p. 257, when Sarnita's full name is given as Antonio Faneca (Ñito being a short form of the familiar 'Antoñito'): the fact that Faneca was Marsé's original surname before adoption produces an additional ironic fusion of narrator and author.[26] The duplication created by the fact that the narrator of the outer frame is the same person as the teller of the 'aventis' contained within it produces a blurring of 'events' remembered by Ñito with fictions told by Sarnita. The boys' interrogations of the orphan girls whom they force to assume the role of Aurora and Java's participation in the church play seem to be 'real events'; but the boundary between fact and fiction is still complicated by the fact that the only 'events' that seem to be real are performances. There is no way of knowing how much of Java's search for Aurora is true since he concocts stories to extort money from Señora Galán; Sarnita concocts additional stories for the benefit of the boys to supplement what Java has told them. It is quite possible that all the encounters with Aurora are fictions invented by the boys and that, for them, she is an entirely mythical creature.

It is equally impossible to establish the extent to which the omniscient narrator who describes Ñito's movements in the hospital intrudes into his narrative. The unacknowledged quotations from Antonio Machado – 'confusa la historia y clara la pena' ['the story confused and the suffering clear'] (168) – and from Pablo Neruda – 'ya no volverán por el cielo a matar niños' ['no more will they come from the sky to kill children'] (71) – cannot be known to either Sarnita who utters them or Ñito who recalls his words.[27] In many chapters it is not specified till halfway through or the very end that what we are reading is spoken by Ñito. Conversely, several chapters that explicitly open with the frame story of Ñito in the hospital end without returning to it. Frequently the fact that a particular chapter is a continuation of a previous one identified as consisting of Ñito's recollections is the only evidence we have for supposing that he is responsible for what we are reading now (chapters 3, 8, 10, 19). In other chapters recounting the boys' 'aventis' there is no evidence at all that Ñito is the frame narrator. In one instance – the first half of chapter 15 which describes Paulina spying on the boys – the narrator is clearly not Ñito but Sor Paulina. The one firm clue (albeit on a second reading) to when Ñito is responsible for the narrative at points when his presence is unannounced is mention of the flowering almond in the Solar Can Compte, which we know is Ñito's touch because at the end of the novel Sor Paulina tells us he has made it up (346). Characteristically, the evidence is itself a lie. In a nice irony Sarnita's final 'aventi' about Aurora and Marcos' death will have them run past the flowering almond 'without even seeing it' (346).

The difficulty of establishing who is speaking – and thus of deciding the degree of reliability of what is said – multiplies when dealing with the chapters about the urban guerrillas and Menchu, in which there is no mention of Ñito and Sor Paulina. It is possible to establish a tenuous narrative frame for most of these chapters in the form of Marcos, who appears in the first person – in conversation with others and participating in several of the armed raids – in chapters 4, 6, 9, 14, 17, 20 and the second part of 21. We know that his conversations with Palau in the Bar Alaska have informed him about episodes involving the guerrillas at which he was not present; we are also told that in all-night conversation in the Bar Alaska Menchu told him her life story (272–3, 309). Marsé has confirmed that Marcos is the narrator of these chapters.[28] But it is not as simple as that. There is a network of cross-references between the chapters about the urban guerrillas and Menchu and those which consist of the boys' 'aventis' about Java and Aurora, which suggest that the former are yet another set of 'aventis' told by the boys. The main link between the two sets of stories is provided by Aurora, who we identify from her attributes as the unnamed lover to whom – in chapters 9, 14 and 17 – Marcos recounts his reminiscences in his hideout. In chapter 10, Java and Sarnita describe Aurora in terms that are a verbatim repetition of Menchu's story as told in the chapters narrated by Marcos (166–7). Conversely in chapter 17, the description of Menchu's room is a verbatim repetition of that given by the boys of Aurora's room (242). In chapter 11, the death of the urban guerrilla Artemi Nin is described as a re-enactment of the execution of Torrijos depicted on Conrado's carpet, otherwise referred to only in the boy's 'aventis' about Java. In the second section of chapter 21 –

the only chapter to mix a story about the boys with episodes involving the urban guerrillas and Menchu – the guerrillas receive Ramón's postcard which we saw him writing under torture in Sarnita's 'aventi' in the first section of the chapter; conversely the *cheka* and El Tuerto's alias as the Siamese Consul, mentioned in this 'aventi', had previously been mentioned by the guerrillas in the preceding chapter (303–4). In their confessions to El Tuerto, the boys had shown they were as interested in piecing together Marcos' story as that of Aurora. Marcos is, of course, Java's brother, walled up in the rag-and-bone merchant's hovel where the boys tell many of their stories and which, with its piles of newspapers, provides the basic information about the urban guerrillas' exploits. The first chapter about the urban guerrillas occurs immediately after the boy's sighting of a figure they take to be Marcos (57), as if generated by the encounter. Mingo tells the boys about the scorpion bracelet he is taking to a luxury prostitute in the Ritz, at which point Java explicitly promises to tell the boys an 'aventi' about it (129). It is in fact specified at the end of the first chapter about the urban guerrillas and Menchu – which up to that point seemed to be narrated by Marcos – that Sarnita (recognizable by the stock formula with which he begins his 'aventis') is responsible for the story:

a partir de ahora, chavales, el peligro acechará en todas partes y en ninguna, la amenaza será invisible y constante. Quien así habla es un muchacho del Carmelo ... En un pequeño desván apenas alumbrado por una vela, dice, alguien sentado en una mecedora hace pajaritas de papel con viejas revistas, de día y noche, pensando en una novia bonita con katiuskas, en los camaradas valientes y fieles hasta la muerte. (71)

from now on, boys, danger will be everywhere and nowhere, its menace constant and invisible. The speaker of these words is a boy from the Carmelo ... In a tiny candlelit garret, he says, someone in a rocking chair is making old magazines into paper birds, day and night, thinking about a pretty lover in wellingtons, about comrades brave and true unto death.

The Marcos who narrates the chapters about the urban guerrillas and Menchu is thus a character in the boys' fictions. As such he may – like Aurora – be a mere fantasy projection.

The reason why Marsé chose to make it so hard to establish whether the two sets of chapters have a common narrator seems to be his desire to give the impression that the text of the novel is the product of an anonymous collective memory. As he himself has said:

'what matters is the collective memory, the voice that belongs to no one and yet to everyone'.[29] Aurora is described as evoking her past 'amid a proliferating memory that was not entirely hers' (243); while Java describes Marcos as 'a voice talking to itself, a memory spreading in ever wider circles, black and vast like the night' (293). The final chapter of the novel – in which Luis Lage and Palau reminisce about the past – cannot be fitted into any narrative frame. It cannot be an 'aventi' remembered by Ñito for it takes place in the 1960s; it cannot be narrated by Marcos for we are told he has lost touch with Luis Lage and Palau, who indeed report rumours of his death. A further complication is introduced by the fact that the final lines of the novel are a re-take of the first paragraph of the initial chapter about the urban guerrillas (63), despite the fact that no common narrator can be established for the two passages. (The climactic phrase in both passages – 'Men of steel, forged in so many battles ... ' – will in Marsé's later novel *Un día volveré* [1982] be attributed to the character Suau, a friend of Palau, whose evocations of the past are notoriously unreliable.)[30] Nor can this last chapter be told by an omniscient narrator, for towards the end it slips into the first person plural: 'when we still had fire in our veins ... we all thought the end was in sight' (359). It has to be recognized that – despite the existence in the novel of a series of tenuous narrative frames (Ñito's memories, the boys' 'aventis', the images in Marcos' head) – there is in the last instance no single frame narrator responsible for the whole text. The first person plural form recurs sporadically throughout the novel. The 'aventis' are frequently constructed by a group of boys working together as a 'we'. Marcos' narration of the urban guerrillas' activities slips on occasions into a first person plural comprising various members of the group. This first person plural voice cannot provide the coherence of a genuine frame narrator because it passes from one group of characters to another. It is the sum of the voices in the novel, rather than a separate voice containing them. As a first person plural voice, it also includes the author and reader outside the novel. Like myth, the text is the product of a disembodied voice that belongs to no one in particular but to the community at large.

It is important that it should be the last chapter which refuses to fit into a narrative frame. For it is the final return to a fixed point of departure that allows a narrative frame to give coherence to the whole work. Initially the final chapter appears to correspond to the traditional 'epilogue' of the realist novel, rounding everything off by telling us what happened to the characters after the end of the story. But this 'epilogue', far from providing closure, opens up further questions as variant versions are given of the characters' fates. An open-ended frame is not a frame at all. The final impossibility of arranging the various stories that comprise the novel in a graded sequence of 'Chinese boxes' breaks down the notion of perspective – central to realist fiction as to realist painting – whereby coherence is provided through the subordination of the component parts of the composition to a hierarchical scheme such that they can be encompassed within a single viewpoint. This breakdown of narrative hierarchy is also a breakdown of narrative authority. If no single voice imposes its viewpoint on the text, all voices have equal validity. The narrative structure of the novel subverts the political structure of the society it describes. If the latter is based on the imposition of falsehood masquerading as absolute truth, the former proposes a collective vision in which all voices are shown to be unreliable and in which, consequently, no single voice is privileged. The vision of reality offered in *Si te dicen que caí* is no less mythical than that of official ideology; the difference is that it has no pretensions to authority.

This one-dimensionality, according to which no voice has more authority than any other, is complemented by another kind of one-dimensionality in the sense that the text frustrates the search for hidden truth. Just as we were teased with the possibility of establishing a narrative frame only to be frustrated, so we are invited to pick up clues and piece them together only to discover they do not fit. Again the conventions of oral and written narrative are played off against one another in order to produce effects alien to both. Oral narrative has to be superficial because without a fixed text to consult the audience is not able to detect a concealed network of references pointing to an underlying meaning. Whereas the written text, consisting of visible signs of sounds that are absent, by definition turns what before was an act of listening into a process of decipherment. It is therefore logical that a central theme of literature should be that of reality and appearance. Ong suggests that it is no coincidence that the nineteenth century, which saw a massive extension of literacy, gave birth to the detective genre.[31] For the thriller depends on the assumption that the text is strewn with clues which will lead the reader, via a process of cross-referencing and deduction, to the final revelation of the truth. It is interesting to compare the detective genre with another product of the nineteenth century: the Romantic view of myth as the revelation of a lost truth. The Romantic obsession with the quest myth is perhaps simply a version of the contemporaneous vogue for the thriller. Ong's observation that the oral transmission of myth necessarily makes it episodic and lacking in depth is in complete opposition to the Romantic view of myth as obeying a linear plot taking the hero towards the final revelation of the truth. By encouraging but at the same time frustrating the search for hidden meaning, *Si te dicen que caí* plays off against one another not only the conventions of literacy and orality but also the two opposing concepts of myth that go with them.

The novel is a detective story in the sense that it does not so much tell the story of Aurora and Marcos as tell the story of the process by which their story is pieced together. But at the end of the detection process there is no revelation. When the bodies are dug up in the final 'aventi' there is no simultaneous unearthing of the truth: the corpses cannot even be identified with any certainty. Appropriately a large number of 'aventis' describe interrogation sessions: at the end all we are left with is, precisely, an interrogation. Throughout, the boys are obsessed with the desire to unearth a hidden truth. Their stories are triggered off by rumours of buried ammunition in the Solar Can Compte. It is this buried ammunition that will blow up Aurora and Marcos (if it is them) in the final 'aventi'; but when the boys go digging for it they find nothing. Many of their stories are told in the bomb shelter whose secret subterranean location is 'terrific for telling stories' (86); but all they find there are Platonic semblances of reality: 'Pero yo no podía verlo, ya le he dicho que estábamos de espaldas y lo único que veíamos eran sus sombras en la pared' ['But I couldn't see what was going on, I've already told you we were facing the other way and all we could see were their shadows on the wall'] (212). The tunnel the boys dig from their hideout leads them only to the theatre dressing-room: a place of illusion. The notion that truth is synonymous with hidden depths is upheld by Ñito's supposition, as he gazes into the 'boggy depths' of the dead Java's eyes (13), that the past is contained within his body;

as morgue attendant, Ñito will extract Java's literal insides (his inner organs) and his figurative insides (his memories). Likewise the boys' torture sessions with the orphan girls combine the interrogation process with an exploration of their internal organs: 'Keep going deeper', Sarnita urges (43). Sarnita in particular is obsessed with getting behind 'the façade of events' (261) to uncover the hidden truth. In Sarnita's 'aventis', Marcos' tattoos and Aurora's scars become ciphers of a concealed past: 'indelible tattoos and scars on the skin of memory' (77). Sarnita's final version of how Aurora got her scars will describe them as the result of sewing a secret document under her skin; but when the scar is opened up to extract the key document it has vanished (268).

The main reason why the 'aventis' do not lead to the final revelation of the truth is that they are not final versions: in order to explain the loose ends in their stories, the boys will create further versions. The variant versions that constitute the 'aventis' are partly a response to the literate convention that a story must have a logically developed plot, and partly a result of their oral delivery, which forces the story-teller to accommodate himself to audience demand. As in the *Quixote*, the characters discuss the verisimilitude of the stories they hear; but in this case they have the power to demand a new version more to their liking. The fact that the characters of the novel are tellers of, and listeners to, stories gives it – like the *Quixote* – a metafictional dimension as a comment on the conventions of story-telling; like the interpolated stories in the *Quixote* the 'aventis' are highly conventionalized, with the difference that the conventions they obey are those of Hollywood rather than Renaissance Italy. But the audience's demand for a further story also makes the reader recognize that in fiction endings are always arbitrary and there is no such thing as a definitive version. The desire to tie up loose ends only leads to the discovery that there is no end. At the same time the demand for a further version will show that there is no such thing as a beginning. The loose ends which the boys wish to have explained usually involve the question of origins: they are constantly asking to hear about the 'original event' which triggered off the sequence of stories in the first place. The 'aventis' thus move backwards at the same time as they move forwards: the inability to produce a final version is the inability to get back to an original source. There can be no original source because the process is circular: it is the story of subsequent events which generates the story of the events leading up to it. The 'original story' is by definition a sequel. The process is without end and without beginning.

If in the Romantic quest myth the search for lost origins leads to enlightenment, in *Si te dicen que caí* it leads precisely to mythification. The reasons for this are partly political: the original source which explains the story of Aurora and Marcos is the Civil War, the truth about which will never be known. The novel describes a society in which there are no original events but only versions: even the Victory Day parade has the theatricality of a 'dress rehearsal' (301). A large number of scenes involve dramatic representations: the church play, the boys' interrogations of the orphan girls – in the theatre dressing-room – in which they enact Aurora's story and the *chekas* of the war, the sexual performances for Conrado, La Fueguiña and Conrado's acting out of sequences from songs, Menchu's career as a chorus-girl. The most poignant case of this replacement of history by representation is that of La Fueguiña, forced to act out her rape by Moorish troops in the Civil War: 'la galleguita se interpretaba a sí misma con lágrimas de verdad' ['the little Galician girl played herself and cried real tears'] (231).

The impossibility of recovering the original event behind the mythifications, except by means of further mythification, is however not a problem exclusive to Spain in the 1940s but one inherent in all fiction that claims to give a faithful portrait of an original reality. *Si te dicen que caí* does say something about the real world of Franco's Spain but it does so by producing a series of versions which are self-consciously mythical. At the same time the novel shows an understanding of the fact that the desire to get back to an original source is a basic factor in the generation of fiction. The 'aventis' frequently double back on their tracks to tell the story of 'the first time'. No sooner are we told in the first 'aventi' in the novel that Java is embarking on his fifth visit to Conrado's flat than we flash back to a description of his first visit. His visit to Aurora starts with him going to her brothel room in the Calle Robadors, flashes back to 'the first time' in Conrado's flat (243) which leads further back to her description of 'the first time' she slept with a man (245), then imperceptibly shifts to a later visit to her by Java in her rented room in the Calle Legalidad ('the first time she had invited him home', 251–2), finally – in response to audience demand: 'Let's get back to the Calle Robadors, to the first time' (253) – returning to the original point of departure. Variant versions will be given of Java's 'first encounter' with both Conrado and Aurora: the concept of the 'original event' is undermined as the 'aventi' in chapter 1 – which purported to describe the 'first meeting' of these three characters – is succeeded by the 'aventi' about Java at the Bishop's Palace, now proposed as the 'really first meeting' of Java and Conrado (104), and by the description of what is now said to be Java's 'really first meeting' with Aurora in the police station (296). The episode of Java's encounter with the Bishop shows that Ñito does not remember the 'aventis' in the order in which they were told, which further complicates the question of which version is the original: in chapter 8 Sarnita promises to tell the story of Java's meeting with the Bishop, but it is actually recalled by Ñito in chapter 7. The recurrence in the episodes set in the Bishop's Palace and in the police station of details and phrases from the 'aventi' in chapter 1 – with the bishop taking on Conrado's attributes and the police watching Java and Aurora through a spy-hole – makes us feel that it is the account of the later meeting narrated in the first chapter that has generated the subsequent accounts of the supposed 'original version'. The spy-hole in the police station is put forward as the explanation of the origin of Aurora's horror of being spied on, but we are given another explanation in the story of Conrado spying on her making love to her boyfriend: the episode in the police station is narrated last as if it were the 'positively first time' but in fact it occurs later (after the war). Yet another version of the spy-hole situation – repeating multiple details and phrases from the 'aventi' in chapter 1 – occurs without Aurora being present, with Java and La Fueguiña grappling with each other in the play directed from behind the curtain by Conrado (119–26). Since this scene is narrated as an 'event', whereas what appears to be its prototype in chapter 1 is clearly an 'aventi', we begin to wonder whether the later scene is not in fact the original. Which would mean that the 'original event' is a theatrical performance. We have the same situation as with the variant versions of the death of Conrado's father, where the film version narrated first (176) may well generate the later account of what is put forward as the 'original event' (250–1). The variant versions of how Aurora originally got her scars – Aurora's account in which El Tuerto accidentally injured her with the corkscrew (247), Sarnita's account of the microfilm sewn under her skin (267–9) – show how the desire to produce the definitive original version leads to even wilder speculation. As Sarnita concludes on this occasion: 'it all sounds like an old conspiracy, sir, a settling of accounts from the distant past whose motives all the conspirators have forgotten' (269). In the same way the urban guerrillas' activities obey 'an ideal whose origin they had almost lost sight of' (357). The original cause is irremediably lost from view: all that is left is to act out a series of performances, or to tell a series of stories. As in the Romantic definition, myth is a re-enactment of a lost original; but it does not recover the past, it merely supplants it with a fictional double.

The notion of doubles is fundamental to the novel. There can be no original because everything comes in doubles. Aurora has two scars; Conrado has two homes; Marcos goes into hiding twice; Java will have twins (further duplicated by their 'exact photographic reproduction' in Java's car [34]). This duplication undermines the uniqueness of the characters and situations, producing the effect of the stereotypes and formulaic clusters of oral narrative. But it also works against oral narrative in that the effect is not to facilitate recognition but to blur identities and locations. What we have is the double in the sense of the stand-in, but it becomes impossible to tell what stands in for what. The fictional version is a stand-in for reality – as Sarnita notes, the cinema 'is a lie, they're doubles' (159) – but the characters' concept of reality is also modelled on fictional prototypes: hence the impossibility of knowing whether the film *Arsène Lupin* generates Aurora's firsthand account of the death of Conrado's father, or vice versa. Appropriately both the film and Aurora's account, which constitutes its double, contain further examples of doubles. Arsène Lupin assumes the false identity of a look-alike duke; Conrado's father is shot in a case of mistaken identity instead of his son.[32] A nice example of this technique of duplication occurs with Sarnita's mention of the same 'sparrows flying above the morning mist' when describing the backcloth in the theatre and his country childhood (328, 337): again the first mention is a representation and the second an autobiographical 'fact', suggesting that the latter may be derived from the former rather than vice versa. As in oral narrative, set epithets are used to introduce the characters – 'marinero' or 'musarañas' for Marcos, 'carota' for Palau, 'legañoso' for Java – but the fact that the epithet is used instead of the proper name rather than in conjunction with it (as in Homer's 'wily Ulysses') complicates matters by giving the impression that the characters have two names, as indeed many have. In some cases is it simply a matter of a nickname and the real name – Sarnita/Antonio, Java/Daniel, Tetas/José María, La Fueguiña/María, El Tuerto or Flecha Negra/Justiniano, El Taylor/ Meneses, Menchu/Carmen – but in others the two names represent the same character in early and later life: Sarnita/Ñito, Aurora/ Ramona (to avoid confusion, I have so far referred solely to 'Aurora'). The novel is of course also divided into two parallel sets of chapters: those about the boys and Aurora, and those about the urban guerrillas and Menchu. Each set is thus in turn subdivided into two parallel stories, which subsequently merge as will the two parallel sets of chapters. This merging takes place not only on account of the urban guerrilla Marcos' relationship with Aurora and Sarnita/Ñito's function as common narrator, but also through the blurring of the characters Aurora and Menchu who become doubles of one another. This duplication cannot be explained by suggesting they are the same person for Marcos will talk to Aurora about Menchu; and although the description of the corpse dug up in the final 'aventi' (identified by Sarnita as Aurora) corresponds to that two chapters earlier of the murdered Menchu (the open neck wound, the turban, the scorpion bracelet), Menchu had been killed in winter while this victim dies in summer and the bomb explosions and additional male corpse do not fit Menchu's story.[33] There is another duplication in this scene with the Ford car, mentioned early on as the urban guerrillas' car in which Menchu was murdered and which Jaime Viñas abandoned in the Solar Can Compte (still with fresh bloodstains and a tuft of blonde hair), and later in the chapter as the rusty Ford chassis already dumped in the Solar Can Compte when the boys told their first 'aventis' nine years before in 1940. Marcos and Aurora ironically run past the Ford without seeing it just as they had failed to notice the flowering almond invented by Ñito, suggesting that one car is a fictional transposition of the other. The point is that it is impossible to say which car is the original and which the secondary version for – like Aurora and Menchu – both appear simultaneously in the final 'aventi'. Throughout the novel there is a network of references linking Aurora and Menchu as doubles: both are dyed blondes and at different points wear turbans

166

(67, 174, 303, 342), a ruby cross (68, 135, 160) and high-heeled green shoes (67, 140, 244). Both are identified as the orphan who creeps under Marcos' blanket in the war (68, 267). La Fueguiña tells us that both of them were at the orphanage at the same time and suggests the boys are confusing them (142). But we cannot conclude that they are two different characters any more than that they are the same character. They are two variant versions of the same possibility: both orphans forced into prostitution, both dying violent deaths, but one successful and the other not. This is made explicit when Sarnita suggests to Java that there are two possible versions of Aurora's life he can give Señora Galán: that corresponding to Menchu and that corresponding to Aurora/Ramona (167–8). At the end of the novel Luis Lage will offer alternative explanations of the prostitute's death in the Solar Can Compte, one of which fits Menchu's story while the other fits Aurora's story. As Palau comments, she was simply 'one of many' (358): her twin incarnation as Menchu–Aurora makes her representative of all those forced into prostitution after the war: not an individual but an archetype.[34]

A similar duplication occurs with Conrado. Apart from the blurring of his description with that of the Bishop, his tortoise-like head will be projected on to the crippled TV detective Ironside (102) and, curiously, on to the tramp Mianet (236). More disconcertingly still, Conrado's attributes fuse with those of his political enemy Marcos. Sarnita's imagined confession will describe Marcos in his hideout striking the ground with Conrado's stick and, like Conrado, needing massage for 'his legs deformed by immobility', continuing with a sentence – 'His was a life viewed in a rearview mirror' (267) – that could apply to either character. In Java's confession, the objects in Marcos' hideout will include Conrado's towel and the bottles he broke when spying on Aurora and her boyfriend; he will then become a dual figure dreaming behind his spy-hole of love (Marcos) and shrapnel (Conrado) and of a joint future blown up by a bomb (Marcos) and watching sexual performances on the carpet depicting Torrijos' execution (Conrado). The description ends with a phrase explicitly referring to both of them: 'Both enveloped in the fire of their impotence and thirst for revenge' (294–5). In this case the blurring of identities serves to break down the political opposition between victor and vanquished in the Civil War, showing that the Nationalist myth of 'the two Spains' is a simplification of a more complex and disturbing reality. The description of characters via a repeated list of set attributes, which in oral narrative serves to create recognizable stereotypes, is used critically to show that stereotypes are a falsification.

The duplication created by this transposition of images from one context on to another also breaks down temporal distinctions, as phrases and motifs move backwards and forwards in time. Lévi-Strauss has observed that mythical narrative uses repetition to produce a static effect, annulling temporality. In *Si te dicen que caí* the effect created is rather that of a 'vertigo of time' (322): a free-floating *perpetuum mobile* moving in all directions simultaneously. For the 'aventis' are as much anticipations of the future as they are a return to an original source: Sarnita tells stories 'based not only on the bloody events of the past but also on events to come' (71). In Java's stories, reality is 'a dense, murky substance that would take some time to float to the surface' (41) partly because the reality at their source cannot be expressed openly but also because, being speculative accounts of 'what might happen', they foreshadow events to come. The novel starts with the end of the story, which it will then attempt to catch up with like a dog – or scorpion – chasing its tail. The characters are trapped in their story because the end has been anticipated from the start. For the boys, the end of the story announced in the first 'aventi' of 1940 – the death of the prostitute in the Solar Can Compte in 1949 – is a fantasy projection; for Ñito looking back with hindsight, it is past history. The double narrative perspective produces an inextricable superimposition of fantasy and memory. The novel makes the point that, no matter how much fiction – as a form of myth-making – may give the impression it is 'recounting', it is in fact inventing. It is this failure to recover the past that makes it progressive as well as regressive.

The two-way process of invention and memory is made explicit in the first two paragraphs – both of which encapsulate in miniature the story to come – starting respectively 'He relates' and 'He remembers". The final bomb explosion is announced twice in chapter 1 and a third time at the end of chapter 4, which means that it is simultaneously anticipated and retold. On the second occasion it is announced from a point of time 'many years later' when what is now the future will be memory (16). Menchu's death will likewise be anticipated – and re-told – three times: in chapters 14, 17 and 21. El

Taylor's death will also be both anticipated and recounted (312, 322–3). The continual mixing of conditional, future, present and past tenses further blurs the difference between imagining and recounting. Frequently – particularly at the beginning of a paragraph – finite verbs will be omitted so we cannot tell from the tense of the verb whether the passage is remembered or anticipated. Different layers of memory and speculation converge at the start of chapter 5, where Sor Paulina tells Ñito her memory of seeing Java and La Fueguiña in the church, into which she inserts her own fantasy reconstruction of Java's fantasy reconstruction – 'he speculated, she said, now I remember' (73) – of La Fueguiña's memory of the church being burnt down during the war. A particularly nice case of a fantasy reconstruction occurs in chapter 12 where Ñito, having been told that Java married an orphan called Pilar, tries to jog his memory by relating a series of invented recollections of the orphanage in which a hypothetical 'Pili' appears. Ironically, a 'Pilar' had figured in Ñito's earlier memories of the orphanage (51, 56) recounted to Sor Paulina before learning that Pilar was the girl Java married. Perhaps the most complex blend of memory and fantasy occurs in chapter 4, the first to deal with the urban guerrillas and Menchu. As in chapter 1, the two opening paragraphs encapsulate in miniature the story to come. The first anticipates a series of guerrilla attacks that will take place in later chapters, again in the form of memories recalled from a point of time 'many years later'. In the second paragraph Menchu's story is anticipated, only to be incorporated within memory as Marcos goes on to recall his conversation with Palau, in which the latter recalls earlier conversations with the other guerrillas, during which Palau has a fantasy vision of his future robbery of Menchu at the Ritz, within which Menchu will recall her past (including the time she slept with Marcos during the war), within which she will in turn look forward to her future as the Baroness' maid. This creates an impossible play of perspective as Marcos remembers Palau's vision of an invented Menchu's memory of having slept with Marcos: an impossibility that will be resolved by our discovery in the final paragraph that the whole chapter is a fantasy reconstruction by Sarnita of the memories inside an imagined Marcos' head. The 'aventis' are precisely that: fantasy reconstructions.

The narrative anticipates the future as well as recounting the past also in that the performances it describes are both re-enactments and rehearsals. The boys make the orphan girls act out what they call 'rehearsals' of Aurora's story, which at the same time are re-enactments of the *chekas* of the past. As Sarnita will say to La Fueguiña: 'es una función muy especial ... son cosas que aún tienen que pasar pero las sabemos de memoria' ['it's a very special kind of performance ... things that have still to happen but we've learnt them off by heart/we know them from memory'] (138). They are literally rehearsing the church play, which is never put on. Everything is a re-enactment or a rehearsal: there is no definitive performance. Java's sexual performances for Conrado become re-enactments and rehearsals through the network of re-takes which makes each individual performance an echo of a previous one and an anticipation of one to come. What in the early stages of the novel are anticipations of a future version, by the end have become re-takes of the previous anticipation: there is no actual event, only a set of self-reflecting mirror-images.

The novel shifts from an initial balance between anticipation and memory to an ever greater reliance on memory. The boys' forward-looking mythifications are systematically juxtaposed with the regressive mythifications of the urban guerrillas, who cling to the ideals of the past to preserve them intact from corruption. By refusing to accept change, they fall into the decay they are trying to avoid. Only Palau is partly exempted because of his capacity for producing fantasy visions of the future: this will not save him from corruption – as he degenerates from resistance fighter to bandit – but at least it allows him to retain a love of life (96). Marsé appears to regard history as an inevitable process of corruption, but the corruption which results from change is preferable to that which results from paralysis. It is Marcos' dread of the future as an annihilation of the past – 'a gravestone of silence coming ever nearer and threatening to entomb him' (293–4) – that unites him with Conrado as an 'ex-future corpse' (204) crippled by the war, for whom the future can hold out nothing but paralysis. Conrado's paralysis is a symbolic consequence of the Nationalist rejection of history for a return to mythical origins; the novel accuses the ex-Republicans of the same stultifying rejection of history for a Paradise Lost.

By the end of the novel, however, the boys' 'aventis' start to lose their dynamic quality as they cease to incorporate new material and start feeding off themselves. The final 'aventi' will kill off its heroes because the story-telling process has exhausted itself. The re-take that Sarnita gives of Aurora and Marcos' death is not a new version but a repetition of the same version; the boys reject it because 'The *aventi* had become one more truth like any other, heard too many times. A story composed of leftovers' (346). The 'aventis' had from the start been constructed from bits of debris – the ruins and detritus of war, the rubbish in the rag-and-bone merchant's hovel – but, as in Lévi-Strauss' definition of myth as *bricolage*, they had previously had the ability through fantasy to turn this debris into something new. The descriptions of the Barrio de Gracia abound with images of disease and dirt, a particularly graphic image being that of 'soiled snow' (26, 314). Sarnita's capacity for fantasy will transform this dereliction by installing in the midst of the rubble of the Solar Can Compte the flowering almond – described as the 'flower of snow' (279) – he has retained from his country childhood as a symbol of the need for illusion: 'If you've had a country childhood, you'll carry a flowering almond inside you for the rest of your life' (335). The scars of war on the almond-tree have been embellished with messages of love (45). It is because the 'aventis' are an embellishment of reality that they are able to redeem the sordidness of the present by keeping alive faith in the possibility of things being otherwise. The need for illusion will make Sarnita present Java's encounter with Aurora as a love story rather than describe 'the disgusting truth' (255), and will make him insist that La Fueguiña caused the fire at the theatre because she was in love with Java (331). It is the episode of the fire – the destruction of the theatre as a chamber of illusion – that marks the beginning of the end for the 'aventis'. Only Sarnita will prefer a fictional version – the fire has appropriately left untouched the theatre backcloth with the 'sparrows flying above the morning mist' that he associates with his country childhood (328) – to an eye-witness account: '"Forget the *aventis*," said Mingo. "Facts are facts, like it or not"' (334). For as the boys grow up, they lose their capacity for illusion and start to make concessions to the sordid reality around them, abandoning Sarnita under his almond-tree (346). Java will go so far as to burn the ingredients of the 'aventis' on his symbolic bonfire (350).[35] But in a sense it was the 'aventis' that, by allowing him to act out the role of hero, had given him his apprenticeship for the future. The urban guerrillas are wrong to

171

reject the future for the past, but Java is also wrong to reject the past for the future. By betraying Marcos, he betrays the past and embraces a future of corruption. His 'obsession with speed' (35) will lead him to a 'naufragio' (a moral as well as a physical drowning) in which his eyes take on the same stagnant look that had terrified him in the eyes of the resigned La Fueguiña (114). For if the rejection of change leads to paralysis, the rejection of the past leads to the death of illusion. The 'aventis' – poised halfway between childhood (looking forward) and adulthood (looking backward) – offer a precarious balance, serving as a testimony to a suppressed past while refusing to become enslaved by it.

This does not mean that, as mythifications, the 'aventis' are not corrupt. All versions are necessarily corrupt in that they supplant an original. But fantasy and memory represent different forms of corruption. Fantasy, in its attempt to transform the world, makes no claim to fidelity. Memory claims to be faithful to an original but in practice betrays it. Fantasy corrupts actively; memory is corrupt. Java will assume the fantasy role of Lucifer, the rebel who opts for corruption rather than submit to God's design. Not only does fantasy actively corrupt the truth; it also seeks to corrupt others in that it is a seduction process. Sarnita's fictions give him 'authority' (329) by captivating the other boys. The authority conferred by fiction – like that of Lucifer – is an illegitimate authority snatched by devious means from those who hold power: it is by telling stories that Java is able to reverse the master–slave relationship in which he stands with regard to Señora Galán, and the boys are able to evade the authority of El Tuerto. But if fantasy is an attempt at mastery, memory is a form of slavery to the past. Fantasy seduces; memory is seduced. The attempt to be faithful that is memory leads by default to the same corruption that fantasy sets out to achieve. By living in terms of the past, the urban guerrillas end up losing 'their true memory' (262). Memory is constantly associated in the novel with death and putrefaction: Ñito remembers the past in the morgue in autumn, looking into the dead Java's eyes in search of 'nameless corruptions' and 'the murky record of a lifetime' (113–14). The corruptibility of Ñito's memory is stressed: his mind is clouded by alcohol; working in a basement, he is blinded by the light (101). He will mix up the pills in Sor Paulina's dispensary just as his memory mixes up people and events (40). Of the two forms of corruption constituted by memory and fantasy, the latter is preferable. It is better to seduce than to be seduced.

The concepts of corruption and seduction are central to the novel. The emphasis on sexual degradation can be read as a statement about the seduction process that is fiction. The heroes and heroines of the novel are prostitutes and voyeurs. Aurora, trapped by the past, incarnates the prostitution process that is memory; Menchu and Java, who succeed in using prostitution to obtain mastery over others and free themselves from the past, incarnate the prostitution process that is fantasy. All the scenes of prostitution described in the novel are performed for the benefit of a voyeur who 'scripts' the performance and is also the recipient of the titillation, functioning as both surrogate narrator and surrogate reader. The pornographic nature of so many of the 'aventis' makes the point that fiction is by definition a peep show, in which 'the real thing' is replaced by a simulation or performance. Marcos – narrator of the stories about Menchu and the urban guerrillas – represents the voyeurism of memory, which compounds impotence. Sarnita – the principal teller of 'aventis', whose characteristic pose is that of the 'mirón' ['peeping tom'] – represents the voyeurism of fantasy, which allows him to seduce others. Almost all the characters become voyeurs at certain points. Paulina's act of voyeurism – spying on the boys torturing La Fueguiña – will lead her to become a nun to obliterate her memories of the past. Aurora will be marked for life by spying on the execution of Conrado's father through the car window. The urban guerrillas' attempts to revive the past reduce them to seeing the outside world via the rearview mirror of their various motor cars, just as Marcos and Conrado view life via the rearview mirror of memory (267). The most ingenious voyeur is Mianet, ex-Republican soldier turned tramp, who sustains a capacity for enjoying life by 'mirando cuadros' ['looking at peep-shows'] in the mirror tucked in his shoe. The 'cuadros' in his mirror parallel the fantasy images contemplated by the girls outside the cinema on whom he spies (237). The voyeurs who see life through the rearview mirror of memory have no control over the images that parade before them; those that live in terms of fantasy are able to compensate for their powerlessness by producing images of their own. In this sense the principal voyeur in the novel – Conrado – stands in an ambiguous position: his paralysis sentences him to viewing life through a rearview mirror, but at the same time –

as director of the performances acted by Aurora, Java and La Fueguiña – he does achieve a measure of release from impotence. The reason why Conrado is able to dictate the performances acted for his benefit is, of course, that as a Nationalist war hero his physical impotence is compensated by social influence. The power of the artistic creator is implicitly likened to the power of those who exercise authority in that both occupy the position of voyeur: the police will spy on Java and Aurora at the police station (297), the cells in the torture centre will be fitted with spy-holes (315). When Java notes 'el caprichoso poder del que dispuso la escena' ['the arbitrary power of the producer/designer'] (285), he is referring both to that of Conrado for whom he is performing sexually ('haciendo cuadros') and to that of the artist responsible for the painting ('cuadro') of Torrijos' execution.

Just as the police force the priest Ramón to perform a series of acts and finally to undress, so fiction is based on the assumption that the characters will go through a series of motions in order finally to reveal their true selves. Annette Kuhn has noted that the concepts of 'dressing up' and 'undressing' are fundamental both to pornography and to the thriller. Pornography requires individuals to be reduced to stock characters acting out prescribed roles in fancy dress in order to defuse the threatening nature of the sexual acts performed by making it clear they are simulated. But at the same time it depends on the assumption that some kind of 'truth' will be revealed when the last item of clothing is removed. In similar fashion the thriller provides its 'thrills' by suggesting that the characters are assuming false disguises which will be 'stripped off' at the end. The climax does come in both pornography and the thriller, but it can never be more than masturbatory because it is achieved by a fictional stand-in (the male stud, the detective who penetrates the mystery). The notion of striptease is essential to both, in that they titillate the reader with the promise of a revelation which is delayed till the last and which, when it comes, provides only vicarious pleasure.[36] By making use of the conventions of both pornography and the thriller, *Si te dicen que caí* suggests an analogy between pornography and fiction. Like fiction, pornography is above all a form of representation. As Susan Sontag, in a classic essay, has said: 'Experiences aren't pornographic; only images and representations – structures of the imagination – are.'[37] Robin Fiddian and Peter Evans note that

174

the cinematographic references in the novel make it a study of forms of representation; its recourse to pornography makes this even more explicit.[38] Just as the boys 'rehearse' with the orphan girls in the dressing-room of the theatre, obliging them to dress up in order to undress them in search of the truth, so in the 'aventis' the voyeuristic scenario will be repeated as different characters dress and undress for the benefit of the reader, who is titillated with the promise that all will finally be revealed. If Java is master of the pornographic art of postponing climax in order to prolong the performance, Sarnita is master of the fictional art of delaying the end of the story for as long as possible in order to achieve maximum excitement. Like Scheherazade he knows that fiction is a seduction process which captivates the listener by keeping him in a state of frustration: 'Así hay que pintarla ante la doña: vivita y coleando, siempre al alcance de nuestra mano pero sin pillarla nunca' ['That's the way to describe her to Señora Galán: alive and kicking, all the time just in sight but just out of reach'] (168).

Pornography is corrupt not only because it replaces reality with a simulacrum but also because the performance is put on for the benefit of a spectator who holds absolute power. *Si te dicen que caí* is an exposure of pornography in that it undermines the degrading power relationships that allow it to function. In an inversion of the usual situation, the pornographic scenes are narrated not from the viewpoint of the voyeur, but from that of the performers forced to enact his will.[39] The novel consistently adopts the viewpoint of the victim: whether La Fueguiña being tortured by the boys, the boys being interrogated by El Tuerto, or Java and Aurora performing for Conrado. The only time events are narrated from El Tuerto's point of view is when he, in turn, becomes the torture victim. When Java performs with Aurora both their points of view, as victims, are given; but when he performs with Ado, his social superior, we see only Java's point of view. This depiction of scenes of victimization from the victim's point of view makes the latter the active party, seducing the voyeur/torturer – placed in the passive position of audience – through his/her performance. Power thus passes into the hands of the dispossessed. The reader is of course also in the position of voyeur looking in on a peep-show. In pornography – as indeed in realist fiction in general – the reader is given the illusion he is in command inasmuch as the sequences acted out on the printed page appear to be presented for his sole attention. In *Si te dicen que caí* the alarming profusion of voyeurs within the text forces the reader to accept that he is not the primary recipient of the performances recounted in it. At the same time the fact that the reaction of the voyeur within the text is not described allows the reader to establish a direct relationship with the performance being acted out, with the result that he too is seduced and loses his position of command. The seduction of the reader is, however, very different from that experienced by the reader of pornography. For the narration of events from the point of view of the performers means that the reader goes 'backstage' and sees for himself their humiliation and capacity for endurance. The reader is seduced not by the pornographic acts but by the emotions of the performers. The fact that the reader is made aware that the performance is not for real makes him reflect on the artificial nature of the power relations that create the pornographic scenario.

The novel's self-conscious recourse to pornography thus serves the cause of demythification. Pornography has been likened to political propaganda in that its stereotypes simplify the complexity of human relationships, giving the impression that people are automatons with a fixed role to play. George Steiner has suggested that pornography is part of 'the general reduction of privacy and individual style in a mass consumer civilization', also raising the issue of the relation between 'the dehumanization of the individual in pornography and the making naked and anonymous of the individual in the totalitarian state (the concentration camp being the logical epitome of that state)'.[40] The use of pornography in *Si te dicen que caí* can be related to its depiction of a society governed by the combined ideology of the Falange and of capitalism, transmitted via Hollywood. The censorship of sexual scenes in the imported movies shown in Spain in the 1940s did not alter the pornographic nature of the stereotyped relations depicted in them. *Si te dicen que caí* uses stereotypes in order to undermine them: by blurring the identities of 'goodie' and 'baddie', of rich and poor, of victor and vanquished; and by inverting the power relations between voyeur/dictator and performer/victim. In her brilliantly argued 'Polemical preface' to *The Sadeian Woman*, Angela Carter likens pornography both to propaganda and to myth in its reduction of human behaviour to a set of archetypes abstracted from the historically determined reality of social relations. Carter argues in favour of a 'moral pornography' that would use its depiction of sexual relations as a means of exposing the social relations that lie behind them.[41] *Si te dicen que caí* is an example of just such a 'moral pornography'. The use of pornography in the novel exposes the mechanics of the seduction process that is fiction at the same time as it exposes the mechanics of the power relations governing society. Fiction is shown to be a form of myth-making, but it can be used to unmask the political myths that encourage us to accept as natural power relations that are man-made and the result of specific historical circumstances: in this case, the Civil War. The depiction of the Nationalist Conrado as a sexual pervert may seem sensationalist, but it is necessary to make the point that the power relations over which he presides are pornographic: that is, a perversion of the natural. By making him a character in their own pornographic stories, the boys create a counter-porno-graphy in which roles are reversed: not only is the voyeur placed in the power of those performing for him but he becomes a performer in turn. The novel takes the reader backstage – into the theatre dress-ing-room where much of the novel takes place – to show him the fictional nature not only of the pornographic scenes he is reading, but also of a society where the falsification of human relations has turned everything into representation. Fiction is a mirror of society precisely because, as a mythification, it reproduces the corruption process.

6

Fiction as release: *San Camilo, 1936,* *Reivindicación del conde don Julián,* *La saga/fuga de J.B.*

The three novels discussed in the preceding chapters provide a critical examination of the various ways in which man converts history into myth. In *Tiempo de silencio*, the characters attempt to give their insecure lives a compensatory solidity; in *Volverás a Región*, reason relegates fear and desire to a mythical exclusion zone, while memory recalls only what failed to happen; *Si te dicen que caí* consists of a string of tall stories that make a mockery of the concept of an official version of history. In all three cases what matters is the suppressed historical reality that makes its presence felt beneath the surface mythifications of the text. All three novels resort to irony to make the reader aware of the unreliability of language. The three novels that will be briefly examined in this chapter also use irony to subvert official versions of Spanish history but in this case the mythical versions are opposed not to an unspoken – perhaps unspeakable – truth, but to a counter-mythification. Martín-Santos, Benet and Marsé regard the gap between language and reality as tragic; it is because language is by definition a tool of mythification that official lies and individual rationalizations are so hard to avoid. But Cela, Juan Goytisolo and Torrente Ballester welcome the divorce between language and reality as a liberation from the 'nightmare of history'. In *Tiempo de silencio* and *Si te dicen que caí*, the humour derived from the ironic contrast between surface mythification and underlying reality is tinged with pathos if not bitterness. In *Volverás a Región*, the ironic exposure of the failure of language to recapture the past is sombre in the extreme; such comic touches as do exist derive from the extravagant use of metaphor which makes the reader all the more aware of the gap between language and reality. Whereas *Reivindicación del conde don Julián* and *La saga/fuga de J.B.* are simply funny; even *San Camilo, 1936* – despite, or perhaps because of, its unpleasantness – produces a reaction of laughter rather than of reflection. In all three novels humour has the function of release. If the use of irony by Martín-Santos, Benet and Marsé falls into the category of what Kierkegaard called Socratic irony, which has the ethical function of making the reader aware of the existence of an alternative truth, that of Cela, Juan Goytisolo and Torrente Balles-ter falls into Kierkegaard's opposing category of Romantic irony, which dismisses everything as illusory.[1] Benet may show the concept of history as progress to be an illusion, but his novel demonstrates the tragic inescapability of history in the form of the destructive passage of time: it is the young Republicans who try to liberate themselves from time by opting for a mythical eternal present of pleasure who suffer the greatest defeat. It is just such a refuge in Eros as a release from history that will be proposed by Cela, Juan Goytisolo and Torrente Ballester. The latter are concerned to demythify official versions of history not because such versions are mythical but because they attempt to pass themselves off as history: that is, because they take history seriously. When Marsé subverts the myths of officialdom by resorting to counter-mythification it is in order to reveal the existence, beneath the proliferation of mythical versions, of a lost original: the historical reality of the Civil War and its aftermath. The three novels studied in this chapter replace official myths with counter-mythification either (in the case of *San Camilo, 1936* and *Reivindicación del conde don Julián*) because Spanish history is written off as beyond redemption, or (in the case of *La saga/fuga de J.B.*) because myth is much more fun. In all three cases history is equated with repression, and myth with liberation.

San Camilo, 1936 (1969) by Camilo José Cela is concerned not with demythifying specific official versions of Spanish history, but with rejecting all accepted accounts whether by historians of the Right or of the Left. It is the writing of history as such that is under attack. The novel's collective vision inevitably brings to mind Unamuno's theory of *intrahistoria*, whereby political change is dismissed as 'surface' agitation leaving untroubled the 'depths' of the sea of history, constituted by the everyday life of the people. What Unamuno meant by this was that historical change was a 'betrayal' of the 'essential roots' of the nation, represented by the folk whose 'closeness to nature' he saw as an antidote to the alienation of history. If Cela rejects political analysis for description of the everyday lives of a cross-section of inhabitants of Madrid before, on and after 18 July 1936 (the Feast of St Camillo de Lellis, Cela's name-day, and the day Franco proclaimed the Nationalist uprising), it is in order to depict a *pueblo* which is not only urban rather than rural but – far from being 'natural' – is degraded and perverted. Cela's gallery of mindless, worthless individuals shows the 'depths' of Spanish history to be every bit as 'superficial' and 'inauthentic' as the historical events in which they are enmeshed. Cela rejects the historian's focus on political figures – here relegated to the status of minor characters; both the Republican and Nationalist martyrs Teniente Castillo and Calvo Sotelo are first introduced anonymously – not in order to show the unsung heroism of the many but because he does not believe in heroism. Even Engracia, who dies for the Republican cause in the assault on the Nationalist-held Montaña barracks, is depicted as 'perverted' by a straightlaced political idealism; her boyfriend's decision after her death to give up politics and open a night-club is related with evident approval. The only other decent couple in the novel – Victoriano and Virtudes – die as victims of a historical accident: the shooting of Victoriano in mistake for a fascist as he runs out into the street to get medical help for his wife in labour. This reduction of historical tragedy to a case of mistaken identity reinforces the notion – implicit in Unamuno's theory of *intrahistoria* and explicit in Ganivet's *Idearium español* – that Spain's history has been a deviation or error. This impression is compounded by the juxtaposition throughout the novel of political and accidental violence. Paul Ilie has accused Cela of irresponsibility in omitting any mention of the political issues that led to the Civil War.[2] What must be stressed is that Cela's presentation of historical events as accidents or mistakes, lacking in any cause or motive, is a direct echo of the Nationalist belief – taken from the 1898 writers – that contemporary history is a deviation or error.[3] Just as José Antonio rejected party politics as divisive and argued for an all-embracing 'totalitarian' state, so Cela goes out of his way to juxtapose events in both political camps not in order to write a non-partisan version of the war but in order to make all political programmes look interchangeable and therefore futile. (The novel's dedication likewise attacks foreign intervention on both sides, further stressing the 'inauthenticity' of Spanish history.) The only 'wholeness' achieved by Cela's breaking down of political divisions is, however, the far from wholesome mingling of Right and Left in the promiscuity of the brothel, the morgue and the cemetery. We have the Falangist desire to overcome the alienating divisions of history without the corresponding belief in a return to purity.

The novel is an attempt to expose the false clarity imposed on historical events by historians writing with hindsight, but its emphasis on the confusion of events as experienced at the time is also an attempt to blur all distinctions and reduce history to a monotonous and meaningless sameness. If *Tiempo de silencio* stressed the need to face the absurdity of history in the sense of the contradictions that produce movement and change, *San Camilo, 1936* reduces history to absurdity in the sense that – as in *La colmena* – it is futile repetition. A large proportion of the text consists of lists of alternatives, not in order to show the multiple possibilities open to the individual, but in order to create the impression that it makes no difference what happens. For Cela history is absurd in the sense that it is random, something which happens to people rather than being the result of their actions. All events are alike in that they are an alien imposition. As in *La colmena*, history is shown to be the product of inertia, habit, tedium and fatigue. Man, being the victim of history rather than its agent, is impotent to change the pattern. As in Unamuno's theory of *intrahistoria*, the emphasis on the common man leads to the idea of a basic unchangeability underlying the nation's history, with the important difference that Cela does not see this as a redeeming feature but as a sign of eternal damnation. Cela's mythical vision coincides with Nationalist ideology in seeing history as the product of original sin, but without the belief in redemption that provided a theoretical justification for the Nationalist uprising. His negative view of history can be seen as the combined result of his early Nationalist associations and subsequent disenchantment with the 'new dawn' held out by Francoism. In *San Camilo, 1936* – as in *La colmena* – dawn rises in a cemetery: in this case as the seal is set on Spain's historical fate with the burial of Teniente Castillo and Calvo Sotelo, whose deaths – in the novel as in the Nationalist version of history – unleash the ensuing violence.[4] Perhaps the most chilling image of this negation of hope for the future is that of the brothel-keeper Doña Sacramento burning on the kitchen stove the corpse of her stillborn granddaughter.

The impression of unchangeability is heightened by the novel's cyclical structure, undermining the superficial chronology of events. Cela rejects the logical linear progression that historians impose on past events. The absence of causal analysis combined with the persistent use of repetition creates a sense of uncontrollable escalation: such progression as there is consists of more of the same but worse. Cela's cyclical view of history – again as in *La colmena* – does not suppose that decay leads to rebirth but that history is doomed to repeat itself: indeed each successive repetition leads to increased exhaustion and decadence. The three parts of *San Camilo, 1936* form a symmetrical structure, with the second part – 18 July – acting as a central pivot, and the first and third parts – the days immediately preceding and following – consisting each of exactly 168 pages.[5] The epilogue forms a coda, suggesting a musical structure: an impression reinforced by the use throughout of recurring motifs or refrains – for example, the references to Napoleon or 'King Cyril of England' – and the contrapuntal interweaving of the vast cast of characters, with the end of Part 3 recapitulating the motifs and characters introduced in Part 1. One is reminded of Lévi-Strauss' likening of myth to music, in that both use repetition to annul linear progression. A musical structure will be explicitly imposed on the historical reality of the Civil War in Cela's later novel *Mazurca para dos muertos* (1983). A similar effect is created by the use of references to nature – 'a lo mejor son las fases de la luna ... o las mareas' ['it's probably the phases of the moon ... or the tides'] (166); 'es como un oleaje, mejor como una marea de histeria colectiva que los guardias no podrán detener' ['it's like a wave or rather a tide of collective hysteria the police will be unable to stem'] (203); 'la gente ya se calmará, las aguas vuelven siempre a sus cauces' ['people will calm down in time, the river always resumes its natural course'] (320); 'los carneros van siempre a donde hay yerba verde' ['the rams always seek out the greenest grass'] (331) – implying that history follows an immutable set of natural laws. Part 2 – the day the war breaks out – ends in the middle of a word, cutting short what promises to be an infinite repetition – 'el destino de las herramientas de las herramientas de las herram' ['the fate of implements of implements of implem'] (259) – reminding the reader of Joyce's *Finnegans Wake* or Octavio Paz's 'Piedra de sol', whose endings flow back into their beginnings in an endless cycle mirroring the natural rhythms structuring the texts. The impression that time is revolving on the spot is reinforced by the description of events taking place simultaneously in different parts of Madrid. Indeed time literally stops with the narrator's watch at the start of the novel. A Republican militiaman – echoing the 1848 July Revolution in Paris – shoots at the clock on the Ministry of the Interior, as if trying to put a stop to politics and with it history.[6] The lack of change brought by the war is suggested by the freezing of dawn breaking over the cemetery, described on p. 139 and again on p. 150 as if left in suspension during the intervening pages. The same sense of time repeating itself is given by the author's final note 'Palma de Mallorca, the week following the Feast of St Camillo, 1969', making the end of the writing of the novel coincide with the week following the Feast of St Camillo thirty-three years before that is described in the last part. This stasis is offset by the use of lists, giving the impression of a frenetic accumulation of events. A similar paradoxical blend of stasis and acceleration is produced by the lack of paragraph divisions and long sentences: it is noticeable that punctuation becomes more and more infrequent – finally almost disappearing – in the course of Part 2 as war is declared. The combined sensation of breakneck speed and paralysis is that of a nightmare in which, no matter how fast one runs, one stays nailed to the spot. The text repeatedly refers to characters – including the narrator – wanting to escape but being unable to. It is above all this reduction of history to a nightmare that makes *San Camilo, 1936* a mythical novel.

It would be a mistake to see the unpleasantness of the novel as a sensationalist gimmick: without it Cela would not have been able to create an impression of the 'nightmare of history'. Paul Ilie pertinently asks whether the novel's pornographic emphasis was approved by the censors because 'coarseness, generally forbidden in Franco's Spain, was nonetheless permissible in the depiction of Republican behaviour'.[7] The novel's view of the last days of the Republic is quite consistent with Nationalist ideology: indeed the equation it draws between the Republic and the whorehouse is directly reminiscent of Giménez Caballero's description of Republican Madrid as a latterday Sodom and whore of Babylon.[8] What is surprising is not that the censors approved Cela's reduction of history to a catalogue of perversion, but that they approved his nihilistic rejection of the possibility of a revolution that would wipe the slate clean. The novel offers no suggestion that the Nationalist uprising will bring anything other than another cycle of blood-letting. Both Right-wing and Left-wing politicians are depicted exclusively in terms of their usually perverse, if not violent, sexual activities. All politics is written off as crime. History offers two options: 'yo soy un asesino o un asesinado ... poco importa, lo malo es el plural, nosotros somos unos asesinos o unos asesinados' ['I murder or am murdered ... never mind, the problem is the plural, we murder or are murdered'] (155). The equation between history and corrup-tion is reinforced by the emphasis on putrefaction, with the refer-ences to excrement, lavatorial detritus, foul smells, and flies drown-ing in an assortment of liquids. Part 3 is dominated by the stench of Matiítas' rotting corpse in the attic, symbolizing the 'skeletons in the cupboard' of Spanish history: the pathetic homosexual's suicide-cum-orgasm as he shoots himself up the arse with the gun handed him by a militiaman stands as a grotesque image of the Republic's self-destructive perversity. The image is all the more unpleasant because, for once, it is not entirely negative. Matiítas dies with a smile on his face: his 'sacrifice' does not purge history but it does afford him a personal salvation through death and oblivion. As well as sexual perversion and violence, the novel insists on venereal and other forms of disease. By a convenient coincidence, St Camillo de Lellis is the patron saint of hospitals. The intercutting of historical events with newspaper advertisements for various elixirs and aphro-disiacs is explicitly reminiscent of the 1898 writers' suggestion that the 'body politick' was 'diseased' and suffering from an atrophy of the will (here literal impotence). The obvious quackery of the advertised remedies emphasizes the lack of a cure. Like the 1898 writers, Cela implies that Spanish history is under a curse: vitiated both in its origins – 'physically, man has not developed beyond the higher paleolithic' (127) – and in its condemnation to repetition, which turns history into an ever more grotesque caricature of itself.

This notion of history as caricature brings to mind Valle-Inclán's theory of the *esperpento*, which in his novels was allied to a cyclical view of history. Like Valle-Inclán, Cela adopts a detached 'demi-urgic' position looking down on his characters as flies (or with the narrator himself as a fly on the brothel wall). The cynical humour of Cela's narrator is that of Valle-Inclán's Devil (alias Gutenberg, the inventor of printing) in *Los cuernos de don Friolera*, laughing at a sinner hanging himself.[9] Valle-Inclán's Gnosticism allowed him to couple

his grotesque, diabolic vision with a messianic belief in revolution as
a way of purging history of evil and breaking out of the infernal cycle
of repetition: in this sense Valle-Inclán is the only writer of the 1898
Generation to combine a view of history as decadence with a positive
political message, albeit one disturbingly close to Falangist ideology.
Cela's vision seems nearer to the fatalism of the other 1898 writers: it
is not Valle-Inclán but Costa, Unamuno, Ganivet, Machado (and
the later Ortega) who are quoted by name in the text. It was
precisely because the 1898 writers and Ortega felt the national
character was congenitally flawed and beyond redemption that they
believed in the need for a 'messiah' to save Spaniards from their
errors. Cela's emphasis on the mediocrity of the 'man in the street' –
together with the immaturity of his twenty-year-old narrator –
likewise implies that Spaniards are not suited to democratic self-
government: 'la política es el arte de ... gobernar a los españoles para
que no se cacen a tiros' ['politics is the art of ... governing Spaniards
to stop them riddling each other with bullets'] (266). At the same
time it is the messianic streak in Spanish politics which is the cause of
Cela's anti-politicism. Cela's contradictions are highlighted by the
fact that it is the Messiah-figure Tío Jerónimo who singles out
'mesianismo' as Spain's 'original sin'. Tío Jerónimo denounces the
'religious incendiary' supposedly inside every Spaniard's soul, making him want to 'burn his history so when nothing is left he can
throw himself on the embers' (298); and insists that 'the answer to
crime is not more crime' (119). But the novel's emphasis on the
contagious chain of violence implies a curse that cannot be broken
(82, 155, 407). The insistence on collective guilt – 'as Spaniards we
are all guilty' (109) – could be taken as an appeal to the conscience
of every Spaniard to accept responsibility for history; but the novel's
view of history as a malign destiny which imposes itself on man –
'cada cual viene al mundo con su destino señalado, nadie puede
escaparse de lo que está escrito' ['everyone comes into this world
with his fate sealed, no one can escape what is written'] (311) –
suggests rather the notion of an original sin which even Spain's
messianic orgies of self-destruction are unable to redeem.[10] This is
perhaps the meaning of Tío Jerónimo's insistence that the Civil War
is not an apocalypse but merely a 'preventive purgation' (422): it
will not lead to the ushering in of a new millennium. Cela is careful
to put the more drastic views of the 1898 writers – Ganivet's

recommendation of blood-letting (283), Machado's description of Spain as a land marked by 'the shadow of Cain' (311) – in the mouth of Jesualdo Villegas, whose advocacy of sacrifice Tío Jerónimo rejects. But Tío Jerónimo's emphasis on the Spaniard's disposition to pyromania leads to an equally pessimistic attribution of the ills of Spanish history to a flawed national character. The novel's confirmation of the theories of national character which formed the 1898 writers' main legacy to Spanish fascism is – as Paul Ilie has warned – its most dangerous contribution to a national mythography.[11] Tío Jerónimo's confusions are those of the Krausista school of thought to which he is said to belong (68–9). While insisting that the answer is not violence but education, he nevertheless sees the remedy as being imposed from above: 'lo que necesitaría España es un hombre íntegro y decente' ['what Spain needs is a solid, upright man'] (119). This is as elitist a solution as the 'quacks and redeemers' he deplores in the same breath. The young and confused narrator oscillates between belief in the need for a purgative revolution – whether of the Right or of the Left makes no difference (116) – and, under his uncle's influence, the belief that all sacrifices are futile: 'deja que sean otros quienes ... prueben a arreglar el mundo, ... te apuntas para golfo superviviente de la tristeza, ... no tienes bastante sentimiento en el alma como para considerarte como chivo expiatorio de los torpes pecados del mundo' ['let others try to fix the world, ... you will appoint yourself the idle survivor of so much suffering, ... there is not enough love in your heart to see yourself as scapegoat for the world's vile sins'] (394). Both views have in common the mythical equation between history and evil. When Tío Jerónimo rejects history as a myth – 'luchemos cipote en ristre contra los mitos que atenazan al hombre, las banderas los himnos las condecoraciones los números las insignias el matrimonio los platos regionales el registro civil, tú y yo tenemos el deber de luchar contra los artificios que adulteran al hombre' ['we must fight prick at the ready against the myths holding man in their grip, flags anthems medals numbers badges marriage regional cooking birth certificates, you and I have the duty to fight against the fabrications adulterating man'] (439) – he does so in the name of a mythical view of history as a perversion of man's original nature.

What Tío Jerónimo is advocating is, of course, a rejection of culture ('marriage regional cooking') for nature in the form of a literally crude sexuality ('prick at the ready'). His rejection of the Spaniard's supposed tendency to 'undo' history through sacrificial violence is complemented with the suggestion that he 'undo' history by returning to animality. The previously lamented inability to break with a primitive atavism – 'physically, man has not developed beyond the higher paleolithic' – is in the epilogue put forward by Tío Jerónimo as the solution. 'Mesianismo' is rejected as a form of self-destruction – 'aquí todo el mundo quiere empezar desde el principio cada mañana' ['everyone here wants to start from scratch every morning'] (110) – but the erotic self-fulfilment Tío Jerónimo proposes is also seen as a return to origins: 'puede ser que haya que empezar por el principio' ['perhaps we ought to start with the beginning'] (435). Tío Jerónimo will literally regress to origins by suckling at the breast of his earth-mother lover Cecilia: 'a woman's milk is the source of life' (435). Throughout the novel asking for a glass of milk, downing yoghourt, fruit juice, raw eggs and vegetables, his return to nature is an advocacy of health. In a significantly Nietzschean gesture, he abandoned his wife because she was ill (69). Tío Jerónimo's ripe old age contrasts with the morbid fantasies of the twenty-year-old narrator, whose tuberculosis is an autobiographical detail on Cela's part but also a sign that he is contaminated by the malaise afflicting his country. In the epilogue Tío Jerónimo clarifies that the 'Spanish disease' is sexual repression. His 'back to the breast' message is a plea for the release of 'leche' not only in the sense of 'milk' but also in that of 'semen': 'éste es un país de leche contenida, de leche a presión, ... aquí se jode poco y mal, si los españoles jodieran a gusto serían menos brutos y mesiánicos, habría menos héroes y menos mártires pero también menos asesinos y a lo mejor funcionaban las cosas' ['this is a country of repressed semen, of pent-up semen, ... Spaniards don't fuck often enough or well enough, if they enjoyed fucking they'd be less violent and messianic, there'd be fewer heroes and fewer martyrs but also fewer murderers and things might work properly'] (319). Spain's proverbial 'cainismo' is quite literally 'mala leche' ('spite'/'bad semen').

In its Reichian suggestion that sexual repression is the cause of political violence, and in its prescription of Buddha plus Nietzsche (17) or Buddha, St Francis plus sexual liberation (438-9), *San Camilo, 1936* is a product of the 1960s.[12] It is also an instructive example of the political ambiguity of 1960s radicalism, whose mystical cult of the natural could all too easily slip into a nihilistic apoliticism. Unlike Reich, Cela equates sexual repression not with political repression in the form of fascism but with politics of any kind: hence the depiction of politicians of all colours in terms of their sexual activities. Reich's theories could have been used to make the point that the Republic made significant advances in the direction of sexual emancipation, and that it was the Nationalists who imposed a retrograde puritanism. But Tío Jerónimo's arguments – presented as the voice of wisdom – suggest that sexual repression was the cause of the Civil War and not its consequence. In practice the novel's almost exclusive focus on sexual activity gives the impression – in line with Nationalist ideology – that if anything the Republic was guilty of sexual excess. The obsession with brothels and perversion may be intended to suggest that Spaniards are repressed in the sense that they associate sex with the taboo – as in the case of Don Joaquín, who can achieve satisfactory relations with his wife only once she has become a prostitute – but Tío Jerónimo's recommendation of free sex seems likewise to be based on the notion of transgression: his earth-mother Cecilia is another man's wife and the mother of another man's children. The ideal proposed is not rejection of marriage for the union of free individuals, but the flaunting of civil and religious bonds through adultery. Cela's answer to 'the fabrications adulterating man' is an alternative adulteration. Tío Jeróni-mo's recommendation of 'natural sex' seems to be a recommenda-tion of a Marcusian 'polymorphous perversity' not in Marcuse's sense of a non-exclusively genital eroticism, but in that of the need to accept that sexual desire is by nature perverted: 'nadie se ve libre jamás de sus propias cochinadas' ['no one is ever free from his own obscenities'] (319). That perversion is not the result of repression but an integral part of nature is suggested by the statement: 'En la naturaleza nada se crea ni se destruye, no hace sino disfrazarse' ['In nature nothing is created or destroyed, but only disguised'] (159). The narrator finds what is described as genuine bliss by making his girlfriend Toisha (whose real name he has replaced with an invented one) submit to sexual practices she finds shameful (278, 375). In a telling example, Tío Jerónimo equates the need for Spaniards to make love 'in the sunlight in the park and in the middle of the street' with the founding of 'the blessed order of the whores of charity' who will dispense sex freely to the crippled and infirm. 'Free sexuality' seems to mean the provision of prostitutes for all males free of charge. In an extraordinary semantic distortion, Cela calls this 'women's liberation' (172–3). It is clear from this that what Cela means by sexual liberation is male self-gratification. When Tío Jerónimo advocates 'love' as the remedy for Spain's 'cainismo', he is not talking about caring relationships but about the physical release of 'making love' indiscriminately to all and sundry: 'da rienda suelta al amor cabalgando a la primer moza que se deje' ['give free rein to love by mounting the first wench who will let you'] (437). Tío Jerónimo insists that love in the sense of emotional commitment is more dangerous even than intellectual conviction, both of which lead men to sacrifice themselves for others: 'se lucha con más ahínco por un sentimiento que por una idea, ... quienes luchan por un sentimiento suelen morir antes, la Engracia murió llena de amor' ['people fight more doggedly for an emotion than for an idea, ... those fighting for an emotion are usually the first to die, Engracia died bursting with love'] (386).

In the place of Engracia's ardent idealism, which leads to self-sacrifice, Cela advocates self-realization in the form of egoistic self-gratification or (to use another Marcusian term) Narcissism.[13] Part 2, describing the outbreak of war, ends with the image of Narcissus: 'todos podéis convertiros en Narciso, la historia está llena de Narcisos, es cuestión de que os propongáis bellos y capaces de recibir amor, el amor más puro y desinteresado es el que siente por sí mismo el hombre que se mira al espejo, que se masturba o se suicida ante el espejo' ['each and every one of you can become a Narcissus, history is peopled with Narcissuses, you just have to convince yourself you are beautiful and capable of receiving love, the purest and most disinterested love is the self-love of the man contemplating himself in the mirror, masturbating or committing suicide in front of the mirror'] (177). Not for nothing is the narrator throughout the novel masturbating while contemplating himself in the mirror. It is hard to see how the Narcissism of masturbating or committing suicide in front of the mirror can be a solution to the perversion and self-destruction which Cela finds characteristic of the nightmare of Spanish history. The same problem is posed by the homosexual Matiítas' suicide – in front of the 'mirror' of the fat Arab prostitute looking at him – depicted simultaneously as an emblem of the ills of Spanish history and as a release. The notion that sex is a release from history is contradicted by its description as an image of the inescapable repetition of history: 'el sexo es como una peonza, como una noria' ['sex is like a spinning-top, like a treadmill'] (44); 'nadie puede librarse de su monótono y violentísimo sexo pero tampoco quiere' ['no one can free himself from his monotonous and violent sexual urges but no one wants to either'] (305). That sex is the condemnation to a curse rather than a cure is also implied by the statement that man's sexual urges are pre-ordained, indeed the result of congenital hormonal factors (371). The Narcissus theme is introduced with the words: 'Nadie se elige a sí mismo, en esto unos tienen suerte y otros desgracia, Narciso no se eligió a sí mismo, se conformó con sí mismo y apoyó su amor en la conformidad' ['No one chooses himself, here some are lucky and others unlucky, Narcissus didn't choose himself, he made do with himself and based his love on conformity'] (177). By opting for Narcissism, Cela locates the solution not in the political arena but in the individual; at the same time the novel's collective emphasis and insistence on the grotesqueness of human behaviour degrades the concept of the individual. What Cela seems to be proposing is self-love (introspection, masturbation) in the sense of acceptance of the perversity that characterizes human nature, and the consequent abandonment of all political attempts at human betterment: 'proclama tu amor a la vida cochina' ['proclaim your love of this disgusting life'] (442); 'creo porque es absurdo dijo San Agustín, la vida también es absurda pero no dejamos de creer en ella' ['I believe because it is absurd said St Augustine, life is absurd too but we still believe in it'] (434). Cela is recommending Narcissism in its Freudian sense, as that infantile stage of human development prior to awareness of the independent existence of others. Just as Tío Jerónimo returns to an infantile self-gratification by suckling at his earth-mother's breast, so the narrator will regress to a foetal position as he contemplates himself in the mirror which turns images of the outside world into projections of the self: 'un espejo ovoide contigo en medio, ... en el que tú flotas en su rara atmósfera dulzona, de sabor dulzón, como un feto en la matriz' ['an oval mirror with you in the middle, ... floating in its strange sickly-smelling and sickly-tasting ambience, like a foetus in the womb'] (265).[14] 'Oval', as the narrator points out on the next page, means 'egg-shaped'. There is, after all, a difference between the 'starting from scratch every morning' of Spanish history, in which self-destruction is seen as a way of wiping the historical slate clean in order to start anew (hence the need to repeat the process 'every morning'), and Tío Jerónimo's 'starting with the beginning', which by taking refuge in a Narcissistic self-indulgence opts out of history for good.

'Esfuérzate por creer en algo que no sea la historia, esa gran falacia' ['Try to believe in something other than history, that great fallacy'] (436) is Tío Jerónimo's final message. The novel is not a purgation of the evil of history in order that it may emerge revitalized, but an exorcism that rejects the traditional concept of history as the record of the past in favour of a concept of history as fiction, as oblivion. Just as it perpetuates the Falangist equation of history with evil but without the corresponding belief in redemption, so it puts into practice Nietzsche's notion of history as myth or 'willed forgetting' but without the latter's aim of making it a source of vital belief. Cela's aim is rather to rid the reader of any vestiges of enthusiasm; not to write history but to write it off. The novel piles repulsive detail upon repulsive detail so that the reader's reaction on finishing it is one of relief that it is over. Don León buries himself in Galdós' historical novel *El equipaje del rey José* to forget the historical events taking place in the street outside (364, 425). In place of the sacrificial heroine Engracia – described as a latterday Agustina de Aragón, the heroine of Spanish history textbooks – the narrator holds up as a model Doña Sacramento, not only for her acceptance as a brothel-keeper of the perversity of human nature, but also for her capacity for forgetting: 'doña Sacra olvida al yerno, quema a la nieta y entierra a la hija, ... doña Sacra es mujer muy entera y valerosa, con mujeres así hubiera podido escribirse la historia sin ideas madrugadoras' ['Doña Sacra forgets her son-in-law, burns her granddaughter and buries her daughter, ... Doña Sacra is a strong, brave woman, with women like that history could have been written without redemptive ideas'] (393). The novel sets up a dialectic between remembering and forgetting. Memory – the persistence of the past – is, it seems, the curse condemning Spain to eternal repetition: 'se dice que el tiempo todo lo borra pero ... el tiempo todo lo fija y la memoria cuando pasa el tiempo es como una fotografía a la que dieron con hiposulfito, que ya no se borra nunca' ['people say things fade with time but ... time puts a seal on things and memory as time goes by is like a photograph treated with hyposulphite to fix its imprint for ever'] (247). It is because memory does not fade with the passing of time that a willed forgetting is necessary. The narrator's mirror, which at the start of the novel – in accordance with conventional assumptions about historical novels – we assume has the function of reflecting history, will by the end explicitly acquire that of blurring or erasing it: 'huye a través de tu espejo, no te importe romperlo ni romper todo, más allá de tu espejo duerme el olvido y quién sabe si la sonrisa' ['escape through your mirror, don't be afraid to break it and break everything, the other side of your mirror oblivion slumbers and maybe laughter'] (385). If insomnia is what causes the living nightmare of Spanish history (102), Tío Jerónimo will end the novel with a recommendation of sleep (443).

In the course of the novel the narrator's mirror – as an image of the process whereby fiction 'reflects' reality – will undergo a series of disturbing transformations.[15] The reader is again reminded of Valle-Inclán's theory of the *esperpento*, according to which a distorting mirror is needed to portray the caricature that is Spanish history.[16] Valle-Inclán argues for a 'mathematical' distortion that, by systematically highlighting the distortions of reality, ceases to be a distortion in that it reveals the true nature of things. Cela's mirror does not give a systematically distorted picture but itself distorts by continually changing shape, so that the reader is never sure what kind of mirror he is facing and is thus unable to interpret the images in its surface. It is worth noting that the problematic nature of the mirror is constituted by the instability of its frame. As Barthes has pointed out, it is the placing of a clearly-defined frame around the text, imposing a fixed perspective on the images contained within it, that creates the illusion of realism.[17] Like *La colmena*, the text of *San Camilo, 1936* provides a commentary on the problem of perspective: 'depende de para dónde miras' ['it depends which way you're looking'] (265); 'lo que pasa es que estamos todos demasiado cerca y carecemos de perspectiva' ['the problem is we're all too close and have no sense of perspective'] (218). The novel not only avoids adopting any political perspective, but blurs all perspectives. The opening warns the reader by stating that 'the mirror has no frame, no beginning or end', only to continue 'yes it has an elegant gilt frame' (13). It is not that the mirror has no frame but that we are given inconsistent information as to whether it has one or not; we do not have the abolition of perspective (which affords a perspective of sorts) but the blurring of it so that we literally do not know where we stand with regard to what we are reading. It is at the start of Part 3, following the outbreak of war, that the frame starts to assume a bewildering succession of forms, with the 'gilt-framed mirror' becoming a 'parallelepipedic mirror' with 'six burnished surfaces', and then an 'oval mirror ... with no bottom or top or sides'. The possibility is also raised that the mirror may have been broken into smithereens (264–5). By chapter 3 of Part 3, the mirror has assumed the form of a 'bloody Medusa', no longer reflecting the narrator's image which has turned into a 'malleable piece of dough' (347). The symbolic flies plaguing Madrid also begin to infest the mirror. At the end of Part 3 (before the final shift of perspective to Tío Jerónimo in the epilogue) the narrator disconcertingly reveals that he has never had a mirror. This does not mean that none of the novel is a reflection of reality but that the narrator has had to resort to 'los espejos del prójimo' ['my neighbour's mirrors']: the novel is a reflection of reality not through the narrator's single perspective but through the shifting perspective of all the characters in the novel. The narrator now announces that these too must be broken 'into a thousand pieces that are no use to anyone' (429). Tío Jerónimo's epilogue reads as the 'voice of wisdom' precisely because, standing outside the narrator's shifting mirror, it is the only part of the novel that obeys a unified perspective. The rest of the novel, by showing us the narrator gazing in his mirror, tricks us into thinking that his voice will provide a coherent frame to the text, only to disabuse us. As his first novel *La familia de Pascual Duarte* (1942) showed, Cela is at his best when playing such Cervantine games with the reader.

The lack of paragraph divisions and infrequency of full stops also create the impossible perspective of a multiplicity of voices which appears to be a continuous, single voice. The uninterrupted flow of the narrative makes it difficult, if not impossible, to work out whether the narrator or a character (and if so which character) is responsible for the conflicting opinions in the text. If we do not know who is speaking we have no way of assessing the validity of what is said. The result is a discourse in which truth, being indistinguishable from falsity, ceases to exist. Apart from the fact that the twenty-year-old narrator is immature and confused (and at the end reveals himself either to have lied before about having a mirror, or to be lying now), it is impossible to know whether the other voices in the text are filtered through his or relayed independently by the author. Being in front of his bedroom mirror (and mentioning only brief sorties into the outside world), the narrator cannot have witnessed even the public – as opposed to private – events described. The confusion as to whether he is a witness or inventor of events is aggravated by his asking himself whether he was in the Plaza de España during the assault on the Montaña barracks, answering with the contradictory information that he was both outside with the Republican assailants and inside with the Nationalist rebels (308). The second person singular form used throughout appears to be the narrator addressing his image in the mirror (the point being that this reduces him to a mere image in the mirror), but could also mean that he is being addressed by the author. This appears to be the case when we encounter the first person intrusion: 'tú tienes mucha memoria, la memoria de los tontos, puede ser que resultaran novelas mis escritos, pero yo sólo me dedico a escribir a Dios dándole cuenta de lo que pasa en la tierra' ['you have a good memory, an idiot's memory, maybe the things I write are novels, but all I do is write to God to let him know what is happening on this earth'] (33). The confusion between narrator (inside the text) and author (outside the text) is compounded by the fact that the narrator is endowed with Cela's autobiographical features (aged twenty in 1936, suffering from tuberculosis), while Cela is also mentioned in the third person as an acquaintance of the narrator (thus placing the author imposs- ibly inside and outside the text) (16, 75). The inclusion as frontis- piece of a photograph of the young Cela in 1936 only adds to the confusion. There is a further problem as to the identity of the alleged editor of the text, responsible for two documentary footnotes, one of which reads like the work of a professional historian while the other is entirely trivial (311, 399): is this editor outside the mirror of the text or inside it as a fictional creation?

The same disconcerting mixture of serious and parodic documen- tation – blurring the boundary between fact and fiction – occurs with the recourse throughout to newspapers and radio broadcasts of the time, mixing news with advertisements and theatre and cinema listings. In addition to politicians, a large number of the characters made to look grotesque through the depiction of their sexual activities are journalists, implying that the reader should be sceptical about the claims to truth of both. It is significant that the send-up of academic scholarship should consist of a list of theses purporting to prove that the characters of Pérez de Ayala's novel *Troteras y danzaderas* are based on real-life figures. The use of lists throughout Cela's novel gives an impression of factuality which is at the same time subverted by jumbling fact and fiction. A similar confusion is created by the lack of distinction between historical figures and fictional characters, the clearest example being the repeated joint mention of a historical Napoleon and a fictitious 'King Cyril of England' (the fact that the latter is loosely based on Edward II only blurs the distinction between history and fiction further, not only because Edward II is known to us largely through Marlowe and Brecht but also because Cela has created a figure which is neither historical nor fictional but both). In the end the use of lists, far from reinforcing the factuality of the text, gives it an incantatory quality which has the effect the narrator attributes to music: 'la música lo bueno que tiene es que permite ... vaciar la cabeza' ['the good thing about music is that it ... lets your mind go blank'] (81). The incorporation of intertextual references to popular and high culture of the day can be seen as an attempt to broaden historiography by depicting all areas of social activity; but at the same time it creates a further blurring of fact and fiction in that the real world introduced into the text itself consists of texts. Furthermore the intertextual references mix writers from different periods (from Heraclitus to Max Aub), producing a collage such that individual quotations are lifted out of their historical context and reassembled in a supra-temporal discourse. (Cela has however taken care to include references only up to July 1936.) The same sensation of timelessness is created by the almost exclusive use of the present tense.

Cela's illusionist use of narrative technique teaches the reader to be sceptical about all language, for it is belief in words that makes people willing to sacrifice themselves in the 'name' of history: 'la palabra llama a la sangre' ['words are a call to blood'] (109). At the same time language is put forward as a mythical antidote on account of its ability to create a continuous flow that transcends the divisions of history. Language is of value only inasmuch as it is not history, only provided one accepts that the mirror of fiction is a mirage. Matiítas is paid to read fiction to a blindman. *San Camilo, 1936* is written to save the reader from seeing a reality which Cela – like T. S. Eliot – feels is more than man can bear.[18]

Reivindicación del conde don Julián (1970) by Juan Goytisolo is an explicit attack on the particular version of Spanish history given by Nationalist ideology: so explicit that it was banned in Spain till Franco's death. The novel shows Francoist historiography to be a mythification not by contrasting it with an alternative view of history, but by debunking it through parody. As in the earlier *Duelo en el Paraíso*, the use of parody introduces a number of ambiguities. Parody depends not on the two-dimensional ironic contrast between opposing sets of values but on the one-dimensional caricature of the values being attacked. The reader interprets praise as meaning condemnation and vice versa: moral values change places but the black and white picture remains. The parody in Goytisolo's novel is effected by taking the values of Nationalist ideology literally so that they turn against their master. Just as the narrator–protagonist hands a rope to the Nationalist child he was brought up to be, forcing him into suicide, so he hands Francoism a metaphorical rope with which to hang itself in the form of its own arguments. The subversion of Nationalist myth is achieved at the expense of endorsing the premises on which it is based. The considerable body of critical studies on the novel – particularly those of Linda Gould Levine – have painstakingly identified the aspects of Nationalist ideology parodied in it.[19] Goytisolo's own lucid essays have also thrown much light on the ideological background to the novel.[20] I shall limit myself here to pointing out the ways in which the novel perpetuates the mythical vision it sets out to subvert.

The main object of parody in *Reivindicación del conde don Julián* is – as in *Tiempo de silencio* – the myth of national character elaborated by the 1898 writers and taken up by Falangist ideology. But if Martín-Santos exposes the psychological drives which have led Spaniards to take refuge in stoicism, Goytisolo rejects causal explanation; as a result the values he mocks appear given and fixed. Goytisolo has stated that it is because he feels unable to change the historical reality of postwar Spain that he has opted in his novel for attacking Francoism via its literary discourse.[21] Historical reality is excluded from the novel: we see Spain through the spectacles of Nationalist myth, presented as a *fait accompli* which cannot be modified but only obliterated. The rigidity of the lawyer Don Alvaro Peranzules – representing the Nationalist ideal of the 'caballero cristiano' ['Christian knight/gentleman'] and also the conformist adult Goytisolo, trained in law, could have become – allows no possibility of change: the text will literally blow him to bits. The fact that the narrator – a clear *alter ego* of the author – feels it necessary also to kill off Alvarito Peranzules Junior – representing the bourgeois child he used to be – further implies that Goytisolo feels his personal rejection of Nationalist morality to have been superficial: the narrator's childhood self accompanies him wherever he goes.[22] The 1898 writers' suggestion that the national character was determined by the Castilian landscape is not refuted in the novel but taken literally, as the narrator and his fellow Arab barbarians destroy the barren *meseta* described by Unamuno, Azorín and Machado, replacing it with a 'northern industrial landscape' (217). (It is curious that Goytisolo's fictional Arab invasion should create a northern landscape: presumably Goytisolo could not have the Arabs importing the desert – glorified in his next novel *Juan sin tierra* – since this would compound the existing barrenness.) This need to destroy the landscape not only implies that the national character is shaped by geographical austerity, but also that the new landscape will in turn produce a new national character. The weather forecast which opens the novel – based on the real-life TV forecaster who, having sworn that if his forecast were wrong he would shave off his moustache, next day appeared clean-shaven – stresses the unpredictability of the climate, thus undermining the 1898 writers' belief in the immutability of the geographically defined national character, but not undermining the concept of geographically defined national character as such.[23] The most successful assault on the concept of national character is the continual metamorphosis to which the figure of Seneca – exalted in Nationalist ideology as the symbol of an innate Spanish stoicism – is subjected, fusing variously with Alvaro Peranzules Junior (Senior being Seneca the Elder), Luis Moscardó (son of the hero of the siege of the Toledo Alcázar in the Civil War, the latter also cast as Seneca the Elder), Little Red Riding Hood, a bullfighter, Unamuno, Sánchez Albornoz, and Franco. Particularly pertinent satires of stoicism are the parodies of press reports of the 1966 Referendum on the Law of Succession, guaranteeing the endurance of Francoist values even beyond death; and the parodic version in the form of scrambled quotations from Calderón and Lope de Vega – playwrights Unamuno had seen as emblematic of an enduring Spanish spiritual nobility – of the telephone conversation

between the heroic defender of the Toledo Alcázar, Colonel Moscardó, and his son Luis threatened with execution ('reproduced' in
school textbooks of the 1940s and shown by Herbert Southworth to
have been a fabrication).[24] Goytisolo's Protean concept of character
is clearly intended to imply that there is no such thing as fixed,
coherent identity; at the same time the multiple guises assumed by
Seneca, being versions of the same stoic endurance, give the impression there is no escape from the proliferation of Senecas. It is
significant that the phrase 'dueño proteico de tu destino' ['Protean
master of your destiny'] (99) is applied to the narrator – who has the
freedom through language to transform himself at will, whether into
Count Julian, the caretaker/snake-charmer, Don Alvaro, Alvarito,
or the final newborn Muslim messiah – and not to any of the
incarnations of 'senequismo', by definition incapable of flexibility,
able only to repeat themselves indefinitely. The implication is that
the narrator, having abandoned Spain for exile in Tangiers, has a
freedom lacking to Spain, sentenced to eternal repetition. The
narrator can become Don Alvaro Peranzules, but not vice versa.
The nickname Figurón given the multiple Seneca figure equates the
rigidity of the national character with a mask, echoing Octavio Paz's
view of Mexico's post-conquest history as an alien imposition on to
authentic roots. But this dismissal of Francoism as a mask is itself a
repetition of the Nationalist view of modern Spanish history –
derived from Ganivet, Unamuno and Ortega – as a deviation from
an authentic destiny. Different sections of Spanish history are
labelled 'deviant', but the mythical view of history as a break with
origins remains the same.

Much of the ambiguity in *Reivindicación del conde don Julián* can be
attributed to the acknowledged influence on Goytisolo of Américo
Castro, whose main contribution to Spanish historiography has been
his rehabilitation of Moorish Spain.[25] In his non-fictional work,
Goytisolo has attacked the Catholic equation of the Arab period of
Spanish history with evil, pointing out the similarities between the
biblical myth of the Fall and the legendary explanation of Arab
invasion as a punishment for lust (the last Visigothic King Rodrigo's
violation of La Cava, daughter of the Governor of Tangiers Count
Julian, who in revenge handed the city over to the Moors, freeing
access to the Straits of Gibraltar), complete with serpent: whether
that which devours Rodrigo's genitals in the ballad or Saavedra

Fajardo's reference to the Arabs letting loose their 'serpents' on Spain.[26] (The 'Ballad of King Rodrigo' and Saavedra Fajardo are quoted in the novel [200, 270].) Like Castro, Goytisolo insists that the eight centuries of Arab rule cannot be dismissed as a 'deviation' from an 'authentic destiny'; but, also like Castro, he proceeds to equate the Arab presence with an 'essential Spain' subsequently 'betrayed' by Castilian domination. (To be precise: Castro equates the 'essential Spain' with the 'three castes' of Jew, Muslim and Christian; in practice he is almost exclusively concerned to prove a Jewish origin for everything he finds significant in Spanish history. Goytisolo is concerned solely with the Arab.) Goytisolo rightly points out that the Nationalists claimed to be descendants of an 'eternal Spain' represented by the Celts, Iberians, Romans and Visigoths in order to dismiss the ensuing Arab presence as a 'usurpation': 'the attempt by our historians to trace back a "glorious national genealogy" is reminiscent of certain dubious *nouveau-riche* businessmen who, to conceal the inglorious origins of their fortune, fabricate a pedigree going back to the time of the Crusades. For this glorification of origins accompanies an unconfessed desire to blot out a stain: the nation's "continuity", stretching from the Tartesians and Iberians to modern times, is broken by an inexplicable intrusion.'[27] Accordingly *Reivindicación del conde don Julián* will compare the Senecan tradition exalted by the 1898 writers and their heirs to the River Guadiana, which flows underground for part of its course (181).[28] Goytisolo's analysis shows the Nationalist concept of an 'eternal Spain', interrupted by Arab rule, to be a perfect example of the mythical scheme analysed by the Islamic historian Bernard Lewis, whereby claimants to power seek to legitimize themselves by alleging descent from a founding tradition, subsequently 'betrayed' by 'usurpers'. But Goytisolo's dismissal of Castilian dominated Spain as a 'mask' or 'straightjacket' imposed on an 'authentic' Arab Spain conforms to the same mythical pattern: the Arab 'usurpers' are simply recast as a 'founding tradition', turning Castilian rule into a 'usurpation'. Bernard Lewis' analysis clarifies the significance of Goytisolo's vindication of the 'traitor' or 'usurper'.[29] Just as Américo Castro adopts an ambiguous attitude to what he diagnoses as Spain's tendency to 'vivir desviviéndose', deploring its self-destructiveness but at the same time implying the need to 'undo' modern Spanish history by reverting to the 'founding tradition' of Arab Spain, so

Goytisolo deplores the Castilian 'undoing' of Arab culture but proposes an alternative 'undoing' of the Castilian tradition. The repeated return to the womb sequences in the novel are in part a parody of the Nationalist emphasis on the need to wipe the slate clean by returning to origins, turning Nationalist myth against itself by 'undoing' the usurpation represented by Nationalist Spain: thus Isabel la Católica's striptease as she throws off the 'corset' of Francoism (Pilar Franco's description of her brother's rule of law and order as an 'orthopaedic corset' comes to mind) will conclude with a journey via her sexual organs back to the womb. But the millenarian demand for an apocalyptic destruction and return to zero remains. When the narrator says 'estáis en el preámbulo de la historia' ['you have entered the preamble to the story/history'] (285) he means not only that the story has not yet run its course but also that he and his childhood self have gone back to the beginning of time. Even when there is no parody of Nationalist myth, the narrator is obsessed with returning to the womb: his bedroom – to which he returns on the last page – is described as a 'comforting foetal penumbra', a 'soothing womb' (87); he will emerge from the doctor's surgery as if 'reborn' (104); and in the darkness of the cinema will plunge into the womb-like scenario of the underwater sequence from *Thunderball* (150). At the end of the novel, having razed Franco's Spain to the ground and 'undone' his childhood self, he is reborn as the new Islamic messiah. The novel inverts the Nationalist demand for a messiah to return the nation to its lost purity by exalting the figure of the traitor; but Goytisolo's traitor figure is also a messiah preaching destruction as the prelude to rebirth (including his own), the difference being that it is purity that is being destroyed in order to usher in a new millennium of corruption.[30] The novel satirizes the Nationalist myth of the siege of the Alcázar, which – being modelled on Guzmán el Bueno's heroic defence of Tarifa against the Moors – perfectly illustrates Bernard Lewis' analysis of how revolutions disguise their illegitimacy by presenting themselves as the reincarnation of a mythical founding tradition; but Goytisolo, by modelling his narrator on Count Julian, is also resurrecting a mythical founder, albeit a notorious one.[31] Goytisolo criticizes Nationalist ideology for imposing the myth of the Fall on to Spanish history, but he also implies that Spain is vitiated by an 'original sin' in the inverse form of puritanism. Indeed the implication is that no redemption is possible for Spain: the latter-day Count Julian redeems the child he used to be from the 'original sin' of birth into a Nationalist family by having him seduced by a social leper, but his invasion of Spain leads simply to destruction. In a phrase which implies impotence at the same time as personal redemption, the narrator describes himself as 'Sisyphus and at the same time phoenix' (204).

If the traitor is a messiah in disguise, so his rejection of purity for corruption will be an inverse form of purification. The narrator precedes his betrayal of Spain with a visit to the Arab baths. His assimilation of the putrefaction of the market is described as a kind of ascesis: 'olores densos, emanaciones agrias que voluntariamente aspiras con fervor catecúmeno, como en una severa y exigente iniciación órfica' ['penetrating smells, acrid emanations which you deliberately inhale with the fervour of a catechumen, as if undergoing some rigorous Orphic initiation rite'] (119). When he takes literally the concept of linguistic purity by eliminating all words of Arabic origin from the Spanish language, the resulting enforced asceticism – as Spaniards are left with nothing to eat – is a parody of Nationalist values; but his pollution of the linguistic purity of the Spanish classics by squashing flies and assorted insects between their pages is an alternative form of purgation or censorship (Goytisolo has recognized the unintended similarity with the priest's inquisitorial book-burning in the *Quixote*).[32] Similarly the novel's replacement of Ganivet's demand for purification in the form of a metaphorical blood-letting by a transfusion of rabid blood provides an inverse 'cure' (here 'poison') for the Spanish 'disease' (here defined as the obsession with 'limpieza de sangre' or racial purity). The parallel syphilitic 'poisoning' of the sexual purity of the narrator's childhood self takes ascesis to the point of martyrdom. Like the 'St Genet, actor and martyr' described by Sartre – who, having been branded a thief as a child, decided to assume the label society had given him – the narrator plays out the role of criminal – donning the dark glasses and false moustache of the movie villain (201) to emphasize the theatrical nature of the 'performance' – so as to cleanse himself of bourgeois prejudices. Goytisolo has described the importance of his friendship with Genet in a moving chapter of his autobiography.[33] The quotation from Genet's *The Thief's Journal* (much of which takes place in Spain) heading the first chapter makes it clear that

Goytisolo's Count Julian is modelled on Genet's exaltation of treachery as the ultimate freedom violating even the 'bond' of friendship, but also the ultimate ascesis resulting in total isolation. Goytisolo's parody of the hell-fire morality drilled into him at school leads not so much to rejection of the association of sex with hell as to the idea that the liberation which lies at the end of the sexual odyssey (the return to the womb that is also entry into the Elysian fields) is reached only after a purgative descent into hell. The Nationalist child will find liberation through reincarnation as a Muslim only after submitting to the scourge of the whip. Liberation consists of imposing punishment on oneself, or of flagrantly violating social norms in order to invite condemnation by society. The novel is a purificatory act of self-punishment, deliberately courting ostracism (it has, of course, brought Goytisolo national and international recognition).

The problem, in Goytisolo's case as in Genet's, is that the adoption of transgression – the deliberate assumption of evil – as a form of liberation inevitably perpetuates the taboos it simulta-neously breaks. Evil is made the object of desire precisely because it is forbidden and punishable. It is appropriate that the entry into the Elysian fields which is the goal of the transgressive sexual acts in the novel should be described via images from the Caribbean carnival scene in *Thunderball*. In his non-fictional work Goytisolo refers to Bakhtin's study of the subversive function of carnival in Rabelais, but – as Geoffrey Kirk reminds us in his analysis of myth – the ritualization of transgression that constitutes carnival has the func-tion of confirming the everyday order.[34] Goytisolo's concept of liberation suffers from the same flaw that rendered ineffective the surrealist call to revolution. Not for nothing do the surrealists' transgressive heroes Sade and Lautréamont – and their equally transgressive heir Buñuel – leave their mark on his text (Sade and Buñuel are quoted [80, 203]; the narrator's corruption, torture and killing of the child is modelled on *Les Chants de Maldoror*).[35] By playing the role of 'enfant terrible' or 'poète maudit' Goytisolo, like the surrealists, makes himself dependent on the continuing existence of the establishment. *Reivindicación del conde don Julián* consists of a succession of transgressive acts (which the end of the novel tells us will be repeated every day) because transgression sets up a literally 'vicious' circle whereby the flouting of taboos reinforces them. The novel's parody of Catholic morality does not allow it to get beyond transgression by ceasing to regard the taboo as forbidden fruit: the rejection of the 'intocables' ('sacred cows') of Goytisolo's Nationalist upbringing leads him to espouse another kind of 'untouchable' in the form of the social pariah. The parodic replacement of the Nationalist concept of a vertical society with that of the underworld Paradise constituted by the 'lower' parts of the body – taking literally López Ibor's unfortunate definition of National Syndicalism as the adoption of an 'erect position' – requires the labelling of sexual activity as 'inferior'.[36] The notion that sex reduces man to bestiality is likewise confirmed by parodic descriptions such as that of the caretaker and flower-seller's 'feline', 'bestial', 'carnivorous' cavortings (170). The recourse to transgression necessarily equates sexual fulfilment with violation, implying that Isabel la Católica and the female congregation at the end of the novel enjoy their rape. The novel exposes the sexual violence of the honour code as represented by Lope de Vega's *El castigo sin venganza*, only to confirm the coexistence of 'el sexo y su violencia desnuda' ['sex and its naked violence'] (278). The difference is that in Lope's play the violence is masked whereas here it is naked. Goytisolo has talked of the need for the writer to rid himself of the 'mask' of the false identity imposed on him by society and to 'define himself negatively, in opposition to the "essences" and myths of his own country'.[37] He has also talked of the need 'to invert the prevailing scale of values, to take the legend from behind, to sodomize the myth': the inversion through parody of Nationalist myth logically leads to the exaltation of the sexual 'invertido' or pervert.[38] But by defining himself as the photographic negative of what he was brought up to be he puts on an alternative mask, in that he is still defining himself according to an external scale of values: the anonymous narrator's constant metamorphosis is perhaps less a sign of liberation than of his condemnation to play a series of theatrical roles. Similarly, by opting for inversion the narrator will embrace homosexuality not so much because it fulfils a natural urge as because it is regarded as a perversion (the Nationalist historian and police chief Comín Colomer had branded Republican politicians not only as Jews and Masons but also as homosexuals).[39] Or rather: the narrator's stripping away of the bourgeois values that warped his natural growth leads to a paradoxical return to nature in the form of artifice and perversion. As in *Duelo en el Paraíso*, nature is seen as corrupt; if in the earlier novel – which rejected myth for history – this led to the contradictory equation of history with nature, in *Reivindicación del conde don Julián* – which rejects history for myth – it leads to the contradictory equation of the return to natural origins with the assumption of the corruption of the fallen world. The striptease – in which the false externals of Nationalist puritanism are peeled away to reveal the 'naked truth' of sexuality – is at the same time a masquerade: the donning in society's eyes of the cloak of evil. The wolf which, in the homosexual parody of *Little Red Riding Hood* (renamed *Caperucita azul* in Nationalist Spain), disguises itself as the bourgeois granny is at the same time a disguise assumed by the narrator to punish himself in the form of the bourgeois child.[40] Spanish culture is rejected as artifice with the renaming of the Golden Age as the 'Age of Gilt-Edged Papier Mâché' (120) and with its reduction to a series of contrived TV programmes; but the narrator's transgressions will also be performed on the inner stage of his mind (referred to as a 'screen' or 'artefact' like the television he is watching). The curtain drawn and closed at the start and end of the novel frames the image of Spain ('a mere cardboard cut-out' [83]) outside the window but also frames the novel, turning both into theatrical representations. The narrator talks of the need to reveal 'the truth beneath the mask', smothered by the 'cancerous proliferation' and 'parasitic excrescence' of Francoist rhetoric (226); but his use of Baroque metaphor and syntax also creates a text that is pure artifice. In a telling phrase in *Crónicas sarracinas*, Goytisolo refers to the Arabist Richard Burton's love of dressing up in Arab robes as a 'second nature'.[41] Goytisolo's rejection of Nationalist myth as an artificial imposition is a return to nature that is in effect the assumption of a 'second nature'. The narrator adopts the transgressive stance of the voyeur not only with regard to his fantasy violation of Spain but also with regard to Tangiers. Just as his rejection of puritanism is a return to nature that is also a perverse theatrical enactment, so his rejection of Spain for Morocco will not be a genuine return to nature because for him, as a Spaniard, the Arab way of life can never be more than a 'second nature' or assumed identity. In *Crónicas sarracinas* Goytisolo talks of the 'intruder's gaze' of the Westerner who tries to enter the Arab world.[42] The narrator's voyeurism is an attempt at liberation via transgression, but it is also the only stance open to him.

Nowhere are Goytisolo's contradictions more apparent than in his demythification of the Western 'myth of the Arab', which for obvious historical reasons has been particularly strong in Spain. Goytisolo has noted that one Nationalist historian – Ignacio Olagüe – went so far in his anti-Arab prejudice as to write a book titled *The Arabs Never Invaded Spain*.[43] The title of Goytisolo's novel is reminiscent of the well-known plea for Spanish imperial expansion in North Africa, *Reivindicaciones de España*, published in 1941 by the Nationalist diplomats José María de Areilza and Fernando María Castiella.[44] In his lucid and well-informed essays in *Crónicas sarracinas*, Goytisolo draws on Edward Said's classic study *Orientalism* to expose the artificiality of the West's views of Islam, which turn it into a theatrical representation or film scenario.[45] But Goytisolo's novel does the same. Apart from the theatrical references, there is constant mention of films (*Thunderball*, *Lawrence of Arabia*, *Tarzan*, *Frankenstein*, *The Birds*, *The Seventh Seal*). The narrator also views the Orient through the lens of European literature: Kipling's *The Jungle Book*, Chateaubriand's *Les Aventures du dernier Abencérage*, as well as the image of the invading Moorish 'barbarians' found in Spanish historiography from Alfonso el Sabio to García Morente. Claudia Schaefer-Rodríguez has criticized Goytisolo for perpetuating the stereotyped Western view of the Oriental as treacherous, violent and sensual.[46] In *Crónicas sarracinas* Goytisolo declares that, in his novels, he has deliberately chosen to depict the Arab world through Western eyes in order to send up 'the traditional collective discourse on Islam'.[47] But Goytisolo is not only parodying the European view of the Oriental (and specifically the Spanish view of the Moor) as the repressed, monstrous 'other' of Western civilization: his attempt to 'define himself negatively' by assimilating Arab culture repeats the view of the Oriental as a Jungian shadow. The narrator's Muslim accomplice Tariq will act as his literal and metaphorical shadow in Tangiers and on his fantasy invasion of Spain. Goytisolo needs the myth of the Arab as 'other' in order not only to destroy Spain but also to liberate himself. Count Julian's latter-day Moorish invasion represents both the vengeful return and the liberating release of the repressed: Goytisolo has described the novel as a 'national psycho-analysis'.[48] If Tariq is throughout compared to a tiger, who takes the narrator to make love to 'a whore from the Rif, wild like a mountain goat' (125), it is not only in order to satirize the Western equation of the Arab with the 'natural' in the form of the 'bestial', but also because the narrator is seeking through Arab culture to release the 'monster within' of his repressed instincts. The re-conquest of Spain by the Arab 'serpents', together with the inversions of *Little Red Riding Hood* and the minotaur myth, permits the triumph of the monster at the expense of perpetuating the equation of the African with the animal.[49] No matter how desirable the monster, the analogy implies that the Arab – as part of nature rather than culture – is an immutable essence. Goytisolo rejects the notion of an 'essential' Spanish character only to fall into the counter-myth of the 'essential', 'natural' Arab.[50] The debunking of Castilian racial purity is met with the exaltation of Count Julian's army of 'pure-blooded Bedouins' (263). The narrator rejects the Hollywood version of the oriental bazaar (118, 120) for the equally fictitious Arcadian images of the lithe young goatherd and the plaintive sound of pan-pipes (89). In *Crónicas sarracinas* Goytisolo shows awareness of the fact that Arab society is just as 'unnatural' and taboo-ridden as any other; his political articles and his involvement with the Algerian independence struggle and the Palestinian cause exempt him from the charges of cultural imperialism he levels against other writers who have used the Arab world as a vehicle for their sexual self-gratification. With his characteristic honesty, he recognizes that his counter-mythification – which in itself he regards as a valid enterprise – may not be entirely free of the exoticism he deplores in others. There are moments in *Reivindicación del conde don Julián* when the narrator does put his discourse at the service of the Arab, rather than use him as the pawn in a European – fundamentally Spanish – game. If in *Crónicas sarracinas* Goytisolo accuses Western Arabists of acting as spies in the service of colonialism, in his novel he will turn the Hollywood spy James Bond against his masters by merging him with Count Julian at the head of the Arabs' pillage of a US-dominated Spain.[51] The novel exposes the parasitic mentality created by colonialism (96) – while at the same time exalting the 'nobility' of the beggars in the market – and recognizes that the insects glorified as a form of pollution are the other side of a poverty in which the child carpetmakers are trapped like flies in a spider's web (137–8). The intrusion of the child carpetmakers into Don Alvaro Peranzules' proclamation of Spain's latest Five Year Plan (232) shows the dependence of the European economic boom of the

1960s on third-world underdevelopment. The ambiguities in Goytisolo's depiction of Islam are the product not only of the equation of Arab culture with sexual freedom (an equation one feels could have been made only by a male writer), but also of the political contradiction between dislike of the backwardness of Franco's Spain and an equal dislike of progress (whether capitalist or socialist).

It is perhaps in this more than anything that Goytisolo echoes the 1898 writers he sets out to debunk. His narrator attacks Unamuno's 'que inventen ellos' ['let other countries do the inventing'] (215) and Azorín's 'pueblos que proclaman su santa alegría de vivir fuera de la Historia' ['villages proclaiming their saintly joy at living outside History'] (182), but also proclaims his own delight at being 'fuera del devenir histórico : del raudo progreso' ['outside the historical process : outside the rush of progress'] (99), embarks on the 'descaracterización histórica' ['undoing of the historical character'] of Spain (214), and admires his young guide's 'elocuente desdén histórico' ['eloquent disregard for history'] (135) as opposed to the US tourists' obsession with their Baedeker. Despite his moving account in *Campos de Níjar* (1960) of the near-starvation existing in Almería in the 1950s, he ridicules the 'Hollywood studios in Almería' and 'Hilton Hotels in Motilla del Palancar' (162). The return to the womb that is also a descent into hell 'undoes' Francoism by turning against it not only the Catholic hell-fire view of sexuality but also the regime's sell-out to US capitalism, as the scenario further metamorphoses into the American tourists' 'profanation' of Hercules' Cave. It is not just US influence that is decried but 'el deslumbrante progreso industrial, la mirífica sociedad de consumo' ['the dazzle of industrial progress, the wonders of consumer society'] (207) as such, satirized via the adverts for luxury chalets in the Sierra Guadarrama where Little Red Riding Hood's granny is anachronistically made to live. The 'quintessentially Spanish' species of 'Carpetovetonic man' and the 'Hispanic goat' will be forced to retreat from the consumer society they have created into the 'womb' of the prehistoric Cave of Altamira; and the invading Arabs – contradicting their introduction of a northern industrial landscape – will provoke a crash on the stock exchange (265) not only to punish Francoism with its own anti-materialist rhetoric but also to 'undo' a material affluence which the author finds repugnant. It is the perennial problem – recognized by Goytisolo in his non-fictional work – of sympathy for the poor being dependent on their remaining poor. Just as Goytisolo attacks the Nationalist messianic conception of history, so he denounces the new US 'saviours' (123). His exaltation of the traitor is in part a rejection of what in *Crónicas sarracinas* he will call 'the redemptive virtues of progress': his traitor is an inverse redeemer leading the nation back to the primitive.[52] Goytisolo attacks Nationalist ideology for its repression of natural sexual urges but is seemingly in agreement with its exaltation of nature in the form of the unspoilt *pueblo*. The problem is that acceptance of the unspoilt *pueblo* means accepting a taboo-ridden morality, while conversely it was the affluence and consumerism of the 1960s that brought about sexual liberation by making pleasure the goal of existence. The description of the advert for luxury chalets in the Sierra Guadarrama sends up consumerism's claim to be affording a return to nature (130), but it was the introduction of mod. cons. that made possible the leisure in which the narrator revels as he wanders round the 'pleasure city' of Tangiers. Goytisolo's break with the Left – whose seeds can be found in *Reivindicación del conde don Julián* and which will become explicit in his next novel *Juan sin tierra* – was motivated not only by his experience of intellectual and sexual repression in the USSR and Castro's Cuba, but also by his rejection of the Socialist emphasis on productivity which he saw as a repetition of the capitalist work ethic.[53] But when he attacks capitalism for its work ethic he is attacking a defunct Victorian version; the emphasis on consumption and obsolescence in contemporary capitalism in fact coincides with Goytisolo's glorification of non-productive self-gratification.

The contradiction is not just Goytisolo's but one which is central to the work of the thinker he has declared to have most influenced him: Marcuse.[54] In *Eros and Civilization* and its post-May 1968 sequel *An Essay on Liberation*, Marcuse recognizes that his libertarian socialist utopia requires the prior existence of capitalist development in order to free man for leisure and pleasure. Goytisolo's novel is virtually a textbook illustration of Marcuse's ideas. As with the Spanish American novels of the 'boom' – Goytisolo's friendship with Carlos Fuentes is decisive here – *Reivindicación del conde don Julián* could have been written only in the 1960s: indeed it was written immediately after the events in Paris of May 1968 which Goytisolo witnessed. Marcuse insists that liberation must take the form of a regression to infancy in order to release the desires that the child has subsequently learnt to repress. He justifies Freud's reduction of history to biology because it shows the 'revolutionary' nature of bodily desire in its permanent opposition to repression. Marcuse's equation of liberation with erotic gratification situates it in a self conceived as being outside society and history, leading to a rejection of culture for nature and of the collective for the individual. Indeed his demand for a return to the 'polymorphous perversity' of infantile Narcissism shows that what he means by gratification is self-gratification: at this point his relationship to Marxism becomes problematic.[55] Goytisolo takes literally Marcuse's demand for the release of repressed infantile desire with his narrator's actualization of the twin Oedipal urges to return to the mother's womb and to kill the father, in the form of his violation of Isabel la Católica and his killing of Don Alvaro Peranzules alias Franco, jointly representing 'la madre patria'. (In his autobiography Goytisolo admits to reacting to Franco's death as if it were the death of a father.)[56] The narrator's killing of the child he used to be is a return to infancy in the sense that he kills his childhood ego and releases his repressed desires: the link between sex and death is again reminiscent of Marcuse's identification of Eros with Thanatos as the demand for stasis. The splitting of the narrator into two selves who make love in a hypnotic mutual fascination puts into practice Marcuse's theory of Narcissism.[57] Marcuse's 'polymorphous perversity' is taken literally with the exaltation of homosexuality (self-love as well as love of the same sex) as a form of liberation, but with the important difference that – as in Cela – perversity is privileged not so much because it is natural as because it is regarded as perverted. Goytisolo's novel also takes literally Marcuse's advocacy of Eros as play: except that again play is not presented as natural but consists of the narrator's staging of a performance and use of Baroque artifice. The notions of Eros as hypnosis, death, homosexuality and play fuse in the figure of the snake-charmer who hypnotizes and kills the child by playing his phallic flute: an actualization of Marcuse's model of non-productive and contemplative eroticism, Orpheus, who charmed nature, descended into the underworld, and was credited with introducing homosexuality into ancient Greece. In chapter 8 of *Eros and Civilization*, Marcuse opposes Orpheus and Narcissus – standing for 'joy and fulfilment; the voice which does not command but sings ...; the liberation from time which unites man with god, man with nature' –

to the Western culture hero Prometheus – representing productivity in its twin aspects of the blessing of progress and the curse of toil – and his female counterpart Pandora – who shows sexuality, beauty and pleasure to be a curse or disease that is 'fatal in the work-world of civilization'. Prometheus and Pandora also figure as negative images of sexual repression in Goytisolo's novel, in the school chaplain's hell-fire sermon: Goytisolo has stated that this sermon is based on a 1940s school text, but the coincidence with Marcuse is felicitous. It is interesting that Marcuse should – like Freud – resort to Greek mythology: both, by reducing history to nature in the form of biology, are indulging in mythical thinking. Marcuse's theory of liberation leads logically to his demand for the release of man from history, indeed from time as such.[58] Goytisolo criticizes the 1898 writers for their reduction of history to nature (182), but his novel, by equating liberation with erotic self-gratification, likewise reduces politics to biology.[59]

The narrative of *Reivindicación del conde don Julián* is designed to create a sense of atemporality. The fixed 'eternal values' of National-ist ideology are replaced with an alternative 'palabra sin historia' ['language without history'] (195) or 'indemne realidad que fúlgida-mente perdura y, a través de los siglos, te dispensa sus señas redentoras' ['unimpaired reality whose time-resisting glow bestows on you its redemptive powers'] (114). This ahistorical discourse is explicitly modelled on the verbal play of Góngora, not only because the latter combines sensuality with artifice (mirroring the narrator's equation of eroticism and perversion) but also because it draws on classical mythology: the text refers repeatedly to this 'Fábula de Polifemo y Galatea'. Allusions to classical mythology – often via Virgil – occur throughout the novel, forming part of a collage of intertextual references that dehistoricize language by lifting it out of its original context to create an 'autonomous verbal order' (195) in which the literary discourse not just of Spain but of the whole of Western civilization is made to coexist. This atemporality is rein-forced by the comic use of anachronism, as when Seneca declares that his philosophy refutes the theories of Marx and Freud (224).[60] The jumble of quotations from Nationalist ideology makes them look ridiculous when taken out of context; the emphasis on the literary discourse of Francoism also emphasizes that it was a man-made product and not 'given' or 'natural'. But at the same time Goytisolo's de-contextualized appropriation of texts echoes the Nationalists' appropriation of Spain's literary heritage for their own purposes.[61] The narrator satirizes the incoherent mixture of 'reportage' and advertising in the Spanish newspaper he reads, but his own text depends on a similar collage technique. It is interesting that the TV announcers should be described as a 'sybil' and 'oracle' respectively, suggesting a Barthesian critique of the media for mythologizing by presenting as 'given' and 'natural' that which is man-made; but Goytisolo's own use of classical mythology creates an autonomous discourse which, despite drawing attention to its artificiality, presents itself as self-sufficient. The narrator's use of parody turns language into another act of betrayal in order to free it from its 'age-old subservience' (195–6) to its historical context. This is, of course, an illusion because you can only betray an original: Goytisolo's text is more obviously dependent on the historical context of Francoism than perhaps any other postwar novel. Indeed its use of parody limits its public to those sufficiently well-informed about Nationalist Spain to recognize the allusions. That Goytisolo is wanting to expose the artificial distortions of history by the Francoist media while producing a text whose artificiality makes it autonomous and therefore unaccountable to history is shown by the narrator's plea for a language which 'hypnotizes' the reader in the same breath as he attacks Spanish television for turning the viewer into a 'blind statue like Lot's wife' (196). If the mass-media hero James Bond is incorporated into the novel, it is not in order to expose Hollywood's mythologizing but to appropriate it. Gould Levine notes that the Bond film *Thunderball* plays a similar role in the novel to that played in the *Quixote* by the romances of chivalry (the sixteenth-century equivalent of the mass media): there is however a crucial difference in that Goytisolo's novel in no way implies a critique of the seductive powers of the popular stereotype.[62]

The cinema is incorporated into the novel also via its use of re-takes, allowing Goytisolo to create a de-contextualized collage not only of other texts but also of his own text. The use of parody is of course itself a kind of re-take. The re-takes of his own text further free the narrator from history by allowing him to 'undo' what he sees in the world around him (as in his re-take of the scene of the American tourist with the snake-charmer), and to 'undo' his own fictional 'undoings' if the result was not satisfactory the first time round (as in his re-take of the death of the Nationalist child he used to be). The re-takes are thus a sign both of freedom and of impotence. The circular structure of the novel on the one hand creates a sense of completeness – through the use, as in Joyce's *Ulysses*, of the classical unities of time and place, confining the action to one day's wanderings round a city – but on the other hand represents an admission of failure: the end of the text announces a return to its beginning not in the sense of a rebirth but in that of the condemnation to an eternal succession of re-takes. The text's circularity is an attempt to subvert the linear irreversibility of time which ends up confirming it. José Manuel Martín nicely describes the text as a fish (serpent would be more appropriate) biting its tail: one thinks less of the mythical uroboros, representing wholeness, than of the scorpion – used as an image in the novel – which stings itself with its own tail when cornered.[63] The continuous flow of the narrative and the lack of full stops can also be interpreted both as a triumph over time and as signifying that there is no end to Sisyphus' trials. The use throughout of the present tense – supplemented by the future and imperative – literally abolishes the past in favour of an eternal present of desire and wish fulfilment. The future and imperative forms, however, turn the text into a spectacle the reader is ordered to witness, laying Goytisolo open to charges of falling into the same dogmatism he deplores in Francoism.[64] The lack of subordinate clauses – with punctuation almost entirely restricted to the colon with a space before as well as after, stressing the equal weight of what precedes and what follows – is presumably intended as a rejection of subordination in all its forms; but it creates a text lacking in intellectual subtlety, in which statements are unqualified and absolute. More seriously, the lack of causal clauses prevents causal analysis, refusing the reader any insight into the historical factors which produced Francoism. This rejection of causal analysis is logically accompanied by the use of Joycean free association, the oneiric quality of which is heightened by the narrator's recourse to drugs and by the use of dream sequences and involuntary memory. The novel takes the form of a monumental surrealist – or 1960s – 'happening', whose irrationalism is a defiance both of common sense and of moral norms. The narrator refuses the 'straight and narrow path' of logical analysis and of bourgeois morality, in order to 'perderse' ('go astray') in the labyrinth of Tangiers whose architecture is 'ajena a las leyes de la lógica y del europeo sentido común' ['alien to the laws of logic and of European common sense'] (143). What starts as an attack on the irrationalist mythifications of Nationalist ideology ends as an equally irrationalist rejection of the Western intellectual tradition.

In an interesting but undeveloped article, Linda Ledford-Miller suggests that *Reivindicación del conde don Julián* should be seen as a putting into practice of Nietzsche's advocacy of an irrationalist historiography, according to which the historian's role is to create a fiction or myth to live by. Like *San Camilo, 1936*, the novel is an exercise in oblivion, literally wiping out Spanish history through a series of parodic re-takes. Again as in Cela the narrator adopts a demiurgic position, standing outside of time in order to 'uncreate' the world: 'en los limbos de un tiempo sin fronteras : en el piadoso olvido' ['in the limbo of a time without frontiers : in merciful oblivion'] (100). He compares himself to Scheherazade (85) not only to situate his text in an Arabic tradition of erotic literature, but also because his fictions are designed to stave off the threat of the outside world. Nietzsche compared the writing of history to the 'invention of ingenious melodies'.[65] The re-takes in the novel function as variations on a theme in a musical score: the narrator describes himself as literally 'composing' his text (85). Music is referred to throughout. The oriental melodies played on the flute by the snake-charmer and the knife-grinder, Haydn's *Farewell Symphony*, Chopin's *Les Sylphides*, Gershwin, Afro-Caribbean *salsa*, the march from *The Bridge over the River Kwai*, the Rolling Stones fuse in a collage of musical styles that defies all logical or chronological classification. The last section of the novel is a musical apotheosis as the newborn Islamic messiah is carried through the streets to the sound of the knife-grinder's flute, which attracts a following of children forming an improvised orchestra of classical, jazz, Afro-Caribbean and Arab instruments, rising to a climax and dying away as the text reaches its end (302). Music is explicitly presented as the voice of Eros: the irresistible 'sirens' song' (174) and ecstatic 'musical erection' (149) that lift man out of time. It is Rimsky-Korsakov's musical version of *Scheherazade* that comes to mind. The narrator's childhood self is hypnotized by the snake-charmer's flute into forgetting the inhibitions imposed on him by his historical conditioning. It is important that the Orpheus-figure of the snake-charmer should be one of the narrator's disguises. His 'composition' likewise attempts to seduce the reader in order to liberate him from the restraints of history. The reader might find the proposition more attractive if Goytisolo did not find it necessary to accompany his musical invitation – in the case of the reader as in that of the child – with the whip.

Of all the novels discussed in this book, *La saga/fuga de J.B.* (1972) by Gonzalo Torrente Ballester is the hardest to pin down. As Torrente Ballester has himself declared, the novel is a jocular exercise in both mythification and demythification: 'yes and no at the same time', 'the expression of my internal contradictions'.[66] The difficulty of distinguishing between what is a satire of mythical attitudes and what is a re-creation of them is matched by the ambiguities of Torrente Ballester's political affiliations: an active member of the Falangist literary establishment during the latter part of the Civil War, as a student in Madrid from 1930–1 he had been editor of an anarchist newspaper and at the start of the war was a member of the Galician regionalist party (banned by the Nationalists on their occupation of Galicia). After the war, he remained closely associated with liberal or disaffected Falangists such as Pedro Laín Entralgo or Dionisio Ridruejo, and incurred frequent official disapproval: despite his re-writing of the conclusion, his first novel *Javier Mariño* (1943) was confiscated after publication; his signature in 1961 of the open letter by Spanish intellectuals demanding reform of the censorship laws led to a ban on his activities as drama critic and on reviews of his novels; after 1962 his brushes with the censor's office were resolved only by direct appeal to the new Minister of Information and Tourism Fraga Iribarne, a former student.[67] What anarchism and Galician regionalism had in common with fascism was their appeal to myth: in the case of anarchism, in the form of its millenarian concept of revolution; in the case of Galician regionalism, in the form of its revival of Celtic folklore to create a racially defined national identity. Torrente Ballester has stated that the concern in much of his work with demythification is the result of his experience in and after the Civil War of the political mythification of José Antonio and Franco.[68] The demythificatory elements of *La saga/fuga de J.B.* can be seen as the direct result of Torrente Ballester's disenchantment with Nationalist Spain: those forms of mythification which have as their end the suppression of plurality and relativity in the name of unity and absolutism are consistently attacked. Galician myth, central to the novel, provokes a more ambiguous response: its political manipulation by regionalist intellectuals is satirized, but its role in keeping alive regionalist sentiment is nevertheless presented positively. The most obviously pro-mythical aspect of the novel is its millenarian concept of revolution as liberation, in which Torrente Ballester's early anarchist leanings and subsequent Falangist involvement join hands with 1960s fringe politics. It is important to remember that Torrente Ballester spent the years 1966–72 – when the United States saw an explosion of radical thought, and when *La saga/fuga de J.B.* was written – as Visiting Lecturer at the State University of New York at Albany.[69] The result is a novel which is curiously modern and old-fashioned at the same time. It is not that its recourse to myth makes it independent of any historical context, but that the political ambiguities inherent in the appeal to myth allow it to straddle different and seemingly incompatible historical contexts.

Torrente Ballester's experience of both ends of the political spectrum places him in an ideal position to appreciate the interested nature of all statements about history. As he notes, there are always at least two versions of any event: that fabricated by the Right and that fabricated by the Left.[70] *La saga/fuga de J.B.* gives a political twist to Lévi-Strauss' notion that myth is founded on a set of binary oppositions by showing how the various versions of Castroforte's past are the result of the political rivalry between the town and the provincial capital Villasanta, representing respectively regional tradition and centralist government. But in this case the function of myth is not to mediate contradiction but to keep alive the struggle. The basis of the political rivalry is shown to be economic: the fight for control over the lamprey trade (the allegedly man-eating fish being ironic versions of the dragon that guards the treasure in the archetypal hero myth). Accordingly the lampreys function as escorts of Castroforte's other treasure: the 'Cuerpo Santo' ['Holy Body'] of St Lilaila of Ephesus, whose religious patronage is from the moment of arrival by sea founded on its financial value to the Barallobre family, given rights in perpetuity to the income generated by its veneration. If the Barallobres are the age-old rivals of the Bendañas (whose mansion, in the rival diocese of Villasanta, faces that of the Barallobres on the other side of the river), it is because the shrine of St Lilaila is a rival centre of pilgrimage to that of the male saint venerated in the 'Holy City' of Villasanta (a fictional version of

Santiago de Compostela). Torrente Ballester has stated that his fictional St Lilaila is intended as a heterodox counter to the orthodox myth of St James of Compostela, whose appropriation by centralist government deprived it of any regional significance.[71] Just as the earlier Bendañas had attempted to destroy Castroforte by military means, Jesualdo Bendaña will devote himself to destroying the myth of St Lilaila in the name of a 'scientific' rationalism that is a cover for jealousy.

It is not only centralist authority (further represented by the series of priests whose names begin with A, and by the team of experts from Villasanta who declare the 'Holy Body' to be a fake) that resorts to rationalist argument: so do the local supporters – or inventors – of Castroforte's myths: the Enlightenment thinker Godofredo Barallobre, the mid-nineteenth-century positivist Torcuato del Río and his fellow historians Doctor Amoedo and Ignacio Castiñeira, the contemporary chemist Perfecto Reboiras and grammarian José Bastida. Like Lévi-Strauss, Torrente Ballester suggests that science and myth are parallel products of reason, the former based on causal analysis and the latter on analogical argument. Also like Lévi-Strauss, Torrente Ballester shows both ways of thinking to be mythical in the sense that they impose arbitrary structures on to reality in order to make sense of its non-sense. If Torrente Ballester sides with the mythmakers it is not because they hold the key to a Romantic or Jungian intuitive wisdom, but because they revel in the potentially infinite proliferation of variant versions offered by myth, as opposed to central authority's 'scientific' insistence on imposing a single 'truth'. The demythifiers of Villasanta and the mythmakers of Castroforte are equally concerned with power, but if the former is centralist the latter is federalist: the mythmakers of the first and second Round Tables declare Castroforte an independent canton at the time of the Federal Republic of 1873 and during the Second Republic (a fictional representation of the approval of Galician Autonomy in the referendum of June 1936, whose implementation was prevented by the outbreak of Civil War). Both falsify the truth for political ends; but the former does so in the name of unity (which in practice means the suppression of dissident Castroforte), while the latter does so in the name of diversity. The contradictions of Castroforte's myths lead to the fabrication of yet more versions; as the local newspaper editor says, there is nothing better than a polemic (375). Whereas Villasanta suppresses deviance by enforcing press censorship; hence the description of Castroforte by Unamuno will end up attributed to the pro-Nationalist Maeztu. It is not that Castroforte is right and Villasanta wrong, for the attribution of such an article to Unamuno is of course equally false, Castroforte being a fictional invention: the point is that Castroforte makes no claim to possess 'the sole truth'. If Castroforte is declared not to exist, it is partly because Villasanta wants to wipe it off the map but also because, as a fictional entity, it replaces the scientific concept of truth (single) with the literary concept of verisimilitude (which allows multiple versions). The religious orthodoxy represented by the priest Don Acisclo is opposed to the heterodoxy of Bishop Jerónimo Bermúdez, whose pantheistic doctrines proclaim God (truth) to be in all things: a proposition vindicated by Don Acisclo's discovery that God keeps changing places (266). Don Acisclo will conclude not that God is plural but that he does not exist: the established Church's 'scientific' concern with a single truth leads it to an equally scientific atheism. It is important that the initial inventors of Castroforte's messianic myth of the multiple returning saviour J.B. – Godofredo Barallobre and Torcuato del Río – should be Masons, combining rationalism with a deviant religious occultism that is a hotchpotch of different sources, Castroforte's first masonic lodge being created out of the heterogeneous ideas picked up by Lilaila Barallobre on her European travels and being named after the St Lilaila who herself is a Christianized version of the Greek goddess Diana. (To compound the incongruous 'blend', Torrente Ballester has named his multiple mythical hero after his favourite brand of Scotch.) Not for nothing do Castroforte's Masons believe in reincarnation: that is, the plurality of identity. The same heterogeneity that denies Castroforte's myths the status of 'truth' allows them to embody the aspirations of the collective: the myth-making of the successive Round Tables will give a sense of identity to the various sectors of the community.

In linking political dissidence with occultism, Torrente Ballester is partly pointing to the historical role played by the secret society in transmitting liberal ideas in late eighteenth- and nineteenth-century Spain, but is also echoing the 1960s fusion of fringe politics with fringe religious cults. It is not surprising that Torrente Ballester should have written the prologue to Fernando Sánchez Dragó's best-selling *Gárgoris y Habidis: Una historia mágica de España* (1978), a hippy vindication – by a repentant ex-communist – of Spanish counter-culture through the ages, combining an exaltation of anarchist millenarianism with a compendium of the clichés inherited by Spanish fascism from the 1898 Generation and Ortega. Sánchez Dragó's aim is to 'liberate' Spanish history by re-writing it in terms not of historical events but of the nation's myths: history 'not as it was but as it might have been'. The one area where he diverges from Falangist ideology is his rejection of the concept of unity in favour of that of marginality: most of his second volume (and parts of the first, retracing 'origins') will be devoted to Galicia, the 'Finisterre' of Europe both because of its geographical location and because of its connection with the Atlantis myth and the Celtic 'fringe'. Sánchez Dragó will exalt the fourth-century Galician Gnostic heretic Priscilian as the expression of an 'essential' Spanish Christianity 'betrayed' by the 'falsifications' of history, and will demand 'a reincarnation of the archetype, another Hercules, a popular hero to give us back strength, gaiety and improvisation'.[72] Sánchez Dragó's attempt to 'invent or recover' the myths and heroes necessary to the rebirth of Spain's lost 'essential soul' reads like a 1960s version of Giménez Caballero's *Genio de España*: indeed Sánchez Dragó would write an admiring preface to the 1983 re-issue of Giménez Caballero's fascist tract. In his prologue to Sánchez Dragó's book, Torrente Ballester restates the Falangist belief that 'The true Spain is neither that of the Right nor that of the Left, but that which failed to realize itself', at the same time pointing out that only part of him sympathizes with Sánchez Dragó's irrationalism, a greater part preferring the exercise of rational thought.[73] The similarities and differences of *La saga/fuga de J.B.* to Sánchez Dragó's *Historia mágica* are instructive. Like Sánchez Dragó, Torrente Ballester stresses Galicia's marginal position as a 'Finisterre', to the extent that Castroforte literally takes off from *terra firma* in an inversion of the Atlantis myth, two variants of which are referred to in the novel: the Galician legend of the sunken city of Doñinos, in which two children ('dos niños') in a cradle survived the deluge (584); and the Gaelic legend of St Brendan's floating isles, which forms the basis of the story of the first priest Don Asclepiadeo (385–8). As in Sánchez Dragó, the links between Galician and Celtic folklore are stressed: Castroforte's 'saviour' Admiral John Ballantyne – an inversion of General John Moore, the

English hero of the Spanish independence struggle against Napoleon, commemorated by a statue in La Coruña – is made into an Irishman who fought for Napoleon to defend his fellow Celts against Castilian domination, his broken sword being erroneously venerated in Fingal's Cave; while the three successive Round Tables of Castroforte impersonate King Arthur and his knights, reviving the search for the Grail in their none-too-chivalric pursuit of the 'Vaso Idóneo' ['Ideal Receptacle'] or female sexual organ. Again like Sánchez Dragó, Torrente Ballester proposes the heretical Christianity of Priscilian (in the form of Bishop Bermúdez) as an antidote to the repressive morality of established Catholicism, and stresses the pagan substratum on which the worship of St James of Compostela (in the heterodox guise of St Lilaila) rests.[74] Not mentioned by Sánchez Dragó on account of its Portuguese provenance, but in keeping with his call for the return of the lost heroes of the past, is the messianic myth of 'sebastianismo' – the belief in the future return of the young Portuguese King Sebastian killed in battle in North Africa in the sixteenth century – on which Castroforte's myth of the defeated J.B.s who will return from over the sea is based. As Torrente Ballester points out, Galicia is the only Atlantic region not to have a myth of the returning saviour: to stress the Atlantic nature of Castroforte's messianic myth, Torrente Ballester will have the various J.B.s disappear on death to a mythical zone 'beyond the Western Isles', taking with them St Lilaila of Ephesus who (like St James) had according to legend originally come by sea from Central Europe; in this way, inverting the centralist appropriation of St James of Compostela, the Celtic 'fringe' appropriates a central myth of orthodox Christianity.[75]

But if Torrente Ballester coincides with Sánchez Dragó in his exaltation of the marginal, he also goes out of his way to 'deconstruct' the process whereby myths are created, destroying any illusions about their value as the expression of an 'essential truth'. Carmelo Urza has shown the novel to be a satire of the mythification of local history undertaken by the nineteenth-century founders of Galician regionalism, Torcuato del Río – whose seven-volume *Historia ... de Castroforte* is published round about 1864 – being based on Manuel Murguía, husband of Rosalía de Castro, whose seven-volume *Historia de Galicia* was published in 1865: 1865 is the date of the founding of the first Round Table, devoted to defending the traditions of Castroforte. Like the Round Table, Murguía had idealized a series of Galician historical figures who had fought for independence, notably the twelfth-century Bishop Gelmírez (another prototype of the fictional Bishop Bermúdez, also from the twelfth century); and had stressed the Celtic inheritance that supposedly made Galicians racially distinct. As Urza notes, Murguía's Galician 'Ossianism' follows the circular logic of inventing a past that fits present separatist aspirations, and then proclaiming such a past to be the manifestation of an 'essential destiny' to be realized in the future.[76] In fact such regionalist mythification is a mirror – with the names changed – of the mythification of national 'essences' that came to constitute Nationalist ideology: Torrente Ballester's double experience of Galician regionalism and the Falange suggests that the novel is a satire of both. Apart from exposing the political motivation underlying the mythmaking process, *La saga/fuga de J.B.* provides a postmodernist critique of the Western obsession with origins, showing – in line with Derrida – the circularity of the process whereby the cause is deduced from the effect, which is then declared to be the result of the cause. It is appropriate that the propagators of Castroforte's myths should be the successive 'Round' Tables. Bastida will invent the story of the circular 'Tren Ensimismado' ['Introverted Train'] after hearing Perfecto Reboiras' theory that Castroforte levitates when it becomes too 'ensimismado' ['involved with its own affairs'] in order then to argue that his derivation was the precursor of the initial thesis; within Bastida's fabrication, Torcuato del Río will in turn deduce the circular train from his theory about the Marathon Runner in order then to argue that the deduction is a prior model proving the initial theory (188–91). Bastida will become trapped in his own circular logic when the circular train he has invented materializes, demonstrating that Castroforte – and he with it – has indeed levitated in the sense that it has lost touch with reality (215–16). The search for origins that underlies Castroforte's mythifications does not 'ground' the town on firm 'foundations', but shows it to be built literally 'on thin air'. In the 'Incipit', the glass case containing the mythical 'Holy Body' and the river containing the mythical 'lampreys' will both be discovered to be empty (13–14). The more the members of the first Round Table (and Bastida as *ex officio* member of the contemporary Round Table) write about Castroforte's beginnings, the more the 'fog' literally thickens. The town has two contradictory founders attributed to it: Argimiro the Ephesian who started the lamprey trade and Celso Emilio the Roman who razed the town to the ground. In the former case it is suggested that Argimiro only capitalized on the lamprey trade that was there already; in the latter case Castroforte's 'beginnings' consist of its destruction (72). Likewise the 'original' arrival by sea of St Lilaila turns out to be a repeat of the earlier arrival by sea of the statue of Diana (196); the cave over which the shrine to St Lilaila is built is a mythical 'womb' that is also an image of hollow foundations, having previously been a shrine to the destroyed image of the 'absent goddess' Diana (319). As in Derrida, origins are indefinitely deferred as they are shown to be the traces of prior origins. Accordingly the 'Holy Body' on which the city's myths are founded is exposed as a fake; within the cave is a further hollow in which the 'original' saint's remains are found, the point being that this 'original' is the product of a dream by Bastida and is corrupt beyond recognition. Origins are by definition corruptions, and are the stuff dreams are made of. Jacinto and Clotilde Barallobre will return to the 'womb' of the cave not once but twice for there is no definitive return to origins; the result will be not the undoing of guilt and rebirth, but Jacinto's murder of his sister. Bastida will reject the option of committing figurative incest by returning to the 'womb' of origins for its promise of rebirth is a false one: if he were reborn he would be somebody else (425–6). The incest on which Jacinto believes his existence to be founded is likewise shown to be a lie. The Barallobres' family history is marked not by incest but by its opposite, adultery: there is no return to origins, only to an infinite sequence of adulterations (479). The genealogical tables included in the 'Secrets' handed down by the Palanganato are partly a parody of Lévi-Strauss' *The Elementary Structures of Kinship*, but can also be seen as a parody of Nationalist and regionalist historians' obsession with tracing a line of descent going back to origins, guaranteeing the 'legitimacy' of those who claim to be the nation's saviours: the lineage of the J.B.s turns out to be a labyrinth of bastardizations. Marriage alliances are shown to be dictated by economic interests rather than by a concern for dynastic legitimacy: Ifigenia – 'destined' from birth to be married to the supposed 'saviour' Joaquín Barrantes – is instead married to Rogelio Barallobre so that her illegitimate offspring by Barrantes may inherit the Barallobres' wealth (97).

The notion of history as a deviation from an 'essential destiny' – central to the 1898 writers and Falangist ideology, as to Galician regionalism – is satirized throughout the novel, making it clear that such an 'essential destiny' is an a posteriori fabrication designed to palliate failure by suggesting that things were 'meant' to have turned out otherwise. The 'meaning' of history thus comes to reside in what did not happen. The speech of Emilio Salgueiro, King Arthur of the second Round Table, defending himself at his court martial at the start of the Civil War, is 'recorded' by Perfecto Reboiras' parrot as a 'significant moment of history' precisely because he was not allowed to pronounce it (54, 211). The myth of the four J.B. figures 'destined' to save Castroforte is created to compensate the fact that they were all defeated: the salvation they failed to bring is deferred to a future date when they will return to realize the 'destiny' frustrated by historical 'accident'. Just as origins are deferred, so too is the 'end' of history. The fact that Jacinto Barallobre bought his life at the start of the Civil War when the other members of the second Round Table died is interpreted as his having 'cheated' a 'destiny' he will 'have' to fulfil in the future. The iron Jacinto throws at Clotilde misses its 'target', whereupon her 'destined' murder is likewise deferred to a later date (562). Jacinto Barallobre aptly terms this view of history as the deferral of destiny 'los hechos desfasados' ['bad timing'] (299). In a nice example of such 'crossed paths', the arrow 'destined' to kill Bishop Bermúdez in the twelfth century and the stone 'destined' to kill Jacinto Barallobre in the twentieth century collide in mid-flight and exchange courses, the arrow killing Jacinto and the stone killing the Bishop (575–6). The repeated motif of 'bizquera' ['squinting'] stands as an image of this notion of a 'destino torcido' ['crossed destiny']. José Bastida will find himself travelling through time in the form of a bent corkscrew, with the result that, on landing back in the present, he misses his 'destined' target and has to walk back to it (424–6). The most graphic image of this notion of history as the deviation from an 'essential destiny' is provided by Torcuato del Río's 'Tubular Homage', consisting of a founding 'Archetype' or 'Matrix' on to which are grafted a succession of tubes twisting in all directions (75). Not for nothing does Don Torcuato describe it as a model of irony (121), the chief irony being that it is a man-made invention.

The novel will show myth to be, not a return to origins, but the suppression of an original by a fraudulent substitute: what Jacinto Barallobre and Jacobo Balseyro graphically call 'gato por liebre' ['a con-trick', literally 'serving up cat instead of hare'] (256, 521). As Jacinto points out, such substitutions are the stuff of religious sacrifice, the prototype being Abraham's substitution of a ram for his son Isaac. Accordingly Jacinto will try to get Bastida to accept the role of sacrificial scapegoat by dying in his place. In order to keep alive the myth of St Lilaila, the necromancer Jacobo Balseyro will remedy the corruption of the original remains by substituting a new 'virgin' corpse: the subversive nature of the fraud – as an undermining of orthodoxy – is highlighted by the fact that the substitute 'saint' died a victim of the Inquisition. This notion of 'gato por liebre' in fact has a basis in the myth of St James of Compostela, of which that of St Lilaila is a subversive echo: in his book *Compostela y su ángel*, Torrente Ballester relates how the 'original' body of St James, which allegedly arrived in Galicia in the first century, was lost and 'rediscovered' in the ninth century; in 1589 the body was hidden to save it from marauding English pirates, again lost and 'rediscovered' in 1878. Both Torrente Ballester and Sánchez Dragó note that a heterodox regionalist tradition claims the relics now venerated at Compostela to be those of the martyred heretic Priscilian.[77] The novel relates the notion of substitution to the Freudian concept of sublimation: myth is a substitute for reality in the sense that it is a sublimation of failure. Hence the successive Round Tables sublimate their desire for the legendary actress Coralina Soto (who probably never visited Castroforte and who, in turn, is a stand-in for the Lilaila Souto whose charms were earlier lost to the town) through the wooden effigy which presides over their sessions, and which functions as a 'succubus' for Carmelo Taboada in hiding during the Civil War (173). The complementary notion of the 'incubus' occurs with two earlier Lilailas: the sixteenth-century Viuda de Barallobre who relieves the frustrations of widowhood with her dead husband's pickled sexual organs, miraculously reanimated by Jacobo Balseyro (482–7); and the early nineteenth-century Lilaila Barallobre who conceives a child by the 'spirit' of the dead Admiral Ballantyne (173). An alternative version replaces Admiral Ballantyne as her lover by the aptly-named 'Lieutenant' Rochefoucauld. Jesualdo Bendaña will relieve his jealousy at the Barallobres' possession of the 'Holy Body' of St Lilaila of Ephesus (also known as St Lilaila de Barallobre) by stealing Jacinto Barallobre's fiancée Lilaila Aguiar as a substitute; conversely Jacinto will relieve the loss of Lilaila Aguiar by making off with the body of St Lilaila. The important point about this last example is that the two Lilailas function as stand-ins for each other: the terms 'stand-in' and 'original' blur. The parodic Freudian symbolism of Bastida's time-travelling – as his elongated form plunges through a succession of tubes – points to the fraudulent nature ('gato por liebre') of the sublimation process whereby frustration is relieved by recourse to a symbolic substitute, but does not detract from the notion that sublimation is the psychological basis of myth. If Lévi-Strauss suggests that myth is the imaginary resolution of a real contradiction, Torrente Ballester suggests that it is the imaginary satisfaction of a real frustration. The various J.B.s function as idealized *alter egos* of the narrator Bastida, sublimating his inferiority complex: whether the tall and socially prestigious mythical figures Jerónimo Bermúdez, Jacobo Balseyro, John Ballantyne and Joaquín Barrantes (exotically remote in time), or his invented interlocutors Monsieur Bastide, Mr Bastid, Bastidoff and Bastideira (exotically remote in space, the Portuguese nationality of Bastideira reminding the reader of the four heteronyms used by the Portuguese poet Fernando Pessoa). Jacinto Barallobre will likewise achieve the success as a linguist denied him when writing under his own name by assuming the four pen-names of Jorge Bustillo, Jaime Barahona, Javier Bocanegra and Jesús Bolaños. Parodying both Freud and Lévi-Strauss, the four mythical J.B.s will further function as totems in the form of Clotilde Barallobre's pet parrot, cat, dog and donkey respectively (268–9). The three successive Round Tables will relieve their provincial mediocrity by assuming the roles of King Arthur and his knights: when sitting in the seat of Bohor, Bastida will feel himself grow in stature and sprout blond Celtic locks (58–9).

As the text repeatedly points out, the assumption of the roles of King Arthur and his knights lifts the members of the successive Round Tables on to a metaphorical plane that confers on them a freedom lacking in real life: Emilio Salgueiro cannot be shot for sedition because the telegram declaring Castroforte's independence was signed by him in his figurative existence as King Arthur (56, 71,

175). Jacinto Barallobre will likewise compare the sacrifice of a symbolic stand-in that is the essence of religious ritual to the linguistic operation of metaphor, whereby the original term is replaced by a figurative substitute (296). If Barallobre chooses Bastida as his symbolic stand-in, it is because – also being a linguist – he shares his understanding of the substitution process whereby language replaces things with words, and then replaces those words with further figurative designations (270). Barallobre will argue that, to release Lilaila Aguiar from her verbal promise to marry him, all that is needed is his verbal – i.e. metaphorical – death in the form of an obituary in the local newspaper: his figurative assumption of the non-existence of a dead man gives him the freedom to do what he likes with impunity (343–4). As Reboiras (appropriately interested in alchemy, the science of transformations) notes, language's metaphorical capacity for substituting one term for another opens up the possibility of an infinite sequence of transformations (182). The value of myth resides precisely in its ability, as a linguistic construct, to replace reality with a potentially infinite series of variant versions. The metaphorical system of transformations that constitutes myth is illustrated by Bastida's travelling through the personalities of the various J.B.s: in fact what we have – in a parody of Jakobson's linguistic theories – is a symbolic system ruled jointly by metaphor (Bastida's figurative adoption of the identity of another) and metonymy (his lateral displacement from one figurative identity to another) (451). The result – as Bastida's various figurative identities get mixed up – is a hilarious sequence of mixed metaphors, whose incongruities point to their lack of literal 'sense' at the same time as demonstrating the infinite potential of the system of transformations. In his mixed figurative identity as Jerónimo Bermúdez and Jacinto Barallobre, Bastida will literally mix his metaphors by describing himself in the same breath as Bécquer's 'olas gigantes que os rompéis bramando' ['giant roar of breaking waves'] and Calderón's 'hipógrifo ... que corriste parejas con el viento' ['hippogryph ... galloping astride the wind'] (462) – the 'hippogryph' itself, of course, being a nice example of a mythical creature that is a hybrid. A further model of metaphorical and metonymical transformation is provided by Bastida's nonsense poems, written in an invented language which is a figurative replacement for Spanish (which in turn is a figurative replacement for reality) whose morphemes can move laterally to create a potentially infinite series of combinations.[78] Bastida's poems are accompanied by their 'translation', the point being that translation purports to offer the 'original' meaning of a text when in fact it is an a posteriori derivation. What we have is another metaphorical relationship – 'metaphor' and 'translation' both meaning 'transferral' – in which we are left with two substitute terms without an original. The analogical process that creates metaphor can work in both directions: the priest Don Acisclo will discover that if his story is analogous with those of the earlier priests Asclepiadeo, Asterisco, Amerio and Apapucio, none can be called the 'original' for they are all variants of each other. Hence Don Acisclo will find his rational train of thought – attempting to establish a one-way causal relationship between an 'original' premise and its consequences – interrupted by a series of free associations linked analogically by rhyme, whose terms are interchangeable (391–3). The analogical – as opposed to causal – nature of Bastida's travelling through the personalities of the various J.B.s is shown by the fact that he moves backwards and forwards rather than in a one-way sequence. A model of this analogical process is provided in his dream – governed by the acausal logic of association – by his two subordinate officers, each a metonymical fusion of the ecclesiastical attributes of Bishop Bermúdez and the naval attributes of Admiral Ballantyne, who comprise mirror-images of each other without there being an original model to generate the reflections (445–6). In his tape-recorded working notes at the time of writing *La saga/fuga de J.B.*, Torrente Ballester declares his aim to be the rejection of causal processes, either through the comic insistence on futile causes, or by creating a reciprocal system of cause and effect such that each is jointly cause and effect to the other.[79]

The novel constitutes a parody of Lévi-Strauss' structuralist analysis of myth, whereby variant versions are seen as analogous and interchangeable rather than related by a process of causal transmission; but the parody in no way implies criticism of Lévi-Strauss' refusal to see variant versions as 'corruptions' of an 'original'. Lévi-Strauss' view of myth as a 'language' whose individual terms are arbitrary designations rather than 'caused' by reality, but which attempts to make sense of reality by re-combining those terms to form meaningful structures, is basic to *La saga/fuga de J.B.* Torrente Ballester's notebooks show him to have a thorough knowledge of

French structuralism and linguistic theory: if he himself has earned his living as a teacher of language and literature, he will make the three contemporary J.B.s – the mythmakers who contribute to the multiple myth of the four earlier J.B.s – linguists by profession.[80] For Jesualdo Bendaña's criticisms of myth are another form of mythification: not only do they revive interest by creating a polemic, but they add to the proliferation of variant versions. Indeed Castroforte's myths are presented to us not as 'original texts' but via a series of secondary critical interpretations: the various historical writings of the first Round Table, and the multiple critical exegeses of the linguists Bastida, Barallobre and Bendaña. Historical writing and critical exegesis – as linguistic versions – are shown to be synonymous with mythification. The various 'Historias' of Castroforte are both its 'history' and its 'story', the point being that there are multiple versions. The phrase 'histórico o mítico' recurs throughout the text: as in the Viking sagas referred to in the title, myth and history are indistinguishable.[81] The historian Torcuato del Río and the critic Bastida are both nominated 'Official Novelists' of the city. Like the *Quixote* – on which Torrente Ballester has published an important critical study – *La saga/fuga de J.B.* consists of the characters' critical discussions on the various 'historias' related within the novel, for criticism adds to the fictional process by creating a further version. The fact that Castroforte's myths are present only via the secondary genres of historiography and criticism also reinforces Lévi-Strauss' notion of myth as *bricolage*: a second-degree cultural system which re-works fragments from prior cultural systems. Accordingly *La saga/fuga de J.B.* consists of texts about texts about texts: there is no original reality, Castroforte – we are reminded – does not exist. Indeed there are not even any original texts. Hence the variant versions that constitute myth cannot be labelled 'right' or 'wrong': the inversion confirms the basic structure by providing a mirror-image of it. The opposition between Castroforte's two rivers – the mobile Baralla and the static Mendo – confirms their common nature as images of the mythical eternal return: if the J.B.s disappear down the Baralla to return in a mythical future, those who drown in the Mendo 'return' via the mythical lampreys who devour them and in turn are eaten by Castroforte's inhabitants. Lilaila Aguiar's ascent to the shrine of St Lilaila, the details of which are a systematic inversion of Coralina Soto's previous ascent, does not contradict but confirms the mythical pattern: both pilgrimages are versions of the ascent of the 'Holy Body' of St Lilaila in the ninth century, narrated simultaneously to make the point that the earlier date of the events described does not mean that it should be seen as the 'original' version (314–23). In this notion that variant versions have equal value – indeed one cannot strictly talk of an 'inversion', for that supposes the existence of an 'original' model – Torrente Ballester comes close to political nihilism. The supposition is not that all positions are equally valid but that all positions are equally false. Torcuato del Río's inversions of history with his journalistic 'canards' – according to which the Paris Commune ended with the massacre of the bourgeoisie by the working classes (125) – have a satirical intention that gives them a certain historical value; but the reduction of Bastida's intervention in the Civil War to a series of inversions as he finds himself reliving the same story on the other side (419–22), or his transformation with minor alterations of a poem to the Popular Front into a poem to the Nationalist Front (337) implies that it makes no difference what side you are on. As in Cela's *San Camilo, 1936* there are echoes here of the Falangist rejection of party politics, with the difference that Falangism is now seen as one of the partisan versions to be rejected.

A more obvious reminiscence is that of Borges, whose total intellectual scepticism leads to a similar apoliticism. As in Borges, Torrente Ballester's principal instrument for demonstrating that all linguistic constructs are mythical versions of versions is parody: either through the use of mock erudition, or through citation of other existing texts. The intertextual references in the novel draw attention to themselves so as to make the point that the text is not an original creation but – as in Lévi-Strauss' definition of myth – an interweaving (literally 'text') of prior cultural fragments. Thus the police chief responsible for Lilaila Barallobre's execution will be named as 'un tal Pedrosa, granadino' ['one Pedrosa, from Granada'] (141), ensuring we notice that her story echoes that of the Mariana Pineda immortalized by Lorca; the constant references to 'niebla' together with the suggestion that Unamuno visited Castroforte likewise ensure we spot the Unamunian games Torrente Ballester plays with the reader.[82] Cultural references from different periods are jumbled up – as in the amalgam of the eleventh-century Pope Hildebrand with the sixteenth-century Pope Aldobrandini to create

228

a fictional early seventeenth-century Pope Aldobrando Hildebran-
dini; or in the blurring of Abelard and Héloïse with Sartre and
Simone de Beauvoir – so that the comic effect makes us aware that
the text is a second-degree cultural construct. The humorous use of
anachronism – as in the opening 'Incomplete and Probably Apocry-
phal Ballad of the Holy Illuminated Body', where the pastiche of
medieval epic includes a comparison of the sea to a swimming pool
(23) – or the incongruous mixing of incompatible literary styles – as
in Barrantes' poetry, 'plagiarized' from a variety of poets who wrote
after his death (372) – similarly makes us realize that what we are
reading is an adulterated version of other versions. The text thus
mirrors the *bricolage* process whereby Castroforte's myths are
created: the best example being the creation of the female secret
society of the Palanganato out of an incongruous mixture of imports
from northern Europe – ranging from Rosicrucianism to the hip
bath – which, when Spain in the mid-nineteenth century becomes
increasingly cut off from the outside world, lose all contact with their
original context, leading to the progressive corruption of the Palanganato's rituals as the concept of reincarnation ('palingenesia') gets
confused with that of ablution ('palangana' being 'washbasin'), the
final stage in the process being the degeneration of the society's cult
of the returning messianic hero J.B. into worship of the 'Havana
lollipop': a nonsensical amalgam of disparate phallic symbols (92–4,
148). A similar process of linguistic corruption leads to the transformation of Admiral Ballantyne into 'Valentín' (37). A large number
of characters have aliases, nicknames or are re-named (as is Castroforte, changed to 'Castrofuerte' by Castilian centralist authority),
emphasizing the fact that all nomenclatures are arbitrary sign-
systems with no direct relationship to reality. Much of the novel is
devoted to parodying Lévi-Strauss' notion of myth as a classification
system which mediates binary oppositions: not only with the various
mock diagrams juxtaposing variant stories or opposing characters,
but also with the inclusion of spoof taxonomies such as Bastida's
division of men into the categories 'clever, dim-witted and half-caste'
(112); or Castroforte's local version of the signs of the zodiac,
replacing the twelve conventional symbols with thirteen disparate
(Spanish 'disparate' means 'nonsense') symbols including Puss in
Boots, the Lamprey, the Bollocks and 'los Tres Pies para un Banco':
a colloquial expression meaning literally 'the Three-Legged Chair'

but used figuratively to mean 'a piece of nonsense' (86–7). In turn Torcuato de Río will replace this substitute taxonomy with a 'modern' version consisting of thirteen scientific references including Curvoisier's Principle (meaning Lavoisier), the Condom and 'la Carabina de Ambrosio': literally 'Ambrosio's Carbine' but used figuratively to designate something that is utterly useless (96). The substitution of new classification systems for old ones highlights their arbitrary nature; while the mixing of literal and figurative designations makes the point that all language – as a sign system – is a form of metaphor. In a lovely joke, the list of sea creatures greeting the various J.B.s as they sail off into the sunset in a final mythical fusion includes 'gambas al ajillo' ['prawns in garlic'], mixing Lévi-Strauss' categories of the 'raw' and the 'cooked' in a mock mediation of binary oppositions. Such spoof taxonomies are obviously reminiscent of Borges, who shares Lévi-Strauss' belief in the arbitrary relation of linguistic constructs to reality but who does not share his faith in man's ability to impose sense on to the non-sense of reality through the creation of structures that have an internal logical coherence. The presence of both writers in *La saga/fuga de J.B.* illustrates Torrente Ballester's own ambivalent attitude to rationalism.

The influence of Lévi-Strauss is most strongly felt in the novel's depiction of myth as an autonomous system which 'speaks through' man rather than being his conscious creation. Torrente Ballester has said that he wrote the novel as a 'medium' whose role was limited to ordering the random occurrences recorded by him on his tape-recorder.[83] The principal (possibly sole) narrator of the novel – José Bastida – also acts as a 'medium' at the spiritualist séances of the innkeeper, the point being that he is a fake medium who invents the 'voices' he transmits in order to earn his supper. This does not imply that he is after all in control; rather that he is a medium for voices that impose themselves from within instead of from without. Lévi-Strauss' notion that myth 'speaks through' man is – as in structuralist criticism – fused with Northrop Frye's suggestion that all literature is the expression of a set of universal archetypes located in the unconscious. *La saga/fuga de J.B.* is a parody of this view but also an illustration of it; what needs pointing out is that the novel's dialogue with structuralism is also a dialogue with myth criticism. Torrente Ballester departs from myth criticism in that, in his novel, the universal archetypes of myth do not provide access to a Jungian intuitive wisdom. Here he is closer to Freud, showing how the fact that language involuntarily betrays the unconscious makes man a prisoner of shameful urges: Bastida will find his nonsense poetry – which dictates itself to him as 'medium' – filling with stereotyped Freudian symbols that betray a filthy mind and aggressive urges he did not know he had; he will conclude that the responsibility for such base emotions lies not with him but with language, over which man has no control (429–31). The novel does however uphold myth criticism's belief that all products of the imagination correspond to a set of universal archetypes. Thus the various stories related in the novel are shown to conform to a basic archetypal pattern – reminiscent of those proposed by Propp – in which a protagonist with the initials J.B. 'saves' a heroine called Lilaila, is opposed by a clerical antagonist whose name begins with A, and defeated by a Bendaña. Not for nothing – in a parodic inversion of structuralist criticism's reduction of all stories to the conflict between a protagonist A and an antagonist B – are the protagonists all called B and the antagonists A. An inverted sub-set of stories relates how a priest whose name begins with A betrays a heroine, makes off with a treasure, and serves a Bendaña. The notion that characters are functions in a structure rather than individuals is illustrated by the variable lovers attributed to Beatriz Aguiar (285) and Coralina Soto (493, 513) in successive versions of their stories. The novel satirizes the scientific pretensions of structuralist criticism by reducing the text to a set of mathematical formulae based on the various possible permutations of a total of 5 priests whose names begin with A, 6 Bendañas, 6 Lilailas and 7 J.B.s (15 if one includes Bastida and Jacinto's heteronyms), not to mention the 3 parrots and 3 Round Tables. The mathematics become literally ludicrous when the 7 J.B.s are turned into a two-dimensional board game with 49 permutations, followed by a three-dimensional model with 343 permutations (the text says '363' which must be an error [207]). At the same time the novel confirms the idea, central to structuralism, that language – being based on inherent 'deep structures' which enable the individual to generate a potentially infinite number of new utterances, while at the same time confining him to the conventions of grammar – is the model for all cultural systems. The three linguists Bastida, Barallobre and Bendaña are the only people capable of decoding the cultural systems of Castroforte. The metaphorical and metonymical

moves that comprise Bastida's travellings through the various combinations of J.B.s are also the paradigmatic and syntagmatic substitutions that comprise the generation of grammatically-valid statements: not for nothing does Bastida keep a prized edition of Bello y
Cuervo's Grammar beside his bed (where of course he dreams – or
his grammar book dictates – his paradigmatic and syntagmatic
travels). The board game of the J.B.s is a model both of myth and of
language, for the latter is proposed as the prototype of the former. In
accordance with structuralism, Bastida's transmigrations through
the various J.B.s show the concept of the individual to be an illusion
for he is the vehicle of cultural systems that have their own
conventions. The novel is the product of Bastida as medium–
narrator: it has no author for the inclusion of Torrente Ballester
within Bastida's text demotes him – in an Unamunian game – to the
status of fictional entity (201–2).[84]

If myth is an autonomous system it has the universal validity of
the archetype, but at the same time the fact that it cannot be
ascribed to an individual voice makes its veracity impossible to
substantiate. Here Borges' scepticism takes over from Lévi-Strauss'
faith in logical systems. The Borgesian image of the labyrinth –
which Torcuato del Río nicely defines as 'reason laughing at itself'
(121) – is central to the novel: in particular that of the stairs leading
to Barallobre's library (another Borgesian image) which go up while
they seem to be going down and vice versa. The same impossible
perspective characterizes the narrative. Torrente Ballester has stated
that Bastida is the narrator of the whole novel, at times disguising
himself in the second or third person.[85] There is however no hint of
Bastida's presence as narrator in the 'Incipit' (where he is mentioned
in the third person) or the 'Coda' (where he appears in the third
person and indeed loses the grammar book which allows him to
perform linguistically). Chapter 1 is ambiguously titled 'Manuscript
or possibly monologue of J(osé) B(astida)', but consists of a relatively
straightforward proliferation of texts within texts in the sense that
the authors of the texts are identified and Bastida's presence as first
person frame narrator is clearly established. Chapter 2 starts as
straightforward third person narrative but halfway through starts –
like Castroforte – to take off from its foundations as Bastida slips into
the second person imagining his conversation next day with Jacinto
Barallobre (313), which then slips back into third person narration

in such a way that we are not sure if we are still inside Bastida's imaginings or have jumped to a later event. We then pass to Jacinto's commentary on the three ascents to the shrine of St Lilaila, Coralina Soto and Lilaila Aguiar which similarly become independent from their speaker as if taking place before the reader's eyes (314–23). After this we return to apparently straightforward third person narration of events, albeit with repeated temporal dislocations and the inclusion of texts within texts, until – in what may be a dream of Bastida having dozed off in the library – we slip into an impossible dialogue in direct speech between Barallobre (in the guise of Jacobo Balseyro) and Bastida (in the guise of Pico della Mirandola in his fictional incarnation as Paco de la Mirandolina) simultaneously witnessing from their flying carpet the War of Independence against Napoleon and the Civil War (414–24), at the end of which Bastida finds himself in the street, implying that the previous sequence was not after all a dream experienced in the library (or else that we have returned to 'reality' still within the dream). Chapter 3 switches to Bastida's first person narration as he lies in bed waiting for Julia (where we left him at the end of the previous chapter) and starts to travel through a series of combinations of the various J.B.s (including himself as Bastida). The supposition (confirmed by Torrente Ballester) that this is a dream allows us to accept the total confusion of time scales with relatively little difficulty.[86] The problems start when (523) we slip in mid-sentence from Balseyro to Bastida as Julia enters his bedroom and they make love: have we moved from the dream back to 'reality', or is this Bastida as himself still inside his dream? Without any transition we then slip into a fantasy Last Judgment which must be a dream sequence (a second dream? a continuation of the same dream?), in which Bastida defends Julia accused by her father of sleeping with Bastida; again without transition this slips back into Bastida and Julia making love for a second time (outside the dream? inside the dream?), jumping (546) to Bastida waking up next morning (still in the first person) and continuing with the narration of that day's events (with Bastida now in the third person). Just as we feel we are back on firm ground, we accompany Bastida and Jacinto to the Cave (nicknamed the 'Cave of Montesinos' by centralist authority [141]) in a parody of the narrative uncertainty of the Cave of Montesinos episode in the *Quixote*: the Freudian symbolism, whose coarseness echoes that of the

Cervantine prototype, suggests that the Cave stands as an image of
the unconscious and that the sequences that follow may be another
dream (or a continuation of the same dream?) in which Bastida is
assuming the double role of himself and Barallobre in order to
'prove' the 'authenticity' of the information learnt by him in his
multiple incarnations as the various J.B.s in the dream sequence
which opened the chapter (a nice echo of Don Quixote's consciousness in Part 2 of the *Quixote* of his fictional adventures in Part 1). This
supposition is reinforced when we switch inexplicably (554) to
Jacinto in the Cave with Clotilde, in the first person attributing to
himself Bastida's dream in the first part of the chapter; and when
Bastida re-enters the narrative in the first person and declares that
he as Bastida in the third person narrated the preceding sequence
between Jacinto and Clotilde in Jacinto's name (562). When Bastida
orders a re-take of the scene between Jacinto and Clotilde (563) –
with Jacinto now appearing in the third person attributing the
dream in the first part of the chapter to Bastida, and with Bastida
appearing in the first person as stage director – we are left not
knowing where we are at all: Bastida's ability to control the course of
the narrative makes it unlikely that the sequence is a dream and
leaves us with no way of naturalizing its strangeness. (Interestingly,
in his book on the *Quixote* Torrente Ballester rejects the critical
assumption that the Cave of Montesinos episode is a dream.)[87] The
impossibility of the narrative perspective now becomes total as
Bastida still in the Cave starts to relate (in the past tense) events that
will take place next day (566), slipping into the final Apocalypse as
the four mythical J.B.s plus Jacinto Barallobre with the 'Holy Body'
sail off to their mythical haven beyond the Western Isles. The
'Coda', narrated by a consistent third person narrator, appears –
apart from the impossibility of the events described – to be quite
straightforward, but this is of course a trick. We assume that both the
'Incipit' and 'Coda', being narrated in the third person, relate 'real
events', and that the mention in both of the crowd gathered in the
Alameda means that they are taking place at the same time. But the
'Incipit' tells us that Barallobre has disappeared with the 'Holy
Body' and that the innkeeper has thrown Bastida and Julia out: both
'events' narrated in the clearly fantastic sequences in chapter 3. In
which case the whole of the 'Incipit' may also be fantasy and, since
they refer to a common 'event', the 'Coda' with it. Of course the

point – as the necromancer Jacobo Balseyro had earlier reminded us (537) – is that 'the Word works miracles'. The novel's impossible narrative perspective obliges us to recognize that the realist habit of distinguishing in a fictional text between what 'really happens' and what is fantasy is an absurd one, because in fiction all events are mythical.[88]

If Torrente Ballester confirms the universality of myth as the expression of a set of archetypes while at the same time undermining its veracity, he will also contradictorily propose myth as a liberation from the limits of time and space while at the same time suggesting that it traps man in a set of infinite repetitions. The Ides of March theme confirms the notion of myth as the expression of Fate, inasmuch as it reduces history to a series of variations on an archetypal pattern: the possibility of reincarnation (central to the J.B. myth) allows one to transcend the limits of the self, but at the same time condemns one to re-living the same old story. Each new J.B. will incarnate the promise of salvation not realized by his predecessors, but is condemned to repeat their defeat by the fact that he is a variation on a theme. If the Ides of March are marked by the conjunction of seven stars, it is because Fate consists of the repetition of a basic pattern (the coincidence of the stories of the 7 J.B.s). The fact that the Apocalypse foretold throughout the novel comes to pass on the Ides of March – completing the millennial cycle since the arrival of the 'Holy Body' – confirms the mythical notion that history is the repetition of what is 'written' in the past in the sense that – as the 'record of the past' – history is a narrative construct and all stories are variants on an archetypal structure. In the case of the priest Don Acisclo, the reduction of history to a series of mythical repetitions clearly denies his freedom: his discovery of Fate – the condemnation to re-live a pre-ordained story (literally 'foretold', i.e. 'told before') – leads to loss of belief in free will and consequent loss of belief in God (390–3). This notion that Fate is in opposition to God reinforces a mythical view of history as the condemnation to evil. Bastida's travels through the various J.B.s, which in one sense liberate him from the limitations of his historical present, in another sense trap him in a temporal labyrinth; his whirlwind tour of different historical periods breaks down the linear sequence by moving back and forth in time, but he is still travelling in time. Chapter 2 will end with his leap out of 'la espiral del tiempo' ['the spiral of time'] (426) in which he has become trapped. It is significant that he lands back in the present in the form of Benito Valenzuela's dustcart, standing as an image of the 'dustbin of history'. The repeated appearance of Benito Valenzuela pushing his dustcart turns him into a Sisyphus condemned to go on pushing the ever-increasing burden of history: at one point (403) his dustcart becomes a train, reminding us of Torcuato del Río's circular 'train of history'. The board game of the J.B.s which Bastida enters in chapter 3 again traps him in a temporal labyrinth: the point of the game is to find a 'way out' of the maze of circular repetitions (as he keeps finding himself at points of time through which he has previously travelled) in order to get back to the present. In his incarnation as Jacobo Balseyro – specialist in alchemy, the science of transformations whose goal is the liberation of spirit from matter – Bastida will learn to fly and will overcome death by revitalizing the Viuda's dead husband's organs, but he can do so only by repeating the Osiris myth (486) just as he is condemned to fly to and fro between previously written stories.[89] Bastida – as linguistic magus – has the freedom to order a re-take of the Battle of Trafalgar depicted in the Barallobres' painting (290) and of Clotilde's murder in the Cave (566), but in neither case is he free to change the end of the story. Words 'work miracles' but also trap man in their implications: Jacinto's remark (echoing Cain) 'Am I my sister's keeper?' inevitably presupposes that he has killed Clotilde (567). Metaphor gives man the freedom of moving on a figurative plane but also traps him in its logic: the figurative King Arthurs of the successive Round Tables are condemned to be cuckolded by the various figurative Lancelots (70–1). The continuous flow of the narrative, with its lack of paragraph divisions and temporal leaps, transcends chronology but at the same time the reader – like Bastida in the board game – gets lost in its labyrinthine convolutions. Bastida's discovery of the sequence of J.B.s will make him have second thoughts about his initial declaration that time is an illusory product of the mind (275).

It is important that Bastida's time-travelling should take the form of a board game, for games are a curious mixture of chance and rules, of the spontaneous and the pre-ordained. Perhaps the primary intertextual presence felt in the novel is that of Lewis Carroll.[90] Like Carroll – a mathematician and author of a book on logic as well as a writer for children – Torrente Ballester is fascinated by the paradoxical similarity of mathematical logic and the infantile imagination. The mythical world of Castroforte – like Alice's 'wonderland' – is based on a mixture of mathematical calculus and children's games.[91] Bastida's fantasy in chapter 3 will end – like *Alice's Adventures in Wonderland* – with a mock trial which disintegrates into harmless unreal figures (539, 544); both novels link the dream world with the unconscious via the use – in Carroll's case, pre-dating Freud – of Freudian symbolism (flying, changing shape); both make use of nonsense verse; and both are concerned with the question of whether man controls language or language controls him. Hence the fascination with verbal play – the debate between Bishop Bermúdez and the priest Don Asclepiadeo over whether 'Everything is God' is the same as 'God is everything' (508) reminds us of Alice's musings over whether 'I say what I mean' is the same as 'I mean what I say' – which both sets man free and traps him in its logic.[92] The notion of myth as verbal play is fundamental to *La saga/fuga de J.B.*: it is this which ultimately makes it – despite, or in a curious way because of, its critique of myth – a mythical novel. For the rules that govern games – like the grammatical rules that govern language – provide a form of release, despite their inexorability, in that they are not 'caused' by reality but arbitrary conventions. Like language, games do not reproduce reality but situate man in an alternative, parallel world. To play a game you have to accept the rules knowing they are arbitrary: the game-player necessarily stands in a position of irony. Even more so the inventor of the game, who obliges others to abide by the arbitrary rules he has created. In this sense the mythmaker is the supreme ironist. In his study of the *Quixote* – titled *El Quijote como juego* [*The Quixote as a Game*], written immediately after *La saga/fuga de J.B.* and based on a course of lectures on Cervantes given immediately before it – Torrente Ballester puts forward the interesting thesis that Don Quixote is not mad but consciously acting out the role of fictional chivalric hero in order to secure a degree of freedom by forcing others to play his game. As Torrente Ballester puts it, Don Quixote's goal is 'the transformation of reality into a stage'; like Bastida in the 'Cave of Montesinos' episode, Don Quixote is an actor in a play he is himself directing.[93] *La saga/fuga de J.B.* will thus view myth from the ironic, ludic point of view of the mythmakers who are fully aware of the fictional nature of their creations. As the inventor of the mythical game that is the whole novel, Bastida frees himself from his role as 'desgraciado' ['butt of others'] by forcing others to 'play the game' in all senses of the phrase. Even when he enters the board game of the J.B.s as a player and is thus himself obliged to respect its logic, as its inventor he retains an awareness of its fictional nature and is thus able to extricate himself from its labyrinth at the right moment. Jacinto Barallobre will likewise force Castroforte to dance to his tune by donning the uniforms of the mythical J.B.s in full knowledge of the imposture. Jacinto's ludic notion that uniforms are theatrical costumes which turn reality into a 'play' (in both senses of the word) is contrasted with that of the café owner who hires waiters to fit the uniform (274), thus making man a prisoner of his role. It is because Jacinto sees all roles as a charade, rather than taking them seriously, that he achieves the freedom of the 'non-existent'. Bastida and Jacinto are rival ironists, each struggling for control over the mythical game in order to make the other assume the role of the J.B. due to die on the Ides of March. In the course of chapter 3, Bastida will succeed in getting Barallobre to suspend his ironic disbelief and take his mythical role seriously: once Jacinto admits – within Bastida's narrative of course – to belief in the J.B. myth, he is doomed to live out its conclusion and die on the Ides of March. The ironic mythmakers Bastida and Jacinto Barallobre are contrasted with the 'scientific' historian Jesualdo Bendaña who believes in the objective validity of his verbal constructs. Jesualdo's lack of a sense of humour links him with the equally humourless priest Don Acisclo and the 'godos' of Villasanta, representing centralist authority. In *El Quijote como juego* Torrente Ballester notes: 'Irony belongs to Socrates, not to Adolf Hitler. Irony is always the product of a clear, critical, sceptical view of reality.'[94] Appropriately the innkeeper, who takes seriously the spiritualist séances which Bastida – as medium – knows to be a fraud, wants to attract the spirit of Hitler (41). Bastida, as ironist, is also the political subversive: imprisoned for three years after the Civil War and still obliged to report regularly to the authorities (305–6). Despite the fact that Torrente Ballester refers to Socratic irony, his belief in the illusory nature of all verbal constructs in fact situates him in the tradition of Romantic irony, as defined by Kierkegaard. In an essay on humour, Torrente Ballester explicitly links irony with modern linguistic theory: 'Modern linguistics, which claims pre-eminence over all the other sciences, has at least served to show us that nothing is as it is but as it is told ... The humorist defends words because only they allow him to show the ambiguity of reality, to expose The Great Platitudes, to undermine The Great Affirmations, to formulate the only truths which are those of contradiction: never "God exists" or "God does not exist" but both at once.'[95] Hence *La saga/fuga de J.B.* will exalt myth precisely because it is not to be believed. It is because Torrente Ballester is against myth that he is for it. The mythical Apocalypse which ends the last chapter is not to be believed because it takes place in a dream, but it allows Bastida to defeat the repressive Don Acisclo by staging a Final Judgment in which – as joint producer and actor – he ousts Don Acisclo from his role as prosecutor. The Brazilian Carnival image – the world upside down: authority reviled, the 'desgraciados' vindicated – which had assailed Bastida after Jacinto Barallobre's impersonation of the poet Barrantes (382) – appropriately dismissed by the humourless Jesualdo Bendaña as a 'Carnival masquerade' (384) – is reintroduced by Bastida in the Final Judgment episode when he interrupts Don Acisclo's 'show' trial with a train of riotous black prostitutes, thus turning it into a 'show' of his own in which Don Acisclo's repressive morality is subverted by fun in the form of Eros (527–8, 539).

This last scene takes place to a musical background as Don Acisclo and his mythical predecessors perform an opening trumpet concerto (530–1), which gets drowned by the thunderings of Jacobo Balseyro 'whose voice sounded like an organ playing', finally pulling out the trumpet stops (536): the trumpet in both cases being the appropriate instrument to accompany a Final Judgment scene. (The 'Incipit' will also start with the clamour of 'voices ... like trumpets'.) The scene will reach its climax with a chorus of the massed voices of all those persecuted by the law (542). The linked motifs of Eros and music – both being forms of play – are central to the novel. Its title explicitly introduces the notion of the 'fuga', appropriately 'playing' on the double meaning of the word as 'fugue' and 'escape'. The figurative organ music of Balseyro reminds us of Bach's toccatas and fugues. Bach is Don Acisclo's favourite composer (266); his love of music – like that of all the priests whose names begin with A, each of whom 'escapes' from a foreign country with his respective musical instrument – is his one redeeming quality: his violin playing will save him from the death sentence pronounced by the Round Table. Appropriately Don Acisclo's favourite hobby is improvising variations on a theme by Bach (282). Lynne Overesch has shown the novel to be structured in terms of a set of themes and variations: the principal theme being the J.B. myth (including the subset of Bastida's imaginary interlocutors, forming a 'wind quartet'), with the story of the priests whose names begin with A – explicitly described as 'variations on a melodic theme' (389) – forming a contrapuntal inversion.[96] The musical variations correspond to the variant versions of which mythical narrative is 'composed'. Torrente Ballester's equation of myth and music – 'saga/fuga' – is clearly taken from Lévi-Strauss' 'Overture' to *The Raw and the Cooked*, where he compares the two not only on account of their common structure as variations on a theme, but also because both are 'languages' which 'transcend articulate expression', and because both 'unfold in time' while at the same time resorting to repetition in order to deny time. Like music, myth provides 'a middle way between aesthetic perception and the exercise of logical thought'.[97] Lévi-Strauss comes close here to reintroducing the Romantic notion of myth as an instrument of integration, overcoming the split between reason and emotion and reconciling the irreconcilable. If music, despite the strictness of its rules, is the freest of the arts in the sense that it is non-referential, so myth – being freed from the restrictions of realist narrative – is able to achieve the impossible: the temporal labyrinth of Torrente Ballester's mythical text creates an impossible perspective that, like the Moebius strip, generates infinity: whether that of the possible permutations of J.B.s, or that of the circularity of the narrative whereby the end of the last chapter provides an 'explanation' of the opening 'Incipit' while at the same time the opening 'Incipit' is deduced from the fantasy sequence that comprises the end of the last chapter. An analogue of this process is provided by Bastida's nonsense poem on the love affair of the nut and the bolt, an incongruous mixture of arithmetic formulae and Freudian symbolism which through its replacement of sense by rhythm generates an 'infernal cycle of indefinite repetition' (202–4). It is an infernal cycle because the nut and the bolt, being different sizes, cannot bring their love affair to a conclusion; but it is also an image of erotic play in which desire is prolonged into eternity. The link between music and Eros is reinforced by the musical associations of the 'Holy Body' of St Lilaila, which functions in the novel as a central image of desire.[98] The 'St Lilaila Royal Society for Music and Poetry' will serenade the contemporary Lilaila Aguiar (307–10). The last chapter – aptly titled 'Scherzo y fuga': a fugue/escape which is also play or jest – will end with the 'Holy Body' revolving eternally to the comic musical rhythm – 'dos destellos, uno, pausa' ['one, two and three, pause'] (580) – created by its flashing light. The humour does not undermine the equation of desire with illumination, for playfulness is the essence of Eros. This final image of rhythmic and erotic play coincides with the final fusion of the various J.B.s – to the musical accompaniment of an incongruous mixture of chorales and popular 'habaneras', fusing conflicting musical styles (577) – for if music is harmony (the resolution, through counterpoint, of difference), Eros is copulation. The play of similarities and differences that comprises the novel is resolved through the rhythmic structure that is language: as Perfecto Reboiras says, 'No hay más lenguaje que el amoroso' ['The only language is the language of love'] (181), for grammar is conjugation.[99] Fate – the subordination of history to a 'design' – is likewise the result of a 'conjunction' of the planets: an erotic encounter – one version of the planetary 'conjunction' being the seven contiguous beauty spots on Coralina Soto's left buttock (473–4) – which also constitutes the 'music of the spheres'. Torcuato del Río's 'Tubular Homage' is a model of Fate which is also a model of Freudian symbolism (with its tubes inserted into holes) and a musical instrument, whose crowning achievement is the 'Smoke Concerto' (145–6).

Torcuato del Río's 'Tubular Homage' is also connected with his declaration of the 'Independent Canton of Castroforte' (74, 77), further linking music and Eros to political subversion. Don Acisclo's attitude towards music is analogous to that of the Round Table towards Eros, in that both are seen as instruments of domination. For Don Acisclo, music 'subdues the masses' (568); the Round Table's erotic pursuits consist of sexual 'conquests'. The pornographic activities of the politically subversive Round Table – whose history is at the same time 'a political history and a pornographic story' (71) – are favourably opposed to the moral repressiveness of Don Acisclo, for whom women are the Devil: his female parrot is accordingly called 'Beelzebub', its virtuoso rendition of Bach's Third Partita for Violin reminding Don Acisclo that the Devil is traditionally depicted as a musician (237–8). Don Acisclo – like centralist authority in Villasanta, with its male saint – represents a repressive patriarchal authority, as opposed to the matriarchal society of Castroforte – exemplified by the worship of St Lilaila, the independent-minded later Lilailas, the female secret society of the Palanganato, not to mention the Round Table's cult of the 'Vaso Idóneo' – which makes Eros the mainspring of its activity. It is likewise in the name of patriarchal authority ('patria potestas') that Julia's father will denounce her for sleeping with Bastida (540). The priest Don Acisclo's violin playing is shown to be a clear case of sexual sublimation ('tocar el violín' being a euphemism for masturbation): his dreams – in which he conducts an orchestra of nuns who escape his control as the music conjures up the mythical J.B. as an incarnation of female desire (232–6) – reveal his repressiveness to be based on an unconscious fear of sexuality. The pornographic pursuits of the Round Table – and the equally pornographic rituals of the Palanganato – are presented as subversive because they are funny. If Don Acisclo's pornographic dreams subvert his repressiveness through their involuntary humour, the rest of Castroforte will consciously cultivate the 'dirty joke' – practical as well as verbal – which Freud showed to be a release for libidinal energies. The prime example is the contest between Castroforte and Villasanta over whether the female sexual organ has more names than the male, which Castroforte (championing the female principle) wins by including figurative designations: that is, because it appreciates the relation of Eros to verbal play (177–82, 215). At the same time this scurrilous form of eroticism, while preferable to repression, is opposed to the wholesome eroticism represented by the 'Holy Body' of St Lilaila and her successors, and by Bastida's union with his 'Holy Body' Julia, the difference being that the former is based on self-gratification and the latter – as a form of worship – on offering oneself to another. It is noticeable that the J.B. figures who receive most attention are the poet Barrantes (with his quixotic, chivalresque love for the loud Coralina Soto whom, in contrast with the rest of the Round Table's cult of a purely physical 'Grail', he transforms into an idealized Dulcinea; the statue of Barrantes will in turn be adorned with flowers each spring by the romantically-inclined maidens of Castroforte), and in particular Bishop Bermúdez (for whom the worship of woman is a form of religious worship). Bermúdez – like his prototype Priscilian – is regarded as a heretic because he advocates marriage for priests and ordains women: he will himself marry his deaconess Lilaila Barallobre, who appropriately is the custodian of the 'Holy Body'. Bermúdez's belief in the sanctity of the body will lead him to a pantheism which is in fact a heresy within a heresy: he will oppose his belief in the divinity of all created things to the Cathars' belief that the world and the flesh are the work of the Devil (508). Ironically Torrente Ballester shows the sexual repressiveness of institutionalized Christianity to be in agreement with the Manichean heresy according to which the Devil, and not God, was responsible for the Creation.[100] In his 'philosophy of love' Bermúdez fuses with Peter Abelard, claiming that 'Cuando un hombre y una mujer cohabitan, Dios está entre ellos ... , y el placer que experimentan es anticipación del Paraíso' ['When a man and a woman cohabit, God is with them ... , and the pleasure they taste is a foretaste of Paradise'] (505–6). Bishop Bermúdez will resolve Bastida's earlier hesitations over whether man can escape the prison of time, stating firmly at the end of chapter 3 that time is an invention of the mind: it is thus the body that provides release (572). In the 'Coda' Bastida and Julia will escape the mythical world of Castroforte as it loses contact with the ground, but they escape into an alternative mythical world of the eternal present of Eros: a Paradise emerging 'cleansed' from the early-morning rain, with the sunflowers turning to greet the dawn (585). Bastida does not escape the fate of the mythical J.B.s but realizes it by saving his St Lilaila. His comic nickname 'Orang-outang' acquires a positive function as he returns to nature, dragged into the wood by Julia in an inversion of the caveman dragging his mate to his lair, for this is a matriarchal paradise in which men give themselves to women. Bastida's other nickname is 'Flat Feet' (32): he and Julia will land with their feet firmly on the ground not in the sense that they have rejected the floating world of myth for historical reality, but in the sense that they have rejected culture for nature. Bastida has lost his grammar book; the last image they have of the Castroforte they have abandoned is El Poncio, representing political authority. The implication is that the mythical world of Castroforte is also the world of history, for history – being a cultural construct which attempts to impose sense on to the non-sense of nature – can never be more than a mythical version. Bastida and Julia's entry into Paradise is accompanied by the loss of language, as they playfully express their love through laughter and Bastida's nonsense language which, because they do not attempt to impose sense on to non-sense, are able to express nature without falsifying it. As Bastida had earlier stated, the aim of his nonsense language is to 'Escandir el silencio, organizarlo en ritmos' ['To scan silence, form it into rhythmic patterns'] (509); significantly this aim was born of his desire to escape the political chatter of the nightwatchman who befriended him in the political capital Madrid. If the mythical world of Castroforte – a verbal, i.e. cultural reality – is represented by play in the form of artifice (disguises, the theatre), the mythical world of Eros into which Bastida and Julia escape is represented by natural play in the form of body language.

It is this final affirmation of Eros – seen as a natural, eternal present outside of history – that most clearly makes *La saga/fuga de J.B.* a mythical novel. Torrente Ballester's sceptical demythification of all verbal constructs is met with an affirmation of belief in Eros as the 'ground' of being. Despite the parodies of Freudian symbolism – Don Acisclo's desire to abolish syringes, volcanoes, hosepipes (304); Barallobre's dream of broken dolls, empty drawers and lances (333); Bastida's castration fantasy of knives, razor blades, saws (436); Abelard and Héloïse's Oedipus and Electra complexes (the Electra complex being frequently attributed to Freud, albeit wrongly) (471–2) – the novel confirms Freud's view of Eros as the foundation of all human activity: not for nothing is Castroforte built over the Cave as an image of the unconscious and of the female sexual organ. In the same way the novel's satire of the notion that destiny is 'what should have happened but didn't' does not prevent it from confirming a Freudian view of history as the frustration of desire: desire is presented as subversive precisely because – as what is not allowed to happen – it stands in opposition to history. The description of Bastida and Julia's union via Bastida's private language further reinforces the Freudian notion that sexuality is an autonomous area of 'authentic' private experience separated off from the 'inauthenticities' of social existence. Here Torrente Ballester is in agreement with the 'Freudian Left' – criticized for its anti-historicism by Frederic Jameson – whose political thought, best exemplified by Marcuse, dominated the 1960s.[101] Torrente Ballester has expressed his disagreement with Marcuse's equation of sexual and political liberation, arguing that restraint is needed to turn sexuality from a biological process into erotic play.[102] In fact this is precisely what

Marcuse – whom Torrente Ballester seems not to have read – meant by his rejection of a purely genital sexuality for a non-productive, playful 'polymorphous perversity'. The difference is that Torrente Ballester – in keeping with much 1960s radical thought – accords eroticism a religious dimension. Eros is seen as analogous to religious experience because it provides release from the temporal and spatial boundaries of the self; in this respect it is also analogous to death. Bastida's union with Julia is an alternative version of the final fusion of the mythical J.B.s in death. It is important to remember that Bastida and Julia experience ecstatic release not only after abandoning the mythical world of Castroforte, but also in the course of Bastida's 'living' of the J.B. myth in chapter 3. The goal of Bastida's time-travelling is his 'meeting' with Julia. If he has to find the 'way out' of the board game to get to her, it is because he has to abandon those forms of mythification that look back to the past as the source of future liberation – that is, those forms of mythification that trap him in the labyrinth of time – in order to find liberation in the equally mythical eternal present of the body. The sexual act does not wake Bastida up from the dream world of myth but leads him into the further dream sequence of the Apocalypse: Eros ushers in the millennium in that – as an eternal present – it puts an end to the sequence of mythifications that comprise history, bringing the cycle of J.B.s to its close. If the millennium that puts an end to history finds its expression in the image of the 'Holy Body' as a central pivot revolving eternally to its silent rhythm, so sexual ecstasy instals Bastida and Julia 'en el centro mismo del silencio, en el centro del cosmos y de la vida' ['in the very centre of silence, in the centre of the cosmos and of life'] (525) and initiates an eternal repetition: '¡ahora y cuando quieras, esta noche y todas!' ['now and whenever you want, tonight and every night!'] (545). In the 'Coda', Bastida experiences in waking reality the sensation of floating previously experienced in dreams, and conversely Julia dreams that she is, as in reality, with Bastida (581–2). For at the end of the novel the mythical and the 'real' world have – through Eros – come to coincide. Bastida's union with Julia is not a rejection of the myths on which Castroforte's history is founded, but their fulfilment. If Castroforte's history is based on the deferral of liberation – the wait for a future saviour who will bring to fruition the unfulfilled promise of the past – Bastida and Julia will put a stop to history by finding release in the here and now. The goal of history – the realization of desire – is literally the 'end' of history. If in the 'Coda' Bastida and Julia 'wake up' from the 'dream of history', it is because they have ended it by realizing its aspirations and making the dream come true.

In its suggestion that Eros provides release from history – and in its related recourse to music as an antidote to the linearity of narrative – *La saga/fuga de J.B.* echoes *San Camilo, 1936* and *Reivindicación del conde don Julián*. There are however important differences. In Torrente Ballester's case, the 'dream of history' is presented not as a nightmare but as huge fun. For in *La saga/fuga de J.B.* the 'dream of history' is chiefly represented not by the repressive official mythifications of centralist authority, but by the subversive counter-mythifications of Castroforte which resort to humour as a weapon against political and moral repression. Bastida and Julia's final escape into Eros is the final stage in the process of liberation: a return to nature which ends the mythifications that comprise Castroforte's history not by rejecting them but by realizing them. Eros provides release not by 'undoing' history but by bringing it to fruition. And if Cela and Juan Goytisolo equate Eros with male self-gratification, Torrente Ballester will propose a mythical eternal present based on the mutual giving of pleasure. The female figures in *La saga/fuga de J.B.* are archetypal images of male desire; but the mythical J.B.s function as reciprocal archetypal images of female desire. It is important that Bastida – chief mythmaker and narrator – should be an androgynous figure whose body is male but whose eyes – and consequently vision – are female (285). Torrente Ballester's escape ('fuga') into Eros is not a withdrawal into self but – in a chivalresque gesture – the surrender of self to other. The image *La saga/fuga de J.B.* proposes of sexual and political liberation is not that of Narcissus but (in the form of the bust of Coralina Soto) that of Queen Guinevere (57, 497).

Notes

Introduction

1 References are to the following editions: *Tiempo de silencio*, 16th edn, Barcelona, Seix Barral, 1980; *Volverás a Región*, Barcelona, Destino, 1981; *Si te dicen que caí*, Barcelona, Seix Barral, 1977; *San Camilo, 1936* (full title *Vísperas, festividad y octava de San Camilo de 1936 en Madrid*), Madrid and Barcelona, Alfaguara, 1969; *Reivindicación del conde don Julián*, ed. Linda Gould Levine, Madrid, Cátedra, 1985; *La saga/fuga de J.B.*, 4th edn., Barcelona, Destino, 1976. The date of publication of *Tiempo de silencio* is given variously as 1961 and 1962. I have followed the breakdown of editions of the novel given in the 15th edition of 1979, which gives 1961 for the 1st edition and 1962 for the 2nd.

2 Ronald Schwartz, *Spain's New Wave Novelists: 1950–1974*; and Margaret E. W. Jones, *The Contemporary Spanish Novel, 1939–1975* respectively.

3 Luis Martín-Santos, *Time of Silence*, trans. George Leeson, London, John Calder, 1965; Juan Benet, *Return to Región*, trans. Gregory Rabassa, New York, Columbia University Press, 1985; Juan Marsé, *The Fallen*, trans. Helen R. Lane, Boston, Little Brown and Co., 1979; and Juan Goytisolo, *Count Julian*, trans. Helen R. Lane, New York, Viking Press, 1974.

4 All the translations from Spanish are my own.

5 A welcome exception here is John White, *Mythology in the Modern Novel*.

6 p. 74.

1 The historical uses of myth

1 p. 20.

2 See William Righter, *Myth and Literature*, pp. 8–9; and Erich Gould, *Mythical Intentions in Modern Literature*, *passim*.

3 Michel Foucault, *The Order of Things: An Archaeology of the Human Sciences*, pp. 328–35.

4 *The Myth of the Eternal Return*; see also José Luis Abellán, *Mito y cultura*.

5 See Jeffrey M. Perl, *The Tradition of Return: The Implicit History of Modern Literature*, pp. 54–7.

6 'What is a historical system?', in *Biology, History and Natural Philosophy*, ed. Allen D. Breck *et al*. See also Allen D. Breck's article 'The use of biological concepts in the writing of history' in the same volume, pp. 217–32.

7 pp. xxi, 224, 297–301.

8 See *The Rise of Modern Mythology*, ed. Burton Feldman *et al*., pp. 297–301.

9 Preface to the 2nd edition, quoted by John B. Vickery in *The Literary Impact of 'The Golden Bough'*, p. 11.
10 *The Rise of Modern Mythology*, pp. 470–1.
11 *Beyond Good and Evil*, p. 75.
12 See Hayden White's chapter on Nietzsche in *Metahistory: The Historical Imagination in Nineteenth-Century Europe*, pp. 331–74.
13 *Collected Papers*, vol. 4, p. 182.
14 Perl, *The Tradition of Return*, p. 224.
15 *The Psychopathology of Everyday Life*, p. 321; *Totem and Taboo*, p. 91.
16 I use the term 'modernist' in its English, not Spanish, sense.
17 K. K. Ruthven, *Myth*, p. 60.
18 *The Tradition of Return*, p. 237.
19 See Mann's essay 'Freud and the future', in *The Modern Tradition: Backgrounds of Modern Literature*, ed. Richard Ellmann *et al.*, pp. 672–9.
20 *Collected Poems 1909–1962*, p. 222.
21 'Ulysses – order and myth' in *James Joyce: Two Decades of Criticism*, ed. Seon Givens, pp. 201–2.
22 *The Tradition of Return*, pp. 9, 256–82.
23 *Modern Essays*, p. 145.
24 See *Man and his Symbols*, pp. 1–94; and *Four Archetypes*.
25 See Furio Jesi, *Cultura di destra*, pp. 38–40.
26 See *Myth and Reality*, pp. 73–4 in particular; and *The Myth of the Eternal Return* in general.
27 p. x.
28 Righter, *Myth and Literature*, p. 77.
29 p. 17.
30 *The Hero with a Thousand Faces*, p. 31. Frye's reductionism is criticized by Ruthven, *Myth*, pp. 75, 324.
31 *The Hero with a Thousand Faces*, pp. 212–13.
32 This is noted by Jonathan Culler in his foreword to Tzvetan Todorov, *The Poetics of Prose*, p. 7.
33 p. 10.
34 'The structural study of myth', in *Structural Anthropology*, p. 229. The Marxist antecedents of Lévi-Strauss' thought are discussed by Edmund Leach in *Mythology*, ed. Pierre Maranda, pp. 46–70.
35 See Jorge Larrain, *The Concept of Ideology*, p. 46.
36 *The Savage Mind*, pp. 233–4; see also *Structural Anthropology*, vol. 2, pp. 321–2.
37 *The Raw and the Cooked: Introduction to a Science of Mythology*, vol. 1, p. 12 and *passim*.
38 Geoffrey Kirk, *Myth: Its Meaning and Functions in Ancient and Other Cultures*, p. 246.
39 *The Concept of Ideology*, p. 144.
40 *The Savage Mind*, pp. 17–22, 67.
41 *Mythologies*, pp. 110, 128, 141–3, 151, 155 in particular.
42 *Life against Death: The Psychoanalytical Meaning of History*, pp. 18, 28, 88–9, 101, 240–4.
43 *The Political Unconscious: Narrative as a Socially Symbolic Act*, pp. 64–8.
44 *Alejo Carpentier: The Pilgrim At Home*, pp. 20–1; *The Voice of the Masters: Writing and Authority in Modern Latin American Literature*, p. 4.
45 pp. 18–21, 32–57.

46 See William Rowe, *Mito e ideología en la obra de José María Arguedas*.
47 For a critical discussion of the 'universal' appeal of myth for Latin American writers, see William Rowe, 'Paz, Fuentes and Lévi-Strauss: the creation of a structuralist orthodoxy'.
48 *Myth*, p. 78.
49 For an analysis of the critical presentation of myth in *Cien años de soledad*, see Edwin Williamson, 'Magical realism and the theme of incest in *One Hundred Years of Solitude*'.
50 pp. 96–104.
51 pp. 91–3, 100–1 in particular.
52 For a clearer account of Derrida's theories than that given by Derrida himself, see Jonathan Culler, 'Jacques Derrida', in *Structuralism and Since*, ed. John Sturrock.
53 Walter J. Ong, *Orality and Literacy: The Technologizing of the Word*.
54 See *Metahistory*.
55 *History – Remembered, Recovered, Invented*, pp. 5–34, 56–69, 96–101.
56 Printed in *Myth and Literature: Contemporary Theory and Practice*, ed. John B. Vickery, pp. 109–18; see p. 110–11 in particular.

2 Myth and Nationalist Spain

1 *En torno al casticismo*, pp. 26–30.
2 *Meditaciones del Quijote*, p. 92.
3 See Julio Rodríguez-Puértolas, *Literatura fascista española*, vol. 1, pp. 90, 288–9, 291, 297, 721.
4 *Genio de España*, p. 14 and *passim*.
5 Rodríguez-Puértolas, pp. 24, 46, 72, 347–54.
6 *El mito de la cruzada*.
7 Rodríguez-Puértolas, p. 332.
8 *Genio de España*, pp. 99–100, 195.
9 Rodríguez-Puértolas, pp. 27, 39, 43, 45, 617, 697. See also Román Gubern, *'Raza': Un ensueño del general Franco*.
10 Rodríguez-Puértolas, p. 48.
11 Rodríguez-Puértolas, pp. 37–8.
12 Rodríguez-Puértolas, pp. 44, 46, 49, 100–11, 297, 363, 346–7.
13 Rodríguez-Puértolas, pp. 49, 99, 253–7, 260, 284, 623–40. See also Carlos Blanco Aguinaga *et al.*, *Historia social de la literatura española (en lengua castellana)*, vol. 3. The classical strand in Falangist aesthetics is examined in Thomas Mermall, 'Aesthetics and politics in Falangist culture (1935–1945)'; and Umberto Silva, *Ideologia e arte del fascismo*, pp. 61–126.
14 See Ignacio Soldevila Durante, *La novela desde 1936*, pp. 144–7; and Robert C. Spires, *La novela española de posguerra*, pp. 246–77.
15 For a discussion of social realism, see Santos Sanz Villanueva, *Historia de la novela social española (1942–75)*; Fernando Morán, *Explicación de una limitación: La novela realista en los años cincuenta en España*; and Pablo Gil Casado, *La novela social española*.
16 *La colmena*, p. 11. For a discussion of Cela's work in the context of Falangist ideology, see Rodríguez-Puértolas, pp. 584–609.
17 See Eduardo Godoy Gallardo, *La infancia en la narrativa española de postguerra*; and Ignacio Soldevila Durante, *La novela desde 1936*, pp. 200–2.

18 Paul Ilie, 'Dictatorship and literature: The model of Francoist Spain', p. 254 and *passim*.

19 *Escrito en España*, p. 245.

20 Joan-Lluís Marfany (review of Cela, *La colmena*, ed. Raquel Asún, p. 377) points out that, even while banned in Spain, *La colmena* received good reviews in the official Spanish press, demonstrating the degree of official protection enjoyed by Cela.

21 'Direcciones de la novela española de postguerra' in *Novelistas españoles de postguerra*, vol. 1, ed. Rodolfo Cardona, pp. 47–65; and 'Juan Goytisolo: La busca de la pertinencia' in Gonzalo Sobejano *et al.*, *Juan Goytisolo*.

22 *La novela desde 1936*, p. 205.

23 *El furgón de cola*, pp. 11–12.

24 *Los bravos*, p. 206.

25 See Francisco García Sarriá, '*El Jarama*: Muerte y merienda de Lucita'.

26 *El Jarama*, p. 249.

27 The mythical function of the river in *El Jarama* is discussed by José Luis L. Aranguren, *Estudios literarios*, p. 247. The references to fate are charted by Edward C. Riley, 'Sobre el arte de Sánchez Ferlosio: Aspectos de *El Jarama*'.

28 See Gonzalo Sobejano, 'Juan Goytisolo: La busca de la pertinencia', in Gonzalo Sobejano *et al.*, *Juan Goytisolo*, pp. 23–51; Kessel Schwartz, *Juan Goytisolo*, pp. 49–59; Gonzalo Navajas, *La novela de Juan Goytisolo*, pp. 49–56; José Luis S. Ponce de León, *La novela española de la guerra civil (1936–1939)*, pp. 78–80.

29 *En los reinos de taifa*, p. 21. For a more detailed discussion, see my article 'The ambiguous implications of the mythical references in Juan Goytisolo's *Duelo en el Paraíso*'.

30 See in particular J. M. Castellet, *Literatura, ideología y política*, pp. 82–95, 135–56; and Monique Joly *et al.*, *Panorama du roman espagnol contemporain (1939–75)*, pp. 219–74. A more complex discussion of myth is found in Aranguren, *Estudios literarios*, pp. 212–310.

31 E. W. Herd, 'Myth and modern German literature', in *Myth and the Modern Imagination*, ed. Margaret Dalziel, p. 51.

3 Fiction as mask: *Tiempo de silencio*

1 Martín-Santos was arrested for political activities four times: in 1957, 1958 (when he spent four months in Carabanchel Prison, Madrid), 1959 (when he spent five months in Carabanchel) and 1962. See Esperanza G. Saludes, *La narrativa de Luis Martín-Santos a la luz de la psicología*, pp. 177–8.

2 The theory of 'objectivism' is outlined in J. M. Castellet, *La hora del lector* (1957) and Juan Goytisolo, *Problemas de la novela* (1959).

3 Much of this chapter is based on ideas developed at more length in chapters 1, 3 and 4 of my book *Ironía e historia en 'Tiempo de silencio'*.

4 See D. L. Shaw, *The Generation of 1898 in Spain*, p. 204; José-Carlos Mainer's introduction to his edition of Luis Martín-Santos, *Tiempo de destrucción*, pp. 17–50; Fernando Morán, *Novela y semidesarrollo*, p. 386; Gemma Roberts, *Temas existenciales en la novela española de la postguerra*, pp. 130, 175; Janet W. Díaz, 'Un par de charlas sobre *Tiempo de silencio*', p. 118; José Ortega, 'La sociedad española contemporánea en *Tiempo de silencio* de Martín-Santos', pp. 256–60; José Domingo, *La novela española del siglo XX*, vol. 2, p. 110.

5   See Sheelagh Ellwood, *Prietas las filas: Historia de Falange Española, 1933–1983,*
     pp. 113–15, 130–4, 203–51; Julio Rodríguez-Puértolas, *Literatura fascista
     española,* vol. 1, pp. 121–9; José Antonio Gómez Marín, 'Los fascistas y el 98';
     Herbert Ramsden, *The 1898 Movement in Spain,* pp. 133–41.
6   I owe this information to Juan Benet.
7   'Baroja-Unamuno', pp. 109–10.
8   Janet W. Díaz, 'Luis Martín-Santos and the contemporary Spanish novel',
     p. 237; interview with Benet.
9   See Julio Caro Baroja, *El mito del carácter nacional.*
10 See Miguel de Unamuno, *En torno al casticismo,* p. 109; Paulino Garagorri,
     Introducción a Ortega, p. 118; José Luis L. Aranguren, *La ética de Ortega,*
     pp. 19, 62–3, 77; and José-Carlos Mainer (ed.), *Falange y literatura: Antología,*
     pp. 16–20.
11 *Idea de la hispanidad* (lectures originally given 1938–42), pp. 36–9.
12 See Martín-Santos, 'Baroja-Unamuno', p. 110; and Pedro Laín Entralgo, *La
     generación del 98,* p. 118.
13 See Thomas Mermall, 'Aesthetics and politics in Falangist culture (1935–
     1945)', p. 47; and Alexandre Cirici, *La estética del franquismo.*
14 Juan José López Ibor, *El español y su complejo de inferioridad,* p. 128.
15 Ramón Menéndez Pidal, *Los españoles en la historia,* p. 17 and *passim*; Angel
     Ganivet, *Idearium español,* pp. 10–11.
16 *César o nada,* p. 158.
17 Américo Castro, *La realidad histórica de España,* pp. 252–63; Claudio Sánchez
     Albornoz, *España, un enigma histórico,* vol. 1, p. 59.
18 José Ortega y Gasset, *España invertebrada,* pp. 164–5; see also his *La rebelión de las
     masas,* p. 94.
19 Sánchez Albornoz, *España, un enigma histórico.*
20 *La realidad histórica de España,* p. 249.
21 *Meditaciones del Quijote,* pp. 59, 71, 82; *España invertebrada,* pp. 140, 149, 151.
22 Ricardo Macías Picavea, *El problema nacional,* p. 77.
23 See Enrique Tierno Galván, *Costa y el regeneracionismo,* p. 241.
24 This is noted by José Ortega, 'La sociedad española contemporánea en *Tiempo
     de silencio* de Martín-Santos', p. 257. In a brilliant if eccentric article ('Repeti-
     tion and excess in *Tiempo de silencio*'), Gustavo Pérez Firmat sees cancer as
     symbolic of the excess linguistic growth that characterizes the novel.
25 See *Apólogos,* p. 104.
26 *Libertad, temporalidad y transferencia en el psicoanálisis existencial,* pp. 232–3, 242,
     245.
27 See Gerald N. Izenberg, *The Crisis of Autonomy: The Existential Critique of Freud,*
     pp. 139–41, 148–9, 222, 248–9; L. Binswanger, 'The Existential Analysis school
     of thought', in *Existence,* ed. Rollo May *et al.,* pp. 191–213; and Rollo May,
     Man's Search for Himself, pp. 134–6.
28 Interviews with Benet and Castilla del Pino.
29 Erich Fromm, *The Fear of Freedom,* pp. 2–5, 24–9, 122–47, 172, 180, 186–91,
     207–21; *The Sane Society,* pp. 120–51, 237–40; and *Beyond the Chains of Illusion,*
     p. 167.
30 Ernesto Giménez Caballero, *Genio de España,* p. 226.
31 Thomas Mermall, *The Rhetoric of Humanism: Spanish Culture after Ortega y Gasset,*
     pp. 56–72, 80–1.
32 May, *Man's Search for Himself,* pp. 126–7.

33 Castro, *La realidad histórica de España*, p. 80 and *passim*.

34 p. 215.

35 See Claude Talahite, '*Tiempo de silencio* de Luis Martín-Santos: Etude des structures sémiotiques'. Talahite is the only critic to have noticed the Freudian substratum to the novel.

36 Juan Villegas, *La estructura mítica del héroe*, pp. 210–17.

37 Sir James Frazer, *The Golden Bough*, pp. 706–68.

38 Sigmund Freud, *Totem and Taboo*, pp. 141–50.

39 *Genio de España*, pp. 198, 226.

40 See Talahite, '*Tiempo de silencio* de Luis Martín-Santos', p. 195.

41 Freud, *Totem and Taboo*, pp. 141–50.

42 Censored on grounds of puritanism: all the brothel scenes were cut except for that of Pedro's arrest, which as a result makes nonsensical reading. Otherwise censorship was limited to isolated phrases. These censored passages were reinstated by the 5th edition of 1969 (I have not seen the 3rd and 4th editions of 1965 and 1967 respectively). The 1980 definitive edition appears to rectify editorial errors. The English translation is taken from the full text as printed in the definitive edition.

43 See Juan Carlos Curutchet, *A partir de Luis Martín-Santos: Cuatro ensayos sobre la nueva novela española*, pp. 38–9.

44 See José-Carlos Mainer's introduction to his edition of Martín-Santos, *Tiempo de destrucción*, p. 17.

45 Martín-Santos declared his admiration for Sartre in his reply to Janet W. Díaz's questionnaire, published in 'Luis Martín-Santos and the contemporary Spanish novel', p. 237. Sartre's influence on *Tiempo de silencio* is studied in detail in my book *Ironía e historia en 'Tiempo de silencio'*; and in Alfonso Rey, *Construcción y sentido de 'Tiempo de silencio'*, Gemma Roberts, *Temas existenciales en la novela española de la postguerra*, and Penelope Prendergast's perceptive PhD thesis 'The exploration and expression of existential awareness in Luis Martín-Santos' *Tiempo de silencio*'.

46 Igor Caruso, *Existential Psychology: From Analysis to Synthesis*, pp. 33–8, 63.

47 *Libertad, temporalidad y transferencia*, pp. 116, 215.

48 Ernst Neumann, *The Origin and History of Consciousness*, pp. 154, 156, 162, 380.

49 Ernst Neumann, *Depth Psychology and a New Ethic*, ch. 2.

50 *La estructura mítica del héroe*, pp. 203–30.

51 Julian Palley, 'El periplo de Don Pedro: *Tiempo de silencio*', pp. 167–83. See also ch. 5 of Prendergast's PhD thesis for an interesting discussion of Martín-Santos' use of Homeric and Joycean 'prefigurations'.

52 T. S. Eliot, '*Ulysses* – order and myth', in *James Joyce: Two Decades of Criticism*, ed. Seon Givens, pp. 198–202; Carl Jung, '*Ulysses* – A monologue', *Nimbus*, 2 (1953), 7–20.

53 See Stuart Gilbert, *James Joyce's 'Ulysses'*, chapter 3; W. B. Stanford, *The Ulysses Theme: A Study in the Adaptability of a Traditional Hero*, pp. 214–21; Harry Levin, *James Joyce: A Critical Introduction*; Samuel L. Goldberg, *The Classical Temper: A Study of James Joyce's 'Ulysses'*; C. H. Peake, *James Joyce: The Citizen and the Artist*; Richard Ellman, *Ulysses on the Liffey*, and *The Consciousness of Joyce*; Hélène Cixous, *The Exile of James Joyce*; Marilyn French, *The Book as World: James Joyce's 'Ulysses'*; Jeffrey M. Perl, *The Tradition of Return*, Part 2, chapter 5; Morton P. Levitt, 'A hero for our time: Leopold Bloom and the myth of Ulysses' and Richard M. Kain, 'The significance of Stephen's meeting Bloom:

NOTES TO PAGES 79-95

A survey of interpretations', both in *'Ulysses': Fifty Years*, ed. Thomas F. Staley, pp. 132–6 and 147–60 respectively.

54 See Fritz Senn, *Joyce's Dislocutions: Essays on Reading as Translation*; Hugh Kenner, *Ulysses*.

55 Ortega y Gasset, *Meditaciones del Quijote*, p. 92.

56 See Rey, *Construcción y sentido de 'Tiempo de silencio'*, pp. 3–23; also Carmen de Zulueta, 'El monólogo interior en *Tiempo de silencio*', p. 298. For Joyce's use of language, see John Gross, *Joyce*; and Anthony Burgess, *Joysprick: An Introduction to the Language of James Joyce*.

57 Jean-Paul Sartre, *Being and Nothingness: An Essay on Phenomenological Ontology*, Part 1, chapter 2.

58 See *Libertad, temporalidad y transferencia*, pp. 47–50; and *Apólogos*, pp. 113–14.

59 See Jonathan Culler, 'Jacques Derrida', in *Structuralism and Since*, ed. John Sturrock, pp. 154–80.

60 See Rey, *Construcción y sentido de 'Tiempo de silencio'*, pp. 10–11.

61 Felisa L. Heller, 'Voz narrativa y protagonista en *Tiempo de silencio*'.

62 '*Tiempo de silencio* de Luis Martín-Santos', pp. 363–77 in particular.

63 *Novela y semidesarrollo*, p. 370.

64 '*Tiempo de silencio* and the language of displacement'.

65 Severo Sarduy, *Barroco*, pp. 50, 67, 70–8. See also Roberto González Echevarría, *Relecturas*, pp. 95–118 on the Baroque in Góngora.

66 p. 134.

67 See Talahite, '*Tiempo de silencio* de Luis Martín-Santos', pp. 249–50.

68 Roberts, *Temas existenciales*, p. 203; Talahite, '*Tiempo de silencio* de Luis Martín-Santos', p. 271.

69 A welcome exception is Prendergast's PhD thesis; see chs. 2 and 3 in particular.

70 *Seven Types of Ambiguity*, ch. 7.

71 D. C. Muecke, *The Compass of Irony*, p. 39.

72 '*Tiempo de silencio* and the language of displacement'.

73 Søren Kierkegaard, *The Concept of Irony*, p. 278.

74 pp. 126, 210.

75 p. 245.

76 Octavio Paz, 'Analogía e ironía', in *Los hijos del limo*, pp. 87–112.

77 *The Compass of Irony*, pp. 126, 246.

78 '*Tiempo de silencio* de Luis Martín-Santos', pp. 31–3.

79 'El psicoanálisis existencial de Jean-Paul Sartre', p. 165.

80 *Dilthey, Jaspers y la comprensión del enfermo mental*, pp. 41–2.

81 pp. 92, 164.

82 See Aquilino Duque, '"Realismo pueblerino" and "realismo suburbano". Un buen entendedor de la realidad: Luis Martín-Santos'; also Ricardo Doménech, 'Luis Martín-Santos'.

83 See Castellet, *Literatura, ideología y política*, p. 145; and Díaz, 'Luis Martín-Santos and the contemporary Spanish novel', p. 237.

84 p. 175.

85 See Guillermo Sucre, *La máscara, la transparencia*.

4 Fiction as echo: *Volverás a Región*

1 Prologue to 2nd edition of *Volverás a Región*, p. 7.

2 Robert C. Spires, *La novela española de posguerra*, pp. 237–45.

3 See *The Golden Bough*, pp. 1–14 and 193–209 in particular.
4 See Plutarch, *Parallel Lives*, vol. 1, pp. 305–83.
5 See *The Golden Bough*, pp. 209–13.
6 *The Golden Bough*, pp. 917–30; and Virgil, *The Aeneid*, p. 125.
7 See *The Divine Comedy*, 1: *Inferno*, pp. 27, 37.
8 *Del pozo y del Numa*, p. 115.
9 Introduction to Benet, *Una tumba y otros relatos*, p. 17.
10 The only critic to have examined in any detail the novel's debt to *The Golden Bough* is Malcolm Alan Compitello (*Ordering the Evidence: 'Volverás a Región' and Civil War Fiction*, pp. 145–76), who does not pick up King Numa's responsibility for founding the worship of Terminus, nor the infernal connotations of Mantua, nor the relation of the gold coin to the golden bough.
11 See Claude Lévi-Strauss, *The Savage Mind*; and *Structural Anthropology*, p. 229.
12 See Jonathan Culler, 'Jacques Derrida', in *Structuralism and Since*, ed. John Sturrock, pp. 154–80.
13 'Prohibition and transgression in *Volverás a Región* and *Una meditación*' in *Critical Approaches to the Writings of Juan Benet*, ed. Roberto C. Manteiga *et al.*, pp. 53–4.
14 *El ángel abandona a Tobías*, pp. 113–30.
15 María-Elena Bravo (*Faulkner en España: Perspectivas de la narrativa de postguerra*, pp. 299–300) remarks that Numa both conquers reason and is the product of it.
16 pp. 85–8.
17 pp. 104–6.
18 *Del pozo y del Numa*, p. 122.
19 p. 108; cf. *The Golden Bough*, pp. 266–71, 294–5.
20 pp. 62, 99–100, 175, 182–3.
21 Benet's analysis is reminiscent of that of Norman O. Brown in *Life against Death*, chapter 15 (particularly Section 4 'Owe and ought'). However Benet implies that the psychological need for defensiveness is essential to the human condition.
22 One is again reminded of Norman O. Brown's equation of sexual liberation with the acceptance of death (*Life against Death*, p. 101), but for Benet the equation is tragic.
23 *Del pozo y del Numa*, pp. 165–7.
24 See Octavio Paz, *Claude Lévi-Strauss: An Introduction*, p. 6.
25 pp. 68, 186.
26 pp. 60, 83–4, 98–9, 139 in particular.
27 'El texto invisible', *Los Cuadernos de La Gaya Ciencia*, p. 10.
28 pp. 135–6. Compare Norman O. Brown's view of Paradise as 'the realm of Absolute Body' (*Life against Death*, p. 89). Again Benet does not share Brown's optimism about the possibility of attaining this lasting release from time.
29 *The Savage Mind*, pp. 256–60.
30 pp. 77, 82–3, 188–9.
31 Benet's view of language is discussed by Robert C. Spires, 'Juan Benet's poetics of open spaces', in *Critical Approaches to the Writings of Juan Benet*, ed. Roberto C. Manteiga *et al.*, pp. 1–7; and by María-Elena Bravo, 'Región, una crónica del discurso literario'.
32 See Luis F. Costa, 'El lector–viajero en *Volverás a Región*'; and Robert C. Spires, *La novela española de posguerra*, p. 227.
33 Robert C. Spires (*La novela española de posguerra*, pp. 235–6) notes the confusion of names, but misreads the novel when he suggests that the woman talking to

Dr Sebastián is identified sometimes as Marré and sometimes as María Timoner.

34 The use of narrative voice is discussed by Esther W. Nelson, 'Narrative perspective in *Volverás a Región*' and Julia Lupinacci Wescott, 'Subversion of character conventions in Benet's trilogy', both in *Critical Approaches to the Writings of Juan Benet*, ed. Roberto C. Manteiga *et al.*, pp. 27–33 and 75–9 respectively. See also Spires, *La novela española de posguerra*, pp. 226–34.

35 '¿Contra Joyce?', pp. 26–8.

36 pp. 98–9, 131–63.

37 See Benet's introduction to the 2nd edition of *Volverás a Región*, pp. 9–10.

38 *The Raw and the Cooked*, pp. 15–16.

39 'El lector–viajero en *Volverás a Región*'.

40 'Enigma as narrative determinant in the novels of Juan Benet'.

41 pp. 18–20.

42 María-Elena Bravo ('Región, una crónica del discurso literario', *Modern Language Notes*, p. 253) notes the photographic nature of Benet's images.

43 See *En ciernes*, p. 77; and *Una meditación*, p. 194.

44 José Luis L. Aranguren (*Estudios literarios*, p. 286) notes the stylistic similarity with Proust. The influence on Benet of Faulkner has been discussed by Randolph D. Pope, 'Benet, Faulkner, and Bergson's memory'; and particularly by María-Elena Bravo, *Faulkner en España*. Benet has himself talked of the impact made on him by Faulkner: see 'De Canudos a Macondo', p. 52; and the interviews with Bravo in *Faulkner en España*, pp. 39–44, 202–5, 266–302. Although Benet's use of language addresses the same problems as Faulkner's work, it seems to me that Benet's style has an intellectual, discursive, indeed classical quality not found in Faulkner.

45 John B. Vickery (*The Literary Impact of 'The Golden Bough'*, pp. 106–19) suggests that Frazer's chief literary influence has been stylistic. Robert C. Spires (*La novela española de posguerra*, p. 238) notes the similarity between the landscape descriptions of Benet and Frazer. Malcolm Alan Compitello (*Ordering the Evidence*, pp. 171–6) notes that several details of landscape description in *Volverás a Región* are taken from *The Golden Bough*.

46 See Benet, 'De Canudos a Macondo'. In a talk at the Spanish Institute, London in May 1978, Benet described how his reading of Cunha's book led him to revise the presentation of landscape in *Volverás a Región*. See also Malcolm Alan Compitello, 'Región's Brazilian backlands: The link between *Volverás a Región* and Euclides da Cunha's *Os sertões*'.

47 *The Savage Mind*, pp. 17–22.

48 p. 193.

5 Fiction as corruption: *Si te dicen que caí*

1 I owe this information to Marsé. *Si te dicen que caí* was first published in Mexico. On its publication in Spain after Franco's death in 1976, it was seized by the police and not allowed back into the bookshops till February 1977.

2 The words of 'Cara al sol' are as follows: 'Cara al sol, con la camisa nueva que tú bordaste en rojo ayer me hallará la muerte si me lleva y no te vuelvo a ver. Formaré junto a los compañeros que hacen guarda sobre los luceros, impasible el ademán, y están presentes en nuestro afán. Si te dicen que caí, me fui al puesto que tengo allí. Volverán banderas victoriosas al paso alegre de la paz, y

traerán prendidas cinco rosas las flechas de mi haz. Volverá a reir la primavera que por cielo, tierra y mar se espera. Arriba, escuadras, a vencer, que en España empieza a amanecer'. The references in the novel to 'Cara al sol' are studied in Nivia Montenegro, 'El juego intertextual de *Si te dicen que caí*'.

3 Geneviève Champeau, 'A propos de *Si te dicen que caí*'.

4 Marsé kindly showed me his collection of press cuttings. The documentary basis of the novel is studied by J. M. Ruiz Veintemilla, 'La transformación de la realidad en *Si te dicen que caí*: el asesinato de Carmen Broto y la guerrilla urbana'. See also the interviews given by Marsé in Samuel Amell, *La narrativa de Juan Marsé*, p. 110; and in Jack Sinnigen, *Narrativa e ideología*, pp. 112, 116–17. Rafael Abella's description of life in Spain in the 1940s in *Por el Imperio hacia Dios: Crónica de una posguerra* provides useful background information to the novel.

5 See Emmanuel Larraz, *Le Cinéma espagnol des origines à nos jours*, pp. 66–73.

6 The exploits of Quico Sabaté are recounted in E. J. Hobsbawm, *Bandits*; and Antonio Téllez Sola, *Sabaté: Guerrilla urbana en España (1945–1960)*.

7 See *Homage to Catalonia*, p. 125.

8 See Juan Benet, *Qué fue la Guerra Civil*, pp. 45–6.

9 The same tongue-in-cheek use of the confessional form is found in Marsé's column 'Confidencias de un chorizo' (published in book form under the same title) in the satirical magazine *Por favor*, of which Marsé was editor from 1974 to its demise in 1978.

10 Marsé – himself an adopted child – told me that Palau was modelled on his adoptive father who was imprisoned several times for his political activities (a member of Esquerra Republicana during the Republic, in the war he joined the Catalan Communist Party, PSUC, which Marsé also briefly joined in 1963). Or as Marsé himself put it: 'He had problems with the police first for political reasons and later for reasons less political'. Palau's son Mingo works, like Marsé as an adolescent, as a jeweller's apprentice. See also Montserrat Roig, 'Juan Marsé o la memoria enterrada', p. 85.

11 See Sinnigen, pp. 111–12; and Marsé's *Confidencias de un chorizo*, pp. 172–3.

12 See Larraz, pp. 105–18; Domènec Font, *Del azul al verde: el cine español durante el franquismo*, pp. 17, 27, 31–47, 80–118; and Félix Fanes, *CIFESA: la antorcha de los éxitos*, pp. 132–42 in particular.

13 For the entertainment available to children after the war, see Josefina R. Aldecoa, *Los niños de la guerra*.

14 Salvador Vázquez Parga, *Los comics del franquismo*, pp. 23, 25, 28, 30, 34, 41, 66, 77–85, 102.

15 This point is made by Amell, p. 11.

16 See interview with Marsé in *Cambio 16*, 539 (29-3-82), p. 95.

17 See William Scherzer's edition of *Si te dicen que caí*, pp. 228, 284.

18 See Amell, p. 21. Marsé's love of the cinema leaves its traces on his later fiction *Un día volveré* (1982) and *El fantasma del cine Roxy* (1985).

19 See Larraz, p. 92.

20 The use in the novel of *Arsène Lupin* and other films is discussed by Robin Fiddian and Peter Evans in '*Si te dicen que caí*: A family affair'.

21 Marsé's later novel *Un día volveré* will undermine the Hollywood hero figure. See J. P. Devlin, 'Killing the hero: image and meaning in Juan Marsé's *Un día volveré*'.

22 Walter J. Ong, *Orality and Literacy: The Technologizing of the Word*, p. 160.

23 See Ong, pp. 22–5, 33–4, 45–6, 70, 142–7, 151, 154, 161, 171.

24 Interview with Marsé.

25 As Amell points out (p. 26), the coincidences between the two writers – technical and thematic – are considerable.

26 See Roig, 'Juan Marsé o la memoria enterrada', p. 86.

27 See Machado, *Soledades, galerías y otros poemas*, p. 25; and Neruda, *España en el corazón*, p. 46.

28 Interview with Marsé.

29 See Roig, 'Juan Marsé o la memoria enterrada', p. 89; also Sinnigen, p. 117.

30 *Un día volveré*, p. 287.

31 Ong, p. 142.

32 Fiddian and Evans ('*Si te dicen que caí*: A family affair') note that the film *Arsène Lupin* – like *The Prisoner of Zenda*, also mentioned in the novel – revolves around the theme of the double.

33 The documentary evidence reproduced by Ruiz Veintemilla ('La transformación de la realidad', p. 192) shows that the explosions do in effect correspond to the story of Carmen Broto's murder, which was discovered as a result of the explosions of the murderers' abandoned car engine. But this detail is not included in the novel's account of Menchu's murder.

34 Marsé has stated that he wanted to show how the official version given of Carmen Broto's murder – according to which she was a red – is undermined by a contrary popular version. In practice the novel gives us two contradictory popular versions. See Sinnigen, p. 111.

35 Diane Garvey ('Juan Marsé's *Si te dicen que caí*: The self-reflexive text and the question of referentiality', p. 385) notes that the contents of the bonfire constitute the basic materials of the 'aventis'.

36 I have here freely paraphrased ideas from chapters 2 and 3 of Annette Kuhn, *The Power of the Image: Essays on Representation and Sexuality*.

37 Susan Sontag, 'The pornographic imagination', p. 96. The same point is stressed by Kuhn; and by Susanne Kappeler, *The Pornography of Representation*.

38 Fiddian and Evans, '*Si te dicen que caí*: A family affair'.

39 I am grateful to my former student Manuel Martínez for making this important point. Marsé has said that he does not like pornographic novels; see Sinnigen, p. 121.

40 George Steiner, *Language and Silence*, p. 91.

41 Angela Carter, *The Sadeian Woman*, pp. 3–37.

6 Fiction as release: *San Camilo, 1936, Reivindicación del conde don Julian, La saga/fuga de J.B.*

1 *The Concept of Irony*, p. 278.

2 'The politics of obscenity in *San Camilo, 1936*'.

3 For an analysis of Nationalist reminiscences in *San Camilo, 1936*, see Rodríguez-Puértolas, *Literatura fascista española*, vol. 1, pp. 601–5.

4 The mythical nature of the claim that the uprising was justifiable as a retaliation for Calvo Sotelo's assassination is shown by the fact that the English plane chartered to take Franco from the Canaries to Morocco to launch the invasion had already left Croydon Airport on 11 July, the day before Calvo Sotelo's death. See Hugh Thomas, *The Spanish Civil War*, p. 168.

5 The use of circular motifs in the novel is studied by Bernardo Antonio González, *Parábolas de identidad*, pp. 69–76.

6 The mythical significance of this episode in the July Revolution is noted by Marcuse, *Eros and Civilization*, p. 163.

7 'The politics of obscenity in *San Camilo, 1936*', p. 26.

8 Patricia McDermott notes that the prostitute Magdalena Inmaculada is a symbolic 'whore of Babylon' representing 'the corrupt city that will be razed'. McDermott also draws some revealing comparisons between Cela's novel and Dalí's paintings on the subject of the Civil War. See '*San Camilo 36*: A retrospective view of the Spanish Civil War', pp. 166 and 172–5.

9 Ramón del Valle-Inclán, *Los cuernos de don Friolera*, p. 67.

10 Gemma Roberts ('La culpa y la búsqueda de la autenticidad en *San Camilo, 1936*') suggests a more positive interpretation of the novel's emphasis on guilt.

11 'The politics of obscenity in *San Camilo, 1936*', *passim*.

12 Roberts ('La culpa y la búsqueda de la autenticidad en *San Camilo, 1936*', pp. 213–14) notes the Nietzschean resonances of the novel.

13 Ilie ('The politics of obscenity in *San Camilo, 1936*', p. 35) uses the word 'Narcissism' in passing but without picking up Cela's explicit use of the Narcissus image or relating it to Marcuse. The use of the Narcissus image is discussed by P. L. Ullman ('Sobre la rectificación surrealista del espejo emblemático en *San Camilo, 1936*', p. 134), again without mentioning Marcuse. McDermott ('*San Camilo 36*: A retrospective view of the Spanish Civil War', p. 173) convincingly relates the novel to Dalí's painting *Metamorphosis of Narcissus*.

14 González (*Parábolas de identidad*, p. 92) notes the 'psychomythic' regression of the narrator to foetal origins.

15 See Ullman, 'Sobre la rectificación surrealista del espejo emblemático en *San Camilo, 1936*'.

16 Ramón del Valle-Inclán, *Luces de bohemia*, Scene 12.

17 Roland Barthes, *S/Z*, pp. 54–5.

18 See T. S. Eliot, *Collected Poems 1909–1962*, p. 190: 'human kind / Cannot bear very much reality'.

19 See Linda Gould Levine, *Juan Goytisolo: La destrucción creadora*; and her edition of the novel, Madrid, Cátedra, 1985.

20 In particular *España y los españoles*, and 'Supervivencias tribales en el medio intelectual español', in *Disidencias*, pp. 137–49.

21 *Crónicas sarracinas*, p. 40.

22 For the autobiographical circumstances surrounding the composition of the novel, see the second volume of Goytisolo's autobiography, *En los reinos de taifa*, ch. 7.

23 I am grateful to my student Pilar Dunster for identifying the incident on which this passage is based.

24 I am grateful to my student Soledad Sprackling for showing me her school textbooks from the 1940s when Goytisolo was educated. The myth of the Alcázar is demolished by Southworth, *El mito de la cruzada*, pp. 50–63. For a compendium of Nationalist clichés on the subject of stoicism, see José Maria Pemán's conversations with an imaginary Seneca in *El Séneca y sus puntos de vista* (originally articles in *ABC*). An interesting rejection of 'senequismo' from a Republican point of view is found in María Zambrano's essay 'Un camino español: Séneca o la resignación', published in *Hora de España* in 1938.

25 See Juan Goytisolo, 'Supervivencias tribales'.

26 See Juan Goytisolo, *Crónicas sarracinas*, p. 35.

27 'Supervivencias tribales' in *Disidencias*, p. 143.

28 Gould Levine discusses Goytisolo's satire of 'la "continuidad" española' in her critical edition, p. 25 and notes 44, 55, 126, 262.

29 Linda Ledford-Miller ('History as myth, myth as history: Juan Goytisolo's *Count Julian*') mentions Lewis' work but does not pick up his theory of the role of usurpers in history.

30 The dual traitor–redeemer figure is discussed by Abigail Lee in her PhD thesis 'Order and chaos in Juan Goytisolo's fictional works from 1966 to 1982', pp. 111–17.

31 See Lewis, *History – Remembered, Recovered, Invented*, p. 60; and Southworth, *El mito de la cruzada*, p. 53. In the 1944 textbook *Historia de España: Segundo grado*, the section on the siege of the Alcázar is actually headed 'Otro Guzmán el Bueno' (p. 223).

32 *Disidencias*, p. 218.

33 *En los reinos de taifa*, ch. 3.

34 See Mikhail Bakhtin, *Rabelais and his World*; Goytisolo, *Crónicas sarracinas*, pp. 45, 53; Kirk, *Myth: its Meaning and Functions in Ancient and Other Cultures*, p. 19. See also Frederic Jameson's criticism of the 'Freudian Left' for its belief in the revolutionary nature of transgression, in *The Political Unconscious*, p. 68.

35 See Gould Levine's introduction to her critical edition, pp. 42–5, 48, 50.

36 For a discussion of Goytisolo's underworld utopias, see Lee's PhD thesis, pp. 145–6 and 168–75.

37 See the introduction to Goytisolo's *Obra inglesa de Blanco White*, p. 97.

38 *Crónicas sarracinas*, p. 40; see also 'Marginalidad y disidencia, la nueva información revolucionaria', in *Libertad, libertad, libertad*, p. 43.

39 See Rodríguez-Puértolas, vol. 1, p. 737.

40 See Rodríguez-Puértolas, vol. 1, p. 358; and Rafael Abella, *Por el Imperio hacia Dios*, p. 28.

41 p. 157.

42 p. 153.

43 *Les Arabes n'ont jamais envahi l'Espagne*, Bordeaux, 1949; there seems not to have been a Spanish edition. See Goytisolo, 'Supervivencias tribales' in *Disidencias*, p. 143; and Rodríguez-Puértolas, vol. 1, p. 666.

44 See Rodríguez-Puértolas, vol. 1, pp. 37, 341–2.

45 pp. 19, 28–9, 143.

46 *Juan Goytisolo: Del 'realismo crítico' a la utopía*.

47 pp. 31–3.

48 Interview with Claude Couffon and 'Declaración de Juan Goytisolo', both in Gonzalo Sobejano *et al.*, *Juan Goytisolo*, pp. 118 and 141; and *Crónicas sarracinas*, p. 32.

49 Sylvia Truxa ('El mito árabe en las últimas novelas de Juan Goytisolo', p. 112) points out that Goytisolo's sexual mythification of the Arab perpetuates the *machismo* of the traditional repressive Spain he is criticizing; see also Gould Levine's introduction to her critical edition, p. 51. Lee analyses Goytisolo's inversion of the dragon-slayer myth in ch. 5 of her PhD thesis.

50 See Schaefer-Rodríguez, p. 60.

51 See *Crónicas sarracinas*, pp. 42, 192, 195–6; 'Tercermundismo hoy', in *Libertad,*

libertad, libertad, pp. 109–18; *El problema del Sahará*; *En los reinos de taifa*, pp. 14–15.

52 See 'La Chanca veinte años después'; *En los reinos de taifa*, p. 23; *Crónicas sarracinas*, p. 145.

53 For a detailed account of Goytisolo's political disillusionment, see *En los reinos de taifa*, chs. 4 and 6 in particular.

54 Interview in *El Viejo Topo*, p. 27. Gould Levine refers to Marcuse's influence in her introduction, pp. 47–8.

55 See *Eros and Civilization*, pp. 11–19, 33, 117, 120-4, 143, 146, 176–8; and *An Essay on Liberation*, ch. 1, 'A biological foundation for socialism?' and p. 92.

56 *En los reinos de taifa*, pp. 82–3.

57 José Manuel Martín ('La palabra creadora: estructura comunicativa de *Reivindicación del conde don Julián*', p. 346) describes the narrator's dialogue with himself as a 'narcissistic act'.

58 Jerome Bernstein ('Reivindicación del conde don Julián y su discurso eliminado', p. 63) points out that the narrator is an Orpheus figure. See *Eros and Civilization*, pp. 120–2, 138; and Gould Levine's critical edition, note 178. Goytisolo's next novel *Juan sin tierra* will show the explicit influence of Norman O. Brown's *Life against Death*, which takes further the idea of sexual liberation as a release from time and history, equated by Brown with anal repression.

59 Schaefer-Rodríguez (pp. 70, 82) criticizes Goytisolo on this score.

60 Gould Levine (*La destrucción creadora*, pp. 178–82) studies the references to Góngora and Virgil. For Goytisolo's use of intertextual references in general, see her book and critical edition, plus Michael Ugarte, *Trilogy of Treason: An Intertextual Study of Juan Goytisolo*, and José Ortega, *Juan Goytisolo: Alienación y agresión en 'Señas de identidad' y 'Reivindicación del conde don Julián'*.

61 This point is made by Martín, 'La palabra creadora', p. 347.

62 *La destrucción creadora*, p. 172.

63 'La palabra creadora', p. 351.

64 This point is well argued by Martín, 'La palabra creadora', p. 346.

65 See Ledford-Miller, 'History as myth, myth as history', p. 26; and Hayden White, *Metahistory*, p. 372.

66 Talk given at the Spanish Institute, London in May 1983; see also Leo Hickey, *Realidad y experiencia de la novela*, p. 221.

67 See Janet Pérez, *Gonzalo Torrente Ballester*, pp. 5, 9, 12, 17. Torrente Ballester insists on the importance of his early anarchist and regionalist sympathies in his untitled contribution to *Novela española actual*, pp. 116–17.

68 Talk given by Torrente Ballester at the Spanish Institute, London in May 1983; and Frieda Blackwell, *The Game of Literature: Demythification and Parody in Novels of Gonzalo Torrente Ballester*, p. 24.

69 Torrente Ballester has stated that the modern aspects of *La saga/fuga de J.B.* are the result of the intellectual stimulation he received from his years in the US; see his untitled contribution to *Novela española actual*, p. 113.

70 Blackwell, *The Game of Literature*, p. 126.

71 Talk given at the Spanish Institute, London in May 1983. In his book *Compostela y su ángel*, first published in 1948, Torrente Ballester justifies the centralist appropriation of the myth of Santiago in the name of national unity; see pp. 42 and 116.

72 *Gárgoris y Habidis: una historia mágica de España*, vol. 1, pp. 25 and 193. For an

analysis of fascist resonances in Sánchez Dragó's book, see Rodríguez-Puértolas, vol. 1, pp. 809–19.

73 *Gárgoris y Habidis*, vol. 1, pp. 12, 16.

74 Sánchez Dragó discusses Galician myths of Atlantis in *Gárgoris y Habidis*, vol. 1,
pp. 97–100; Galicia's Celtic tradition in vol. 1, pp. 208–26; the myth of the
Grail in vol. 2, pp. 191–226; Priscilian's Gnostic heresy in vol. 2, pp. 77–102;
and the myth of St James in vol. 2, pp. 103–89. See also Leandro Carré
Alvarellos, *As lendas tradizonaes galegas*, pp. 14–16, 51–3, 77–83. The modelling
of Bishop Bermúdez on Priscilian is discussed by Carmelo Urza, 'Historia, mito
y metáfora en *La saga/fuga de J.B.*', pp. 194–202; see also Torrente Ballester's
interview with Montserrat Roig, 'Gonzalo Torrente Ballester, escritor en
libertad', p. 48. The best account of the myth of St James is given by Torrente
Ballester himself in *Compostela y su ángel*. He notes that the 'flying city' of
Castroforte is an inversion of the Atlantis myth (inspired by a Goya painting in
Washington National Gallery) in *Los cuadernos de un vate vago*, pp. 216–17; and
in his interview in *Ínsula*, 317 (1973), p. 4.

75 This point was made by Torrente Ballester at his talk at the Spanish Institute,
London in May 1983.

76 See Urza, 'Historia, mito y metáfora en *La saga/fuga de J.B.*', pp. 39, 57, 99–
110, 116–41 in particular; the whole of Urza's thesis is essential reading.
Torrente Ballester confirms that Torcuato del Río is modelled on Murguía
(also in his sexual promiscuity) in *Los cuadernos de un vate vago*, p. 186. The
twelfth-century Bishop of Santiago de Compostela, Diego Gelmírez, is discussed by him in *Compostela y su ángel*, pp. 68–76, where he points out that it is
an anachronism to see Gelmírez as a champion of Galician separatism, also
noting that Gelmírez's stealing of the relics of various saints from Braga
Cathedral to add them to the shrine at Compostela would make 'a good
chapter in a novel'.

77 See Torrente Ballester, *Compostela y su ángel*, pp. 29–40, 87–9; and Sánchez
Dragó, *Gárgoris y Habidis*, vol. 2, pp. 94–5.

78 Torrente Ballester points out that Bastida's poems are a parodic application of
the principles underlying Jakobson's literary criticism in *Cuadernos de La
Romana*, p. 72; see also Roig, 'Gonzalo Torrente Ballester, escritor en libertad',
p. 48.

79 *Los cuadernos de un vate vago*, pp. 152, 170. One has of course to be wary of taking
too seriously the comments that Torrente Ballester – an inveterate leg-puller
and equator of criticism with fiction – makes about his work.

80 For Torrente Ballester's knowledge of French structuralism and linguistic
theory, see *Los cuadernos de un vate vago* (his tape-recorded comments on work in
progress between 1961 and 1976); and *Cuadernos de La Romana* and *Nuevos
cuadernos de La Romana* (his daily newspaper column in *Informaciones* from
1973–5).

81 In *Compostela y su ángel* (p. 61), Torrente Ballester points out that the Viking
sagas mention Galicia.

82 Torrente Ballester identifies some of his intertextual sources in Roig, 'Gonzalo
Torrente Ballester, escritor en libertad', pp. 48–9.

83 *Los cuadernos de un vate vago*, p. 24.

84 Robert Spires (*La novela española de posguerra*, pp. 304–37) attempts a Jungian
reading of *La saga/fuga de J.B.*, arguing that the novel traces Bastida's mythical

journey towards the acquisition of individualized identity. Torrente Ballester has rejected this interpretation: see Blackwell, *The Game of Literature*, p. 105.

85 Interview in *Ínsula*, 317 (1974), p. 14.

86 Talk at the Spanish Institute, London in May 1983.

87 See *El Quijote como juego y otros trabajos críticos*, pp. 169-72.

88 Blackwell (*The Game of Literature*, pp. 107-19) makes the mistake of supposing that Bastida's travels through the mythical J.B.s in chapter 3 'proves' their existence and the truth of Castroforte's myths. In any case, some of the information given by the mythical J.B. figures in chapter 3 contradicts the earlier accounts of the myths.

89 Balseyro is based on the thirteenth-century Bishop of Santiago de Compostela, Pedro Muñiz, an alleged necromancer credited with flying through the air to appear in Santiago while at the same time being in Rome. See Torrente Ballester, *Compostela y su ángel*, p. 79.

90 Torrente Ballester mentions reading a book about Lewis Carroll in *Los cuadernos de un vate vago*, p. 182.

91 In *Los cuadernos de un vate vago* (pp. 182-3), Torrente Ballester states that the nonsensical chants of the Palanganato are based on children's songs.

92 Lewis Carroll, *The Annotated Alice*, p. 95. Colin Smith, in his helpful comments on my typescript, notes the additional debt of *La saga/fuga de J.B.* – as a great comic novel – to Sterne's *Tristram Shandy*: an observation worth exploring.

93 *El Quijote como juego*, p. 93.

94 p. 86.

95 *El Quijote como juego*, p. 418.

96 'Fugal structure in Gonzalo Torrente Ballester's *La saga/fuga de J.B.*'

97 *The Raw and the Cooked*, pp. 14-16 and 28 in particular.

98 In *Los cuadernos de un vate vago* (p. 129), Torrente Ballester describes the image of St Lilaila as 'la imagen poética fundamental de la novela'.

99 Torrente Ballester has talked of the importance in his writing of the musical cadences of his native Galician; see his untitled contribution to *Novela española actual*, p. 103.

100 Sánchez Dragó notes that in this respect Priscilian's doctrines deviate from the Gnosticism for which he was martyred; see *Gárgoris y Habidis*, vol. 2, pp. 83-4.

101 Frederic Jameson, *The Political Unconscious*, pp. 64-8.

102 *Nuevos cuadernos de la Romana*, pp. 109-13.

Select bibliography

Martín-Santos

Martín-Santos, Luis. *Apólogos*, Barcelona, Seix Barral, 1970
'Baroja-Unamuno' in *Sobre la generación del 98: Homenaje a don Pepe Villar*, San Sebastián, Ed. Auñamendi, 1963
Dilthey, Jaspers y la comprensión del enfermo mental, Madrid, Paz Montalvo, 1955
Libertad, temporalidad y transferencia en el psicoanálisis existencial, Barcelona, Seix Barral, 1964
'El psicoanálisis existencial de Jean-Paul Sartre', *Actas Luso-Españolas de Neurología y Psiquiatría*, 9 (1950), 164–78
Tiempo de destrucción, ed. José-Carlos Mainer, Barcelona, Seix Barral, 1975
Tiempo de silencio, 16th edn, Barcelona, Seix Barral, 1980 (*Time of Silence*, trans. George Leeson, London, John Calder, 1965)
Curutchet, Juan Carlos. *A partir de Luis Martín-Santos: Cuatro ensayos sobre la nueva novela española*, Montevideo, Alfa, 1973
Díaz, Janet W. 'Luis Martín-Santos and the contemporary Spanish novel', *Hispania*, 51 (1968), 232–8
'Un par de charlas sobre *Tiempo de silencio*', *Hispanófila*, 62 (1978), 109–19
Doménech, Ricardo. 'Luis Martín-Santos', *Insula*, 108 (1964), 4
Duque, Aquilino. '"Realismo pueblerino" y "realismo suburbano". Un buen entendedor de la realidad: Luis Martín-Santos', *Índice*, 108 (1964), 9–10
Heller, Felisa L. 'Voz narrativa y protagonista en *Tiempo de silencio*', *Anales de la Novela de la Posguerra*, 3 (1978), 27–37
Labanyi, Jo. *Ironía e historia en 'Tiempo de silencio'*, Madrid, Taurus, 1985
Ortega, José. 'La sociedad española contemporánea en *Tiempo de silencio* de Martín-Santos', *Symposium*, 22 (1968), 256–60
Palley, Julian. 'El periplo de Don Pedro: *Tiempo de silencio*' in *Novelistas españoles de postguerra*, vol. 1, ed. Rodolfo Cardona, Madrid, Taurus, 1976, pp. 167–83
Pérez Firmat, Gustavo. 'Repetition and excess in *Tiempo de silencio*', *PMLA*, 96 (1981), 194–209
Prendergast, Penelope. 'The exploration and expression of existential awareness in Luis Martín-Santos's *Tiempo de silencio*', University of Cambridge, 1987 (doctoral thesis)
Rey, Alfonso. *Construcción y sentido de 'Tiempo de silencio'*, 2nd revised edn, Madrid, Porrúa Turanzas, 1980
Roberts, Gemma. *Temas existenciales en la novela española de la postguerra*, Madrid, Gredos, 1973, pp. 129–203

Saludes, Esperanza G. *La narrativa de Luis Martín-Santos a la luz de la psicología*, Miami, Ediciones Universal, 1981

Talahite, Claude. '*Tiempo de silencio*, une écriture de silence', *Co-Textes*, 1 (1980), 1–58

'*Tiempo de silencio* de Luis Martín-Santos: Etude des structures sémiotiques', Paris, Université de la Sorbonne, 1978 (doctoral thesis)

Ugarte, Michael. '*Tiempo de silencio* and the language of displacement', *Modern Language Notes*, 96 (1981), 340–57

Villegas, Juan. *La estructura mítica del héroe*, Barcelona, Planeta, 1973, pp. 203–30

Zulueta, Carmen de. 'El monólogo interior en *Tiempo de silencio*', *Hispanic Review*, 45 (1977), 297–309

Benet

Benet, Juan. *El ángel abandona a Tobías*, Barcelona, La Gaya Ciencia, 1976

'¿Contra Joyce?', *Camp de l'Arpa*, 52 (1978), 26–28

'De Canudos a Macondo', *Revista de Occidente*, 24 (1969), 49–57

Del pozo y del Numa, Barcelona, La Gaya Ciencia, 1978

En ciernes, Madrid, Taurus, 1976

Una meditación, Barcelona, Seix Barral, 1970

Qué fue la Guerra Civil, Barcelona, La Gaya Ciencia, 1976

Una tumba y otros relatos, ed. Ricardo Gullón, Madrid, Taurus, 1981

Volverás a Región, Barcelona, Destino, 1981; and 2nd end, Madrid, Alianza, 1974 (prologue by Benet, pp. 7–11) (*Return to Región*, trans. Gregory Rabassa, New York, Columbia University Press, 1985)

Untitled contribution in *Novela española actual*, ed. Andrés Amorós, Madrid, Fundación Juan March/Castalia, 1977, pp. 173–88

Azúa, Félix de. 'El texto invisible', *Los Cuadernos de La Gaya Ciencia*, 1 (1975), 7–21; and in *Juan Benet*, ed. Kathleen M. Vernon, pp. 147–57

Bravo, María-Elena. 'Región, una crónica del discurso literario', *Modern Language Notes*, 98 (1983), 250–8; and in *Juan Benet*, ed. Kathleen M. Vernon, pp. 177–87

Compitello, Malcolm Alan. *Ordering the Evidence: 'Volverás a Región' and Civil War Fiction*, Barcelona, Puvill, 1983

'Región's Brazilian backlands: the link between *Volverás a Región* and Euclides da Cunha's *Os sertões*', *Hispanic Journal*, 1 (1980), 25–45

Costa, Luis F. 'El lector–viajero en *Volverás a Región*', *Anales de la Narrativa Española Contemporánea*, 4 (1979), 9–19

Herzberger, David K. 'Enigma as narrative determinant in the novels of Juan Benet', *Hispanic Review*, 47 (1979), 149–57

The Novelistic World of Juan Benet, Clear Creek, Indiana, American Hispanist, 1976

Manteiga, Roberto C., Herzberger, David K. and Compitello, Malcolm Alan (eds.) *Critical Approaches to the Writings of Juan Benet*, Hanover and London, University Press of New England, 1984

Ortega, José. 'La dimensión temporal en *Volverás a Región*' in *Ensayos de la novela española moderna*, Madrid, Porrúa Turanzas, 1974, pp. 137–52

Pope, Randolph D. 'Benet, Faulkner and Bergson's memory' in *Critical Approaches to the Writings of Juan Benet*, ed. Roberto C. Manteiga *et al.*, pp. 110–19; and in *Juan Benet*, ed. Kathleen M. Vernon, pp. 243–53

Summerhill, Stephen J. 'Prohibition and transgression in *Volverás a Región* and *Una meditación*' in *Critical Approaches to the Writings of Juan Benet*, ed. Roberto C. Manteiga *et al.*; and in *Juan Benet*, ed. Kathleen M. Vernon, pp. 93–107

Vernon, Kathleen M. (ed.) *Juan Benet*, Madrid, Taurus, 1986

Villanueva, Darío. Untitled contribution in *Novela española actual*, ed. Andrés Amorós, Madrid, Fundación Juan March/Castalia, 1977, 133–72

Marsé

Marsé, Juan. *Confidencias de un chorizo*, Barcelona, Planeta, 1977

 Un día volveré, Barcelona, Plaza y Janés, 1982

 El fantasma del cine Roxy, Madrid, Almarabu, 1985

 Si te dicen que caí, Barcelona, Seix Barral, 1977; and ed. William Scherzer, Madrid, Cátedra, 1982 (*The Fallen*, trans. Helen R. Lane, Boston, Little Brown and Co., 1979)

 Interview in *Cambio 16*, 539 (29.3.82), 95

Amell, Samuel. *La narrativa de Juan Marsé*, Madrid, Playor, 1984

Campbell, Federico. 'Juan Marsé o el escepticismo' in *Infame turba*, Barcelona, Lumen, 1971, pp. 218–27

Champeau, Geneviève. 'À propos de *Si te dicen que caí*', *Bulletin Hispanique*, 85 (1984), 359–78

Devlin, J. P. 'Killing the hero: image and meaning in Juan Marsé's *Un día volveré*' in *Essays in Honour of Robert Brian Tate*, ed. Richard A. Cardwell, University of Nottingham, pp. 29–37

Fiddian, Robin W. and Evans, Peter W. '*Si te dicen que caí*: A family affair' in *Challenges to Authority: Fiction and Film in Contemporary Spain*, London, Támesis, 1988, pp. 47–60

Garvey, Diane. 'Juan Marsé's *Si te dicen que caí*: The self-reflexive text and the question of referentiality', *Modern Language Notes*, 95 (1980), 376–87

Gould Levine, Linda. '*Si te dicen que caí*: Un calidoscopio verbal', *Journal of Spanish Studies: Twentieth Century*, 7 (1979), 309–27

Montenegro, Nivia. 'El juego intertextual de *Si te dicen que caí*', *Revista Canadiense de Estudios Hispánicos*, 5 (1981), 145–55

Roig, Montserrat. 'Juan Marsé o la memoria enterrada' in *Los hechiceros de la palabra*, Barcelona, Martínez Roca, 1975, pp. 84–91

Ruiz Veintemilla, J. M. 'La transformación de la realidad en *Si te dicen que caí*: el asesinato de Carmen Broto y la guerrilla urbana' in *Estudios dedicados a James Leslie Brooks*, ed. J. M. Ruiz Veintemilla, Barcelona, Puvill, 1984, pp. 191–206

Sinnigen, Jack. *Narrativa e ideología*, Madrid, Nuestra Cultura, 1982, pp. 111–22

Cela

Cela, Camilo José. *La colmena*, Barcelona, Noguer, 1967

 La familia de Pascual Duarte, Barcelona, Destino, 1971

 Mazurca para dos muertos, Barcelona, Seix Barral, 1983

 Vísperas, festividad y octava de San Camilo de 1936 en Madrid, Madrid and Barcelona, Alfaguara, 1969

Ilie, Paul. 'The politics of obscenity in *San Camilo, 1936*', *Anales de la Novela de la Posguerra*, 1 (1976), 25–63

McDermott, Patricia. '*San Camilo 36*: A retrospective view of the Spanish Civil War' in *1936: The Sociology of Literature*, vol. 1: *The Politics of Modernism*, Colchester, University of Essex, 1979

Marfany, Joan-Lluís. Review of Cela, *La colmena*, ed. Raquel Asún, *Bulletin of Hispanic Studies*, 63 (1986), 377

Roberts, Gemma. 'La culpa y la búsqueda de la autenticidad en *San Camilo, 1936*' in *Novelistas españoles de postguerra*, vol. 1, ed. Rodolfo Cardona, Madrid, Taurus, 1976, pp. 205–18

Ullman, P. L. 'Sobre la rectificación surrealista del espejo emblemático en *San Camilo, 1936*', *Neophilologus*, 66 (1982), 377–85

Juan Goytisolo

Goytisolo, Juan. 'La Chanca veinte años después', *Voces*, 1 (1981), 12–13
   Campos de Níjar, Barcelona, Seix Barral, 1975
   Crónicas sarracinas, Barcelona, Ibérica de Ediciones, 1982
   Disidencias, Barcelona, Seix Barral, 1977
   Duelo en el Paraíso, Barcelona, Destino, 1974
   En los reinos de taifa, Barcelona, Seix Barral, 1986
   España y los españoles, Barcelona, Planeta, 1979
   El furgón de cola, Barcelona, Seix Barral, 1976
   Libertad, libertad, libertad, Barcelona, Anagrama, 1978
   Obra inglesa de Blanco White, Barcelona, Seix Barral, 1982
   El problema del Sahará, Barcelona, Anagrama, 1979
   Problemas de la novela, Barcelona, Seix Barral, 1959
   Reivindicación del conde don Julián, ed. Linda Gould Levine, Madrid, Cátedra, 1985
   (*Count Julian*, trans. Helen R. Lane, New York, Viking Press, 1974)
   Interview in *El Viejo Topo* (November 1985), 26–31

Bernstein, Jerome S. '*Reivindicación del conde don Julián* y su discurso eliminado', *Voces*, 1 (1981), 55–66

Blanco Aguinaga, Carlos. 'Sobre la *Reivindicación del conde don Julián*: la ficción y la historia' in *De mitólogos y novelistas*, Madrid, Turner, 1975, pp. 51–71

Gould Levine, Linda. *Juan Goytisolo: La destrucción creadora*, Mexico City, Mortiz, 1976

Ilie, Paul, 'A case history of self exile: Juan Goytisolo' in *Literature and Inner Exile (Authoritarian Spain, 1939–1975)*, Baltimore and London, Johns Hopkins University Press, 1980, pp. 114–34

Labanyi, Jo. 'The ambiguous implications of the mythical references in Juan Goytisolo's *Duelo en el Paraíso*', *Modern Language Review*, 80 (1985), 845–57

Ledford-Miller, Linda. 'History as myth, myth as history: Juan Goytisolo's *Count Julian*', *Revista Canadiense de Estudios Hispánicos*, 8 (1983), 21–30

Lee, Abigail E. 'Order and chaos in Juan Goytisolo's fictional works from 1966 to 1982', University of Cambridge, 1986 (doctoral thesis)

Martín, José Manuel. 'La palabra creadora: estructura comunicativa de *Reivindicación del conde don Julián*' in Juan Goytisolo, *Reivindicación del conde don Julián*, ed. Linda Gould Levine, Madrid, Cátedra, 1985, pp. 309–52

Navajas, Gonzalo. *La novela de Juan Goytisolo*, Madrid, Sociedad General Española de Librería, 1979

Ortega, José. *Juan Goytisolo: Alienación y agresión en 'Señas de identidad' y 'Reivindicación del conde don Julián'*, New York, Torres, 1972

Pérez, Genaro J. *Formalist Elements in the Novels of Juan Goytisolo*, Madrid, Porrúa Turanzas, 1979

Romero, Héctor. *La evolución literaria de Juan Goytisolo*, Miami, Ediciones Universal, 1979

'Los mitos de la España sagrada en *Reivindicación del conde don Julián*', *Journal of Spanish Studies: Twentieth Century*, 1 (1973), 169–85

Schaefer-Rodríguez, Claudia. *Juan Goytisolo: Del 'realismo crítico' a la utopía*, Madrid, Porrúa Turanzas, 1984

Schwartz, Kessel. *Juan Goytisolo*, New York, Twayne, 1970

Sieburth, Stephanie. 'Reading and alienation in Goytisolo's *Reivindicación del conde don Julián*', *Anales de la Literatura Española Contemporánea*, 8 (1983), 83–93

Sobejano, Gonzalo. '*Don Julián*: iconoclasta de la literatura patria', *Camp de l'Arpa*, 43–44 (1977), 7–14

Sobejano, Gonzalo et al. *Juan Goytisolo*, Madrid, Fundamentos, 1975

Spires, Robert C. 'La autodestrucción creativa en *Reivindicación del conde don Julián*', *Journal of Spanish Studies: Twentieth Century*, 4 (1976), 191–202

Truxa, Sylvia. 'El mito árabe en las últimas novelas de Juan Goytisolo', *Ibero-Romania*, 11 (1980), 96–112

Ugarte, Michael. 'Juan Goytisolo: unruly disciple of Américo Castro', *Journal of Spanish Studies: Twentieth Century*, 7 (1979), 353–64

Trilogy of Treason: An Intertextual Study of Juan Goytisolo, Columbia, Missouri University Press, 1982

Torrente Ballester

Torrente Ballester, Gonzalo. *Compostela y su ángel*, Barcelona, Destino, 1984

Cuadernos de La Romana, Barcelona, Destino, 1975

Los cuadernos de un vate vago, Barcelona, Plaza y Janés, 1982

Nuevos cuadernos de La Romana, Barcelona, Destino, 1976

El Quijote como juego y otros trabajos críticos, Barcelona, Destino, 1984

La saga/fuga de J.B.., 4th edn, Barcelona, Destino, 1976

Interview in *Ínsula*, 317 (1973), 4, 14–15

Interview in *Ínsula*, 452–3 (1984), 11–12

Untitled contribution in *Novela española actual*, ed. Andrés Amorós, Madrid, Fundación Juan March/Castalia, 1977, pp. 93–113

Blackwell, Frieda Hilda. *The Game of Literature: Demythification and Parody in Novels of Gonzalo Torrente Ballester*, Valencia and Chapel Hill, Albatros-Hispanófila, 1985

Giménez, Alicia. *El autor y su obra. Torrente Ballester*, Barcelona, Barcanova, 1981

Torrente Ballester en su mundo literario, Salamanca, Ediciones Universidad de Salamanca, 1984

Homenaje a Gonzalo Torrente Ballester, Salamanca, Caja de Ahorros y Monte de Piedad de Salamanca, 1981

Marco, Joaquín. Untitled contribution in *Novela española actual*, ed. Andrés Amorós, Madrid, Fundación Juan March/Castalia, 1977, pp. 65–113

Overesch, Lynne E. 'Fugal structure in Gonzalo Torrente Ballester's *La saga/fuga de J.B.*', *Anales de la Literatura Española Contemporánea*, 9 (1984), 71–80

Pérez, Janet. 'La función desmitificadora de los mitos en la obra literaria de Gonzalo Torrente Ballester' in *Actas del VIII Congreso de la Asociación Internacional de Hispanistas (Brown University, 22–27 August 1983)*, ed. David Kossof *et al.*, Madrid, Ediciones, Istmo, 1986, pp. 437–46

Gonzalo Torrente Ballester, Ballester, Twayne, 1984

Roig, Montserrat. 'Gonzalo Torrente Ballester, escritor en libertad' in *Los hechiceros de la palabra*, Barcelona, Martínez Roca, 1975, pp. 41–50

Urza, Carmelo. 'Historia, mito y metáfora en *La saga/fuga de J.B.*', University of Iowa, 1981 (doctoral thesis)

General studies of the postwar Spanish novel

Blanco Aguinaga, Carlos, Rodríguez-Puértolas, Julio and Zavala, Iris M. *Historia social de la literatura española (en lengua castellana)*, vol. 3, Madrid, Castalia, 1984

Bravo, María-Elena. *Faulkner en España: Perspectivas de la narrativa de postguerra*, Barcelona, Península, 1985

Buckley, Ramón. *Problemas formales en la novela española contemporánea*, 2nd edn, Barcelona, Península, 1973

Cardona, Rodolfo (ed.). *Novelistas españoles de postguerra*, vol. 1, Madrid, Taurus, 1976

Domingo, José. *La novela española del siglo XX*, vol. 2, Barcelona, Labor, 1973

Fiddian, Robin. 'The Spanish "chronomorph": Developing structures in the contemporary novel', *Ibero-Romania*, 2 (1975), 137–48

Gil Casado, *La novela social española*, 2nd revised edn, Barcelona, Seix Barral, 1973

Godoy Gallardo, Eduardo. *La infancia en la narrativa española de postguerra*, Madrid, Playor, 1979

González, Bernardo Antonio. *Parábolas de identidad: Realidad interior y estrategia narrativa en tres novelistas de posguerra*, Potomac, Scripta Humanistica, 1985

Hickey, Leo. *Realidad y experiencia de la novela*, Madrid, CUPSA, 1977

Joly, Monique, Soldevila, Ignacio and Téna, Jean. *Panorama du roman espagnol contemporain (1939–75)*, Montpellier, Etudes Sociocritiques, 1979

Jones, Margaret E. W. *The Contemporary Spanish Novel, 1939–1975*, Boston, Twayne, 1985

Morán, Fernando. *Explicación de una limitación: La novela realista en los años cincuenta en España*, Madrid, Taurus, 1971

Novela y semidesarrollo, Madrid, Taurus, 1971

Ponce de León, José Luis S. *La novela española de la guerra civil (1936–1939)*, Madrid, Ínsula, 1971

Sanz Villanueva, Santos. *Historia de la novela social española (1942–75)*, 2 vols, Madrid, Alhambra, 1980

Historia de la literatura española, vol. 6 (ii): *El siglo XX. La literatura actual*, Barcelona, Ariel, 1984

Tendencias de la novela española actual (1950–1970), Madrid, Edicusa, 1972

Schwartz, Ronald. *Spain's New Wave Novelists: 1950–1974*, Metuchen, NJ, Scarecrow Press, 1976

Sobejano, Gonzalo. *Novela española de nuestro tiempo*, 2nd revised edn, Madrid, Prensa Española, 1975

Soldevila Durante, Ignacio. *Historia de la literatura española actual*, vol. 2: *La novela desde 1936*, Madrid, Alhambra, 1980

Spires, Robert C. *Beyond the Metafictional Mode: Directions in the Modern Spanish Novel*, Lexington, University Press of Kentucky, 1984

La novela española de posguerra, Madrid, CUPSA, 1978

Ynduráin, Domingo (ed.). *Historia y crítica de la literatura española*, vol. 8: *Época contemporánea: 1939–1980*, Barcelona, Editorial Crítica, 1980

Other works mentioned

Abella, Rafael. *Por el Imperio hacia Dios: Crónica de una posguerra*, Barcelona, Planeta, 1978

Abellán, José Luis. *Mito y cultura*, Madrid, Seminarios y Ediciones, 1971

Aldecoa, Josefina R. *Los niños de la guerra*, Madrid, Anaya, 1983

Aranguren, José Luis L. *Estudios literarios*, Madrid, Gredos, 1976

La ética de Ortega, Madrid, Taurus, 1959

Aronne Amestoy, Lida. *Utopía, paraíso e historia: Inscripciones del mito en García Márquez, Rulfo y Cortázar*, Amsterdam and Philadelphia, John Benjamins, 1986

Bakhtin, Mikhail. *Rabelais and his World*, Cambridge, Mass., MIT Press, 1965

Baroja, Pío. *El árbol de la ciencia*, Madrid, Alianza, 1967

César o nada in *Las ciudades*, Madrid, Alianza, 1967

Barthes, Roland. *Mythologies*, London, Granada, 1973

S/Z, London, Jonathan Cape, 1975

Breck, Allen D. and Yourgrau, Wolfgang (eds.) *Biology, History and Natural Philosophy*, New York and London, Plenum Press, 1972

Brown, Norman O. *Life against Death: The Psychoanalytical Meaning of History*, London, Sphere, 1968

Love's Body, New York, Vintage, 1966

Burgess, Anthony. *Joysprick: An Introduction to the Language of James Joyce*, London, André Deutsch, 1973

Calvo Serer, Rafael. *España, sin problema*, Madrid, Rialp, 1949

Campbell, Joseph. *The Hero with a Thousand Faces*, London, Sphere, 1975

Camus, Albert. *The Plague*, Harmondsworth, Penguin, 1979

Caro Baroja, Julio. *El mito del carácter nacional*, Madrid, Seminarios y Ediciones, 1970

Carpentier, Alejo. *Los pasos perdidos*, Barcelona, Barral, 1974

El siglo de las luces, Barcelona, Barral, 1970

Carré Alvarellos, Leandro. *As lendas tradizonaes galegas*, Oporto, Museu de Etnografia e História, 1975

Carroll, Lewis. *The Annotated Alice*, ed. Martin Gardner, Harmondsworth, Penguin, 1972

Carter, Angela. *The Sadeian Woman*, London, Virago, 1979

Caruso, Igor. *Existential Psychology: From Analysis to Synthesis*, London, Darton Longman and Todd, 1964

Cassirer, Ernst. *Language and Myth*, New York, Dover, 1953

Castellet, J. M. *La hora del lectors*, Barcelona, Seix Barral, 1957

Literatura, ideología y política, Barcelona, Anagrama, 1976

Castro, Américo. *La realidad histórica de España*, Mexico City, Porrúa, 1968

Chase, Richard. *Quest for Myth*, Baton Rouge, Louisiana State University Press, 1949

Cirici, Alexandre. *La estética del franquismo*, Barcelona, Gustavo Gili, 1977

Cixous, Hélène. *The Exile of James Joyce*, London, John Calder, 1976

Cohn, Norman. *The Pursuit of the Millennium*, London, Paladin, 1970

Cortázar, Julio. *Rayuela*, Buenos Aires, Editorial Sudamericana, 1972

Culler, Jonathan. *On Deconstruction: Theory and Criticism after Structuralism*, London, Melbourne and Henley, Routledge and Kegan Paul, 1983

Cunha, Euclides da. *Revolt in the Backlands*, trans. Samuel Putnam, London, Gollancz, 1947

Dalziel, Margaret (ed.). *Myth and the Modern Imagination*, Dunedin, University of Otago Press, 1967

Dante, *The Divine Comedy*, 1: *Inferno*, trans. John D. Sinclair, London, Oxford and New York, Oxford University Press, 1971

Delibes, Miguel. *El camino*, Barcelona, Destino, 1980
Castilla, lo castellano y los castellanos, Barcelona, Planeta, 1979
Las ratas, ed. Leo Hickey, London, Harrap, 1969

Delzell, Charles F. (ed.) *Mediterranean Fascism, 1919–1945*, London, Macmillan, 1971

Díez del Corral, Luis. *La función del mito clásico en la literatura contemporánea*, Madrid, Gredos, 1957

Eliade, Mircea. *Myth and Reality*, London, Allen and Unwin, 1964
The Myth of the Eternal Return, Princeton University Press, 1971

Eliot, T. S. *Collected Poems 1909–1962*, London, Faber and Faber, 1963

Ellmann, Richard. *The Consciousness of Joyce*, London, Faber and Faber, 1977
Ulysses on the Liffey, London, Faber and Faber, 1972
and Feidelson, Charles (eds.). *The Modern Tradition: Backgrounds of Modern Literature*, New York, Oxford University Press, 1965

Ellwood, Sheelagh. *Prietas las filas: Historia de Falange Española, 1933–1983*, Barcelona, Editorial Crítica, 1984

Empson, William. *Seven Types of Ambiguity*, Harmondsworth, Penguin, 1973

Fanes, Félix. *CIFESA: la antorcha de los éxitos*, Valencia, Institución Alfonso el Magnánimo, 1982

Feldman, Burton and Richardson, Robert D. *The Rise of Modern Mythology 1680–1860*, Bloomington and London, Indiana University Press, 1972

Fernández Retamar, Roberto. *Calibán: Notas sobre la cultura de nuestra América*, Mexico City, Diógenes, 1971

Fernández Santos, Jesús. *Los bravos*, London, Harrap, 1974

Font, Domènec. *Del azul al verde: el cine español durante el franquismo*, Barcelona, Avance, 1976

Foucault, Michel. *The Order of Things: An Archaeology of the Human Sciences*, London, Tavistock Publications, 1970

Frazer, Sir James. *The Golden Bough*, abridged edn, London, Macmillan, 1963

French, Marilyn. *The Book as World: James Joyce's 'Ulysses'*, Cambridge, Mass. and London, Harvard University Press, 1976

Freud, Sigmund. *Civilization and its Discontents* in *The Pelican Freud Library*, vol. 12, Harmondsworth, Penguin, 1985
Collected Papers, vol. 4, London, Hogarth Press and Institute of Psychoanalysis, 1925
The Interpretation of Dreams, New York, Avon, 1971
Moses and Monotheism in *The Pelican Freud Library*, vol. 13, Harmondsworth, Penguin, 1985
The Psychopathology of Everyday Life in *The Pelican Freud Library*, vol. 5, Harmondsworth, Penguin, 1975
Totem and Taboo, London, Routledge and Kegan Paul, 1972

Fromm, Erich. *Beyond the Chains of Illusion*, New York, Simon and Schuster, 1962
The Fear of Freedom, London, Routledge and Kegan Paul, 1977

The Sane Society, London, Routledge and Kegan Paul, 1956

Frye, Northrop. *Anatomy of Criticism: Four Essays*, Princeton University Press, 1973
  Fables of Identity: Studies in Poetic Mythology, New York, Harcourt, Brace and World, 1963

Fuentes, Carlos. *La nueva novela hispanoamericana*, Mexico City, Mortiz, 1969
  Terra Nostra, Barcelona, Seix Barral, 1975

Gallegos, Rómulo. *Doña Bárbara*, Mexico City, Fondo de Cultura Económica, 1977

Ganivet, Ángel. *Idearium español*, Madrid, Espasa-Calpe, 1970

Garagorri, Paulino. *Introducción a Ortega*, Madrid, Alianza, 1970

García Márquez, Gabriel. *Cien años de soledad*, Buenos Aires, Editorial Sudamericana, 1971

García Morente, Manuel. *Idea de la hispanidad*, Madrid, Espasa-Calpe, 1961

García Sarriá, Francisco. 'El Jarama: muerte y merienda de Lucita', *Bulletin of Hispanic Studies*, 53 (1976), 323–37

Genet, Jean. *The Thief's Journal*, trans. Bernard Frechtman, Harmondsworth, Penguin, 1971

Gilbert, Stuart. *James Joyce's 'Ulysses'*, revised edn, London, Faber and Faber, 1960

Giménez Caballero, Ernesto. *Genio de España*, prologue by Fernando Sánchez Dragó, Barcelona, Planeta, 1983

Givens, Seon (ed.) *James Joyce: Two Decades of Criticism*, New York, Vanguard Press, 1963

Goldberg, Samuel L. *The Classical Temper: A Study of James Joyce's 'Ulysses'*, London, Chatto and Windus, 1961

Gómez Marín, José Antonio. 'Los fascistas y el 98', *Tiempo de Historia*, 1 (1974), 26–39

González Echevarría, Roberto. *Alejo Carpentier: The Pilgrim At Home*, Ithaca, Cornell University Press, 1977
  Relecturas, Caracas, Monte Avila, 1976
  The Voice of the Masters: Writing and Authority in Modern Latin American Literature, Austin, University of Texas Press, 1985

Gould, Eric. *Mythical Intentions in Modern Literature*, Princeton University Press, 1981

Goytisolo, Luis. *Las afueras*, Barcelona, Seix Barral, 1971

Gross, John. *Joyce*, London, Fontana, 1971

Gubern, Román. *'Raza': un ensueño del general Franco*, Madrid, Ediciones 99, 1977

Güiraldes, Ricardo. *Don Segundo Sombra*, Buenos Aires, Losada, 1966

Harrison, John R. *The Reactionaries*, London, Gollancz, 1966

Historia de España: Segundo grado, Zaragoza, Editorial Luis Vives, 1944

Hobsbawm, E. J. *Bandits*, Harmondsworth, Penguin, 1972

Ilie, Paul. 'Dictatorship and literature: the model of Francoist Spain', *Ideologies and Literature*, 4 (1983), 238–55

Izenberg, Gerald N. *The Crisis of Autonomy: The Existential Critique of Freud*, Princeton University Press, 1976

Jacobi, Jolande. *The Psychology of C. G. Jung*, London, Routledge and Kegan Paul, 1968

Jaffé, Aniela. *The Myth of Meaning: Jung and the Expansion of Consciousness*, New York and Baltimore, Penguin, 1975

Jameson, Frederic. *The Political Unconscious: Narrative as a Socially Symbolic Act*, London, Methuen, 1981

Jesi, Furio. *Cultura di destra*, Milan, Garzanti, 1979
  Mito, Milan, Mondadori, 1980

Joyce, James. *Ulysses*, Harmondsworth, Penguin, 1972
Jung, Carl. 'Approaching the unconscious' in *Man and his Symbols*, London, Picador, 1978, pp. 1–94
    Four Archetypes, London, Routledge and Kegan Paul, 1972
    '*Ulysses* – A monologue', *Nimbus*, 2 (1953), 7–20
Kappeler, Susanne. *The Pornography of Representation*, Cambridge, Polity Press, 1986
Kenner, Hugh. *Ulysses*, London, Allen and Unwin, 1980
Kermode, Frank. *Modern Essays*, London, Fontana, 1970
Kierkegaard, Søren. *The Concept of Irony*, London, Collins, 1966
Kirk, Geoffrey S. *Myth: its Meaning and Functions in Ancient and Other Cultures*, Cambridge, Berkeley and Los Angeles, Cambridge University Press and University of California Press, 1970
Kuhn, Annette. *The Power of the Image: Essays on Representation and Sexuality*, London and Boston, Routledge and Kegan Paul, 1985
Laín Entralgo, Pedro. *España como problema*, Madrid, Aguilar, 1962
    La generación del 98, Madrid, Espasa-Calpe, 1970
Larrain, Jorge. *The Concept of Ideology*, London, Hutchinson, 1979
Larraz, Emmanuel. *Le Cinéma espagnol des origines à nos jours*, Paris, Cerf, 1986
Levin, Harry. *James Joyce: A Critical Introduction*, London, Faber and Faber, 1960
Lévi-Strauss, Claude. *The Raw and the Cooked: Introduction to a Science of Mythology*, vol. 1, Harmondsworth, Penguin, 1986
    The Savage Mind, London, Weidenfeld and Nicolson, 1972
    Structural Anthropology, Harmondsworth, Penguin, 1968
    Structural Anthropology, vol. 2, London, Allen Lane, 1977
Lewis, Bernard. *History – Remembered, Recovered, Invented*, Princeton University Press, 1975
López Ibor, Juan José. *El español y su complejo de inferioridad*, Madrid, Rialp, 1951
López Salinas, Armando. *La mina*, Barcelona, Destino, 1977
McCormack, W. J. and Stead, Alistair (eds.) *James Joyce and Modern Literature*, London, Boston, Melbourne and Henley, Routledge and Kegan Paul, 1982
Machado, Antonio. *Soledades, galerías y otros poemas* in *Poesías*, Buenos Aires, Losada, 1965
Macías Picavea, Ricardo. *El problema nacional*, Madrid, Alianza, 1972
Mainer, José-Carlos (ed.) *Falange y literatura: Antología*, Barcelona, Labor, 1971
Mallada, Lucas. *Los males de la patria*, Madrid, Alianza, 1969
Maranda, Pierre (ed.) *Mythology*, Harmondsworth, Penguin, 1972
Marcuse, Herbert. *Eros and Civilization*, London, Sphere, 1972
    An Essay on Liberation, Harmondsworth, Penguin, 1973
May, Rollo. *Man's Search for Himself*, London, Allen and Unwin, 1953
May, Rollo, Angel, Ernest and Ellenberger, Henry F. (eds.) *Existence*, New York, Basic Books, 1960
Menéndez Pidal, Ramón. *Los españoles en la historia*, Madrid, Espasa-Calpe, 1959
Mermall, Thomas. 'Aesthetics and politics in Falangist culture (1935–1945)', *Bulletin of Hispanic Studies*, 50 (1973), 45–55
    The Rhetoric of Humanism: Spanish Culture after Ortega y Gasset, New York, Bilingual Press, 1976
Muecke, D. C. *The Compass of Irony*, London, Methuen, 1969
Murray, Henry A. (ed.) *Myth and Mythmaking*, Boston, Beacon Press, 1960
Neruda, Pablo. *Alturas de Macchu Picchu* in *Canto general*, vol. 1, Buenos Aires, Losada, 1975

España en el corazón in *Tercera residencia*, Buenos Aires, Losada, 1972
Neumann, Ernst. *Depth Psychology and a New Ethic*, London, Hodder and Stoughton, 1969
The Origins and History of Consciousness, Princeton University Press, 1970
Nietzsche, Friedrich. *Beyond Good and Evil*, New York, Vintage, 1966
The Birth of Tragedy, New York, Doubleday, 1956
Ong, Walter J. *Orality and Literacy: The Technologizing of the Word*, London and New York, Methuen, 1982
Ortega y Gasset, José. *España invertebrada*, Madrid, Revista de Occidente, 1975
Meditaciones del Quijote, Madrid, Revista de Occidente, 1970
La rebelión de las masas, Madrid, Revista de Occidente, 1981
Orwell, George. *Homage to Catalonia*, Harmondsworth, Penguin, 1970
Partridge, Colin. *The Making of New Cultures: A Literary Perspective*, Amsterdam, Rodopi, 1982
Paz, Octavio. *Claude Lévi-Strauss: An Introduction*, London, Jonathan Cape, 1971
Los hijos del limo, Barcelona, Seix Barral, 1974
El laberinto de la soledad, Mexico City, Fondo de Cultura Económica, 1973
Peake, C. H. *James Joyce: The Citizen and the Artist*, London, Edward Arnold, 1977
Pemán, José María. *El Séneca y sus puntos de vista*, Jérez de la Frontera, Jérez Gráfico, 1953
Perl, Jeffrey M. *The Tradition of Return: The Implicit History of Modern Literature*, Princeton University Press, 1984
Plutarch. *Parallel Lives*, vol. 1, London, Heinemann, 1914
Primo de Rivera, José Antonio. *Textos revolucionarios*, Barcelona, Ediciones 29, 1984
Propp, Vladimir. *Morphology of the Folktale*, Austin and London, University of Texas Press, 1975
Ramsden, Herbert. *The 1898 Movement in Spain*, Manchester University Press, 1974
Reich, Wilhelm. *The Function of the Orgasm*, London, Panther, 1972
The Mass Psychology of Fascism, London, Souvenir Press, 1972
Ridruejo, Dionisio. *Escrito en España*, Buenos Aires, Losada, 1962
Righter, William. *Myth and Literature*, London and Boston, Routledge and Kegan Paul, 1975
Riley, Edward C. 'Sobre el arte de Sánchez Ferlosio: aspectos de *El Jarama*' in *Novelistas españoles de postguerra*, vol. 1, ed. Rodolfo Cardona, Madrid, Taurus, 1976, pp. 123–41
Rivera, José Eustasio. *La vorágine*, Buenos Aires, Losada, 1981
Rodríguez-Puértolas, Julio. *Literatura fascista española*, vol. 1, Madrid, Akal, 1986
Rowe, William. *Mito e ideología en la obra de José María Arguedas*, Lima, Instituto Nacional de Cultura, 1979
'Paz, Fuentes and Lévi-Strauss: the creation of a structuralist orthodoxy', *Bulletin of Latin American Research*, 3 (1984), 77–82
Rulfo, Juan. *Pedro Páramo*, Barcelona, Planeta, 1972
Ruthven, K. K. *Myth*, London, Methuen, 1976
Said, Edward G. *Orientalism*, Harmondsworth, Penguin, 1985
Sánchez Albornoz, Claudio. *España, un enigma histórico*, 2 vols, Buenos Aires, Editorial Sudamericana, 1956
Sánchez Dragó, Fernando. *Gárgoris y Habidis: una historia mágica de España*, 4 vols, Madrid, Hiperión, 1980 (1st edn 1978)
Sánchez Ferlosio, Rafael. *El Jarama*, Barcelona, Destino, 1975

Sarduy, Severo. *Barroco*, Buenos Aires, Editorial Sudamericana, 1974
Sartre, Jean-Paul. *Being and Nothingness: An Essay on Phenomenological Ontology*, London, Methuen, 1969
The Flies, in *Three Plays*, Harmondsworth, Penguin, 1981
Saint Genet, Actor and Martyr, New York, George Braziller, 1963
Sebeok, Thomas (ed.) *Myth: A Symposium*, Bloomington, Indiana University Press, 1965
Senn, Fritz. *Joyce's Dislocutions: Essays on Reading as Translation*, Baltimore and London, Johns Hopkins, 1984
Shaw, D. L. *The Generation of 1898 in Spain*, London and New York, Ernest Benn, 1975
Silva, Umberto. *Ideologia e arte del fascismo*, Milan, Gabriele Mozzotta, 1973
Sontag, Susan. 'The pornographic imagination' in Georges Bataille, *Story of the Eye*, London, Marion Boyars, 1979, pp. 83–118
Southworth, Herbert. *Antifalange*, Paris, Ruedo Ibérico, 1967
El mito de la cruzada, Paris, Ruedo Ibérico, 1963
Staley, Thomas F. (ed.) *'Ulysses': Fifty Years*, Bloomington and London, Indiana University Press, 1972
Stanford, W. B. *The Ulysses Theme: A Study in the Adaptability of a Traditional Hero*, Oxford University Press, 1954
Steiner, George. *Language and Silence*, Harmondsworth, Penguin, 1979
Stivers, Richard. *Evil in Modern Myth and Ritual*, London, University of Georgia Press, 1983
Storr, Anthony. *Jung*, Fontana, London, 1973
Sturrock, John (ed.) *Structuralism and Since*, Oxford University Press, 1979
Sucre, Guillermo. *La máscara, la transparencia*, Caracas, Monte Ávila, 1975
Téllez Sola, Antonio. *Sabaté: Guerrilla urbana en España, 1945–1960*, Barcelona, Plaza y Janés, 1978
Thomas, Hugh. *The Spanish Civil War*, 2nd revised edn, Harmondsworth, Penguin, 1965
Tierno Galván, Enrique. *Costa y el regeneracionismo*, Barcelona, Barna, 1961
Todorov, Tzvetan. *The Poetics of Prose*, Oxford, Blackwell, 1977
Unamuno, Miguel de. *En torno al casticismo*, Madrid, Espasa-Calpe, 1968
Valle-Inclán, Ramón del. *Los cuernos de don Friolera* in *Martes de carnaval*, Madrid, Espasa-Calpe, 1968
Luces de bohemia, Madrid, Espasa-Calpe, 1971
Valls Montes, R. *La interpretación de la historia de España y sus orígenes ideológicos en el bachillerato franquista (1938–1953)*, Universidad Literaria de Valencia, 1984
Vargas Llosa, Mario. *La guerra del fin del mundo*, Barcelona, Caracas and Mexico City, Seix Barral, 1981
Vázquez Parga, Salvador. *Los comics del franquismo*, Barcelona, Planeta, 1980
Vickery, John B. *The Literary Impact of 'The Golden Bough'*, Princeton University Press, 1973
Myth and Literature: Contemporary Theory and Practice, Lincoln, Nebraska University Press, 1966
Virgil. *The Aeneid*, trans. C. Day Lewis, London, New English Library, 1962
White, Hayden. *Metahistory: The Historical Imagination in Nineteenth-Century Europe*, Baltimore and London, Johns Hopkins University Press, 1973
Tropics of Discourse: Essays in Cultural Criticism, Baltimore and London, John Hopkins University Press, 1978

White, John. *Mythology in the Modern Novel*, Princeton University Press, 1971

Whitmont, Edward C. *The Symbolic Quest: Basic Concepts of Analytical Psychology*, London, Barrie and Rockliff, 1969

Williamson, Edwin. 'Magical realism and the theme of incest in *One Hundred Years of Solitude*' in *Gabriel García Márquez: New Readings*, ed. Richard Cardwell and Bernard McGuirk, Cambridge University Press, 1987, pp. 45–63

Zambrano, María. 'Un camino español: Séneca o la resignación' in *Los intelectuales en el drama de España: Ensayos y notas (1936–1939)*, Madrid, Hispamerca, 1984, pp. 117–28

Index